Lecture Notes in Computer Science

Lecture Notes in Computer Science

Edited by G. Goos and J. Hartmanis

429

A. Miola (Ed.)

Design and Implementation of Symbolic Computation Systems

International Symposium DISCO '90
Capri, Italy, April 10–12, 1990
Proceedings

Springer-Verlag

Berlin Heidelberg New York London Paris Tokyo Hong Kong

Editor

Alfonso Miola
Dipartimento di Informatica e Sistemistica
Università di Roma "La Sapienza"
Via Buonarroti, 12, I-00185 Roma, Italy

CR Subject Classification (1987): D.1, D.2.1, D.2.10, D.3, I.1, I.2.2-3, I.2.5, I.3.5-6

ISBN 3-540-52531-9 Springer-Verlag Berlin Heidelberg New York
ISBN 0-387-52531-9 Springer-Verlag New York Berlin Heidelberg

Printing and binding: Druckhaus Beltz, Hemsbach/Bergstr.
2145/3140-543210 – Printed on acid-free paper

Foreword

The growing importance of systems for symbolic computation has greatly influenced the decision to organize the International Symposium on Design and Implementation of Symbolic Computation Systems, DISCO '90. It takes place in Capri, Italy, April 10-12, 1990, and is the first international event in the field, organized and sponsored by Italian Universities, Institutes of the Italian National Research Council and industry.

DISCO '90 focuses mainly on the most innovative methodological and technological aspects of hardware and software system design and implementation for symbolic and algebraic computation, automated reasoning, geometric modeling and computation, and automatic programming.

The symposium has grown out of the research developed within a five-year national project on software systems and parallel computing, funded by the Italian National Research Council, and of the unanimous intention of presenting and discussing new trends in the development of symbolic computation systems, according to the projects funded by the Italian Ministry of University and Research.

The international research communities have recognized the relevance of the proposed objectives and topics which are generally not well covered in other conferences in the areas of symbolic and algebraic computation, automated reasoning, geometric modeling and computation, and automatic programming.

DISCO '90 includes papers on theory, languages, software environments, architectures and in particular, papers on the design and the development of significant running systems.

The general objective of DISCO '90 is to present an up-to-date view of the field, while encouraging the scientific exchange among academic, industrial and user communities on the development of systems for symbolic computation. Therefore it is devoted to researchers, developers and users from academia, scientific institutions, and industry who are interested in the most recent advances and trends in the field of symbolic computation.

The Program Chairman received 91 contributions to DISCO '90 and organized the reviewing process with the cooperation of the Program Committee. Each paper was sent to two Program Committee members and it was then carefully reviewed by at least three independent referees, including Program Committee members. The Program Committee met on 3 to 4 January, 1990 at the Scuola Superiore G. Reiss Romoli, L'Aquila (Italy), to reach the final decision on acceptance of the submitted papers. During the meeting a deep discussion on the scope of DISCO allowed us to design and build this new conference in a very precise way. The resulting DISCO '90 Scientific Program corresponds well to the initial objectives.

Among the submissions, 25 papers were selected as full contributions for presentation at the conference, as well as in this volume, under classified sections. Ten further papers were selected as contributions for a short presentation at the conference, concerning work in progress or running systems relevant to the themes of the symposium. Short papers are presented at the conference in the appropriate scientific sections, while in this volume they are included in a separate section.

All my personal appreciation goes to both the Program Committee and the Organizing Committee members for their indefatigable and valuable cooperation.

On behalf of the Program Committee, I would like to thank the authors of the submitted papers for their significant response to our proposal, the invited speakers for having agreed to make their outstanding contributions to DISCO '90, and the referees for their cooperation in timely and precisely reviewing the papers.

I would also like to express all my recognition to our sponsors which have made this event possible; in particular, University "La Sapienza", Roma, the Italian National Research Council, which also supported the preparation of the present volume, Olivetti Systems and Networks, Ivrea, and Fondazione Ugo Bordoni, Roma, especially for having supported the students' attendance.

Roma, February 1990 — Alfonso Miola

Symposium Officers

General Chairman

A. Miola (Italy)

Program Committee

B. Buchberger (Austria), L. Carlucci-Aiello (Italy), G. Gonnet (Canada), C.M. Hoffmann (USA), J. Hsiang (USA), A. Kreczmar (Poland), A. Miola (Chairman, Italy), F. Parisi-Presicce (Italy), P.S. Wang (USA), M. Wirsing (W. Germany)

Organizing Committee

- Centro Interdipartimentale di Calcolo Scientifico,
    Universita' "La Sapienza", Roma, Italy
- Dipartimento di Informatica e Sistemistica,
    Universita' "La Sapienza", Roma, Italy
- Dipartimento di Matematica, Universita' L'Aquila, Italy
- Dipartimento di Scienze dell'Informazione, Universita' Milano, Italy
- Istituto di Analisi dei Sistemi ed Informatica, CNR, Roma, Italy
- Istituto per la Matematica Applicata, CNR, Genova, Italy
- Olivetti Systems & Networks, Ivrea, Italy
- Scuola Superiore G. Reiss Romoli, L'Aquila , Italy

In cooperation with:
ACM, AICA, AiiA, EATCS, ECCAI, SAME, SIGSAM

Symposium Topics

Theory:
    Specification and verification logics
    Specification languages
    Abstract data types and type inference
    Executable specifications

Languages:
    Language design
    Language implementation
    Language constructs for different computing paradigms
        (numeric, non-numeric, logic)
    Integration of programming paradigms

Software Environments:
    System design and implementation
    Software development tools
    Systems for different computing paradigms
        (numeric, non-numeric, logic)
    Visual and graphic tools
    User interface

Architectures:
    Parallel and specialized architectures
    Software/Hardware interface

List of Referees

D. Arnon

G. Attardi

L. Bachmair

A. Bansal

T. Becker

W. Bibel

C. Bohm

M.P. Bonacina

G. Bongiovanni

A. Bossi

R. Breu

J. Calmet

P. Chang

H. Chen

G. Cioni

A. Colagrossi

L. Console

M. Coppo

J.H. Davenport

F. Dederichs

Y. Deleh

U. Fraus

U. De' Liguoro

A. De Luca

E.E. Doberkat

R. Fateman

J. Fitch

J. Gallier

M. Gengenbach

A. Geser

A. Giacalone

L. Giordano

E. Giovannetti

T. Gruenler

A. Hearn

R. Hennicker

H. Hussmann

T. Ida

H. Kredel

K. Kusche

M.J. Lao

M. Lenzerini

F. Lichtenberger

R.E. Lynch

A. Martelli

G. Mascari

A. Mathur

H. Melenk

P. Mello

T. Mora

D. Nardi

A. Natali

E.G. Omodeo

P. Padawitz

A. Paoluzzi

R. Pavelle

A. Pettorossi

A. Piperno

M. Proietti

G. Rossi

C. Ruggieri

A. Salwichi

D. Sannella

P. Sguazzero

R. Sigal

G. Sofi

S. Steinberg

M. Stillman

T. Streicher

J. Tiuryn

F. Ulrich

G. Vanecek

M. Vanneschi

M. Venturini-Zilli

K. Weber

T. Weigert

Contents

Symbolic and Algebraic Computation - Systems Design

Symbolic and Algebraic Computation - Implementation Methods and Techniques

Theory

Automated Reasoning

Software Environments and Languages

Software Environments and User Interfaces

Short Papers

Current Problems in Computer Algebra Systems Design

J.H. Davenport
School of Mathematical Sciences
University of Bath
Bath BA2 7AY
England

Summary. Computer Algebra systems have been with us for over twenty years, but there is still no consensus on what an "ideal" system would look like. There are all sorts of trade-offs between portability, functionality and efficiency. This paper discusses a few of these issues.

Introduction

Computer Algebra systems form a unique area of software, combining large amounts of mathematics, often the latest research, with sophisticated software techniques needed to handle the requirements of

- Efficiency;
- Expressiveness;
- Friendliness.

It is very difficult to get all of these in one package, of course, and part of the designer's art consists in achieving a suitable compromise.

Storage Management

This is a perennial problem in Computer Algebra systems, and the new-comer to the field is always surprised how much of a problem this proves to be. Why is it such a problem in Computer Algebra, when it is not such a significant problem in, say, numerical software? One reason is the unpredictability of the size of answers to Computer Algebra problems.

This can be seen in a variety of examples. One is polynomial factorisation, where the factorisation of $x^{1155} - 2$ (typically stored as a polynomial of two terms, occupying four cons cells in Reduce's representation) is "irreducible", occupying one bit from the information-theoretic point of view, and certainly not much more space than the original problem. However, the factorisation of $x^{1155} - 1$, a very similar polynomial, is

$$(x-1)(x^2+x+1)(x^4+\cdots+1)(x^6+\cdots+1)(x^8-\cdots+1)(x^{10}+\cdots+1)(x^{12}-\cdots+1)(x^{20}-\cdots+1)$$
$$(x^{24}-\cdots+1)(x^{40}-\cdots+1)(x^{48}+\cdots+1)(x^{60}-\cdots+1)(x^{80}+\cdots+1)(x^{120}+\cdots+1)$$
$$(x^{240}+\cdots-3x^{120}-\cdots+1)(x^{480}+\cdots+3x^{240}-\cdots+1).$$

More surprisingly, a similar variation can happen in the case of greatest common divisors. The first example of this was found by Rényi [1947]. Based on his construction, we consider the polynomial

$$p := \left(5376x^{24} - 896x^{20} + 160x^{16} - 32x^{12} + 8x^8 - 4x^4 - 1\right)\left(4x^4 + 4x^3 - 2x^2 + 2x + 1\right)$$

which expands to

$$-21504x^{28} - 21504x^{27} + 10752x^{26} - 10752x^{25} - 1792x^{24} + 3584x^{23} - 1792x^{22} + 1792x^{21}$$
$$+256x^{20} - 640x^{19} + 320x^{18} - 320x^{17} - 32x^{16} + 128x^{15} - 64x^{14} + 64x^{13} - 32x^{11} + 16x^{10} - 16x^9 + 8x^8$$
$$+16x^7 - 8x^6 + 8x^5 + 8x^4 + 4x^3 - 2x^2 + 2x + 1$$

While p has 29 terms, p^2 has only 28. Let us consider the computation

$$\gcd(p^2, (p^2)').$$

The two input polynomials have 28 and 27 terms respectively, while the answer p has 29. Examples can be produced when the number of terms in the gcd is arbitrarily greater than in either input (either an arbitrary number more, or an arbitrary factor as many) [Coppersmith & Davenport, 1989]. Similar problems can be found in integration, where the result of integrals can be the word "failed", or a formula of almost any size: for example

$$\int \frac{5x^4 + 60x^3 + 255x^2 + 450x + 274}{x^5 + 15x^4 + 85x^3 + 225x^2 + 274x + 120}$$
$$= \log(x^5 + 15x^4 + 85x^3 + 225x^2 + 274x + 120)$$
$$= \log(x+1) + \log(x+2) + \log(x+3) + \log(x+4) + \log(x+5);$$

but

$$\int \frac{5x^4 + 60x^3 + 255x^2 + 450x + 275}{x^5 + 15x^4 + 85x^3 + 225x^2 + 274x + 120}$$
$$= \frac{25}{24}\log(x+1) + \frac{5}{6}\log(x+2) + \frac{5}{4}\log(x+3) + \frac{5}{6}\log(x+4) + \frac{25}{24}\log(x+5)$$

whose expression with a single logarithm is too long to write here, since it contains the logarithm of a polynomial of degree 120, of which the largest coefficients have 68 decimal digits.

Other subjects, such as Artifical Intelligence, have the same propensity to allocate storage, and interactive statistics packages allocate variable-sized objects. Why is Computer Algebra special? The main reason is that the natural data structures of computer algebra, in order to cope with this variation in data size, and the requirements for sparse polynomials, recursing down polynomials etc., tend to consist of a large number of small items, rather than one large one — in other words of linked lists rather than vectors. Many of the algorithms involved tend to turn over storage at a high rate. These two factors combine to give a very rapid turn-over of small blocks.

There are three possible strategies for storage management in such a system:

- **Explicit Return**, in which the program "knows" at each moment when a piece of storage is of no more use to it and can be recycled;
- **Reference Counting**, in which the program maintains a record of the number of references to a particular data structure, and recycles the space as soon as this count drops to zero;
- **Garbage Collection**, in which a separate phase of the program investigates all data structures, decides which are unreachable, and whose space can therefore be recycled.

Explicit Return is only suited to a small system, and, as far as the author knows, is not the exclusive technique of any current system, though CAMAL [Fitch, 1974] uses a combination of high-level Reference Counting and low-level Explicit Return.

Reference Counting

This is conceptually quite straight-forward, but, as any-one who has implemented it knows, is fraught with technical difficulties. The essential problem is that the entire program has to satisfy the invariant *the reference counts are all correct*. Any error in this leads to one of two mysterious problems: "storage leaks" where the amount of free space decreases inexplicably; random corruptions, where an object has been freed (and therefore used again) when it was actually still in use. The place where the error is detected (if any) is normally a long way from where the error occurred, and tracking down such an error is extremely difficult.

There are also performance problems associated with reference counting. The simple operation $a := b$ (where a and b are variables whose values are pointers) has to become the sequence of operations:

```
decrease_reference_count(a)
if reference_count(a) = 0
    then free(a)
a:=b
increase_reference_count(a)
```

Reference counts must also be adjusted when variables come into scope or go out of scope, or when pointers are passed as parameters or returned as function values. If pointers are not heavily used then these extra costs can be ignored. But if most of the programming consists in pointer manipulation, as is the case in typical computer algebra systems, these extra costs are substantial.

There are various tricks that can be used to decrease the cost of this process [Deutsch & Bobrow, 1976]. These reference-counting operations add complexity and conditional branches to the code generated: a feature of considerable concern with today's RISC processors, though they are less of a problem for interpreters (including micro-coded systems [Deutsch, 1980]). Direct coding of the reference-counting operations by hand is probably a mistake, since any error is likely to have obscure ramifications far from the point at which the error actually took place. For this reason interpreters or special-purpose compilers are generally used with reference counting techniques.

Garbage Collection

This is conceptually an attractive idea: the rest of the program is written assuming an infinite amount of memory, and occasionally a part of the program called the *garbage collector* re-cycles that memory which is not actually referenced. Once this small (at least by comparison) program is debugged, the rest of the system can assume that memory is infinite, and need not worry about storage management. There are many potential techniques for garbage collection, for which we refer the reader to Cohen [1981].

Again, life is not quite so simple in practice. In order to determine what is "referenced", the garbage collector has to scan all potential roots of references: principally the global and local variables (including routine parameters). The global parameters require some kind of management scheme to ensure that the collector knows where to find them, but are otherwise not much of a problem. However, the local variables are more of a problem, since they are stored on the stack. Hence we are driven to the necessity of scanning the stack — an operation that is essentially non-portable, and can be complicated by various kinds of register windows or stack cacheing.

There are varying degrees of sophistication that can be employed in scanning the stack. At one extreme, the entire stack structure is described by code-words associated with the routine using the frame (or maybe even with the routine and address within it) indicating precisely how the frame is laid out. The garbage collector knows the type of every entry on the stack, and descends only those which it should. This scheme is potentially neat, but requires a great deal of co-operation from the compiler.

At the other extreme, we can imagine a system which knows nothing about the structure of the stack, and descends every word on it. This means that return addresses and links must either be distinguished from ordinary data, or it must not matter if we get this wrong. Either of these decisions is likely to be highly machine-dependent.

A convenient half-way house is that of systems which know enough about the structure of stack frames (typically as much as a debugger knows) to distinguish control information from data information, but which descends all data items on the stack. This scheme is often adopted in practice, as within a limited range of machines it provides a reasonable degree of portability.

All these schemes suffer, in one way or another, from the defect known as "holes in the stack", when a place in a stack is allocated, but not yet used. At best, this hole points by accident to something that is not actually referenced. In the worst case, it can point into the middle of a structure, and cause the garbage collector to crash. This requires all sorts of precautions in the system's construction: Lisp compilers have to initialise the stack explicitly, and systems hosted in other languages have to take special precautions: KCL [Yuasa & Hagiya, 1985] uses a separate stack, not the system stack, for garbage-collectible references, and Cambridge Lisp [Fitch & Norman, 1977] had to modify the host BCPL compiler to prevent it from generating these kinds of holes.

The "totally independent garbage collector" is in fact somewhat of a myth: although this particular piece of code is small, it is relying on the rest of the system's obeying certain conventions. These are typically conventions that:

(a) only legitimate data items (with any form of tagging that identifies them as what they really are) are on the stack — see the previous paragraph;

(b) those registers that the garbage collector examines always contain legitimate values.

We have already mentioned the problems of the first assumption: the second can also cause substantial problems, especially in the area of big-number arithmetic, when arbitrary binary values are being manipulated. In fact over 50% of the PSL "garbage collector" bugs found over the past few years are in fact cases of the arithmetic code not adhering to these conventions [Neun, 1990].

It is the author's general experience that, no matter which scheme of storage management is used, there is a substantial shake-down period required in order to produce a completely reliable system.

Which Language?

While computer algebra systems have been written in many languages (COBOL [Fitch et al., 1976] being perhaps the most impressive example of the fact that one can do computer algebra in any language), the main contenders today are clearly Lisp and C. Lisp is used by Macsyma, Reduce and Scratchpad, as well as many smaller systems, while C is used by Maple and Mathematica, as well, again, as many smaller systems. What are the pros and cons?

C

These days, C is a very widely available language, with good quality C compilers present on almost all computers: the possible exceptions of IBM mainframes and some super-computers (depending on one's precise definition of "quality"). It is the host language for Unix, which de facto is the standard operating system family for work-stations. This tends to mean that C is the first language available on many of the new processor chips that are rapidly coming on the market, and are appearing in the new high-performance work-stations on which computer algebra is being done.

C has suffered from the absence of standardisation. The old de facto standard [Kernighan & Ritchie, 1978] was imprecise in some areas, and many compilers implemented features not in that standard (in particular the ability of functions to return structures), often in slightly different ways. The handling of functions with a variable number of arguments also varies considerably. These problems should now be solved by the reference to the ANSI standard for C, though it will take time for ANSI-conforming compilers to emerge. In general, careful programmers can write C with a very high degree of portability, using macros and the C pre-processor to handle machine-specific or compiler-specific features.

Another problem with C-based systems is that of operating system interface. C has historically been very closely coupled to its operating system, which means that operating system details show through very easily. This can affect the design of friendly algebra systems in areas such as:

- interrupt processing;
- file system interface and file-name handling;
- screen handling;
- memory allocation and memory expansion.

Again, the experienced programmer can generally isolate these dependencies.

Lisp

Lisp is not so much a language as a family of languages, and portability between different Lisps can be extremely difficult. Historically there have been several families of Lisp dialects: the two of practical importance for computer algebra system designers today are the "Standard Lisp" family and the "Common Lisp" family. The "Scheme" family generally does not have compilers and big-number systems of the efficiency required to support computer algebra systems, though this is a judgement about the implementations of the language, not about the abstract language, which may well become more influential in the computer algebra community.

The "Standard Lisp" family of languages is actually the product of computer algebra: the "Standard Lisp Report" [Marti et al., 1978] was an attempt to secure a portability base for Reduce. There are several standard Lisp systems available: the two which are still undergoing development, or at least transport to new machine architectures, are Cambridge Lisp [Fitch & Norman, 1977] and Portable Standard Lisp [Griss et al., 1982]. Standard Lisp can be described as following a minimalist approach: the facilities of the language are those required to support computer algebra (in particular Reduce). PSL has indeed shown itself to be reasonably portable, being available on machines from the Cray to the 80386-based PC machines (under Unix).

The "Common Lisp" family of languages [Steele, 1984] is essentially an attempt to standardise the Babel of dialects that grew out of MacLisp. Common Lisp has much wider goals than Standard Lisp, and Common Lisp systems tend to be much larger. The additional facilities offered are not always those required by computer algebra systems, and it can be argued that using such a system means paying (in terms of memory at least, and possibly in terms of speed as well) for something that is not actually required in a production computer algebra system. While there are many implementations of Common Lisp, one of particular note in Kyoto Common Lisp (KCL) [Yuasa & Hagiya, 1985], which is itself implemented in C. Hence the choice of Lisp verses C is not quite as clear-cut as it seems, and it can be argued that that Common Lisp (admittedly a relatively large and slow implementation) is as available as C is.

Whichever Lisp family is chosen, we can immediately observe the following advantages of Lisp: the storage management (typically garbage collection), debugging tools (typically very good ones) and big number processing are built in, and the algebra system designer can concentrate on the algebra. On the other hand, these things are fixed, and may not be done to the precise requirement of the designer. In particular, many Lisp system builders who do not come from the computer algebra area may well not implement big numbers as efficiently as we would like. If one considers machines with n-bit words, it is easy and portable to build big number arithmetic using $(n/2 - 1)$-bit "digits", because partial products will have $(n - 2)$ bits, and any addition performed on them will still yield $(n - 1)$-bit numbers, and avoid any risk of carry. If one wishes to implement big numbers with $(n - 2)$ or $(n - 1)$-bit "digits", then one has to solve the problem of multiplying two such digits together. While this can often be done, the solutions tend to be machine-dependent, and not accessible from a high-level implementation language. Hence Lisp system designers often choose $(n/2 - 1)$-bit "digits", despite the performance advantages of $(n - 1)$-bit "digits".

Need we make a choice?

We have already mentioned that writing a system in KCL might have the advantages (and disadvantages) of both Lisp and C. Fitch [1990] proposes an alternative mixture: *develop* in Lisp, where the interactivity and debugging tools are excellent, but *deliver* in C, for reasons of portability and efficiency. We refer the reader to his paper for details.

Interfacing

It is generally accepted these days that a computer algebra system should be more than a black box using a "glass teletype" style of interaction with a user. It should interface to other software systems, and should provide a "modern" interface to the user.

Many users use computer algebra as one component of a more general problem-solving arsenal. Other components of this might include: numerical software, for producing numbers, tables or graphs; graphical software, for visualising various formulae, or numbers produced by the numerical software; and text-processing software, to produce the final report or paper, often incorporating automatically-generated formulae form the computer algebra component.

Interfacing to Numerical Software

Whether one likes it or not, the vast majority of high-quality numerical libraries or software packages are written in Fortran. Hence the ability of a computer algebra system to generate Fortran code directly is essential. Nearly all such systems have a primitive mechanism (on `fort` in Reduce) for producing expressions capable of being fed to numerical languages (typically), but such mechanisms are far from ideal. Anderson *et al.* [1979] discuss Macsyma in this context, and Steinberg & Roache [1986] provides a more recent point of view. There are several problems with this simplistic approach, which we consider in subsequent paragraphs.

Languages such as Fortran do not deal with expressions, but rather with complete programs. A program in such a language may well *incorporate* an automatically-generated expression, but will certainly not be limited to it. Indeed, a complete program may well require several automatically-generated expressions, held together by various kinds of linking glue. For example, let us suppose that we wish to use a NAG library routine such as E04LBF to determine the range of a function such as

$$f(x, y, z, w) = (x + 10y)^2 + 5(z - w)^2 + (y - 2z)^4 + 10(x - w)^2$$

over an interval (this is not the best way to do this — see Wallis [1990] for a more suitable method). The first remark is that we will need two calls, one to calculate the minimum value of f, and the other to calculate its maximum value, which can be obtained as the minimum of $-f$. E04LBF takes one subroutine parameter which returns the function value and its first derivatives, and another which returns the matrix of second derivatives (as well as 22 other parameters, but now is not the time to go into this!). Hence, our program will consist of the main program and four subroutines, each of the four subroutines containing either five or ten expressions derived from f. This is a far cry from the naïve approach of just evaluating a one-line expression, and clearly cannot be done by hand for more than a very small number of expressions, especially as Wolfe [1982] points out that there is a high error rate in the writing of these programs.

This problem has been tackled in general by the Gentran package [Gates, 1985; 1986] for Macsyma and Reduce, which can process a complete "template" file and add the expressions (in Fortran or other languages) as required. There are other approaches to more specific areas by Wang (see, e.g. Sharma & Wang [1988]). The interactive approach to the use of numerical libraries is typified by the Irena project ([Dewar, 1989], [Dewar & Richardson, 1990]). There are also requirements to optimise the numerical code generated, which are pointed out by van Hulzen [1981; 1983] — see also [Hulshof & van Hulzen, 1985].

Interfacing with Text Processing

In practice, this tends to mean generating TeX or `troff` output, with the former being much more common these days. Here again, the problem is not so much one of doing *something*, but rather one of doing something *reasonable*. The challenges of this are described by Antweiler *et al.* [1988].

Much of this transcends the design of computer algebra systems specifically, and is rather in the domain of designing an integrated work-station. This is an area in which there has been more talk than action, though there is hope that the Euromath project will result in a useful marriage of text processing, bibliographic databases, communication tools and computer algebra.

Interfacing with Graphics

Here the undoubted winner among existing computer algebra systems is Mathematica, many versions of which have quite good graphical capabilities. There are severe practical portability problems with graphics applications at the moment, but emerging international standards may well help in this area.

Graphics should not stand apart from numerical processing, since very often one wants the computer algebra to generate the program to compute the numbers that the graphics should draw. This is typified by the Desir project, where the Desir package in Reduce generates a Fortran program which evaluates the appropriate series and calls the Uniras graphics system to draw the curves. The graphical side is described by Richard [1987; 1988], and a general over-view of the system is provided by Tournier [1987].

How Much Mathematics?

While we have left this question until last, it is certainly one of the most important questions for the designer to face. Many small (or early) systems took a very simple view: they treated $\mathbf{Z}$ or $\mathbf{Z}[x_1, \ldots, x_n]$, or its field of fractions $\mathbf{Q}(x_1, \ldots, x_n)$, or matrices with elements in this field. To the purely algorithmic treatment of these domains, one might add re-write rules of some kind. Reduce-2 is a typical example of this genre of system. These systems are, in their own way, quite powerful — after all many engineers graduate without ever doing algebra in a more complex domain.

However, one may wish to go further. There are a variety of reasons for this — naïve user pressure, expert user pressure ("I know you have modular arithmetic in there somewhere: I want to use it") and the implementers own needs: modular arithmetic for factorisation, distributed polynomials for Gröbner bases, univariate polynomials whose coefficients are rational functions for integration, and so on. This can be done by a sequence of *ad hoc* extensions, but one rapidly falls across the mounting complexity: Why don't polynomials whose coefficients are rational functions work properly if the coefficients of them are modular numbers?

Reduce's theory of *domains* [Bradford *et al.*, 1986] is one example of a somewhat more integrated approach for the treatment of "constant" domains. Here one an treat one of a wide range of domains, including user-supplied domains, as R, and the system will them work over R, $R[x_1, \ldots, x_n]$, its field of fractions $R(x_1, \ldots, x_n)$, or matrices with elements in this field. This certainly provides a reasonably clean interface. But it has two limitations:

- it is currently inherently limited to constant domains, which causes problems with people who wish to have algebraic functions, truncated power series, or polynomials over rational functions;
- domains are viewed as monolithic objects, so that, although the user appears to see a single switch complex which will give him a complex version of the domain he is already in, in fact there are separate domains for complex integers, complex floats and complex bigfloats, with the system switching between them to maintain the illusion to the user.

Scratchpad [Jenks, 1985] is a system designed *ab initio* to remove some of these limitations. Scratchpad would view the equivalent of the on complex statement as the application of the functor Gaussian to whatever the current domain of computation was, and this would create a new domain, the complex equivalent of the previous one. Functors can be nested arbitrarily, so that the mathematical structure $\mathbf{Z}[i](x, y)[z]$ would be represented as

    UP(QF(MP(G(I),OV(x,y))),z)

where we have used the Scratchpad abbreviations:

  G Gaussian — creates the complex equivalent;
  I Integer — a nullary functor which builds the integers;
MP MultivariatePolynomial — takes a coefficient ring and a description of the variables;
OV OrderedVariables — describes the ordering imposed on a set of variables;
QF QuotientField — converts an integral domain into its field of fractions;
UP UnivariatePolynomial — takes a coefficient ring and a single variable.

The generality available is obviously enormous: equally obviously, this system is going to be more difficult to use (unless the complexity can be concealed by suitable defaults) than one of the simpler systems.

References

[Anderson *et al.*, 1979] Anderson,J.D., Lau,E.L. & Hellings,R.W., Use of Macsyma as an Automatic Fortran Generator. Proc. 1979 MACSYMA Users' Conference (M.I.T., Cambridge, Mass., 1979) pp. 583–595.

[Antweiler *et al.*, 1988] Antweiler,W., Strotmann,A. & Winkelmann,V., A REDUCE-TEX-Interface. University of Cologne Computer Center Technical Report, April 1988.

[Bradford *et al.*, 1986] Bradford,R.J., Hearn,A.C., Padget,J.A. & Schrufer,E., Enlarging the REDUCE Domain of Computation. Proc. SYMSAC 86 (ACM, New York, 1986) pp. 100–106.

[Cohen, 1981] Cohen,J., Garbage Collection of Linked Data Structures. Computing Surveys **13** (1981) pp. 341–367.

[Coppersmith & Davenport, 1989] Coppersmith,D. & Davenport,J.H., Polynomials whose Powers are Sparse. IBM Research Report RC 14859, August 21, 1989

[Deutsch, 1980] Deutsch,P., Bytelisp and its Alto Implementation. Proc. LISP 80, pp. 231–242.

[Deutsch & Bobrow, 1976] Deutsch,P., & Bobrow,D., An efficient, Incremental Automatic Garbage Collector. Comm. ACM **19** (1976) pp. 522–526.

[Dewar, 1989] Dewar,M.C., IRENA - An Integrated Symbolic and Numerical Computation Environment. Proc. ISSAC 89 (ACM, New York, 1989), pp. 171–179.

[Dewar & Richardson, 1990] Dewar,M.C. & Richardson,M.G., Reconciling Symbolic and Numeric Computation in a Practical Setting. To appear in Proc. DISCO 90.

[Fitch, 1974] Fitch,J.P., CAMAL Users' Manual. University of Cambridge Computer Laboratory, 1974.

[Fitch, 1990] Fitch,J.P. & Hall,R.G., A Delivery System for Reduce. Submitted to ISSAC '90.

[Fitch & Norman, 1977] Fitch,J.P. & Norman,A.C., Implementing LISP in a High-level Language. Software - Practice and Experience, **7** (1977) pp. 713–725. CR 33,698 (Vol. **19** (1978)).

[Fitch *et al.*, 1976] Fitch,J.P., Herbert,P. & Norman,A.C., Design Features of COBALG. Proc. SYMSAC 76 (ACM, New York, 1976) pp. 185–188.

[Gates, 1985] Gates,B.L., GENTRAN: An Automatic Code Generation Facility for REDUCE. SIGSAM Bulletin **19** (1985) 3, pp. 24–42.

[Gates, 1986] Gates,B.L., A Numeric Code Generation Facility for Reduce. Proc. SYMSAC 86 (ACM, New York, 1986) pp. 94–99.

[Griss *et al.*, 1982] Griss,M.L., Benson,E. & Hearn,A.C., Current Status of a Portable LISP Compiler. Proc. SIGPLAN '82 Symposium on Compiler Construction (SIGPLAN Notices **17** (1982) No. 6) pp. 276–283.

[Hulshof & van Hulzen, 1985] Hulshof,B.J.A. & van Hulzen,J.A., An Expression Compression Package for REDUCE based on Factorization and Controlled Expansion. Proc. EUROCAL 85, Vol. 2 (Springer Lecture Notes in Computer Science Vol. 204, Springer-Verlag, 1985) pp. 315–316.

[van Hulzen, 1981] van Hulzen,J.A., Breuer's Grow Factor Algorithm in Computer Algebra. Proc. SYMSAC 81 (ACM, New York, 1981) pp. 100–104.

[van Hulzen, 1983] van Hulzen,J.A., Code Optimization of Multivariate Polynomial Schemes: A Pragmatic Approach. Proc. EUROCAL 83 [Springer Lecture Notes in Computer Science 162, Springer-Verlag, 1983] pp. 286–300.

[Jenks, 1985] Jenks,R.D., A Brief Introduction to Scratchpad II. Scratchpad II Newsletter **1** (1985) 1, pp. 1–3.

[Kernighan & Ritchie, 1978] Kernighan,B.W. & Ritchie,D.M., The C Programming Language. Prentice-Hall, 1978.

[Marti *et al.*, 1978] Marti,J.B., Hearn,A.C., Griss M.L. & Griss,C., Standard LISP Report. Utah Symbolic Computation Group Report UCP-60, University of Utah, Salt Lake City, Jan. 1978. SIGSAM Bulletin 14 (1980) 1, pp. 23–43.

[Neun, 1990] Neun,W., Private Communication 8 Feb. 1990

[Rényi, 1947] Rényi,A., On the Minimal Number of Terms of the Square of a Polynomial. Hungarica Acta Math. 1 (1947) pp. 30–34.

[Richard, 1987] Richard,F., Graphical Analysis of Complex O.D.E. Solutions. Computer Graphics Forum 6 (1987) 4, pp. 335–341.

[Richard, 1988] Richard,F., Représentations graphiques de solutions d'équations différentielles dans le champ complexe. Thèse de Doctorat, Strasbourg, 16.9.88 (IRMA Publication 1988 368/TS-08).

[Sharma & Wang, 1988] Sharma,N. & Wang,P.S., Symbolic Derivation and Automatic Generation of Parallel Routines for Finite Element Analysis. Proc. ISSAC '88 (ed. P. Gianni) Springer lecture Notes in Computer Science 358, pp. 33–56.

[Steele, 1984] Steele,G.L.,Jr., Common LISP: The Language. Digital Press, 1984.

[Steinberg & Roache, 1986] Steinberg,S. & Roache,P.J., Using MACSYMA to Write FORTRAN Subroutines. J. Symbolic Comp. 2 (1986) pp. 213–216.

[Tournier, 1987] Tournier,E., Solutions Formelles d'Equations différentielles: Le Logiciel de Calcul Formel: Desir Etude Théorique et Réalisation. Thèse d'Etat, University of Grenoble, 2 April 1987.

[Wallis, 1990] Wallis,P.J.L.W. (ed.), Improving Floating Point Programming. Wiley, 1990

[Wolfe, 1982] Wolfe,P.S., Checking the Calculation of Gradients. ACM TOMS 8 (1982) pp. 337–343. Zbl. 493.65027. CR 8412-1021.

[Yuasa & Hagiya, 1985] Yuasa,T. & Hagiya,M., The Kyoto Common Lisp Report. Research Institute for Mathematical Sciences, Kyoto University. June 1985.

The Design of Cayley - a Language for Modern Algebra[*]

Greg Butler[†] and John Cannon[‡]

University of Sydney

Abstract

Established practice in the domain of modern algebra has shaped the design of Cayley. The design has also been responsive to the needs of its users. The requirements of the users include consistency with common mathematical notation; appropriate data types such as sets, sequences, mappings, algebraic structures and elements; efficiency; extensibility; power of in-built functions and procedures for known algorithms; and access to common examples of algebraic structures. We discuss these influences on the design of Cayley's user language.

Introduction

Mathematical computation has been one of the major application areas of computers, and has lead to the design of specialised programming languages. A major design criterion of these languages is to provide users with the mathematical data types and operations appropriate to their particular domain of mathematics. For example, numerical computation is concerned with real numbers, vectors, and matrices, so Fortran provides the types REAL, DOUBLE, and ARRAY together with control structures to iterate over vector and matrix entries. Furthermore, the parallel derivatives of Fortran provide vector and matrix parallel operations.

Symbolic algebra languages, such as Macsyma, Reduce, Scratchpad, and Maple, support computation in the domain of classical 19th century algebra, which is primarily the algebra of polynomials and the elementary calculus. Hence, they provide their users with data types for arbitrary precision real numbers and integers, polynomials, functions other than polynomials, lists and/or arrays. The languages support symbolic differentiation and integration, as well as the taking of limits, and the provision of arithmetic. The implementation of these operations often involves simplification and pattern matching.

Modern algebra as a domain is concerned with axiomatically defined structures such as groups, rings, and fields. An algebraist is concerned with issues such as

---

[*]This research was supported in part by the Australian Research Council.

[†]Basser Department of Computer Science. Currently visiting Universität Bayreuth.

[‡]Department of Pure Mathematics.

1. Find examples of structures which satisfy the defining axioms for a particular class of algebraic structures.

2. Given a particular algebraic structure A, what properties does this structure have? For example, does it have a finite or infinite number of elements?

3. Classify all structures which satisfy a particular set of defining axioms.

4. Given a particular algebraic structure A, identify A in terms of known classifications.

Languages and systems for modern algebra generally require algebraic structures to be defined by a concrete representation such as permutations or matrices over finite fields. Computation with these concrete representations offers orders of magnitude gains in efficiency over inference from the defining axioms.

Cayley is a system designed to support research in modern algebra - primarily group theory - and to support applications of modern algebra to related disciplines such as combinatorics and topology. In contrast to classical algebra systems, whose emphasis is on computing with individual elements of an algebraic domain, Cayley is concerned with investigating the properties and relationships of complete algebraic structures. A beta test version was available in 1978, and production versions have been in distribution since 1982. Cayley is now used at about 150 universities and research establishments in 21 countries. We are now in the process of a major redesign to produce the next version, to be called version 4. The version includes

- a user language,

- a library of implementations of algorithms for modern algebra, which are accessible as built-in functions of the user language,

- libraries of user defined functions and procedures implementing algorithms and algebraic structures,

- catalogues of groups and combinatorial structures classified by various properties,

- a deductive facility, and a knowledge base of definitions and theorems for group theory.

The Cayley project has always aimed at a production quality system that would be widely accepted and widely used by the research community. To this end the users and their domain of research have had a large influence on the design of the facilities, particularly the user language. In this paper, we wish to discuss some of those influences and their impact on the language design. The design and implementation of the internal aspects of the Cayley system will not be discussed.

Influences on the Design

The users of Cayley are researchers or students in scientific or engineering disciplines. Most are not interested in Cayley but rather in the results of their computations and the application of these results to their problem. For them Cayley is a tool, which should be easy to learn and use, and which can be used interactively in an exploratory fashion. However, a number of users apply Cayley deeply and intensively in their own research. They are more likely to develop their own algorithms and algebraic domains to explore. Their long computations will be batch processed. The feedback from the users comes via teachers and demonstrators, through individual correspondence, or through contact at workshops and conferences. The feedback is vital and is actively sought. The users have indicated many varying and often conflicting requirements. The user requirements that will be discussed here are

- provide data types for the domain of modern algebra,

- support standard mathematical notation,

- support the informal style adopted by working mathematicians,

- provide control structures natural to mathematical processes,

- allow access to existing catalogues or libraries of examples,

- power, and

- efficient extensibility.

Of course, as a language for a specialised domain, Cayley must provide the objects which are a natural part of the discourse in that domain. The **data types** for modern algebra are

- algebraic structures,

- elements of algebraic structures,

- homomorphisms between algebraic structures,

- sets, sequences, and maps.

The fundamental operations for finite structures are to determine membership of an element in a structure, to determine the order of a structure, and to enumerate the elements of a structure. For algebraic elements, the language must provide the 'arithmetic' operations such as addition, multiplication, and inversion. The operations with homomorphisms include composition, determining the kernel and image as well as taking images and preimages of elements, sets of elements, and substructures.

A wide variety of sets are required. Sets of integers, algebraic elements, structures, homomorphisms, maps, and sets of sets all have a natural place in modern algebra.

The kinds of algebraic structures supported in the language depend not only on their relevance to group theory and its applications, but also on the practicality of representing the structures and performing the operations. This second requirement suggests that the algebraic structures be defined in concrete terms. In many cases, algebraic structures can be described in terms of a small set of elements, called *generators*, or *basis elements*. Therefore, the system is designed around the principle that the algebraic structures definable in it must be given explicitly by a finite set of concrete generators or basis elements. That is, an explicit set of generators must be supplied, and the generators must be well-defined concrete objects such as permutations or matrices. Furthermore, for practical purposes, the set of generators should be finite.

There is a wide variety of algebraic structures that have been defined in modern algebra, and more are being introduced as the area develops. However, it turns out that a small number of algebraic structures suffice to support most applications. We have adopted the following principle.

Principle :

Introduce an algebraic structure into the language only when

1. *user applications indicate a clear need for the structure;*
2. *the structure can be finitely generated;*
3. *there exists a suitable representation for the algebraic structure and its elements; and*
4. *there exist effective algorithms for the fundamental operations.*

Users may define other algebraic structures in the language, but they must provide a representation for the structure, and provide algorithms for the operations. In this way they may explore new domains, and perhaps convince us that the structure should be more fully supported by the language.

The users of Cayley are mathematicians, scientists, and engineers familiar with **standard mathematical notation**. There are substantial benefits, such as reducing learning time and increasing user acceptance, in being consistent with this notation. Furthermore, the notations have been developed and refined over many years to be useful aids to mathematical thought. Such experience should not be lightly discarded.

There are, however, problems in wholeheartedly adopting standard notation. Keyboards and character sets are limited and do not include many mathematical symbols. Some mathematical notation, such as matrices, require two-dimensional layout. There are often several competing schools of well-developed notation, and there is always developing notation which has not yet standardised. For example, sets are universally enclosed in braces {}; the commutator of two elements x and y (defined as $x^{-1}y^{-1}xy$) is commonly denoted by (x,y) or $[x,y]$; while there is no generally accepted notation for sequences. The principles we adopt are

Principle :

Within the limitations of the character set,

1. *if there is one standard notation for a concept then use it,*

2. *if there are several common standard notations then select one and use it, and*

3. *if there are no commonly accepted standard notations then feel free to improvise.*

Principle :

If there is a common symbol used as notation but that symbol is not in the character set, then prefer a meaningful word for the symbol over a string of symbols.

As an example of the latter, we use in rather than $<=$ for the inclusion operator $\subseteq$.

The other issue which affects the adoption of standard mathematical notation is the limitations of machine parsing when compared to a human's use of context and common sense. For example, humans have no trouble with the elision of operators in a finite presentation like $< x,y \mid x^2 = y^2 = (xy)^2 >$ but the Cayley equivalent must include them :

$$\textbf{finitely presented} < x,y \mid x\char`\^ 2 = y\char`\^ 2 = (x * y)\char`\^ 2 >$$

A very important part of mathematical notation is the description of sets by the properties satisfied by the elements. For example, $\{\ x \in G \mid x^2 = identity\ \}$ defines the set of involutions in the group G, and $\{\ 2^n - 1 \mid n \in Z\ and\ n\ prime\ \}$ defines the Mersenne numbers.

While mathematical notation has the possibility to be very precise and pedantic, the everyday use of mathematics is informal. For example, people will identify an algebraic structure with its underlying set of elements and use the same identifier to refer to both objects. Another common example is to identify a group of transformations with the actual transformations. In this case, a group element might also be used as a map. This is well and good for humans who can identify the type of objects from context and perform the necessary coercions or shift of views. It is also very convenient for users. Hence, Cayley supports such informal behaviour wherever possible. For the remaining cases, Cayley provides a simple coercion facility for users to specify their shifts of view.

There are several **control structures natural to mathematics**. For example, it is very natural to iterate over sets as well as over subranges of the integers. Furthermore, it has been observed in user behaviour that it is very common to iterate over a set and to only execute the body for elements of the set with a given property.

for each x **in** S **do if** x **has the required property then**

...

end if; end for;

Another very common mathematical construct is to use the existential and universal quantifiers in conditions. For example,

```
if all elements of the group G have order 2 then
print 'the group', G, 'is elementary abelian 2-group';
end if;

if there exists an integer i less than q which divides q then
print 'the integer', q, 'is composite';
else
print 'the integer', q, 'is prime';
end if;
```

There are several **catalogues or libraries of groups** in existence. Some examples are Hall and Senior's list of 2-groups of order up to 64, the list/catalogue/database of groups of order 2^7, the Atlas of finite simple groups, the primitive permutation groups of degree less than 50, and more are envisaged in the future. Furthermore, users often have a library of their own favourite examples.

Given that a natural task of a research algebraist is the search for examples or counterexamples to conjectures, these catalogues should be available online, and via Cayley.

Users are forever in search of more **power** in a system. It is only recently, with the increased speed of computers and improvements in software, that computer algebra systems have made a non-trivial contribution to non-numerical mathematics. The system must solve problems of interest to the user with the minimum effort, and work 'instantaneously' no matter how large the problem is. (Remember, there is always a larger problem to solve once the current one is out of the way!) Generally this power is provided by the system's built-in functions and procedures. The built-in functions must cover as wide a range of properties and constructions as possible, and their implementations must be very efficient.

If the system can not solve the problem with the built-in machinery, then it must be **extensible** enough for the truly dedicated problem solver to still tackle the problem. This not only includes supporting the development of new functions and procedures, but also the introduction of new algebraic structures if they are appropriate. Furthermore, the cost of this approach over the built-in implementations must not be too great because the interesting problems are still going to be large.

Some Resulting Language Features

This section does not attempt to be complete in its description of the language or the individual language features. Instead, we wish to impart the flavour of the features via examples, and show that they address the requirements raised in the previous section.

The Cayley system is designed for interactive use. There are no declarations of variables or types, rather there are constructors which define structures, homomorphisms, sets, and sequences of various kinds. The kinds of structures supported by Cayley include groups, integers, finite fields, matrix rings, polynomial rings, vector spaces, geometries and incidence structures.

The groups may be defined by permutations, matrices, a power-commutator presentation, or a finite presentation.

The definition of structures consists of three parts: a keyword indicating the kind of structure (its *class*); parameters qualifying the kind of structure; and generators or basis elements describing the structure. For example, the definition

$A := $ **permutation group**$< 5 \mid (1,2)(3,4), (1,2,3,4,5) >;$

has a parameter 5 indicating the degree of the permutation group, and a set of two permutations which generate A, the alternating group of degree 5.

For a vector space, the parameters indicate the dimension of the vectors, and the field from which the vector entries come. For example, the Golay code of dimension 6 can be defined as

$golay := $ **vector space**$< 12, $ **field**$<3> \mid $ **vec**$(0,0,0, 0,0,0, 1,1,1, 1,1,1),$
vec$(0,0,0, 0,1,1, 0,0,1, 1,2,2),$ **vec**$(0,0,0, 1,0,1, 0,1,0, 2,1,2),$
vec$(0,0,1, 0,0,1, 0,1,2, 0,2,1),$ **vec**$(0,1,0, 0,0,1, 0,2,1, 2,0,1),$
vec$(1,0,0, 0,0,1, 0,2,2, 1,1,0) >;$

Substructures can be defined by specifying their generators, which must be elements of an existing structure. For example,

$Z2 := < (1,2)(3,4) >;$

would define the cyclic group of order 2 as a subgroup of A.

Each structure defined is contained in a universal structure, which is the largest algebraic structure with the parameters used in the definition. Hence, the universal structure for A is the largest permutation group of degree 5, which is the symmetric group S_5. The universal structure for $golay$ is the full 12-dimensional vector space over GF(3). The universal structures together with the defined structures and substructures form a hierarchy. An element belongs to a structure S and all the structures above S in the hierarchy. Coercion supports shifts of view of an element amongst the structures of the hierarchy.

The definitions of maps and homomorphisms follow the syntax of structure definitions. The definition specifies the domain, the range, and the image of the elements in the domain. The images may be specified by exhaustively listing the pairs [element of domain, image]; by specifying the image with the arrow operator; by giving a formula; by supplying a user defined function which calculates the image given the element of the domain; or, in the case of homomorphisms, giving the images of the generators of the domain. For example,

$f := $ **map**$< \{1..3\} -> \{1..3\} \mid [1,1], [2,3], [3,3] >;$
$m := $ **map**$< \{1..3\} -> \{1..3\} \mid 1 -> 1, 2 -> 3, 3 -> 3 >;$
$r := $ **map**$< Z2 -> $ **field**$<2> \mid $ identity $-> 0, (1,2)(3,4) -> 1 >;$
$i := $ **homomorphism**$< A -> A \mid A.1 -> A.1, A.2 -> A.2 \char`^ -1 >;$

where $A.j$ denotes the jth generator of A.

Sets can be constructed by listing their elements between braces, or by specifying an overlying set and a property that must be satisfied by the elements. For example,

> { 1, 3, 5, 7 }
> { n : n in {1..8} | odd(n) }

are two ways to define the odd integers between 1 and 8 inclusive.

Set elements may be integers, structure elements, structures, maps, homomorphisms, and sets. A structure may be used wherever a set can be used. In this case it is identified with its underlying set of elements. For example, in

> { <x,y> : x, y in A | order(x) eq 2 and order(y) eq 2 and order(x^*y) eq 5 }

the group A is treated as a set, and we construct a set of subgroups of A.

The set constructors serve as models for boolean expressions involving the existential and universal quantifiers. For example,

> exists{ x in A | order(x) eq 3 }

is true precisely when there is an element of A that has order 3. The universal quantifier uses the keyword **forall**.

There is an obvious influence of SETL on the way maps, sets (and similarly sequences) are defined. However, Cayley has significantly generalized the constructors and their domains of application.

The control structures of Cayley are modelled on those of Pascal and Modula-2. The selection and iteration constructs are extended to interact with sets and set constructors. The **for** loop may iterate over sets, and when sets are defined by properties there is a special syntax. Some examples are,

```
for each x in A do
print 'the order of', x, 'is', order(x);
end for;
```

```
for each x in A | x ^ 2 eq A.1 do
print x, 'is a square root of', A.1;
end for;
```

The **if** statement adapts to the set constructors by having special cases for the boolean expressions involving existential and universal quantifiers. This allows access to the value which is the example or counterexample of the property being tested. For example,

```
if exists{ x in S | x ^ 2 eq identity } then
"the variable x is defined here"
"it is an example in S for which the condition holds"
```

```
...
else
"the variable x is undefined here"
...
end if;

if forall{ x in S | x ^ 2 eq identity } then
"the variable x is undefined here"
...
else
"the variable x is defined here"
"it is a counterexample in S for which the condition does not hold"
...
end if;
```

Extensibility of the language's functionality is provided by user-defined packages, procedures, and functions. Packages are modelled on the modules of Modula-2. They can protect the implementation details of objects defined within the package, thus supporting abstract data types.

Extensibility of algebraic domains is provided by both built-in and user-defined varieties, classes, and structures. A *variety* provides a theoretical definition by specifying the fundamental operators of the variety, and (optionally) some derived operators. It may provide methods for the derived operators in terms of the fundamental operators. A *class* of a variety provides a particular machine definition of the variety, so that computations can be efficiently performed. A class specifies a representation for the elements of an algebraic structure belonging to the class (and variety). It may also specify representations for substructures and quotients of such algebraic structures. Methods for the fundamental and derived operators of the variety may be overridden by class methods which use the particular machine representation. Those methods not re-defined in the class will be inherited from the variety. An algebraic structure is then defined by specifying its class (such as **permutation group**), by specifying the parameters of the class (such as the degree of a permutation group), and by specifying a set of generators or basis elements.

Databases are viewed as generalizations of sets. Their elements are virtual elements, in that they are stored in files, and there may be a heterogeneous collection of elements. This view allows database queries to be formulated using the set constructor mechanisms. For example, suppose the file /cayley/lib/groups contained a database of groups then

```
D := database( '/cayley/lib/groups' );
```

would bind the variable D to the database.

```
if exists{ G in D | simple( G ) } then
print 'a simple group is', G;
end if;
```

would locate a simple group G in the database, if one exists, and print it, while

```
for each G in D | simple( G ) do
print 'a simple group is', G;
end for;
```

would print all simple groups in the database.

Conclusion

The state of the project at this time is that the language design is (almost) complete, a grammar has been written, and an interpreter for version 4 is up and running. The interpreter does not yet implement packages, user-defined varieties and classes, file I/O, or database facilities. The implementation of packages has however been designed. A prototype deductive database in Prolog is under construction, and will lead to an interface between Cayley and the prototype.

Cayley, in its existing version, has already gained wide user acceptance. With the language design for version 4, we feel that user acceptance can only be enhanced. Furthermore, the language provides a solid foundation for users to devise their own algebraic domains and algorithms within the language, and for experimentation with the use of sophisticated database facilities.

References

John J. Cannon, **A Language for Group Theory**, Department of Pure Mathematics, University of Sydney, 1982, 300 pages.

John J. Cannon, *An introduction to the group theory language, Cayley*, **Computational Group Theory**, M.D. Atkinson (ed.), Academic Press, 1984, 145-183.

Bruce W. Char, Keith O. Geddes, W. Morven Gentleman, Gaston H. Gonnet, *The design of Maple : a compact, portable, and powerful computer algebra system*, **Computer Algebra**, J.A. van Hulzen (ed.), *Lecture Notes in Computer Science 162*, Springer-Verlag, 1983, 101-115.

J.H. Conway, R.T. Curtis, S.P. Norton, R.A. Parker, R.A. Wilson, **Atlas of Finite Groups**, Clarendon Press, Oxford, 1985.

M. Hall, Jr and J.K. Senior, **The Groups of Order 2^n**, ($n \leq 6$), Macmillan, New York, 1964.

A.C. Hearn (editor), **REDUCE User's Manual**, version 3.2, The Rand Corporation, Santa Monica, California, April 1985.

Richard D. Jenks, *A primer : 11 keys to New SCRATCHPAD*, **EUROSAM 84**, J. Fitch (ed.), *Lecture Notes in Computer Science*, **174**, Springer-Verlag, 1984, 123-147.

K. Kennedy and J. Schwartz, *An introduction to the set theoretical language SETL*, Comp. and Maths with Appls, 1 (1975) 97-119.

M.F. Newman and E.A. O'Brien, *A Cayley library for the groups of order dividing 128*, submitted to Proceedings of the Singapore Group Theory Conference, June 1987.

C.C. Sims, *Computational methods in the study of permutation groups*, **Computational Problems in Abstract Algebra**, J. Leech (ed.), Pergamon, Oxford, 1970, 169-183. (and unpublished manuscript)

Symbolics Inc., **MACSYMA Reference Manual**, Version 10, Volumes 1 and 2, December 1984.

N. Wirth, **Programming in Modula-2**, Springer-Verlag, Berlin, 1982.

CoCoA: a User-Friendly System for Commutative Algebra

Alessandro Giovini & Gianfranco Niesi[*]
Department of Mathematics, University of Genova
viale Leon Battista Alberti 4, 16132, Genova – Italy

0. Introduction

CoCoA[1] is a small special-purpose system for doing computations in commutative algebra which runs on any computer of the Macintosh[2] family. Several motivations led us to the development of an entirely new system for symbolic computations. We noticed that mathematicians working in the fields of the commutative algebra and algebraic geometry and who do not have much experience of computers do not use very frequently (or effectively) existing general-purpose powerful systems (like Macsyma, Maple, Mathematica, Reduce, Scratchpad...); in our opinion the main reason is that these packages run essentially on microcomputers or mainframes and their use implies an account on a machine and some knowledge of its operating system; very often instead one needs a software system for sophisticated but reasonably simple tasks for which a microcomputer (not to say a mainframe) is really oversized; indeed up to now the system most widely used by researchers in the quoted fields is probably Macaulay [SSB], which is a small specialized system running on both Sun workstations and on Macintoshes, but not making use of its user interface. (recently another small system, the AlP*I* system, is being developed; it is due to C. Traverso [T], is written in muLisp and is being ported to Common Lisp; it is however a tool for the study of Buchberger's algorithm rather than a user-oriented system); we noticed that instead many mathematicians use frequently a computer of the Macintosh family due to its very cleverly designed user interface. Finally, we felt the need of a system entirely developed within our research group to test and check algorithms and theoretical ideas.

There is a lot of recent work on systems and algorithms for algebraic computation; an extended bibliography can be found in the book "Computer Algebra", [DST]. The purpose of that book is "to demonstrate the existing possibilities, to show how to use them, and to indicate the principles on which systems of non numerical calculations are based, to show the difficulties which the designers of these systems had to solve" (p. vi).

In late 1987 we started to work on the prototype of a small system capable of handling multivariate polynomial rings, embodying algorithms which use the most recent algebraic techniques and completely integrated within the Macintosh environment. The design and implementation of the user interface and of the basic algorithms started in parallel, and during the first months of 1988 we had a prototype running the fundamental user interface, the kernel and the main algorithm for the computation of the Gröbner basis of an ideal. We felt that the small prototype was worth some more work since, although its absolute computation speed was less than that of the Macaulay system, nevertheless the total time spent by a generic user in writing, changing and correcting the input data was very low compared to that needed for performing the same tasks on the Macaulay system: the user interface proved to be very effective. We continued then polishing and speeding up the system while adding more and more functionalities (data structures and algorithms), while the system was being used and commented by our colleagues, and at the beginning of 1989 a version of the system was ready to be given to "external users"; since then the system has been presented at the COCOA II meeting (Genova, May 29 - June 3, 1989) and at the Computers & Mathematics 1989 conference (MIT, Cambridge, Massachusetts, June 13 - 17, 1989) within the tutorial minicourse 'Gröbner

[*] Work partially supported by CNR–Progetto Strategico "Matematica Computazionale"

[1]The CoCoA system has been developed by the authors with the collaboration of Anna Bigatti and Massimo Caboara for the part related to Poincaré series and Hilbert function; it is freely distributed to anyone who requests it by simply sending a blank diskette to the authors. Questions and suggestions can be also sent to the email address cocoa@igecuniv.bitnet

[2]Macintosh is a trademark of Apple Computer, Inc.

bases: A Foundation for Commutative Algebra' given by L. Robbiano [Ro5].

The main characteristics of CoCoA can be, in our opinion, so summarized:

- it is a small system, and we make any effort in keeping it small; it runs on a machine one can have on the desktop, and even at home, but takes advantage of additional hardware provided;
- it uses consistently the classical Macintosh user interface and it is integrated within that environment;
- it gives the user great freedom in organizing the computations and in writing commands and expressions in a very intuitive way while being very forgiving w.r.t. errors ;
- it implements advanced algorithms and strategies without supposing the user knowing them;
- and, yes!, it is reasonably fast.

Presently CoCoA is being used in several research centres in Canada, England, France, Germany, Italy, Japan, Nigeria, Spain, Sweden and USA (up to now we have distributed about 150 copies of it), and even though we will not turn CoCoA into a "software product", we will continue to improve it and to make it more and more sophisticated; but we especially hope that at least some of the ideas we have put into it will be accepted by the community of mathematicians as a reasonable starting point of a "user-friendly" symbolic computation system one would like to have on his desktop.

The paper is structured as follows: in section 1 we summarize the basic mathematical prerequisites needed to understand the description of the system; in section 2 we give an overview of the architecture of the system; in section 3 we outline the implementation of some of the algorithms; in section 4 we give some examples and timings and finally in section 5 we suggest which could be the future of the system.

1. Technical Preliminaries

Let $A = k[X_1,...,X_n]$ be a polynomial ring over a field k in the indeterminates $X_1,...,X_n$ having weights $w_1,...,w_n$. Let $T(A)$ be the set of *terms* (i.e. monic monomials) of A. Then $T(A)$ is a commutative semigroup isomorphic to $\mathbb{N}^n$ via $X_1^{a_1}...X_n^{a_n} \to \log(X_1^{a_1}...X_n^{a_n}) = (a_1,...,a_n)$.

A *term ordering* on A is a total ordering > on $T(A)$ such that for all $t, t_1, t_2 \in T(A)$:

a) $t > 1$; b) $t_1 > t_2 \Rightarrow t t_1 > t t_2$.

A classification of the orderings on $\mathbb{N}^n$ (and hence on $T(A)$) and a characterization of the term orderings can be found in [Ro1]. Essentially each ordering > corresponds to a (not uniquely determined) array $(u_1,...,u_s)$ of vectors in $\mathbb{R}^n$ and $t > t' \Leftrightarrow (\log(t) \cdot u_1,...,\log(t) \cdot u_s) >_{lex} (\log(t') \cdot u_1,...,\log(t') \cdot u_s)$, where $>_{lex}$ is the ordering on $\mathbb{R}^s$ given by $(a_1,...,a_s) >_{lex} (b_1,...,b_s)$ iff the first leftmost non zero coordinate of $(a_1-b_1,...,a_s-b_s)$ is positive; moreover > is a term ordering iff the matrix whose columns are the vectors $u_1,...,u_s$ has the following property: the first non zero element of each row is positive.

Let M be a free A-module of finite rank r. We may assume $M = A^r$. A *term* of M is an element of the form $t e_i$ where $t \in T(A)$ and $\{e_i\}_{i=1,...,r}$ is the canonical basis of M. Hence the set of terms $T(M)$ of M is in one-to-one correspondence with $T(A) \times \{1,...,r\}$. In [Tr, MM3] *module term orderings* are defined as total orderings > on $T(M)$ such that for all $t, t_1, t_2 \in T(A)$, and $i, j \in \{1,...,r\}$

a) $t t_1 e_i > t_1 e_i$; b) $t_1 e_i > t_2 e_j \Rightarrow t t_1 e_i > t t_2 e_j$.

A term ordering on A induces several module term orderings on A^r. We just give two examples:
1) 'TO-Position' : $t_1 e_i >_M t_2 e_j \Leftrightarrow t_1 >_A t_2$ or, if $t_1 = t_2$, $i < j$;
2) 'Position-TO' : $t_1 e_i >_M t_2 e_j \Leftrightarrow i < j$ or, if $i = j$, $t_1 >_A t_2$.

Up to now, however, there is no complete classification of module term-orderings.

From now on assume that a term ordering > is given on A. Then each polynomial f of A has a unique canonical representation as $\Sigma c_i t_i$ where $c_i = c(f, t_i)$ is a non zero coefficient, $t \in T(A)$ and $t_1 > t_2 > ....$

In this case we call $Lt(f) = t_1$, $Lc(f) = c_1$, $Lm(f) = c_1 t_1$ resp. *leading term, leading coefficient, leading monomial* of f and the set $Supp(f) = \{t \in T(A) \mid c(f,t) \neq 0\}$ *support* of f.

These and the successive notions can be adapted with minor changes to the case of the modules.

Given a finite subset $G = \{g_1,...,g_s\}$ of A, a polynomial f is called *reduced* w.r.t. G (resp. *completely reduced*) if $Lt(f)$ (resp. any term in $Supp(f)$) is not multiple of the leading term of any element in G. If f is not completely reduced, then there exists $t \in Supp(f)$, $g_i \in G$ such that $t = \tau Lt(g_i)$, for some $\tau \in T(A)$; the polynomial $h = f - c(f,t)Lc(g_i)^{-1} \tau g_i$ is said to be a *reduction* of f w.r.t. G, its leading term is less than or equal to the leading term of f and it is equivalent to f modulo the ideal generated by G.

The *division algorithm* for f and G is the iterated application to the polynomial f of the previous reduction procedure with elements of G until a completely reduced polynomial, denoted by remainder(f, G), is obtained. In general remainder(f, G) is not uniquely determined by f and G but it depends on which elements of G are chosen for the reduction when various choices are possible.

A *Gröbner basis* [Buc1, Buc2], or briefly a *Gbasis*, of an ideal I (w.r.t. the term ordering >) is a finite system of generators G of I such that $f \in I$ iff remainder(f, G) = 0. We recall also that G is a GBasis iff for all $f \in A$ remainder (f, G) is uniquely determined by f and G. Hence a Gbasis of I solves the ideal membership problem for I.

Other characterizations of Gbases in polynomial ring theory can be found in [Buc4, Bay, MM3, Ro2].

An algorithm for computing a Gbasis from a set of generators $F = \{f_1, ..., f_r\}$ for I was first given by Buchberger ([Buc1], [Buc2]). His algorithm is based on the following characterization of the Gbasis: G is a Gbasis iff for all f, $g \in G$ remainder(Sp(f,g), G) = 0 where the S-polynomial Sp(f,g) is defined as

$$\frac{Lm(g)}{GCD(Lt(f),Lt(g))} f - \frac{Lm(f)}{GCD(Lt(f),Lt(g))} g.$$

The simplest form of the Buchberger's algorithm, which takes in input the polynomials $\{f_1, ..., f_r\}$ and returns a Gbasis G of the ideal generated by them, is the following:

```
G = {f₁,..., fᵣ};
B = {(i,j) / 1 ≤ i < j ≤ r }
while B ≠ ∅ do
    Choose (i,j) ∈ B
    B = B-{(i,j)}
    h = remainder(Sp(fᵢ,fⱼ), G)
    if h ≠ 0 then
        r = r+1
        f = h
        G = G ∪ {fᵣ}
        B = B ∪ {(i,r) / 1 ≤ i < r }.
```

This algorithm can be optimized giving criteria for detecting a priori useless pairs (i.e. pairs (i, j) such that remainder(Sp(f_i,f_j), G) = 0) and choosing a 'good strategy' for selecting the pair to be next processed (see [Buc3], [GM] and section 3).

We report some results (without proofs) about Gbases that lead to a computational solution of some classic problems in the theory of polynomial rings. It should be noticed that in some problems (ideal membership, syzygies...) it suffices to know a Gbasis w.r.t. any term ordering while in some others (elimination, homogeneization...) particular term orderings are required. For more details see for example [Ro4, Ro5].

Ideal membership and canonical representation of the elements of A/I

A Gbasis of an ideal I solves, by definition, the problem "$f \in I$". Let $I = \{f_1, ..., f_r\}$ be an ideal of A, let Lt(I) be the monomial ideal generated by $\{Lt(f) / f \in I-\{0\}\}$. Then $Lt(I) \supset (Lt(f_1),...,Lt(f_r))$ and the equality holds if and only if $\{f_1, ..., f_r\}$ is a Gbasis of I.

Let $\mathbf{B} = \{t \in T(A) / t \notin Lt(I)\}$. Then the image of **B** in A/I is a k-basis of A/I. Hence, fixed a Gbasis of I, each residue class $\bar{f}$ of A/I has a canonical representative, remainder(f, G), which is the (only) completely reduced polynomial (w.r.t. G) in the class.

Hilbert function and Poincaré series

If I is a homogeneous ideal, then A/I is a graded ring and for all $d \in \mathbb{N}$ $(A/I)_d$ is a finite k-vector space. The function $H_{A/I}: \mathbb{N} \to \mathbb{N}$ defined by $H_{A/I}(d) = \dim_k(A/I)_d$ is called *Hilbert function* of I. It is an important numerical invariant of I and gives informations about I like dimension and multiplicity. It is well known that, for $d \gg 0$, $H_{A/I}(d) = P(d)$ where P is a polynomial with rational coefficients called *Hilbert polynomial*.

From the canonical representation of the elements of A/I it follows immediately that the homogeneous ideal I and the monomial ideal Lt(I) have the same Hilbert function. There are several algorithms about Hilbert function computation (see for instance [MM2]).

The series $\mathbf{P}_{A/I}(z) = \Sigma_i H_{A/I}(i) z^i$, associated to the function $H_{A/I}$, is called *Poincaré series*. It is well known that $\mathbf{P}_{A/I}$ is rational of type $Q(z)/(1-z)^n$ where $Q(z)$ is a polynomial with integer coefficients, and can be easily computed being $H_{A/I}$ an additive function. The Hilbert function and the Hilbert polynomial can be derived from the Poincaré series.

Syzygies

Given a finite subset $F = \{f_1,\ldots, f_r\}$ of A, the syzygy module of F is the sub A-module $Syz(F) = \{(h_1,\ldots, h_r) \in A^r \mid \Sigma h_i f_i = 0 \}$ of A^r. In [Zac] it is shown how to derive a system of generators of $Syz(F)$ from a system of generators of $Syz(G)$, where G is a Gbasis of the ideal generated by F. On the other hand a system of generators of $Syz(G)$ can be easily computed, indeed if $G = \{g_1,\ldots, g_s\}$ is a Gbasis and we put $h_{ij} = Sp(g_i,g_j) = m_i g_i - m_j g_j$, then for all i, j we have remainder(h_{ij}, G) = 0, so $h_{ij} = \Sigma p_k g_k$ and the set $\{\Sigma p_k e_k - m_i e_i - m_j e_j\}$ is a basis of $Syz(G)$.

Syzygies play a fundamental role in commutative algebra; they allow, among other things, to construct minimal free resolutions, to minimize a given set of generators, to compute the intersection of ideals or modules, to compute GCD of multivariate polynomials (even if, perhaps, this is not the best way to do it).

Elimination

Let $A = k[X_1,\ldots,X_n,Y_1,\ldots,Y_m]$ and let T(X) (resp. T(Y)) be the set of terms in the variables $X_1,\ldots,X_n$ (resp. $Y_1,\ldots,Y_m$). Given two term orderings, $>_X$ on T(X) and $>_Y$ on T(Y), the corresponding *elimination term ordering* $>_A$ on A is defined in the following way:

$$X^A Y^B >_A X^C Y^D \Leftrightarrow (Y^B >_Y Y^D) \text{ or } (Y^B = Y^D \text{ and } X^A >_X X^C).$$

The key point is that if I is an ideal of A and G is a Gbasis of I w.r.t. an elimination term ordering on A, then $G \cap k[X_1,\ldots,X_n]$ is a Gbasis of $I \cap k[X_1,\ldots,X_n]$ ([Tr], [GTZ]).

Elimination is a very powerful tool in commutative algebra and algebraic geometry. It may be used in several circumstances, for instance in the computation of projections of subvarieties on a subspace, cartesian equations of varieties given parametrically, zeros of a 0-dimensional ideal ([Tr]), dimension of an ideal ([Ca], [KW]), intersection of ideals ([GTZ]), standard bases ([La1]), primary decomposition ([La2], [GTZ]), etc.

Homogeneization

Consider the overring $B = k[X_0,X_1,\ldots,X_n]$ of A and assume that X_0 has weight 1. If $f(X_1,\ldots,X_n) \in A$ is a polynomial of degree d, then $^h f = X_0^d f(X_1/X_0,\ldots,X_n/X_0) \in B$ is the homogeneization of f. The homogeneization of the ideal I of A is defined as the ideal $^h I$ of B generated by $\{^h f / f \in I - \{0\}\}$. If $I = (f_1, \ldots, f_r)$, then $^h I \supset (^h f_1, \ldots, ^h f_r)$. But if $>_A$ is a degree compatible term ordering on A, i.e. such that its first vector is $(1,w_1,\ldots,w_n)$ (w_i is the weight of X_i), and $G = \{g_1,\ldots,g_s\}$ is a Gbasis of I w.r.t. $>_A$, then $^h I = (^h g_1,\ldots,^h g_s)$ ([RV]).

2. An Overview of the System

The release 0.993β of the CoCoA system consists of about 20,000 lines of Pascal code and has been developed on and for the Macintosh personal computer. The programming style and the implementation of the data structures have been chosen to make the system open and easy to improve and modify having preferred the ease of maintenance to very advanced optimization techniques, the emphasis being on the optimization of the algorithms from a strictly mathematical point of view.

The system is composed of a *kernel* and of a *library*.

The kernel consists of the following two components:

- the *user interface kernel*, which is about 20% of the system and deals primarily with implementing the user interface (including the scanner and the parser of the input data) and provides the basic standard functionalities of the Macintosh environment;

- the *algebraic kernel*, which is about 20% of the system and implements the basic data structures and algorithms underlying nearly every operation of the system.

The library is built directly on top of the algebraic kernel; while the algorithms of this one are not likely to change very often (and indeed they did not change during the last few releases of the system), the library is a continuously increasing collection of algorithms which are subject to frequent modifications.

The connection between the user interface and the library is established primarily by the *command handler*: a typical CoCoA user types, selects, cuts, pastes and modifies data within a CoCoA window, and eventually decides that a certain portion of text is a command that needs to be executed: at this point the text can be selected and by hitting a key the selection is passed to the command handler; this part of the system interprets the input text and, if no errors are encountered, it decides which algorithms to invoke and which strategies to apply. The selection of the strategy depends on several factors:

- first, it depends on the calculations which have been previously performed (for example, many algorithms compute values as a side effect, and these values can be sometimes reused in later computations without computing them from scratch);
- second, it depends on the know–how of the authors (and of those which collaborate to the system) which has been embodied in the system;
- finally, it depends on the value of some parameters which can be directly changed by the user.

It should be stressed that a design goal of the system is that the selection of the (optimum) strategies should be done in the background, and the (average) user should never be concerned with the problem of choosing the best values of the parameters; only to some specialized extent one should need the direct access to the value of the inner parameters.

Once the invoked algorithms are done with their job, the resulting value, if any, is displayed on the screen; the syntax for the output values is essentially a subset of the syntax for the input values, so the results can be re-input in the system by a simple selection.

The syntax of the input commands and expressions is a simple Pascal-like syntax which takes benefit from the graphic capabilities of the Macintosh; so the user can enter and evaluate a sequence of commands like

$$F = t^{31}-t^6-t-x;\ G = t^8-y;\ H = t^{10}-z;$$
$$I = ideal(F, G, H)\ ;$$
$$J = elim(t, I);\ J$$

In the picture it is shown is how the Macintosh screen looks like after their execution.

 File   Edit   Keyboard   Ring

CoCoA 1

$F = t^{31}-t^6-t-x;\ G = t^8-y;\ H = t^{10}-z;$
$I = ideal(F, G, H)\ ;$
$J = elim(t, I);\ J$

Ideal J

$y^5 - z^4$,
$xy^4z^5 + 1/2yz^7 - 2xy^4z^2 - xy^4 - 2x^2y^2z - x^3z^2 - yz^4 - 1/2x^2y^2 - 1/2yz^2 + 1/2yz$,
$x^3y^4z^4 - 1/2x^2yz^7 + xy^3z^5 - 2x^3y^4z + x^2yz^4 + 1/2z^7 - 3/2x^4y^2 - x^5z - 2xy^3z^2 + 1/2x^2yz^2 - xy^3 - 5/2x^2yz - z^4 - 1/2x^2y - 1/2z^2 + 1/2z$,
$z^8 - 2z^5 - 2xy^3 - x^2yz - z^3 + z^2$,
$y^2z^6 - 1/2xz^7 - 2y^2z^3 + xz^4 + 1/2x^3y - y^2z - 3/2xz^2 + y^2 - 1/2xz$,
$x^6y^4z^3 + 3x^4y^3z^5 - 2x^5yz^6 + x^4y^3z^4 - 2x^6y^4 + x^3z^7 - 6x^4y^3z^2 + 4x^5yz^3$
$+ 2xy^4z^4 + x^2y^2z^5 - x^8 - 2x^4y^3z - yz^7 - 3x^4y^3 - 4x^5yz - 2x^3z^4 + yz^6 - 5x^5y -$
$4xy^4z - 2x^2y^2z^2 - x^3z^2 + 2yz^4 - 4x^2y^2 - 3x^3z - 2yz^3 + yz^2 - 2yz + y$

Superscripts, subscripts and special symbols appear as such on the screen, and hence expressions are very easy to read, understand and correct, since their notation is very similar to the usual mathematical one.

The following is an example of a rather complex expression, together with the resulting value:

```
Resultant(NormalForm(-x³(y²+z)+x²-yz, Ideal(x³-y,x⁴-z)∩Ideal(y+z,x²)),
         Der((x²+y⁵)², x), x)
```

$- 128y^{12}z^2 - 128y^{11}z^3 + 64y^{10}z^4 - 128y^{12}z - 128y^{11}z^2 + 64y^{10}z^3 - 32y^{12} - 32y^{11}z + 16y^{10}z^2 - 32y^9z^2 - 96y^8z^3 - 80y^7z^4 + 16y^5z^6 - 256y^9z - 512y^8z^2 + 256y^6z^4 - 64y^5z^5 - 128y^9 - 256y^8z + 128y^6z^3 - 32y^5z^4 - 128y^6 - 384y^5z - 192y^4z^2 + 256y^3z^3 + 96y^2z^4 - 96yz^5 + 16z^6$

A command can be either an expression to be evaluated, an assignment of an expression to an identifier or a call to a procedure; finally commands can be separated by semi-colons.

All the command are executed within the *current ring*; this is determined by the following items:

- the *field* of the coefficients: it can be either Q or Z_p; but please note that Q is a *proper subset* of the field of rational numbers implemented by using the built–in long integers, so there is possibility of overflow; whether or not to implement arbitrary precision integers is a design topic which is still under analysis;
- the *indeterminates*: an indeterminate is a single letter possibly followed by a subscript;
- the *weights* of the indeterminates;
- the *term-ordering* (an n×n integer matrix, where n is the number of indeterminates); the most common term orderings are predefined and can be selected by simply pressing a button; the user can anyway directly fill in the matrix with a custom ordering.

The system defaults upon startup to the ring $Q[t, x, y, z]$, to all the weights equal to 1 and to the "degree reverse lexicographic" term–ordering. The user can change at any time these values, and another design goal is that the system should be able to "smoothly transfer" already entered or computed data from a ring to another (whenever this makes sense); presently this is true if the user limits itself to changes to the weights or to the term–ordering or to the addition of variables.

An outline of the algorithms of the library is given in next section; we give here a short overview of the algebraic kernel. Multivariate polynomials are represented as dynamic-length lists of monomials, which are themselves dynamic-length lists; this representation has been preferred since most algorithms dealing with Gröbner bases are naturally implemented with it. The presence of dynamic data enforces garbage collection and we do immediate and total garbage collection to allow the system to work when little memory is available. Moreover, due to compatibility problems with the Macintosh operating system (which "prefers" relocatable blocks to nonrelocatable ones), we independently maintain a private heap in which all nonrelocatable blocks used by the algebraic kernel are allocated; this allows CoCoA to work smoothly even under MultiFinder, with desk accessories and so on. The size of the private heap is determined upon startup depending on the available memory, but leaving at least enough space in the public heap for loading the code, some desk accessories and printing routines. Currently CoCoA runs with a minimum of 390K of application memory.

Polynomials are always kept sorted w.r.t. the current term–ordering, and the operations of the kernel benefit of and preserve this ordering; but notice that during some computations the term–ordering changes temporarily without the user ever knowing.

The other data structures are built on top of those of the kernel: these are polynomial lists, ideals, matrices, modules and Poincaré series. For the benefit of the algorithms, there is often a lot of information associated with these structures; for example, a value of type ideal consists of the generators, and, possibly, of its Gröbner basis, its standard basis, its Poincaré series, its dimension and so on; whenever for some reason one of these values is computed it remains associated with the ideal and can be hence reused for later computations.

3. The Library

The most important module of the library is the implementation of Buchberger's algorithm for computing the Gröbner basis of an ideal or of a module. The implementation includes several "local" optimizations, the criteria of Gebauer and Möller [GM] for detecting useless pairs and a strategy for selecting the pair to be next processed, due to Robbiano, based on the following fact: if we order the critical pairs so that they are processed by increasing degree of the l.c.m. of the corresponding leading terms, then, *in the homogeneous case*, the algorithm produces only non redundant elements of the Gbasis, i.e. each new polynomial is such that its leading term does not divide the leading term of any other polynomial already in the basis. So it seems suitable (and the experience confirms it) to force the general case to a similar behaviour. Although one could add a new variable, homogenize the given generators, compute the Gbasis and then go back to the initial situation ([MM1]), in practice it is not convenient to increase the number of variables. Robbiano's strategy consists of ordering the pairs with an ordering which is very close to the order which would have been chosen if we had homogenized the generators.

The system can compute a truncated Gbasis, i.e. it can carry out the computation until a polynomial of degree greater than a fixed number has been found.

The other main building block of the system is the algorithm for computing syzygies, which is essentially that of [Zac] and consists in a small variation of Buchberger's one. More precisely, we keep in the basis the given generators $g_1,...,g_r$, we keep track of how the new polynomials $g_{r+1},...,g_s$ can be expressed in terms of $g_1,...,g_r$, and, for each critical pair (g_i,g_j) such that remainder$(S(g_i,g_j), G) = m_ig_i - m_jg_j -\Sigma_i h_ig_i = 0$ we add to the syzygy module the relation among $g_1,...,g_r$ obtained lifting the relation $m_ie_i - m_je_j - \Sigma_i h_ie_i$ among all the g_i's.

The library contains also several procedures that using Gbasis and syzygies computations allow to compute:

- the elimination of one or of a block of variables; the system automatically changes the term-ordering to an elimination term-ordering, applies the algorithm outlined in section 1 and then returns the result in the original setting;
- the standard basis of an ideal (at the moment we use Lazard's algorithm [Laz1], an implementation of Mora's tangent cone algorithm [M] is planned for the next months); here *standard basis* of I means a basis $f_1, ..., f_t$ of I s.t. $I^* = (f_1^*, ..., f_t^*)$ where f^* denotes the homogeneous form of f of minimal degree, and I^* denotes the ideal generated by $\{f^* \mid f \in I\}$.;
- the homogeneization of an ideal, using the result of Robbiano–Valla quoted in section 1;
- the intersection of ideals or of submodules of a free module;
- the division of an ideal by another ideal;
- the Poincaré series, Hilbert function, and Hilbert polynomial of homogeneous ideals and, hence, their dimension, multiplicity and index of regularity;
- the GCD of multivariate polynomials.

For a complete list of the operations available in the system see CoCoA User's Manual ([GN]).

4. Performances

In this section we give some execution times of the CoCoA system; we use as bench-mark the computation of some Gröbner bases; we compare our execution times with those of the AlP*I* system [T] instead of those of the Macaulay system since Macaulay does only work on (and hence it is optimized for) homogeneous ideals, while our algorithm has been especially fine tuned for the generic non homogeneous case (in the homogeneous case Macaulay is in the average 3–4 times faster than CoCoA).

The examples are take from [T] where the source of the example and the AlP*I* timings on a Toshiba–5100 are given. For each example we give the generators of the ideal, the variables of the ring, the term-ordering (L for total lexicographic, DR for degree reverse lexicographic), the time in seconds for CoCoA (on a Macintosh SE/30) and for AlP*I*.

A comparison between CoCoA and Mathematica [W] is not very significant; first of all Mathematica works with a unique term-ordering – the lexicographic term-ordering – which is almost never used in the applications for which our system has been designed; secondly, the implementation of the GroebnerBasis procedure appears not very efficient: example 1 is computed in 2.48 seconds, while during the computation of examples 3 and 6 the available memory on the Macintosh SE/30 is exhausted after respectively 58' and 20'.

Example 1: $(x+y+z+t, xy+yz+zt+tx, xyz+yzt+ztx+txy, xyzt+1)$; variables xyzt

Example 2: $(x+y+z+t+u, xy+yz+zt+xu+tu, xyz+yzt+ztu+tux+uxy,$
$\quad\quad xyzt+yztu+ztux+tuxy+uxyz, xyztu+1)$; variables xyztu

Example 3: $(t^{31}+t^6+t-x, t^8-y, t^{10}-z)$; variables txyz

Example 4:

$(l_1(l_4-1/2l_5+l_6),$

$(2/7l_1{}^2-l_4)(-10l_1+5l_2-l_3),$

$(2/7l_1{}^2-l_4)(3l_4-l_5+l_6),$

$(-2l_1{}^2+l_1l_2+2l_1l_3-l_2{}^2-7l_5+2l_6)(-3l_1+2l_2)+21(7l_7-2l_1l_4+3/7l_1{}^3),$

$(-2l_1{}^2+l_1l_2+2l_1l_3-l_2{}^2-7l_5+2l_6)(2l_4-2l_5)+(7l_7-2l_1l_4+3/7l_1{}^3)$
$\quad\quad (-45l_1+15l_2-3l_3),$

$2(-2l_1{}^2+l_1l_2+2l_1l_3-l_2{}^2-7l_5+2l_6)l_7+(7l_7-2l_1l_4+3/7l_1{}^3)(12l_4-3l_5+2l_6),$

$(l_1(5l_1-3l_2+l_3))(2l_2-l_1)+7(l_1(2l_6-4l_4)),$

$(l_1(5l_1-3l_2+l_3))l_3+7(l_1(2l_6-4l_4)),$

$(l_1(5l_1-3l_2+l_3))(-2l_4-2l_5)+(l_1(2l_6-4l_4))(2l_1-8l_1)+84(1/2l_1l_7),$

$(l_1(5l_1-3l_2+l_3))(8/3l_5+6l_6)+(l_1(2l_6-4l_4))(11l_1-17/3l_2+5/3l_3)-168(1/2l_1l_7),$

$15l_7(l_1(5l_1-3l_2+l_3))+(l_1(2l_6-4l_4))(5l_4-2l_5)+1/2l_1l_7(-120l_1+30l_2-6l_3),$

$-3(l_1(5l_1-3l_2+l_3))l_7+(l_1(2l_6-4l_4))(-1/2l_4+1/4l_5-1/2l_6)+1/2l_1l_7(24l_1-6l_2),$

$3(l_1(2l_6-4l_4))l_7+1/2l_1l_7(40l_4-8l_5+4l_6))$; variables $l_1l_2l_3l_4l_5l_6l_7$

Example 5 $(y^2z+2xyt-2x-z, 2yzt+xt^2-x-2z,$
$\quad\quad -x^3z+4xy^2z+4x^2yt+2y^3t+4x^2-10y^2+4xz-10yt+2,$
$\quad\quad -xz^3+4yz^2t+4xzt^2+2yt^3+4xz+4z^2-10yt-10t^2+2)$; variables xyzt

Example 6 $(x(y+z+t)-a, y(x+z+t)-b, z(x+y+t)-c, t(x+y+z)-d))$; variables xyztabcd

Example 7 $xb-ya$, $(x-1)d-y(c-1)$, $b^2+a^2-r^2$, $(c-1)^2+d^2-s^2$, $(a-c)^2+(b-d)^2-t^2$, variables xyabcdrstu

	CoCoA Timing	AIPI Timing
Example 1	DR=0.46	DR=8.0
	L=0.51	L=1.2
Example 2	DR=48.91	DR=114.0
	L=?	L=128
Example 3	DR=1.23	DR=8.00
	L=15.55	L=113.0
Example 4	L=245.18	L=96.0
Example 5	DR=12.63	DR= 67.0
Example 6	DR=10.73	DR=28.0
	L=372.14	L= 2257
Example 7	DR=40.65	DR=137
	L=433.0	L=2157

Notes:

- In examples 5 and 6, the computations done by AlP/ with the lexicographic ordering make use of secondary storage since the intermediate values exceed the available RAM.
- Macaulay takes 7 seconds to eliminate the variable t in example 3, CoCoA takes 10.1 seconds; however to try the example with Macaulay the ideal has to be first homogeneized.
- Example 6, with the lexicographic term-ordering and without the optimization due to Robbiano on the selection of the next critical pair to be processed takes 494.0 seconds.

For what concerns the overall implementation of the algebraic kernel, it should be noted that the execution speed of some basic operations is faster than in a general-purpose system like Mathematica (release 1.2, running on the same configuration as CoCoA). For example, the computation of the GCD of the following two polynomials

$$f = 2x^7t^4 - 4x^7zt^2 - 3x^6t^4 - 6x^5yt^4 + 2x^7z^2 + 6x^6zt^2 + 12x^5yzt^2 + 9x^4yt^4 + 6x^3y^2t^4$$
$$- 3x^6z^2 - 6x^5yz^2 - 18x^4yzt^2 - 12x^3y^2zt^2 - 9x^2y^2t^4 - 2xy^3t^4 + 9x^4yz^2 + 6x^3y^2z^2 +$$
$$18x^2y^2zt^2 + 4xy^3zt^2 + 3y^3t^4 - 9x^2y^2z^2 - 2xy^3z^2 - 6y^3zt^2 + 3y^3z^2$$

$$g = 2x^5y^7 - 4x^5y^6 - 3x^4y^7 - 4x^3y^8 - 4x^5y^4t^2 + 6x^4y^6 + 8x^3y^7 + 6x^2y^8 + 2xy^9 +$$
$$8x^5y^3t^2 + 6x^4y^4t^2 + 8x^3y^5t^2 + 2x^5yt^4 - 12x^2y^7 - 4xy^8 - 3y^9 - 12x^4y^3t^2 - 16x^3y^4t^2$$
$$- 12x^2y^5t^2 - 4xy^6t^2 - 4x^5t^4 - 3x^4yt^4 - 4x^3y^2t^4 + 6y^8 + 24x^2y^4t^2 + 8xy^5t^2 + 6y^6t^2 +$$
$$6x^4t^4 + 8x^3yt^4 + 6x^2y^2t^4 + 2xy^3t^4 - 12y^5t^2 - 12x^2yt^4 - 4xy^2t^4 - 3y^3t^4 + 6y^2t^4$$

takes 2.5 seconds in Mathematica and 1.36 seconds in CoCoA; similarly, $(x+y+z+t)^{11}$ is computed in 14.5 seconds in Mathematica and in 8.80 seconds in CoCoA (Macaulay takes 4 seconds).

5 The Future

We plan to add in the immediate future many new algorithms; among these we have:

- Mora's tangent cone algorithm;
- a set of algorithms specialized to monomial subalgebras (the current release of the system embodies already an algorithm for computing the Hilbert function of an affine monomial curve);
- minimal free resolutions.

For what concerns the user interface, we plan to handle more smoothly the transfer of values between different rings; we are also experimenting a version of the system capable of performing the computations in the background (under the MultiFinder).

Two big holes in the system are the lack of programmability and of arbitrary precision integers. We do not plan to fill them in the immediate future; we fear that the system would become too large w.r.t. our goal of a "desktop symbolic computation system". Nevertheless we plan to make some experiments in those directions.

Finally, although the algebraic kernel and the library are written in standard Pascal, and hence are largely independent from the Macintosh environment, we are not planning to port CoCoA to other machines. First of all, it would be too difficult for us to develop and maintain different releases, second, no machine offers currently the kind of features the Macintosh does and which are essential part of our view of the system.

Acknowledgements: It is for us a pleasure to thank Lorenzo Robbiano; his constant encouragement and enthusiasm convinced us in bringing CoCoA to its current state; needless to say, many algorithms embody his ideas and suggestions; we would also like to thank Teo Mora for his contribution to the system progress and for having been one of the first users and critics; finally, thanks also to Anna Bigatti and Massimo Caboara, who undertook the heavy task of reading and understanding the code of CoCoA for adding the modules related to Poincaré series and Hilbert functions.

Bibliography

[Bay] D. A. BAYER, The Division Algorithm and the Hilbert Scheme, Ph. D. Thesis, Harvard Univ.,Cambridge, Mass., 1982.

[Buc1] B. BUCHBERGER, Ein Algorithmus zum Auffiden des Restklassenringes nach einem nulldimensionalen Polynomideale, Ph. D. Thesis, Univ. Innsbrück, Austria, 1965.

[Buc2] B. BUCHBERGER, Ein algorithmisches Kriterium für die Lösbarkeit eines algebraischen Gleichungssystems, Aequationes Math. 4 (1970), 364-383.

[Buc3] B. BUCHBERGER, A criterion for detecting unnecessary reductions in the construction of Gröbner bases, in "Proc. EUROSAM '79", 3-21, Lect. Notes in Comp. Sci., vol. 72, 1979.

[Buc4] B. BUCHBERGER, Gröbner bases: An algorithmic method in polynomial ideal theory, in "Recent Trends in Multidimensional System Theory" (N. K. Bose, Ed.), Reidel, Dordrecht, 1985.

[Ca] G. CARRA' FERRO, Some upper bounds for multiplicity of an autoreduced subset of INm and their applications, in "Proc. AAECC-3", 306-315, Lect. Notes in Comp. Sci., vol. 229, 1986.

[DST] J. H. DAVENPORT, Y. SIRET, E. TOURNIER, "Computer Algebra", Academic Press, London, 1988.

[GM] R. GEBAUER - M. MÖLLER, On an Installation of Buchberger's Algorithm, J. of Symb. Comp. 6 (1988), 275-286.

[GN] A. GIOVINI - G. NIESI, CoCoA User's Manual (v. 0.99b - May 1989), University of Genova

[GTZ] P. GIANNI - B. TRAGER - G. ZACHARIAS, Gröbner bases and Primary Decomposition of Polynomial Ideals, J. of Symb. Comp. 6 (1988), 149-167.

[KW] H.KREDEL - V. WEISPFENNING, Computing Dimension and Independent Set for Polynomial Ideals, J.of Symb. Comp. 6 (1988), 231-247.

[La1] D. LAZARD, Gröbner bases, Gaussian elimination, and resolution of systems of algebraic equations, in "Proc. EUROCAL '83", 146-156, Lect. Notes in Comp. Sci., vol. 162, 1983.

[La2] D. LAZARD, Ideal bases and primary decomposition: case of two variables, J. of Symb. Comp. 1 (1985), 261-270.

[MM1] H.M. MÖLLER - F. MORA, Upper and lower bounds for the degree of Gröbner bases, in "Proc. EUROSAM '84", 172-183, Lect. Notes in Comp. Sci., vol.162, 1983.

[MM2] H.M. MÖLLER - F. MORA, The computation of the Hilbert function, in "Proc. EUROCAL '83", 157-167, Lect. Notes in Comp. Sci., vol.174, 1984.

[MM3] H.M. MÖLLER - F. MORA, New Constructive Methods in Classical Ideal Theory, J. Alg. 100 (1986), 138-178.

[M] F. MORA, An algorithm to compute the equations of tangent cones, in "Proc. EUROCAM '82", 158-165, Lect. Notes in Comp. Sci., vol.144, 1982.

[Ro1] L. ROBBIANO, Term Orderings on the Polynomial Ring, in "Proc. EUROCAL '85", 513-517, Lect. Notes in Comp. Sci., vol.204, 1985.

[Ro2] L. ROBBIANO, On the theory of graded structures, J.of Symb. Comp. 2 (1986), 139-170.

[Ro3] L. ROBBIANO, Introduction to the theory of Gröbner Bases, in "Queen's Papers in Pure and Applied Mathematics", n. 80 (1988).

[Ro4] L. ROBBIANO, Computer and Commutative Algebra, in "Proc. AAECC 6", 157-167, Lect. Notes in Comp. Sci., vol.357, 1988.

[Ro5] L. ROBBIANO, Gröbner Bases: a Foundation for Commutative Algebra, notes of a tutorial given at MIT in June 1989.

[RV] L. ROBBIANO - G. VALLA, On set theoretic complete intersections in the projective space, Rend. Sem. Mat. Fis. Milano 53 (1983), 333-346.

[SSB] M. STILLMAN - M. STILLMAN - D. BAYER, Macaulay User Manual, May 25, 1989

[T] C. TRAVERSO, Experimenting the Gröbner basis algorithm with the AlPI system, in "Proc. of ISSAC '89", ACM Press, 192-198

[Tr] W. TRINKS, Über B. Buchberger's Verfahren, Systeme algebraischerm Gleichungen zu Losen, J. of Number Theory 10 (1978), 475-488.

[W] S. WOLFRAM, "Mathematica, A System for Doing Mathematics by Computer", Addison Wesley, Reading, Mass, 1988

[Zac] G. ZACHARIAS, Generalized Gröbner basis in commutative polynomial Rings, Bachelor Thesis, MIT, 1978.

The design of SISYPHE : a system for doing symbolic and algebraic computations

A.Galligo *, J.Grimm, L.Pottier

Institut National de Recherche en Informatique et Automatique

2004 route des Lucioles, Sophia Antipolis 06565 Valbonne CEDEX FRANCE

1 Introduction

SISYPHE is a new general purpose Computer Algebra System under development at INRIA and University of Nice since 1988.
The system can be used interactively as a mathematical calculator and new procedures and packages can be added using a programming language.
SISYPHE is written in Le-Lisp [J.Chailloux and al.], the syntax of the command language and the names of the user functions are Macsyma like.
The system is made from a set of compiled modules and contains a pre-compiler and a compiler. Mathematical objects admit various typed internal representations with associated conversion functions.
SISYPHE is designed to be used by engineers as well as researchers.

Why do we develop yet another system?

Computer Algebra Systems such as Macsyma [The Mathlab' Group 83] or Reduce [A.Hearn 83] have been used successfully and widely since the early seventies in reaserch and (more recently) in engineering.
These systems are written in a dialect of Lisp and provide a command language, with a Pascal like syntax, which allows extensions of the system with new functions. In 20 years these two systems have accumulated impressive libraries of auxillary functions for specialized scientific computations.

In the eighties, besides the compact program mu-Math and specialized softwares, essentially three new general systems appeared : Maple, Mathematica (in the continuation of SMP) and Scratchpad II (see [B.Char,K.Geddes,W.Gentleman,G.Gonnet], [S.Wolfram 88],
[D.Jenks 84], [D.Jenks, S.Sutor, M.Watt]).

The first two, written in dialects of the C language, brought significant improvements but in separate directions.
Very briefly :
Maple has a compact kernel, its efficiency relies on hashing and use of dynamic vectors. Maple provides easy access to almost all its (readable) algebraic code and provides clean tools for eventual

---

*INRIA and Université de Nice: Dép. de Math. 06034 Nice CEDEX FRANCE.

extensions.

Mathematica was designed to run on a work station, it takes advantage of its graphic facilities and of a well-optimized pattern matching procedure.

Scratchpad II is completely different from the previous ones : it looks like a sophisticated language with parametrized types and it has a powerful compiler. These facilities allow the creation of new computational domains together with their adapted data structures, and the satisfactory incorporation of new algorithms in the system.

Experiences with Scratchpad II and specialized softwares have shown clearly that for new useful algorithms (such as Gröbner basis computation for multivariate polynomial equations and related topics dealing with matrices of polynomials) the algebraic data type and data structures of the other "classical" systems were too limited. Unfortunately, Scratchpad II is rather big, with restricted portability, its unusual syntax and semantics make it more difficult to use than other systems.

We think that recent progress in the field and a greater use of Computer Algebra for industrial applications imply a need for designing new Computer Algebra Systems (both specialized and "general purpose"). A first task will be to start filling the gap between Scratchpad II and the other more classical systems.

Now, we discuss our current solutions to several design issues.

Our target was to design a modular Computer Algebra System easy to use, in the continuation of the classical ones (almost "compatible") but which takes advantage of some recent progresses realised in

- Software Engineering and man-machine interface

- Rewriting Techniques

- Computer Algebra

Also, we wanted to provide the possibility, for industrial users, to produce safe compiled code.

Let us list some new features already implemented (the first three) or in process of implementation (compare with the corresponding features of Macsyma) :

- extend the RAT representation
  in order to obtain the same kind of features than in Scratchpad II for this crucial computational domain. (See section 3 or [M.Gaetano 87]). We used object oriented programming facilities of Le-Lisp to build the needed structured types.

- extend the notion of simplification
  in order to provide the principal facilities of a rewrite system together with the classical optimizations for usual functions in Computer Algebra. Hashing is used to speed up sorting and associative-commutative operations. We payed special attention to get a good pattern matching. As an application, our simplifyer allows efficient manipulation of matrices given by formal properties (without looking at the entries).

- provide separate compilation into machine code.

- build a simple language of module
  disjoint from the command language and from Lisp.

- create facilities for communicating with others Computer Algebra Systems .

- develop a high level graphic interface for work-stations [N.Kajler 89].

SISYPHE is developed by a group of computer scientists, mathematicians and engineers from INRIA or University of Nice, also attached to the GRECO 60, CNRS.

Our group includes J.M. Chalindar, C. Faure, M. Gaetano, A. Galligo, J. Grimm, N. Kajler, L. Pottier.

An adapted version of SISYPHE constitutes the Computer Algebra module of the PTAIA ("Poste de Travail pour l'Automatique et l'Intelligence Artificielle") an integrate software for a specialized work-station of the company CETIA.

In the text, we describe the organisation and facilities of the version dated on January 1st 1990. A version with a suited graphic interface will be available in Summer 1990.

SISYPHE is called after the hero of the greek mithology $\Sigma\iota\sigma\nu\varphi\sigma\varsigma$. We agree with Albert Camus [A.Camus 42] :

"La lutte elle-même vers les sommets suffit à remplir un coeur d'homme. Il faut imaginer Sisyphe heureux"

2 The system

As usual the top-level loop consists of : Read , Simplify , Display .

- The simplification will be explained in section 4.

- The parsing program is rather classical and can be interfaced with other similar programs.

- The display procedure receive three arguments describing the object to be displayed, where and how. Several modes of display are possible : linear, Sisyphe, 2D,TEX , Fortran, (C forthcoming). The system can be viewed like a black box with an input flow and an output flow. The second one consists of independant channels. To each channel is attached a list of files with their own mode of display.
  The display procedure is decomposed into three steps : formatting, box building, printing , so that the data are gradually converted.
  In order to make the printing looks familiar to users, we have two ordering for the expressions. One for internal use and one for display.

- Evaluation is decomposed into three phases : pre-compilation (interpretation of the commands starts), compilation (creation of machine code), execution.
  Compilation is made by Complice (Le-Lisp compiler using lexical binding of variables) and a main task of the pre-compiler is to provide Complice with suited objects.
  The pre-compiler does macro-expansion, static tests on the number of arguments, test for permission level, variable substitution and creation of closure.
  (At a given time the system has permission level N, $0 \leq N \leq 3$, and all functions of higher level are forbidden. One can check and change this level.)
  Thus, in Sisyphe, all commands are compiled either to be executed immediately or to be kept for later use.

- Trace facilities and error management which can be extended by functional parameters.

3 Data structures

The objets manipulated in SISYPHE are the following: rational numbers, terms (formal expressions), rings, polynomials and rational fractions, matrices, system objects, and various classical objects in a computer system (lists, arrays, functions,...). These objects are structured objects, which are implemented with the object-oriented functionalities of Le-Lisp, constitued of a type hierarchy, and a inheritance of fields and methods.

Most of these objects are hashcoded, in order to quickly decide the equality and the ordering beetwen objects.

SISYPHE also provides functions of conversions beetwen types and subtypes of objects.

A type is defined as sub-type of an existing type, with additional fields. An object of type T is then a lisp typed vector $T : [., ..., .]$. Its components correspond to fields of T, and contain the values of these fields.

We now describe the type hierachies used to implement the main objects of SISYPHE .

3.1 Terms

A *term* is a formal expression with an operator and arguments, i.e. of the form $f(a_1, \ldots, a_n)$ where f, called the *root*, is a SISYPHE object of functional type, and the a_i (*arguments*) , are SISYPHE objects.

The operator may have algebraic properties, like associativity, commutativity, group law, boolean law, ..., and then the arguments have a corresponding structure (list for associativity, ordered multi-set for associative-commutativity, ordered set for boolean operator, ...). This formalizes when possible the notion of canonical form modulo a set of equational axioms (cf section 4). Terms are represented by the lisp type **term** with the following fields:

root : the operator.

args : a description of the arguments.

canonical-form : the function (depending of the operator) setting the term into canonical form.

hashcode : terms are hashcoded, in order to test quickly order and equality.

We will explain in section 4 the motivations for these implementation of formal expressions.

3.2 Concrete rings, polynomials and rational fractions

The principal operators in a Computer Algebra System are the addition and the multiplication. Thus the main mathematical structure is the structure of *ring*. We have choosen in SISYPHE to allow the manipulation of *arbitrary rings*, with *arbitrary implementations*. The notion of *abstract ring* covers the mathematical properties of rings. An abstract ring with a particular implementation of its objects and of its operators is then called *concrete ring*.

Typically, in an concrete ring the operators $+$ and $*$ do not make conversions beetwen arguments.

Objects of a concrete ring are usually typed vectors with two fields **cring** containing the concrete ring where they live, and **num** containing their effective value.

SISYPHE provides *ring constructors* which allows to construct arbitrary rings, from *ground rings* like $Z, Q, \frac{Z}{pZ}$, contructors of ring of polynomials, rings of fractions, quotient rings, rings of matrices, and various choices of implementations (density, orderings on monomials, for example in the case of polynomial, number of rows, of column with the matrices,...).

More generally, we allow the definition *concrete algebras*, in the sense of universal algebra, with arbitrary implementation of objects and operators.

3.2.1 Hierarchy of abstract rings

The root type of abstract rings is `#:ring` whith the following fields :
`f+` (addition), `f*` (multiplication), `f-` (symetric element for addition), and `f/` (quotient, which is a partial function).
Under this type we have many subtypes which correspond to mathematical hierarchy of rings : fields, fractions' rings, factorial rings, polynomial rings,... with various new fields in each case (for example fields `ffactor`, `fgcd`, `flcm` for euclidian rings).

3.2.2 Hierarchy of concrete rings

The root type of concrete rings is `#:cring` whith the following fields :
`f+` (addition), `f*` (multiplication), `f-` (symetric for addition), `f/` (quotient, which is a partial function), `zero` (the object zero in the ring), `one` (the unity of the ring), `fmake` (creates an object of the ring with parameters), `fgetnum` (gets the unstrutured value of an object of the ring).
For example there is a concrete ring belonging to this root type: `%freering` which contains all the SISYPHE objects, and use the generic addition and multiplication.
The main subtypes are organized as follows :

`#:cring:numb:` the rings of numbers (for example Z and Q, called `%z` and `%q` in SISYPHE).

`#:cring:rat:` the rings of polynomials and rational fractions. They have various fields giving the kernels (= indeterminates) used, the dense or sparse representation, the concrete ring of coefficients (which can be arbitrary), the order used on monomials (given by an arbitrary linear form), the gcd and factor functions,...

`#:cring:rquo:` the quotient rings, with a field `fnormal-form` , which compute canonical forms of elements (for example with a *standard basis* in quotient of polynomial rings). Here are for example the rings $\frac{Z}{pZ}$ (in subtypes).

`#:cring:matrix:` the rings of matrices, with fields giving the concrete ring of elements (arbitrary), the number of rows and columns, and subtypes as `#:cring:matrix:square`,...

3.2.3 Polynomials and rational fractions

The root type of these objects is `#:rat` with fields `cring` which is the concrete ring where the object lives, and `num` which is his representation (for example a vector of integers for a dense polynomial of $Z[X]$). All the informations about the representation and the manipulation of objects are then contained in their concrete ring.

The subtypes are `#:rat:pol1`, the polynomials in one indeterminate, `#:rat:poln`, the polynomials in several indeterminates, and `#:rat:frac`, the rational fractions.

3.3 Matrices

Matrices are objects of root type `#:matrix` with two fields `cring` which is the concrete ring where the matrix lives, and `num` which is his representation (for example a two dimensional array in dense representation). All the informations about the representation and the manipulation of matrices are then contained in their concrete ring (sizes, dense or sparse or other representations, ring of coefficients,...).

3.4 System objects

System objects are essentially objects used by the *display* functions of SISYPHE which provides printable structured objects, for matrices, sums, products, integrals, differentials, fractions, and in general all SISYPHE objects.

4 Simplification

4.1 The problem

A mathematical expression has many equivalent forms, which are of various interest in practice (factorised or expanded form of polynomials for example). The context where one works determines the possible equivalences and the transformations (*simplifications*) applied to an expression to obtain an interesting equivalent form. Some simplifications are always done, and form the basis of the simplifiers of Computer Algebra Systems , for example :

$$x + 0 \rightarrow x$$
$$x * 1 \rightarrow x$$
$$x - x \rightarrow 0$$
$$log(1) \rightarrow 0$$

More complex transformations are useful simplifications in some contexts but not in others, for example :
$a^3 - b^3$ in expanded form can be more interesting than $(a - b)(a^2 + ab + b^2)$ in factorized form, while the factorized form $(a + 1)^3$ can be more interesting than the expanded form $a^3 + 3a^2 + 3a + 1$. Complex system flags are often used to choose or inhibit them. Our choice is to use understandable sets of *rewrite rules* depending of the context.

4.2 SISYPHE approach

In SISYPHE we distinguish three types of simplifications:

Computations : which uses specialized algorithms attached to some operators on "non formal" objects like numbers, polynomials, rational fractions, matrices, lists, functional expressions.

Canonical simplification : Some algebraic properties like associativity, commutativity can be expressed by *equations* and *term rewrite rules*, and we know in some cases (sums, products for example) how to compute quickly *canonical forms* (we recall that then two terms are equal modulo properties if and only if their canonical forms are syntacticly equal). The user in SISYPHE can give properties to operators, among **associativity, commutativity, monoid law, group law, idempotency, involution, homomorphism, distributivity, ring laws**. Setting expressions with such operators in canonical forms is called "canonical simplification".

Rewriting simplification : Whe use *equational term rewriting* to formalize more complex algebraic properties with *equations* and *term rewrite rules* (cf [J.P.Jouannaud and P.Lescanne 86] and [G.Huet 80]). Then simplification consists in applying rewrite rules (using matching modulo equations), with a choosen strategy. Rules , equations, and rewriting strategies can be easly modified by the user.

The SYSIPHE's simplifier is then composed of two simplifiers used together : the *standard simplifier* (computations on/of canonical forms of objects) and the *rewrite simplifier* (rewriting with rewrite rules and equations). We describe now these simplifiers.

4.3　The rewrite simplifier

The equivalence relation on terms is given by a set of *equations* beetwen terms :

$$tr(a.b) = tr(b.a) \text{ (the trace of a product of matrices)}$$
$$\cdots$$

and the possible simplifications by a set of *rewrite rules* :

$$tr(a.b.a^{-1}) \rightarrow tr(b)$$
$$rotation(x, theta1).rotation(x, theta2) \rightarrow rotation(x, theta1 + theta2)$$
$$\cdots$$

A simplified expression is an expression on which no rule applies modulo the set of equations.

4.3.1　Advantages

- The mecanism of simplification is simple: it is the application of a rule, which is performed with pattern matching modulo the set of equations.

- The simplifications are understandable (looking at the rules and the equations), modifiable (adding or removing rules or equations), controllable (choice beetwen rules which can be applied simultaneously).

- To a particular domain, one can associate a specialized simplifier (trigonometry, Fourier transforms,...), by giving equations and rules, the simplification mecanism remaining the same.

- One knows how to formally manipulate term rewrite systems to make them *noetherian* (no infinite chain of simplifications, [N.Dershowitz 87]), *convergent* (unicity of simplified form, with Knuth-Bendix-like completion). So we can define specialized simplifiers, prove their termination, and even try to complete them in order to define canonical forms (and decide equivalence beetwen expressions, by equality of simplified forms).

4.3.2　Improvements and extensions

Some improvements and extensions of the usual simplification with rewrite rules are already made or in process in SISYPHE :

Sharing subexpressions:　Terms are not only viewed as trees but also as direct acyclic graphs.This considerably speeds up the rewrite process (matching and substitution) and restrict memory allocations (see [P.W.Purdom and C.A.Brown 87] for example).

Compilation of systems, rules and patterns:　We compile systems of rules by optimization of matching (left linear rules,etc), and *term generalization* (the dual notion of unification, see [L.Pottier 89a] or [L.Pottier 89b]), and generate an equivalent lisp function.

Conditional rules:　We allow extra conditions (logical conditions, conditions on types,...) in the application of rules (not only pattern matching).

Optimization of term matching algorithms:　Especially in the Associative, Commutative, Boolean, Group, Ring, Endomorphisms cases, and in general in syntactic theories [C.Kirchner 85].

Already made packages of rules of simplification: In mechanics (matrix simplification), trigonometry, fonctional analysis,...

4.4 The standard simplifier

The simplification process of an expression $f(a_1, \ldots, a_n)$ is briefly the following:

- simplify the arguments a_i.

- **if** there exists an Sisyphe function computing f and the a_i have the good types,
  then the computation of this function is made,
  else the expression is transformed in a term in canonical form with the appropriate function, depending directly of the operator f.

In particular, the classical functionalities of Computer Algebra Systems like simplifications of sums, products, powers, logarithms, etc, are performed by the standard simplifier, taking advantages of the SISYPHE data structures of formal expressions (hashcoding), and rational numbers (improved algorithms).

4.5 Mixing the two simplifiers

An expression is completely *simplified* when it is simplified for each of two simplifiers. The whole simplification is then simply made by using the rewrite simplifier only on simplified expressions relatively to the standard simplifier, and looping if the result is not a standard simplified expression.

5 Forthcoming extensions

The following features are under development :

- extended debug facilities.

- graphic interface [N.Kajler 89].

- modules.
  A module can be considered as package containing a group of functions. This package as a specification corresponding to one or several signatures allowing different views on the module. Modules can be created from other modules and parametrized by modules.
  So, modules are elements of software. They can be used for representing a computational domain. This mecanism is used to express clearly import-export relations. At the instantiation of parametrized modules, there will be a signature check.
  The module language will have a very simple syntax and will be harmoniously integrated in the system without modifying the already existing part.

- static type inference on expressions.

- expression compression.

- improved Fortran generation.

- "exact" real numbers.

- pre-made computational domain.

- communication with others systems.

6 Conclusion

We have presented the SISYPHE system and its forthcoming extensions.
We emphase that the system was designed to give priority to the following three properties:

- conviviality

- high level data structures
  suited for modern useful algorithms

- production of efficient and safe compiled code

The current version of SISYPHE is particuliarly well suited for mathematical developments using multivariate rational functions. Good examples are the new formal integration package to be implemented in SISYPHE by J.A. Abbott and J.Davenport, and a new algorithm of D.Lazard [D.Lazard 89] for solving algebraic systems of positive dimension,to be implemented in SISYPHE by C.Gontard.

In the futur, we shall describe the implementation of new algorithms or original implementation of classical algorithms.

References

[A.Camus 42] "Le Mythe de Sisyphe. Essai sur l'absurde", Gallimard ed. 1942.

[J.Chailloux and al.] "Le-Lisp de l'INRIA Version 15.22 Le manuel de référence", INRIA, FRANCE, avril 1989.

[J.Grimm and al.] "Eléments de documentation SISYPHE", technical report, INRIA, may 1989.

[D.Bayer,M. and M.Stillman] "Macaulay user manual"

[B.Char,K.Geddes,W.Gentleman,G.Gonnet] "The design of Maple: A compact,portable and powerful computer algebra system".

[N.Dershowitz 87] "Termination" , Journal of Symbolic Computation, 1987.

[M.Gaetano 87] "BASTA: un système de manipulation de polynômes en plusieurs indéterminées" Thèse de Doctorat, Université de Nice, 1987.

[A.Hearn 83] "REDUCE-3 User's Manual". Rand Corporation, 1983.

[G.Huet 80] "Confluent reduction: abstract properties and applications to term rewrite systems", J.ACM 27 4 pp 787-821, oct.80.

[D.Jenks 84] "A primer : 11 keys to New Scratchpad", Proceeding of EUROSAM '84, LNCS, Springer.

[D.Jenks, S.Sutor, M.Watt] "Scratchpad II: An abstract Datatype System for Mathematical Computation" IBM technical report 1986.

[J.P.Jouannaud and P.Lescanne 86] "La réécriture", Techniques et Sciences Informatiques, AFCET-Gauthier-Villard, juin 86.

[N.Kajler 89] "Conception d'une interface utilisateur graphique pour un système de calcul algébrique formel", submitted to DISCO 89.

[C.Kirchner 85] "Méthodes et Outils de Conception systématique d'Algorithmes d'Unification dans les Théories équationnelles" , Thèse d'Etat, Univ. Nancy, France, 1985.

[D.Lazard 89] "A new method for solving algebraic systems of positive dimension", rapport LITP, Univ. Paris VI, France, 1989.

[The Mathlab' Group 83] "Macsyma user manual, version 10" M.I.T. ed. 1983.

[L.Pottier 89a] "Algorithmes de complétion et généralisation en logique du premier ordre", Thèse de Doctorat, Université de Nice, février 1989.

[L.Pottier 89b] "Term generalization, general and associative-commutative cases", proc. UNIF'89, Third International Workshop on Unification, Lambrecht, June 1989.

[P.W.Purdom and C.A.Brown 87] "Tree Matching and Simplification", Software-Practice and Experience, Vol 17(2),pp105-115, Feb 1987.

[S.Wolfram 88] "Mathematica : A system for doing Mathematics by Computers", Addison-Wesley 1988.

Scratchpad's View of Algebra I:
Basic Commutative Algebra

J.H. Davenport   and   B.M. Trager

School of Mathematical Sciences   Department of Mathematical Sciences

University of Bath BA2 7AY   IBM Thomas J. Watson Research Center

Claverton Down   P.O. Box 218

Bath   Yorktown Heights

England   10598 NY, U.S.A.

Abstract. While computer algebra systems have dealt with polynomials and rational functions with integer coefficients for many years, dealing with more general constructs from commutative algebra is a more recent problem. In this paper we explain how one system solves this problem, what types and operators it is necessary to introduce and, in short, how one can construct a computational theory of commutative algebra. Of necessity, such a theory is rather different from the conventional, non-constructive, theory. It is also somewhat different from the theories of Seidenberg [1974] and his school, who are not particularly concerned with practical questions of efficiency.

Introduction

This paper describes the constructive theory of commutative algebra which underlies that part of Scratchpad which deals with commutative algebra. We begin by explaining the background that led the Scratchpad group to construct such a general theory. We contrast the general theory in Scratchpad with Reduce–3's theory of domains, which is in many ways more limited, but is the closest approach to an implemented general theory to be found outside Scratchpad. This leads us to describe the general Scratchpad view of data types and categories, and the possibilities it offers. We then digress a little to ask what criteria should be adopted in choosing what types to define. Having discussed the philosophical issues, we then discuss commutative algebra proper, breaking this up into the sections "up to Ring", "Integral Domain", "Gcd Domain" and "Euclidean Domain". It should be noted that, while most of the decisions taken in Scratchpad have a sound mathematical foundation, some, such as the decision not to define various devleopments of semi-groups, such as quasi-groups, are not so soundly based, and reflect the authors' prejudices as much as anything else. We will endeavour to distinguish these decisions from those with a more mathematical foundation. This brings us to the heart of the matter: the definitions used in Scratchpad. Since we are more interested in the theory than in the practical details of Scratchpad, we will often simplify the details of implementation. The full details can be found in Davenport & Trager [1990].

Do we need a new theory? Why can't Scratchpad just use the conventional definitions of, say, "ring", "field", "integral domain" or "unique factorisation domain" found in any text-book on abstract algebra? The reason is that these definitions are fundamentally non-constructive. They say that things exist, but do not give any algorithms for constructing them. Furthermore, such algorithms may well not exist. For example, it is well-known in abstract algebra that, in the presence of noetherianity, the existence of greatest common divisors is equivalent to the existence of unique factorisation. However, as was first shown by Fröhlich & Shepherdson [1956], there exist domains with algorithms for computing greatest common divisors, but for which there cannot exist algorithms for computing unique factorisation. Their example made use of a recursively enumerable, non-recursive sequence to generate a field K which might be $\mathbf{Q}$ or $\mathbf{Q}[i]$, but such that one couldn't tell which. $K[x]$ is certainly noetherian, since K is a field. Then it is certainly possible to compute greatest common divisors in $K[x]$, since Euclid's algorithm is purely rational in its inputs. But, computing the factorisation of $x^2 + 1$ is equivalent to deciding what K is, and so is impossible. We will make use of several such constructions as we show why we need to make certain distinctions which the non-constructive theory doesn't make.

The Problem

The handling of polynomials with integer coefficients is one of the oldest problems of computer algebra [Collins, 1966]. The difficulties encountered in the implementation of polynomials with integer coefficients were largely ones of efficiency, especially for the computation of greatest common divisors and the factorisation of polynomials. While improvements continue to be made in these areas, it is fair to say that these problems are largely solved in principle, though the algorithms are not as easy to implement as one would like:

> We found that, although the Hensel construction is basically neat and simple in theory, the fully optimised version we finally used was as nasty a piece of code to write and debug as any we have come across   [Moore & Norman, 1981].

Once $Z[x_1, \ldots, x_n]$ has been implemented, it is possible to implement $Q(x_1, \ldots, x_n)$ as the quotient field of $Z[x_1, \ldots, x_n]$. To ensure canonical forms, we need merely verify that there is no common factor between the numerator and the denominator (hence one major use of the computation of gcds) and that the leading coefficient of the denominator is positive. $Q[x_1, \ldots, x_n]$ is generally treated as a special case of $Q(x_1, \ldots, x_n)$, in other words, a global denominator is used rather than local denominators. This is generally justified by arguing that the cost of repeated gcd calculations between the numerators and denominators of the rational numbers greatly outweighs the cost of carrying the lcm of the individual denominators as a global denominator. Hence, in principle, all questions of algebra with rational coefficients are solved.

In practice, things are not so simple. Let us consider Hermite's algorithm [Hermite, 1872] for the integration of a rational function $f(x)$ in $Q(x)$ (or, more precisely, for finding the rational part of the integral of such a function). The algorithm (given fully in Davenport & Trager [1990]) is fundamentally based on the algebra of $Q[x]$: the divisions, the partial fraction decomposition, the solution of Bézout's equality and the remainder calculations all take place in $Q[x]$ rather that in $Z[x]$. This is not to say that the algorithm cannot be implemented over $Z[x]$: many authors have done that in many algebra systems. But the implementation becomes much more complicated: every variable must be replaced by a pair consisting of a polynomial in $Z[x]$ and a denominator in Z, and a twelve-line algorithm becomes several pages of code.

Worse, consider what happens when we have a parametric integral, so that $Q[x]$ is replaced by $Q(y)[x]$. We have to embed $Q(y)[x]$ in $Q(y, x)$, the quotient field of $Z[y, x]$. If our system insists on treating y as the main variable, rather than x, in some recursive polynomial representation, or adopts a distributed representation, operations such as the initial synthetic division, which are mathematically trivial in $K[x]$ for any field K, become software nightmares, since the data structure is not representing the underlying mathematics.

More generally, there are many rings between $Z[x_1, \ldots, x_n]$ and $Q(x_1, \ldots, x_n)$, and many algorithms which are naturally set in one of these intermediate rings rather than in either of the extremities. Furthermore, there are quotients of these intermediate fields, such as algebraic number fields. Davenport [1981] describes the difficulty of trying to manipulate algebraic extensions in a system (Reduce-2) which was essentially purely polynomial.

Before we proceed much further in this direction, we should sound a note of warning. It is certainly true that the ability to talk about objects like $Q(x_1, \ldots, x_n)[y]$ is useful when it comes to expressing algorithms. However, these algorithms may not be the most efficient possible. For example, it is possible to use Euclid's algorithm to compute greatest common divisors in $Q(x_1)(x_2) \ldots (x_n)[y]$, regarding each extension (x_i) as the field of fractions of the polynomial extension $[x_i]$, and using Euclid's algorithm to calculate greatest common divisors every time fractions have to be added or multiplied. But it is far more efficient to clear denominators, and to use a modular or p-adic algorithm in $Z[x_1, \ldots, x_n][y]$.

System Requirements

The two major computer algebra systems in which this has been treated are Scratchpad [Jenks & Trager, 1985] and Reduce–3 with its theory of domains [Bradford *et al.*, 1986]. These systems differ substantially in their approach to the problem: Scratchpad is a system designed *ab initio* to handle this view as abstractly as possible, whereas the theory of domains in Reduce–3 (more precisely Reduce–3.3) was intended as an extension to an existing successful system to enable it to handle a wider range of ground objects: earlier versions of Reduce were limited to polynomials (and rational functions) with integer or (machine-precision) floating-point coefficients, and the theory of domains extends this to allow user-defined types, as well as system-defined types such as "arbitrary-precision floating-point numbers", rational numbers, Gaussian integers (or Gaussian rationals, or Gaussian floating-point numbers or ...) and algebraic numbers. In the Reduce model, domains are either rings or fields, the sole difference being that division is always possible in fields, but not in rings. The whole of the "polynomial arithmetic" part (and packages which are based on it, such as the matrix manipulation package) of Reduce works with respect to any domain (except that the g.c.d. algorithm, which is sub-resultant based [Hearn, 1979] has severe problems with inexact domains, such as floating-point numbers), but packages such as factorisation and integration work with only a subset of the domains, with special-case code for each domain — for example, factorisation works directly with integers as the domain, converts rationals to integers first, and reduces Gaussian problems to non-Gaussian ones by taking the norm [Trager, 1976].

Scratchpad, on the other hand, allows any set of operators (and corresponding axioms) to form a definite class of types (the Scratchpad phrase is *category*), of which there are over 100 named ones currently defined in Scratchpad. Categories can in fact be parametrised by other types — the first instance of this in this paper is the definition of LeftModule, where the concept is explained. These are viewed as forming a multiple-inheritance hierarchy: a new category is defined as being the union of the operators and axioms of certain previously-defined categories, together with some new operators and axioms (of course, any of these components may be empty). We say that this category is the *direct descendant* of these previously-defined categories, which are the *direct ancestors* of the category just defined. The concepts *descendant* and *ancestor* are the reflexive-transitive closure of *direct descendant* and *direct ancestor* respectively.

New types (or domains: the two words are used almost interchangably in Scratchpad, but we will use "type" to avoid confusion with Reduce's theory of domains) are constructed by means of *functors*: functions which take some (possibly none) parameters, which may themselves be types, and return a new type. The parameters of a functor are themselves typed, so that an object is defined to come from some type, and a type from some category. For example, the type Z is created by applying the functor Integer (a function with no parameters), the type Q is created by applying the functor Fraction to the type Z (belonging to the category IntegralDomain), and the type* $Z[x]$ is created by applying the functor UnivariatePolynomial to two arguments: the object x (belonging to the type Symbol) and the type Z (belonging to the category Ring).

A functor defines the implementation of the various operators that are defined on the resulting type. In general, the resulting type is defined to belong to a nonce category, generally a named one with some additional operations. For example, Integer could be defined to return an object that belonged to the category EuclideanDomain with an additional operator positivep that said whether or not the integer was positive (the actual definition is far more complicated). Hence the body of Integer would have to define operations such as +, / and gcd as well as positivep.

With such a rich language available, how do we decide which categories to define, and what functors should be available, and what categories should their arguments belong to? It is this question that this paper addresses, for that part of Scratchpad which implements commutative algebra. First, we must ask ourselves what criteria we should use to choose among the various possibilities.

---

* More precisely, one of the many types in Scratchpad which is abstractly isomorphic to the abstract mathematical type $Z[x]$. Other types can be created by using DenseUnivariatePolynomial, or by creating multivariate polynomials in only one variable, or in many other ways.

A Little Philosophy

Why does "abstract algebra" insist so much on the definition and use of concepts (*algebras* in the sense of the subject Universal Algebra: *categories* would be another word, and is the word Scratchpad has borrowed) such as "ring", "integral domain" and "field"? One answer, it seems to us, is *economy of effort*: for example, rather than proving many different theorems, such as "polynomials in one variable over the integers have a unique factorisation property", "polynomials in two variables over the integers have a unique factorisation property", "polynomials in two variables over the integers modulo 7 have a unique factorisation property" and so on, we need only prove one theorem — "polynomials in one variable over a unique factorisation domain form a unique factorisation domain". We will ask later whether this particular piece of generality can in fact be achieved constructively.

There are other reasons as well, which explain why a particular category is "successful". The first reason is one of *interest*: there must be some significant interest in various objects which belong to this category. Furthermore, the interest must have something to do with the property: for example, **Z** is interesting, as is **Z**/n**Z** for odd n, but one is unlikely to find much interest in a theory of "rings which, when viewed as abelian groups, have an involution with precisely one fixed point".

Another reason is what we will call *functoriality*: there should be operations (functors) which construct new objects of the category from old objects of this category, or maybe from old objects of another category. For example, the functor [x] (construct polynomials in one indeterminate over) takes integral domains into integral domains, and takes fields into Euclidean domains.

How does this translate into the computational setting? We certainly want *economy of effort*, by which we mean now that one implementation of an algorithm will work over several different types: for example one sorting algorithm working over all types belonging to the category OrderedSet. This is provided to some extent by the Reduce model, since the whole of polynomial arithmetic is provided over all domains by one piece of code (with the occasional dependence on whether the domain in question at the moment is a field or not). This would be easy to provide in Scratchpad, if all that was wanted were polynomial and rational function calculations over constant domains. But, as was pointed out in the introduction, we would like to see polynomials and rational functions defined over other domains, in particular over domains which are themselves polynomial or rational function domains.

We also want *interest*: it should be possible to implement difficult algorithms over many different types. For example, we would like to implement polynomial factorisation as few times as possible, and then have it operate over as wide a range of different types as possible. Hence we need to define a category such that:

a) It is possible to implement polynomial factorisation over this category;

b) As many types as possible belong to this category.

Such a goal may not be easy, but it is surely worth aiming for.

The types up to Ring

Scratchpad implements a fundamental category SetCategory, of which almost all other categories are descendants. Two operations are defined on types $ (the standard Scratchpad notation for the type one is defining at the moment) belonging to this category

$$= \; : \$ \times \$ \mapsto \text{Boolean}$$

$$\text{coerce} : \$ \mapsto \text{OutputForm}$$

where Boolean is a built-in type of truth values, and OutputForm is a built-in type which is used in printing and other general-purpose expression-manipulation tasks. The assumption that almost all types contain an equality operator is extremely convenient for most purposes, though it could be argued that it is too restrictive. Note that we do *not* require that mathematical equality be represented by Lisp equality, though it will generally be more efficient if this is the case. Domains in which Lisp equality is the same as mathematical equality are said to be *canonically represented*, and are declared to have the attribute `canonical`. This attribute is useful when it comes to considering the use of hashing, to quote but one example, since the hashing functions built into a Lisp system will not give the correct results unless the domain is canonically represented. Another way of viewing this attribute is to say that it asserts that objects that print (in terms of the coercion to `OutputForm`) differently really are different. We discuss the propagation of this attribute further in the section "What does it mean to be an Integral Domain?".

From this we can develop a straight-forward sequence which covers elementary commutative algebra:

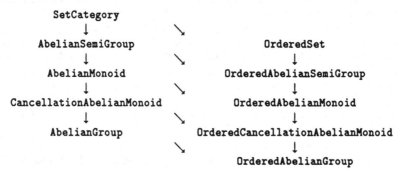

where the arrows indicate a "direct descendant" relationship.

`AbelianSemiGroup` is defined to have one new operator:

$$+ \ : \ \$ \times \$ \mapsto \$$$

satisfying the associative and commutative axioms:

$$a + (b + c) = (a + b) + c$$
$$a + b = b + a.$$

`AbelianMonoid` introduces a new nullary operator

$$0 :\mapsto \$$$

satisfying the obvious axiom

$$0 + a = a.$$

`CancellationAbelianMonoid` is the category of abelian monoids with the cancellation axiom:

$$a + b = a + c \Rightarrow b = c.$$

Constructively, this is represented by a partial subtraction operator, whose signature is defined as:

$$- \ : \ \$ \times \$ \mapsto \text{Union}(\$, \text{"failed"}).$$

The right-hand side of $\mapsto$ is Scratchpad's notation for what other languages sometimes call a "disjoint union". `"failed"` is a distinguished symbol, which can be tested for by seeing which branch of the union is returned. While such an operation could be defined for any `AbelianMonoid`, or even any `AbelianSemiGroup` (as was indeed done in some earlier versions of Scratchpad), it is the cancellation axiom that ensures that $-$ has a unique value. This operator is subsumed in the $-$ operation defined on `AbelianGroups`, so is not of immediate interest in the development of commutative algebra. When we come to define polynomial data types, we will rely on the existence of this operation in the exponent domain.

`AbelianGroup` adds one further unary operator:

$$- \ : \ \$ \mapsto \$.$$

This operator satisfies the axiom

$$a + (-a) = 0.$$

The first $\searrow$ introduces an operator

$$< \ : \$ \times \$ \mapsto \text{Boolean}$$

satisfying the usual axioms:

$$a < b \wedge b < c \Rightarrow a < c$$
$$\neg(a < b) \wedge \neg(b < a) \Rightarrow a = b$$
$$a < b \Rightarrow \neg(b < a).$$

Subsequent $\searrow$ in this diagram introduce no new operators, but one more axiom is introduced, when OrderedAbelianSemiGroup is defined:

$$a < b \Rightarrow a + c < b + c.$$

This is typical of what happens when two categories are merged to form a new named category: we keep the same operators, but are interested in the interaction between them, which requires the introduction of new axioms to define this interaction. Subsequent $\searrow$ in the chain represent the straight-forward merging of ancestors.

In Scratchpad, we have also defined types SemiGroup and Monoid, with the obvious multiplicative operations. We can now start defining ring-like objects properly. There is substantial disagreement (at the notational level) amongst mathematicians as to whether a ring need or need not contain a unity: we have chosen to require that a Ring needs to. Hence our first definition is of a Rng, which is defined to be both an AbelianGroup and a SemiGroup, with two additional axioms:

$$a * (b + c) = a * b + a * c$$
$$(b + c) * a = b * a + c * a.$$

If this domain has the property that the product of two non-zero elements is always non-zero, then we assert the additional attribute noZeroDivisors.

It would be pleasant to proceed now to the definition of a Ring, but we are caught here by a conflict between the Scratchpad requirement that a category be defined in terms of previously-defined categories, and the mathematical statement that *a ring is a (left-)module over itself*. We break the dilemma by defining a NaiveRing to be both a Rng and a Monoid, with operations

$$\text{characteristic} : \ \mapsto \text{NonNegativeInteger}$$
$$\text{recip} : \$ \mapsto \text{Union}(\$, \text{"failed"}).$$

The right-hand side of the last $\mapsto$ again includes a "disjoint union" and the distinguished symbol "failed".

For an arbitrary NaiveRing, characteristic is defined as being the least positive integer n, if one exists, such that 1 added to itself n times is 0, otherwise 0. recip satisfies the axiom

$$\text{recip}(x) \neq \text{"failed"} \Rightarrow x * \text{recip}(x) = \text{recip}(x) * x = 1.$$

Clearly recip cannot be defined any earlier than this, since we need to have a definition of 1. It could be argued that the definition should be later, but it seems in practice to be convenient to define it here.

If R is any NaiveRing, we can define the category LeftModule(R) of all left-R-modules* to be sets \$ which are members of the category AbelianGroup equipped with an extra operation

$$* \ : R \times \$ \mapsto \$$$

and the corresponding axioms:

$$(a * b) * x = a * (b * x)$$
$$(a + b) * x = a * x + b * x$$
$$a * (x + y) = a * x + a * y.$$

---

* We could equally well have chosen to work in terms of right-R-modules.

The category Ring is then both a NaiveRing and a LeftModule over itself. A Module over a Ring R is then both a LeftModule and a RightModule.

A CommutativeRing is both a Ring and a BiModule over itself, with the additional axiom that multiplication is commutative.

What does it mean to be an Integral Domain?

The usual definition of an Integral Domain is rather non-constructive:

$$\nexists a, b \neq 0 : ab = 0.$$

Another way of saying this is to regard it as a property of multiplication: $a, b \neq 0 \Rightarrow ab \neq 0$. A third way is to see that it is much the same as "cancellation" in the type CancellationAbelianMonoid, since if $pq = pr$, then $p(q - r) = 0$, and if $p \neq 0$, then $q = r$. Knowing this property may well help in implementing an operation: for example the definition of multiplication of a sparse polynomial by an element of the underlying ring is defined as

```
if R has noZeroDivisors then
  r * x ==
      r = 0 => 0
      r = 1 => x
      [[u.k,r*u.c] for u in x]
  else
  r * x ==
      r = 0 => 0
      r = 1 => x
      [[u.k,a] for u in x | (a:=r*u.c) ^= 0$R]
```

where the knowledge of the noZeroDivisors property obviates the test to see whether any product has become zero. A Ring with this property is an EntireRing.

However, this is far from realising the full power of integral domains. For example, we would like to be able to implement Bareiss' [1968] fraction-free matrix algorithms, which are only valid over integral domain, not over general rings, and we would like to be able to implement quotient fields of integral domains. None of the definitions given above is very helpful from this point of view, though we can be inspired by the algorithmic rendering we gave "cancellation". We choose to give "integral domain" an algorithmic flavour by using the following corollary to the usual definitions: if R is an integral domain, then a/b, if it exists at all, is unique. Hence we choose to define an IntegralDomain to be a CommutativeRing, an EntireRing and an Algebra over itself, with an (infix) operator exquo:

$$\text{exquo} : \$ \times \$ \mapsto \text{Union}(\$, \text{"failed"}).$$

In this context, a exquo $b = $ "failed" should be interpreted as meaning "there is no element c of the current domain such that $bc = a$, but there's no reason why one shouldn't enlarge the domain to add one". For many domains, in particular euclidean domains, exquo could be defined in terms of a "quotient and remainder" operation, but it is often not very efficient to calculate an enormous remainder and then discover that it is non-zero*. exquo gives a hard error if the second argument is zero, since then there is no legal enlargement of the IntegralDomain to permit the division. There are various axioms associated with this aspect of being an integral domain:

$$a * b = b * a$$
$$a, b \neq 0 \Rightarrow a * b \neq 0$$
$$b \neq 0 \wedge a \,\text{exquo}\, b \neq \text{"failed"} \Rightarrow b * (a \,\text{exquo}\, b) = b$$
$$a = b * c \Rightarrow a \,\text{exquo}\, b \neq \text{"failed"}.$$

---

* This is discussed by Davenport & Padget [1985a,b] and by Abbott *et al.* [1985]. The latter introduced the concept of "early abort" trial division.

As we remarked earlier, there is no very good reason why we have forced all integral domains to be commutative: it is just that we haven't seen any need for a category of non-commutative integral domains with **exquo**. It would certainly not be difficult to add such a category, but one would have to be careful as to whether one meant left-division or right-division. Whether or not this is done, the **exquo** operator is quite powerful.

Proposition. *In any* **IntegralDomain**, *it is possible to determine if two elements are associates or not.*

The proof is obvious.

But, from a computational point of view, there's more to being an integral domain than the existence of the **exquo** operator. We have already discussed the importance of *functoriality* in the abstract and here we have a good concrete example: there ought to be a functor **Fraction**, taking any **IntegralDomain** into its field of fractions (we describe this functor later). The obvious representation for such a functor is to represent a fraction by its numerator and denominator. What would it mean for this field of fractions to be canonically represented?

(1) The **IntegralDomain** itself must clearly be canonically represented.

(2) We must be able to suppress common divisors from the numerator and denominator of a fraction. This question is discussed in the next section: "Greatest Common Divisors".

(3) We must be able to choose which associate of the denominator to use, since a fraction is the same whatever unit we multiply the numerator and denominator by.

It is this last point that concerns us for the moment. We will require some form of operator which returns a distinguished associate of any element. Such operators are sometimes easy to find, and sometimes very difficult. For example, the normal choice for the integers would be "absolute value", and the normal choice for a polynomial domain is to ensure that the leading coefficient is, recursively, canonical. For the Gaussian integers we could choose one quadrant of the Argand diagram, say $x > 0, y \geq 0$.

Theorem. *There exist integral domains such that there cannot exist an algorithm for computing a canonical associate of every element.*

Proof. As Fröhlich & Shepherdson [1956] did, we construct a domain D which may be either $\mathbf{Z}$ or $\mathbf{Z}[\sqrt{2}, 1/\sqrt{2}]$. If it is $\mathbf{Z}$, then 1 and 2 are not associates, and the canonical form for 2 must be ± 2. If, however, it is $\mathbf{Z}[\sqrt{2}, 1/\sqrt{2}]$, then 1 and 2 are associates, and so must have the same canonical form. Asking the question "do 1 and 2 have the same canonical form" is equivalent to deciding on the nature of D, which is impossible.

We note that D is not an **IntegralDomain** in the Scratchpad sense, since it doesn't possess an **exquo** algorithm either, since knowing the value of 1 **exquo** 2 would determine D. In fact, using Brown's trick [Brown, 1969], we can equip any **IntegralDomain** with a canonical associate operator: we keep a list of every canonical element encountered, and, every time the "canonical associate" question is asked of x, we return the first element of this list which is an associate of x. If there is no such element, x is deemed to be canonical, and is added to the list of canonical elements. Algorithms such as this, while in some sense they work, are not to be regarded favourably: partly because of their expense, but also because of their fundamentally non-canonical nature — organising a calculation in a different way, or a different choice of random numbers, can change the definition of "canonical", which is not particularly helpful.

Hence, from the point of view of efficient algorithms, we can see that some **IntegralDomains** will have efficient algorithms for finding canonical associates, and some will not. It turns out to be more practical in Scratchpad to say that all **IntegralDomains** should have an operator **canonical**, which always satisfies the axiom

$$x, \mathtt{canonical}(x) \text{ are associates,}$$

but that the truly canonical nature of this, viz. that

$$x \text{ and } y \text{ are associates} \Rightarrow \mathtt{canonical}(x) = \mathtt{canonical}(y)$$

should be optional — if we know that this holds in a particular domain, we declare the attribute `canonicalUnitNormal` in that domain.

There is an additional question that has to be considered here: are the canonical elements closed under multiplication? This can be expressed axiomatically in the following way:

$$\text{canonical}(\text{canonical}(x) * \text{canonical}(y)) = \text{canonical}(x) * \text{canonical}(y).$$

Some domains have this property, e.g. the integers with the usual definition of canonical as "absolute value". The Gaussian integers don't have this property with the choice of a quadrant of the Argand diagram, but it is possible to find definitions of `canonical` which do have this property — choose, once and for all, a canonical associate for each prime of the Gaussian integers (for example, this could be in a particular quadrant), and then define the canonical associate of an arbitrary element to be the product of the canonical associates of its prime factors. This set of canonical associates is then closed under multiplication, but the algorithm for finding them is hardly efficient. Hence the axiom mentioned above is given a name — `canonicalsClosed`, and some domains assert its validity, while others don't. It is only asserted in the presence of `canonicalUnitNormal`. It is a consequence of this axiom that

$$x \text{ exquo } y \neq \text{"failed"} \Rightarrow \text{canonical}(x) \text{ exquo } \text{canonical}(y) \text{ is canonical.}$$

Proof. Let $z = \text{canonical}(x) \text{ exquo } \text{canonical}(y)$. Since $z * \text{canonical}(y) = \text{canonical}(x)$, $z * y$ is an associate of x. Hence

$$\text{canonical}(x) = \text{canonical}(z * y) = \text{canonical}(\text{canonical}(z) * \text{canonical}(y))$$
$$= \text{canonical}(z) * \text{canonical}(y),$$

so $\text{canonical}(x) \text{ exquo } \text{canonical}(y) = \text{canonical}(z)$. Since the result of the `exquo` operator is unique, $z = \text{canonical}(z)$.

Greatest Common Divisors

As was explained in the introduction, we have to distinguish between the existence of algorithms for the computation of greatest common divisors and the existence of algorithms for the computation of unique factorisation. A `GcdDomain` is defined to be an `IntegralDomain` with an additional operator

$$\gcd : \$ \times \$ \mapsto \$$$

satisfying the following axioms:

$$x \text{ exquo } \gcd(x, y) \neq \text{"failed"}$$
$$y \text{ exquo } \gcd(x, y) \neq \text{"failed"}$$
$$x \text{ exquo } z \neq \text{"failed"} \wedge y \text{ exquo } z \neq \text{"failed"} \Rightarrow \gcd(x, y) \text{ exquo } z \neq \text{"failed"}$$
$$\text{canonicalUnitNormal} \Rightarrow \gcd(x, y) = \text{canonical}(\gcd(x, y)).$$

It is a consequence of these axioms that $\gcd(x, y)$ and $\gcd(y, x)$ are associates, and hence that

$$\text{canonicalUnitNormal} \Rightarrow \gcd(x, y) = \gcd(y, x)$$

but this condition is not imposed more generally, since without `canonicalUnitNormal`, it is hard to ensure that the correct associate of the gcd has been found. This question can be seen as another illustration of the importance of associates in the constructive multiplicative theory.

It follows from the classical theory that, in a `GcdDomain`, factorisations into irreducible elements are unique (up to order and up to choice of associates). Such factorisations will exist if the domain is Noetherian, but we have not found any useful algorithmic categorisation* of "Noetherian". There is an attribute `Noetherian`, which is asserted by some domains, and propagated by some functors (e.g. `SparseUnivariatePolynomial`).

---

* One could imagine an operator `increase` which, given an ideal, either returned a larger ideal, or the word `"failed"`, indicating that the ideal was maximal. The axiom of Noetherianity would

The Functor Fraction

We are now able to describe the structure of the functor Fraction. The declaration of Fraction requires an IntegralDomain D as input, and essentially returns a Field. The representation chosen is that of an ordered pair: numerator and denominator. If x belongs to the quotient field then these are referred to within the functor as x.num and x.den: conversely, if n and d are two elements of D, then the fraction n/d in $ is denoted [n,d]. In fact, operations for accessing these components, known as numer and denom are exported. This is in fact the triumph of pragmatism over purism, since these are not necessarily algebraic operations (in the sense of $ being canonical). By this we mean that $a = b$ does not necessarily imply that $\text{numer}(a) = \text{numer}(b)$, as can be seen from the Scratchpad example quoted in Davenport & Trager [1990].

If D is a GcdDomain, then one defines auxiliary functions cancelGcd and normalize, both with signature $ \mapsto $. The first makes use of the gcd operation, while the second ensures that the denominator is canonical (of course, if the attribute canonicalUnitNormal is not present, this doesn't mean very much). Both operators update their argument, and return it as result. The propagation of canonical is dealt with by a clause:

```
if D has canonical and D has GcdDomain and D has canonicalUnitNormal
    then $ has canonical
```

in the declaration of the functor.

The basic arithmetic operators come in two varieties: for domains which aren't GcdDomains, and for those which are. The definitions of the second variety cancel common divisors and use the normalize function. These are stated as separate operations, since it is generally more efficient to cancel greatest common divisors during an operation, rather than at the end, while this is not true for normalisation. Thus multiplication for GcdDomains is defined as

```
x * y ==
            xx := [x.num,y.den]
            yy := [y.num,x.den]
            cancelGcd xx
            cancelGcd yy
            normalize [xx.num*yy.num,xx.den*yy.den]
```

making two small gcd calculations rather than one large one. The canonicalsClosed attribute would render the call to normalize unnecessary, but the extra complexity of a further set of conditional definitions seems too high for the small gain in run-time efficiency. Of course, this decision could be changed at any time just by changing the code of the functor Fraction.

The rest of the arithmetic operations are not worth considering in detail, but there are a couple of operations whose definitions are worth looking at. The first is =, defined as

```
x = y == x.num = y.num & x.den = y.den
```

if D is a GcdDomain with canonicalUnitNormal, otherwise* as

```
x = y == x.num * y.den = y.num * x.den
```

---

then translate into the assertion that the loop

$$\text{while } I \neq \text{"failed" do}$$
$$I := \text{increase}(I)$$

always terminates (at least if I isn't the whole domain). However, this requires the introduction of "ideal" as a type (one might restrict oneself to finite-generated ideals from the point of view of representation, though the axiom should certainly apply to infinitely-generated ideals), and it's not clear how to turn this and the GcdDomain properties into an efficient algorithm for the factorisation of *elements*, rather than *ideals*. Of course, there is no problem in principal ideal domains.

* It could be argued that we should find a better default definition, since doing two large multiplications may well be unnecessary. For example, we could verify things like degree compatibility if the underlying domain were a polynomial domain.

The second is the operator `retractIfCan` with signature $\$ \mapsto$ `Union(D, "failed")`, satisfying the axiom

$$x = \frac{n}{1}, n \in D \Leftrightarrow \texttt{retractIfCan}(x) = n.$$

If D is a `GcdDomain` with `canonicalUnitNormal`, the definition is

```
retractIfCan x == if x.den = 1 then x.num
                               else "failed"
```

If D is a `GcdDomain`, but without `canonicalUnitNormal`, the definition is

```
retractIfCan x == (z:=recip x.den) case "failed"=> "failed"
                  z * x.num
```

If D is not a `GcdDomain`, then the definition is

```
retractIfCan x == x.num exquo x.den
```

Unique Factorisation Domains

If R is any `IntegralDomain`, we define the functor `Factored` to map R onto another structure, which can be viewed as "partially-factored elements of R". We then define a `UniqueFactorisationDomain` to be a `GcdDomain` with the following additional operators:

$$\texttt{prime} : \$ \mapsto \texttt{Boolean}$$
$$\texttt{squareFree} : \$ \mapsto \texttt{Factored(\$)}$$
$$\texttt{factor} : \$ \mapsto \texttt{Factored(\$)},$$

satisfying the obvious axioms, viz. that `prime` is true only if the element is prime (in the sense that it is not a unit, but any factorisation of it must contain a unit), `squareFree` and `factor` return elements with the same value, containing relatively prime square-free factors in the first case, and non-associate prime factors in the second, with the additional proviso that, if $\$$ has the `canonicalUnitNormal` attribute, then the factors are canonical.

Mathematically speaking, the operator `factor` would suffice, since `prime` could test whether the result of factoring its argument had length 1 or not, and `squareFree` could call `factor` and then regroup all factors having the same multiplicity. But this would be over-kill. It might also seem surprising that `squareFree` is not defined earlier: surely for polynomial domains (though not for the integers) this is equivalent to the computation of greatest common divisors. Regrettably, this is not true for two reasons: the first is that, for polynomials over a ring, we should compute the square-free decomposition of the content as well as of the primitive part, and this is not necessarily equivalent to greatest common divisor calculations. The second is that, even for polynomials over a ring, the problem of computing square-free decomposition may be insoluble, even though greatest common divisors can be computed.

Proof. Let K be $(\mathbf{Z}/p\mathbf{Z})[y]$. As Fröhlich and Shepherdson [1956] did, we construct a domain L which might be K, or might be $K[y^{1/p}]$, and the consider the factorisation of $x^p - y$ in $L[x]$. If L is K, this is irreducible, and *a fortiori* square-free. The other possibility is that this factors as $\left(x - y^{1/p}\right)^p$, in which case it is not square-free.

Euclidean Domains

In the normal development of commutative algebra, the sequence of refinement goes

$$\text{Unique Factorisation Domain} \longrightarrow \text{Principal Ideal Domain} \longrightarrow \text{Euclidean Domain}.$$

In practice, there are few examples of principal ideal domains which are not Euclidean domains, and in fact there are no such domains in Scratchpad.

The example of Fröhlich & Shepherdson shows that it is possible to have constructive Euclidean domains which are not constructive unique factorisation domains, so that our hierarchy will look like

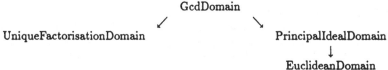

PrincipalIdealDomain is defined to be a GcdDomain with an operator principalIdeal which, given a list of elements, finds a generator of the ideal they define This only ensures that finitely generated ideals are principal, but there are (non-constructive) axioms asserting that all ideals are principal.

The conventional definition of a Euclidean domain involves a function ϕ from the domain to some ordered (abelian) monoid, with the property that

$$x, y \neq 0 \Rightarrow \phi(xy) \geq \phi(x), \phi(y).$$

If one declares that $\phi(0)$ is not defined, one can regard the non-negative integers as the range of ϕ. EuclideanDomains are defined to be extensions of GcdDomain with two additional fundamental operators:

$$\text{euclideanSize} : \$ \mapsto \text{NonNegativeInteger}$$

$$\text{div} : \$ \times \$ \mapsto \$ \times \$,$$

where div is infix, and the two components of the return type are called quotient and remainder. These satisfy the axioms:

$$y \neq 0 \Rightarrow x = y * (x \operatorname{div} y).\text{quotient} + (x \operatorname{div} y).\text{remainder}$$

$$y \neq 0 \Rightarrow (x \operatorname{div} y).\text{remainder} = 0 \lor \text{euclideanSize}((x \operatorname{div} y).\text{remainder}) < \text{euclideanSize}(y)$$

$$x, y \neq 0 \Rightarrow \text{euclideanSize}(xy) \geq \text{euclideanSize}(y),$$

In such a domain, there are obvious default definitions for the functions exquo* and gcd:

```
x exquo y ==
  qr:=x div y
  qr.remainder = 0 => qr.quotient
  "failed"
```

and

```
gcd(x,y) ==
  x:=canonical(x)
  y:=canonical(y)
  while y ^= 0 repeat
    (x,y) = (y,(x div y).remainder)
    y:=canonical(y)
  x
```

Proposition. *This algorithm does in fact compute the greatest common divisor of its inputs.*

Proof. The partial correctness (i.e. the fact that, if the algorithm terminates, then it computes the correct result) of the algorithm follows exactly as in the classical case. If z is a common

---

* As was remarked earlier, this may well not be the most efficient definition for exquo.

divisor, then it divides x and y initially, and hence it divides x and y throughout the running of the algorithm, and in particular it divides the final value of x, which is the result. On the other hand, the result divides the last pair (x, y) (since $y = 0$). But each pair is a linear combination of the elements of the next pair, so by induction, the result divides the elements of every pair.

Hence we need merely show that the algorithm terminates, which is obvious since $\phi(y)$ is strictly decreasing. Furthermore, the guard $y \neq 0$ ensures that the division always succeeds.

Inside EuclideanDomain, we can give principalIdeal a default definition in terms of the extended Euclidean algorithm.

The Functor SparseUnivariatePolynomial

We are now able to describe the structure of the functor SparseUnivariatePolynomial. This is defined to take as parameter a ring R, and the return the ring of polynomials in one "anonymous" variable over this ring. In fact, the return type is not simply a ring, rather it is at least a Ring and an Module over R, with various other properties:

(1) If R is an IntegralDomain, then so is \$;
(2) If R is a GcdDomain, then so is \$;
(3) If R is a Field, then \$ is a EuclideanDomain;
(4) If R has the canonicalUnitNormal attribute, then so does \$;
(5) If R has the canonicalsClosed attribute, then so does \$;
(6) If R is a CommutativeRing, the so is \$, which is also an Algebra over R.
(7) If R has the canonical attribute, then so does \$;
(8) If R has the Noetherian attribute, then so does \$;

The representation chosen is that of a List of objects called Terms, each of which is a record with a component from R (known as c) and a non-negative integer (known as k). In the terminology of Stoutemyer [1984], the representation is sparse, and implicit in variables. Of course, R could itself be the result of calling SparseUnivariatePolynomial, so the representation is also capable of being recursive. Given this representation, most of the algorithms are fairly obvious (though a little care has to be taken, since it is not assumed that R is always commutative): the important point for this paper is to note how the correct properties of R let us define the correct operations for \$.

For example, the function canonical for \$ is defined to return 0 if the input is 0, otherwise $(\mathtt{canonical}(\mathtt{lc}(x)) \mathtt{\,exquo\,} \mathtt{lc}(x)) * x$, where lc is the "leading coefficient" operator. Of course, this is not the only choice possible, but it is both natural and fairly efficient. It certainly does ensure the correctness of the propagation of the attribute canonicalUnitNormal, and indeed that of canonicalsClosed.

Conclusions

We see that, up to the category IntegralDomain, the conventional theory and the constructive theory are pretty much in step. When it comes to IntegralDomain, we have to convert a non-effective axiom into an operation, the uniqueness of whose result is guaranteed by the non-effective axiom. Every IntegralDomain can be extended to a quotient field, and the functor Fraction does precisely this. In order to get an efficient extension, and in particular to ensure that domains with the canonical attribute extend to fields with the canonical attribute, we require that the domain should be a GcdDomain, and that it should have the canonicalUnitNormal attribute. The first of these is fairly obvious, the second is a feature of the constructive theory. With these definitions, we have a general functor which has all the efficiency of the special cases "rational number" and "rational function" of traditional computer algebra systems, where this is possible.

From the constructive point of view, the categories GcdDomain and UniqueFactorisationDomain are very different. This is partly due to the fundamental difference between the operations: gcd depends only on its inputs (at least up to the choice of associates), whereas factor depends also on the ambient domain, and, as the example of Fröhlich and Shepherdson shows, this difference is crucial when it comes to questions of effectivity. The difference is also partly due to the fact that we do not have an effective formulation of "Noetherian". We can formulate this as a question for future research:

- Does "Noetherian" have a useful constructive definition?

The major difference from the classical theory follows from the previous paragraph: a EuclideanDomain is not necessarily a UniqueFactorisationDomain. With this, we can build a successful abstract functor SparseUnivariatePolynomial, which models the classical theory, with one significant exception.

The classical theorem *polynomials over a unique factorisation domain form a unique factorisation domain* has no part in the constructive theory we have elaborated. There are two obvious reasons for this. The first is that it is false: in the Fröhlich–Shepherdson example, K is a field, hence a UniqueFactorisationDomain, but $K[x]$ cannot be a UniqueFactorisationDomain. The second is that it is unreasonable: the efficient algorithms that we know for factoring polynomials over the integers don't rely on the factorisation of integers (unless one insists that the content be completely factored), but do rely on other properties of polynomials over the integers (reduction modulo p; Hensel's Lemma) which our formulation does not capture at all. We can set this as a future research topic:

- Find a formulation of "unique factorisation" such that polynomials over a unique factorisation domain become a unique factorisation domain. It may be useful to consider condition (F) of Seidenberg [1974] in this context.

Acknowledgements.

Both authors are grateful to many past and present members of the Scratchpad group for their input to the theory described in this paper. Many of the orignal ideas were worked out in conjunction with D.R. Barton. The stimulus for writing the first version of this paper was provided by the Computer Algebra Group of Nice/Antipolis. Much discussion of this material took place while the authors enjoyed the hospitality of Mrs. Barbara Gatje.

References

[Abbott *et al.*, 1985]   Abbott, J.A., Bradford, R.J. & Davenport, J.H., A Remark on Factorisation. SIGSAM Bulletin **19**(1985) 2, pp. 31–33, 37.

[Bareiss, 1968]   Bareiss, E.H., Sylvester's Identity and Multistep Integer-preserving Gaussian Elimination. Math. Comp. **22**(1968) pp. 565–578.

[Bradford *et al.*, 1986]   Bradford, R.J., Hearn, A.C., Padget, J.A. & Schrüfer, E., Enlarging the REDUCE Domain of Computation. Proc. SYMSAC 86 (ACM, New York, 1986) pp. 100–106.

[Brown, 1969]   Brown, W.S., Rational Exponential Expressions, and a conjecture concerning π and e. Amer. Math. Monthly **76**(1969) pp. 28–34.

[Collins, 1966]   Collins, G.E., PM, a system for polynomial multiplication. Comm. ACM **9**(1969) pp. 578–589.

[Davenport, 1981a]   Davenport, J.H., On the Integration of Algebraic Functions. Springer Lecture Notes in Computer Science 102, Springer-Verlag, Berlin-Heidelberg-New York, 1981 [Russian ed. MIR, Moscow, 1985].

[Davenport, 1981b]   Davenport, J.H., Effective Mathematics — the Computer Algebra viewpoint. Proc. Constructive Mathematics Conference 1980 (ed. F. Richman) [Springer Lecture Notes in Mathematics 873, Springer-Verlag, Berlin-Heidelberg-New York, 1981], pp. 31–43.

[Davenport & Padget, 1985a]   Davenport, J.H. & Padget, J.A., HEUGCD: How Elementary Upperbounds Generate Cheaper Data. Proc. EUROCAL 85, Vol. 2 (Springer Lecture Notes in Computer Science 204, Springer-Verlag, Berlin-Heidelberg-New York, 1985) pp. 18–28

[Davenport & Padget, 1985b]   Davenport, J.H. & Padget, J.A., On Numbers & Polynomials. Computers and Computing (ed. P. Chenin, C. Dicrescenzo, F. Robert), Masson and Wiley, 1985, pp. 49–53.

[Davenport & Trager, 1990]   Davenport, J.H. & Trager, B.M., Scratchpad's View of Algebra I: Commutative Algebra. IBM Research Report RC 14897 and University of Bath Computer Science Technical Report 90-31, January 1990.

[Fröhlich & Shepherdson, 1956]   Fröhlich, A. & Shepherdson, J.C., Effective Procedures in Field Theory. Phil. Trans. Roy. Soc. Ser. A 248(1955-6) pp. 407–432.

[Gianni et al., 1988]   Gianni, P., Trager, B.M. & Zacharias,G., Gröbner Bases and Primary Decomposition of Polynomial Ideals. J. Symbolic Comp. 6(1988) pp. 149–167.

[Hearn, 1979]   Hearn,A.C., Non-Modular Computation of Polynomial Gcd Using Trial Division. Proc. EUROSAM 79 (Springer Lecture Notes in Computer Science 72, Springer-Verlag, Berlin-Heidelberg-New York) pp. 227–239.

[Hermite, 1872]   Hermite, E., Sur l'intégration des fractions rationelles. Nouvelles Annales de Mathématiques, 2 Sér., 11(1872) pp. 145–148. Ann. Scientifiques de l'École Normale Supérieure, 2 Sér., 1(1872) pp. 215–218.

[Jenks & Trager, 1981]   Jenks, R.D. & Trager, B.M., A Language for Computational Algebra. Proc. SYMSAC 81 (ACM, New York, 1981) pp. 6–13. Reprinted in SIGPLAN Notices 16(1981) No. 11, pp. 22–29.

[Moore & Norman, 1981]   Moore, P.M.A. & Norman, A.C., Implementing a Polynomial Factorization and GCD Package. Proc. SYMSAC 81 (ACM, New York, 1981) pp. 109–116.

[Seidenberg, 1974]   Seidenberg, A., Constructions in Algebra. Trans. AMS 197(1974) pp. 273–313.

[Stoutemyer, 1984]   Stoutemyer, D.R., Which Polynomial Representation is Best: Surprises Abound. Proc. 1984 MACSYMA Users' Conference (ed. V.E. Golden), G.E., Schenectady, pp. 221–243.

[Trager, 1976]   Trager,B.M., Algebraic Factoring and Rational Function Integration. Proc. SYMSAC 76 (ACM, New York, 1976) pp. 219–226.

Design Issues for a Computed-aided Environment for Constructive Mathematics

Gerard Huet
INRIA,
Rocquencourt, France

The Calculus of Constructions is a logical formalism in the spirit of AUTOMATH, which is being developed at INRIA as the basis for a proof assistant. The talk will discuss various design issues arising in the construction of this proof assistant, and will describe its current CAML implementation.

The present system consists of a proof checker, the Constructive Engine, a high-level declarative language for mathematical theories, the Mathematical Vernacular, a Theorem Prover which attempts to synthesize proofs interactively under the mathematician's guidance, and and which may be extended by user's defined tactics written in CAML, and a Program Extractor, which extracts a program from the computationally relevant part of the proof of satisfiability of its specification. The issues discussed are relevant to logic-based knowledge representation systems, and to the design of programming environments for strongly typed modular programming languages.

Efficient Type Inference and Coercion in Computer Algebra

Albrecht Fortenbacher

Scientific Center Heidelberg, IBM Deutschland GmbH
EARN: FORTE at DHDIBM1

Abstract

Computer algebra systems of the new generation, like SCRATCHPAD, are characterized by a very rich type concept, which models the relationship between mathematical domains of computation. To use these systems interactively, however, the user should be freed of type information. A type inference mechanism determines the appropriate function to call. All known models which allow to define a semantics for type inference cannot express the rich "mathematical" type structure, so presently type inference is done heuristically. The following paper defines a semantics for a subproblem therof, namely coercion, which is based on rewrite rules. From this definition, an efficient coercion algorithm for SCRATCHPAD is constructed using graph techniques.

1 Type Inference in Computer Algebra

Early computer algebra systems did not have a sophisticated type system, mainly due to the small number of computational domains. With the progress in computer algebra, the number of applications, and so the number of domains, grew significantly. A type concept was needed for two reasons: first, to organize the domains of computation according to their algebraic relationship, and second, to allow polymorphism and generic functions, e.g. polynomial addition is implemented once for all polynomial domains using the underlying coefficient domain functions.

In the following, the type system of SCRATCHPAD is used to present the problems of type inference and coercion. SCRATCHPAD is an experimental computer algebra system currently under development at the IBM Thomas J. Watson Research Center, which has a very clean concept of mathematical data types. Nevertheless, the following results and algorithms, especially the undecidability result of section 2, are independent of the choice of SCRATCHPAD; they hold for any similar computer algebra system. For a description of SCRATCHPAD see [4,2,5], and [1] for a comparision of the major computer algebra systems.

The programming language of SCRATCHPAD combines concepts of abstract data type theory and object oriented programming. Function specifications and attributes form *categories*, e.g. Monoid consists of functions "+" and "0" (a constant) as well as of an attribute indicating that "+" is associative. More complex categories like Ring inherit the above function specifications from Monoid.

Each *domain* can be seen as one possible implementation of a specific category (abstract data type), i.e. a domain provides data representations and implementations for all functions defined in the category. For example the domain P implements polynomial operations, including addition of polynomials. P is parameterized by a coefficient domain of category Ring, so the *generic* function "+" is defined in terms of functions of the category Ring.

Domains, categories and *packages* (which are not described here) form the type concept of a programming language, which is adequate to implement algebraic algorithms. But can an interpreter of this language also serve as an interactive user interface?

A user interface which requires strong typing is not very convenient. To manipulate $3 + x$, which is of type P(I), the user has to define two polynomials 3 and x, then call the polynomial addition. For more complex computations, this becomes very tedious. Instead, a user wants to get rid of all this type information, and determining an appropriate function should be achieved by a type inference mechanism. Nevertheless, omitting type information must not give wrong results.

Even worse, there need not be one unique result of a formula. Given an implementation of the function "+" (from category Monoid) in a string domain, the result of above formula could also be the concatenated string $3x$. Therefore, the type inference algorithm used for function selection is not (and cannot be!) "exact" in the sense that it always leads to one uniquely determined "best" function invocation. Instead, the SCRATCHPAD interpreter chooses heuristically one of several appropriate function definitions, and the user can provide more type information if he dislikes the choice. This is a conservative strategy, because all answers given by the interpreter are correct, in the sense that only functions are called which are applicable w.r.t. type information derived in a bottomup process [5].

To select an appropriate function, the interpreter starts with some basic types (very much like a mathematician). In the formula $3 + x$, the number 3 is assumed to be of type I, the symbol x of type VAR. But neither in the computational domain I nor in the domain VAR exists an applicable function "+". So the next step is to *coerce* x or 3 to some other types. Mathematically this means to look at the objects in a different way, without changing them. There is no coercion from I to VAR or vice versa, but there is a "common" domain P(I). Both x and 3 can be coerced to polynomials, and there is an appropriate addition which yields the polynomial $3 + x$.

In SCRATCHPAD, the process of function selection (and type inference) depends on built-in heuristics, if no type information is provided. How does this conform with exact computations, which is one of the basic ideas of computer algebra? Type inference semantics can be defined for a restricted type system, which eliminates all "irregular" cases [3], as opposed to existing computer algebra systems with their variety of domains of computation. But ambiguity in function selection seems to be inherited directly from mathematical notation, where function symbols are heavily overloaded and the semantics of a formula depends very much on its context.

Coercion, as a special case of type inference, is much more regular. In the next section, we define its semantics based on rewrite rules, which allows to decide the predicate coercibility and furthermore

2 The Coercion Graph

As indicated in the last section, coercion is a basic tool for type inference. Also, in a system with hundreds of computational domains, coercion poses a real performance problem, so it is crucial to test coercibility very efficiently.

A coercion algorithm as presented below, which bases on a well-defined semantics, makes coercion transparent to the user (as opposed to a purely heuristic algorithm) and helps in understanding type inference and function selection. On the other hand, we will describe conditions on "admissible coercions" in order to have a decidable coercibility predicate and an efficient coercion algorithm.

Having introduced coercion intuitively in the previous section, we shall now define it. First a convention: the computational domain an object lives in is called the *type* of that object. In a mathematical sense, coercing an object from one domain to another means changing its type without changing its value. As an example, the number 3 (of type I) can be coerced to RN or P(I), i.e. it can be seen as rational number or polynomial.

In SCRATCHPAD, a domain D can be coerced to a domain D', if there exists a function *coerce* : $D \rightarrow D'$. So coercion can be formulated within the strongly typed language.

Naturally we want coercion of domains to be unique, independent of the coercion functions we use. Given (overloaded!) coercion functions

$$
\begin{array}{rccl}
coerce: & \mathtt{I} & \rightarrow & \mathtt{RN} \\
coerce: & \mathtt{I} & \rightarrow & \mathtt{P(I)} \\
coerce: & \mathtt{RN} & \rightarrow & \mathtt{P(RN)} \\
coerce: & \mathtt{P(I)} & \rightarrow & \mathtt{P(RN)}
\end{array}
$$

this means that the following diagram has to commute:

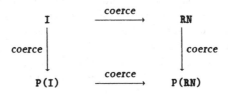

A computer algebra system, which allows parameterized types and genericity, can have infinitely many domains, and infinitely many coercion functions. Our goal is to describe an algorithm which, given two domains D and D', can determine whether there is a coercion from D to D', i.e. whether we can reach D' from D by successively applying coercion functions.

Coercion functions define a binary relation $\Rightarrow$ on domains: $D \Rightarrow D'$ if there is a function $coerce : D \rightarrow D'$. The predicate $canCoerce$ on domains can be defined as the the reflexive and transitive closure $\Rightarrow^*$. By definition, $\Rightarrow^*$ is a (partial) preorder, but not necessarily an order: there might exist distinct domains D und D' which are coercible in either direction.

The relation $\Rightarrow$ can be represented as directed *coercion graph*. Nodes are labelled by domains, vertices by coercion functions. Coercibility is now the question whether there exists a *coercion path* from a domain D to D'.

This problem is undecidable (in general), as the word problem of a Chomsky-0 language can be reduced to it. Nevertheless, if the coercion graph obeys some (reasonable) conditions, we not only gain decidability but also get an efficient algorithm. The rest of this section deals with these conditions.

Given two domains D and D', we want to construct a coercion path from D to D' (in case $D \Rightarrow^* D'$) or find out that there is no coercion path, otherwise. If this can be done algorithmically, we call the coercion graph *admissible*.

In the next section, we will see how coercion functions in SCRATCHPAD can be used as conditional rewrite rules to construct coercion paths. Because coercion is unique (c.f. the diagram in section 1), it can be applied along any path from D to D'. Constructing coercion paths is a semidecision procedure for the predicate $canCoerce$, and to decide it we further have to limit the number of paths to examine.

Let ι be any map (*interpretation*) from the set of all domains into the natural numbers, and $f : \mathcal{N} \times \mathcal{N} \rightarrow \mathcal{N}$ an arbitrary function. A coercion path $D_1 \Rightarrow \ldots \Rightarrow D_n$ is *bounded* (w.r.t. ι and f), if interpretation of all domains is limited by the interpretation of D_1 and D_n:

$$
\forall 1 \leq i \leq n : \quad \iota(D_i) \leq f(\iota(D_1), \iota(D_n))
$$

Having defined bounded coercion paths, we can present sufficient conditions for admissibility: A coercion graph is admissible if functions ι and f exist with:

1. a bounded coercion path $D \Rightarrow \ldots \Rightarrow D'$ exists for any two coercible domains (i.e. $D \Rightarrow^* D'$)

   and

2. the construction of bounded coercion paths is a terminating process (for any domains D and D')

The concept of bounded coercion paths depending on functions ι and f seems to be very general. The SCRATCHPAD type system, for example, represents an admissible coercion graph with f realized as the maximum function and the interpretation ι as a depth function, i.e. a non-parameterized domain has interpretation 0, otherwise the interpretation is $1 + n$, where n is the maximum of all parameter domain interpretations.

A final remark: instead of defining the predicate *canCoerce* in full generality through the relation $\Rightarrow^*$ and providing conditions for an admissible graph, we could have regarded any coercion graph where the construction of bounded paths terminate. Then coerciblity must be defined by the existence of a bounded path (as opposed to any path). In practice, these two approaches seem to coincide, because admissibility is very general and can be achieved easily.

3 Coercion Functions as Rewrite Rules

Given infinitely many domains and coercion functions, how can a coercion path between domains D and D' be constructed? Clearly, this depends on the representation of coercion functions. Given a SCRATCHPAD-like type system (see section 1), coercion functions can be regarded as conditional rewrite rules. Hence we can construct coercion paths in a transparent and efficient way by applying rewrite rules to domains. These rules are labelled by coercion functions, which are called when we actually coerce values along a coercion path.

Unary functions on parameterized domains can easily be expressed as rewrite rules, where variables stand for parameter domains. To guarantee validity w.r.t. category information, conditions have to be fulfilled before applying a rule. For example coercion to a polynomial from its coefficient domain would look like

$$x \Longrightarrow P(x) \text{ if x is of category Ring}$$

A coercion rule can be applied in two directions. From left to right (as written above) applied to domain D, this yields a new domain $\bar{D}$ with $D \Rightarrow \bar{D}$ and a new coercion problem from $\bar{D}$ to D'. But it can also be applied from right to left to yield $\bar{D}'$ with $\bar{D}' \Rightarrow D'$ and a new coercion problem from D to $\bar{D}'$. An example shall illustrate this.

To determine whether domain I can be coerced to P(RN), we can apply the rule $x \Longrightarrow P(x)$ to I (I is of category Ring) and proceed to P(I). Then we have to find a coercion path from P(I) to P(RN). Equally, we could have applied the rule from right to left, which yields a different coercion path $I \Rightarrow^* RN \Rightarrow P(RN)$.

For computer algebra systems, it is crucial to select appropriate functions efficiently. In a system like SCRATCHPAD, with several hundreds of domains, the predicate *canCoerce* is called very frequently. Efficiency of this algorithm can be improved by two means:

1. avoiding computation of unnecessary coercion paths, especially dead end paths

2. saving already computed vertices in a hash table

Each coercion rewrite rule can be restricted to left-right (right-left) application only. E.g. a rule $I \Longrightarrow D$, where D is some infrequently used domain, should only be applied when a coercion to D is requested, i.e. from right to left. This reduces the number of unnecassary paths significantly. However, coercion rewrite rules have to be constrained very carefully, because it can reduce the number of coercion paths which can be constructed, and thus change the way coercion works.

Finally, we scetch an algorithm which realizes the predicate *canCoerce* using coercion rewrite rules. Given two domains D and D', we want to determine whether an object of D can be coerced to D'. First, coercion rules are applied from left to right to D (or vertices from D are looked up in a hash table which represents the graph). If this yields domain D', a coercion was found. Otherwise, rules are applied from right to left to D. If still no coercion is found, all new domains, which do not violate the condition on bound paths, are used to create new coercion problems, which are solved recursively.

When a coercion path from D to D' was found, it is straightforward to actually perform the coercion: all coercion functions along the coercion path are applied the object of type D.

This algorithm is currently under implementation for the SCRATCHPAD type system. First tests look very promising: the algorithm is not only very fast, but also transparent to all SCRATCHPAD users, because the behaviour of coercion solely depends on the coercion rewrite rules (and on functions ι and f used to state conditions for bounded paths).

References

[1] Buchberger, B., Collins, G.E., and Loos, R., "Computer Algebra, Symbolic and Algebraic Computation", *Springer Verlag*, 1982.

[2] Jenks, R.D., Sutor, R.S., and Watt, S.M., "Scratchpad II: An Abstract Datatype System for Mathematical Computation", in: *Proceedings Trends in Computer Algebra*, Bad Neuenahr, LNCS 296, Springer Verlag, 1987.

[3] Comon, H., Lugiez, D., and Schnoebelen, P., "Type Inference in Computer Algebra", *Proceedings EUROCAL 87*, Leipzig, 1987.

[4] Jenks, R.D. and Trager, B.M., "A Language for Computational Algebra", *Proceedings of SYMSAC 81, Symposium on Symbolic and Algebraic Manipulation*, Snowbird, Utah, August 1981. Also *SIGPLAN Notices*, New York: Association for Computing Machinery, November 1981, and *IBM Research Report RC 8930* (Yorktown Heights, New York).

[5] Sutor, R.S., and Jenks, R.D., "The Type Inference and Coercion Facilities in the Scratchpad II Interpreter", Proceedings of the SIGPLAN 87 Symposium on Interpreters and Interpretive Techniques, *SIGPLAN Notices* 22, 7, New York: Association for Computing Machinery, July 87, and *IBM Research Report RC 12595* (Yorktown Heights, New York).

ABSTRACT SPECIFICATION OF
MATHEMATICAL STRUCTURES AND METHODS

Carla Limongelli +, *M. Beatrice Mele* †, *Mauro Regio* †, *Marco Temperini* ‡

+ Dipartimento di Informatica e Sistemistica, Università degli Studi di Roma "La Sapienza", Via Buonarroti 12, 00185 Roma, Italy.

‡ Istituto di Analisi dei Sistemi ed Informatica del C.N.R. Viale Manzoni 30, 00185 Roma, Italy; student of Dottorato in Informatica at Università degli Studi "La Sapienza", Roma.

Abstract

This paper presents several methodological and technological aspects for the treatment of mathematical objects by very high level abstract specification of data and methods. A homogeneus environment is defined for the design and implementation at the highest abstract level. The presentation is developed from the point of view of both formal specification and implementation languages. Indeed specification and programming are considered as uniform actions under the same general conceptual model. The conceptual model is completely supported by the Object-Oriented methodology. Particular interest is devoted to Algorithmic Logic, as a logic specification language, and to Loglan as an innovative Object-Oriented programming language.

1. Introduction

The aim of this work is to discuss and experiment with a methodology for axiomatization and implementation of mathematical structures and methods. The selection of specification formalisms and programming methodologies has been considered, having in mind a general model to guarantee good level of uniformity between the stage of analysis and formal definition of structures and methods and the stage of consequent correct implementation. The selected specification model corresponds to some essential requirements for the specification language:

- it should have enough expressive power to capture properties of a large variety of structures;

- it should allow for a translation as simple and correct as possible into the implementation language.

Those requirements can be achieved by an integrated system supporting direct executable specifications. From the specification point of view the Algorithmic Logic (AL) [MiSa] is a well known formal instrument for the specification of Abstract Data Types (ADT); in particular, it can be used, in an Object-Oriented (OO) framework to design axiomatic specifications of mathematical structures. The language of AL can be shortly described as the least extention of the language of the First-Order Logic, such that expressions of the form ⟨*program*⟩ ⟨*formula*⟩ are

Research partially supported by MURST: "Calcolo Algebrico, Sistemi di Manipolazione Algebrica"; CNR: "Matematica Computazionale", Progetto Finalizzato "Sistemi Informatici e Calcolo Parallelo"; Olivetti System and Networks.

also regarded as formulas. An example is given in section 4, showing the use of AL in the axiomatization of the matrix structure. A second example shows the possibility to enrich the specification of a data structure with the definition of a method at its highest level of abstraction. From the implementation language point of view, Loglan [Log] has been taken into consideration, because of its characteristics of object-orientedness, and for the possibility to state an automatic method for the translation from AL specifications to Loglan executable code.

As far as the effective construction of a running system is concerned, some main factors have been considered to constrain the implementation language: correctness, dynamic typing (as the two most important ones), easy-to-useness, efficiency, extendibility and general reliability of the system. According to these needs and consequently to the specification environment, Loglan has been chosen as the appropriate language for the implementation of structures specified in AL.

The following section presents an overview of OO methodology, stating some characteristics of particular interest to our purpose. Then, in the third section, the Loglan programming language is described, recalling the use of *prefixing* and *virtual definition* as two peculiar constructions. The section 4 contains two examples of the specification of structures, of the related Loglan implementation, and of the structure enrichment by the definition of computational methods.

2. Object-Oriented methodology

Having to deal with a general applicative problem, whose solution can be obtained by the manipulation of mathematical objects, it is necessary to consider two specification levels: an "object level" in which the objects manipulation has to be defined, and a "specification level" in which the properties of the classes of the objects are described: actually each object is an instance of some of these classes. From the design methodology point of view these requirements are satisfied by the OO methodology for ADT treatment. In fact the ADT is defined at the higher level and instanciated at the object level.

In the following, we show that this methodology gives rise to richer algebraic structures in which the computing methods become a characteristic component of the abstract structures themselves.

This very-high-level of abstraction constitutes the formal definition layer that finds its activation in the ground level, where the objects are instanciated to represent the defined ADT. An OO approach can be used for both specification and implementation of ADT, because it offers an adequate tool for the hierarchization, by the inheritance mechanism. In fact as far as the method abstraction is concerned, the inheritance allows us to use the code provided for a higher structure, in all its sub-structures, without any redefinition. Actually the OO programming paradigm can be considered as a general philosophy for both designing and implementing mathematical computation systems. It can support natural mechanisms for manipulating mathematical objects, by its intrinsic hierarchical organization, conforming to the original hierarchization of the mathematical objects as proposed in formal algebra.

The main concepts of the general OO conceptual model can be stated as

$$\langle Objects + Classes + Inheritance \rangle$$

where the three most important abstraction mechanisms are included: *classification, generalization* and *aggregation*.

From the point of view of our objectives, the crucial concept to be explored is the dynamic use of ADT, which can be interpreted as actual abstract algebraic structures.

The following example (see [TeVi] for more details) shows the correspondence between the logical model of data (given by ADT specifications) and the physical one (given by classes hierarchy). Let us suppose to require the representation of some algebraic elementary data (e.g. matrices, polynomials, integers) and elementary operations on their instances (e.g. addition, multiplication). Let us also consider that an element as a matrix or a polynomial can be viewed as composite data, built upon some ground elementary structures. Therefore, a system for those composite data has to deal (in a dynamic way) with, for example, matrices having polynomial over integers as components, and with polynomials having matrices of integers as coefficients. Once we have recognized that different data types (e.g. Matrix, Polynomial, Integer) have some commonalities, a type hierarchy can be designed. For example, matrices, polynomials and integers, composed by addition and multiplication operators, belong to the ring abstract structure.

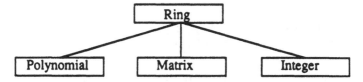

The implementation of these data structures can exploit the polymorphism induced by the hierarchy of the data type definition. When a suitable management module is programmed for such a data system, by using the parametric polymorphism, requirements for a dynamic treatment of objects of the specified types are supplied. Therefore dynamic types can be managed (e.g. matrix of polynomials over ... matrices of integers).

The previous example explicitly shows the reason for the choice of an OO model in the design of data structures, based on the possibility of fruitfully using polymorphism and inheritance for the correct use of ADT instances.

Further considerations on the class inheritance mechanism, in particular on strict and non-strict inheritance, can be made. As a matter of fact, two main relations do exist between ancestor and descendant classes, namely "is-a" or "is-like", according to *strict* or *non-strict* inheritance respectively [Weg].

The strict inheritance allows us to enforce the *generalization* abstraction method: classes are viewed as generalization of all their descendant ones. In non-strict inheritance, the properties of a new class can be obtained by inclusion, exclusion or modification of properties from inherited ones. Furthermore, in this case, an object is not always a member of its parent class, so the "is-a" relation between classes not always holds, and it can be substituted by an "is-like" relation. Therefore with non-strict inheritance the "similarity" relation generally substitutes the "specialization" one.

The *aggregation* mechanism of abstraction can be included in OO systems by the multiple inheritance mechanism: a class may inherit its properties from many parent classes. Either an "is-a" or an "is-like" relation may exist between child and parents. The relation between aggregated and aggregating classes is very similar to the set cartesian product, where the aggregating classes are "part-of" the aggregated ones.

In a strict inheritance framework the class mechanism can powerfully support he use of ADT in the manipulation of mathematical objects. It is also important to stress how this hierarchical organization principle offers a relevant general method for code reuse.

In the following figure, each node inherits properties while adding some others. The inherited properties label the arcs, and the added properties are indicated between braces next to the structure names.

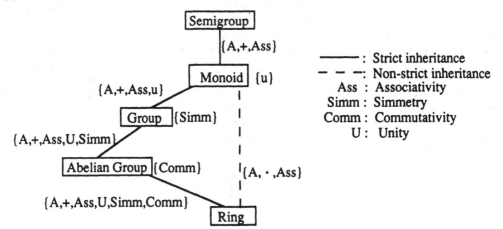

For instance, Group is obtained by strict inheritance from Monoid (i.e. inheriting *all* the properties of monoid) adding a new property, namely the existence of the inverse of each element. Ring can be obtained by multiple and non-strict inheritance from Monoid and Group; let us note that this is an enforcement: Ring could be also obtained following a more proper algebraic pattern, via multiple strict inheritance, by aggregating the Abelian Group and Semigroup properties.

Type hierarchy is a powerful tool for incremental design, a way to express similarities between various ADT and a basis for implementing a simple and safe type system in the target language. However what strict inheritance can preserve in terms of correctness of the data system, can be lost in terms of flexibility of the software production. Indeed strict inheritance is not a very flexible mechanism to report ADT correlations. Moreover if these relations are discovered only after the ADT hierarchy has been completely specified then it might be necessary to reconsider the type hierarchy and the implementation itself [Lis]. On the other hand, relations between mathematical objects are often known before their implementation, and new classes are always specializations of existent ones. Therefore system rigidity induced by strict inheritance is mainly a way to preserve correctness.

In conclusion aggregation mechanism of abstraction seems very useful for our purposes, provided that it is achieved by a multiple strict inheritance mechanism.

Basically two approaches, namely bottom-up and top-down, can lead the work in formal specification. Both of them can be supported by the OO programming style. However the bottom-up construction can be considered as a peculiar characteristic of the OO paradigm. In fact, the modular composition of the software elements (which can be freely combined together to derive new elements) is a general property of this style. In this way it is possible to build mathematical objects using the natural increasing behaviour of the formal definition.

Such an approach allows to take advantage from the structured organization with many levels, which is suggested by the problem itself. Furthermore the existence of a type checking at both compile-time and run-time can guarantee a correct use of the dynamic data typing [Goo]. If the programming language supports a high degree of modularity and abstraction, we can pursue the required flexibility which is given by the dynamic typing in a homogeneous and semantically correct way.

3. Loglan: a suitable implementation language

The AL represents an axiomatic method for the definition of programming language semantics, and in particular has been emploied for the definition of different semantic aspects of the OO programming language Loglan. Therefore Loglan is considered a suitable programming language for the implementation of structures which have been axiomatized in AL. We use AL to define formal and correct specifications. Once axioms are consistently defined, we can translate them into an executable Loglan code, without loss of correctness. Examples of this natural translation from axioms into Loglan code are shown in the section 4.

Loglan supports data abstraction and OO programming in addition to traditional programming techniques. In this programming language, the fundamental structure is the *class*, as a template concept, in which both a declarative part and an executive part exist. A class is a kind of pattern: once it is defined, objects (instances of the class) can be generated during the execution. A class can have attributes (e.g. variables, procedures, functions) that can be used by remote access. Classes themselves can be defined like attributes of other classes, that is class definition can be nested. In this way we can enclose a class definition into its peculiar context, and we can reduce its instances lifetime to that of the instances of the class where it is defined.

Prefixing is one of the main features in Loglan. It offers the possibility of linking units in a hierarchy, providing the inheritance of attributes and instructions. For example, the prefixing of a class to another class creates a "prefixed class" having all the attributes of the "prefixing class" (plus the local attributes properly defined in the declarative part of the new class). The same can happen in the executive part of the new class, which can embed the inherited instructions. In particular, Loglan supports "multi-level prefixing". This feature avoids some non trivial problems and, mainly, the suffering from redundancy in some unit declaration.

Since instances can be dynamically defined at run-time, the inheritance represents a dynamic feature and a very flexible mechanism to define new data types. Furthermore, it is also possible to define, in an abstract way, by means of the "virtual" definition feature, the operation attributes of a unit, and the specialization of the different operations can be delayed until the definition of the inheriting unit.

Combining prefixing and virtual definition it is possible to define a generic structure as a unit (class) by just enumerating its general characteristics (e.g. the names of its operations). Then, when one or more sub-structures have been declared, the operations defined in the generic structure can be inherited by the sub-structures and they can be implemented according to the specialization of the sub-structures.

Referring to the previous example, a simple class definition of the abstract structure of Ring and of its sub-structure Integer-number is given in the following. For instance, the general concept of multiplication in a generic ring can be specialized both for the multiplication in a multivariate polynomials ring and for the multiplication in the ring of integer.

```
unit ring: class;
  virtual unit ADD: function(A: ring): ring; end ADD;
  virtual unit MULT: function(A: ring): ring; end MULT;
end ring;
unit integer-number: ring class;
 var n:integer;
  virtual unit ADD: function(A: integer-number): integer-number;
   begin
    result := new integer-number;
    result.n := n + A.n;
   end ADD;
  virtual unit MULT: function(A: ring): ring;
   begin
    result := new integer-number;
    result.n := n * A.n;
   end MULT;
end integer-number;
```

4. Experiments with the proposed methodology

Let us present here the axiomatization of structures and methods by sketching the application of the proposed methodology to two specific problems. In this way we give the flavour of how OO principles can be applied to structures and methods definition, and how specifications can be translated into executable code. The first example partially presents the axiomatization of a particular mathematical object (the Matrix structure), by using AL and the related Loglan code. The second example introduces the Hensel method for polynomial equations, showing how it is possible to extend an abstract data structure by including in it an algebraic computational mechanism. This extension defines to a more powerful algebraic structure in which the computing method becomes a newly introduced characteristic component for the abstract structure itself.

4.1 The axiomatization and the implementation of the matrix structure

Here only two sample axioms are showed (with the aim to illustrate that the translation to Loglan code can be automatic; no general method is given here to automatically perform this trasformation). For a complete axiomatization refer to [TeVi].
Here, the underlying model is given with the notations

Max-row, Max-col	$: \text{Mat} \to \text{N}$
New-mat	$: \text{N} \times \text{N} \to \text{Mat}$
Put	$: \text{Mat} \times \text{N} \times \text{N} \times \text{E} \to \text{Mat}$
Get	$: \text{Mat} \times \text{N} \times \text{N} \to \text{E}$
Empty-mat	$\in \text{Mat}$
Empty	$\in \text{E}$
$=_m$	$: \text{Mat} \times \text{Mat} \to \text{Bool}$
$+_m$	$: \text{Mat} \times \text{Mat} \to \text{Mat}$

where Mat denotes the set of the matrices; E is the generic matrix elements set (provided by an order relation and two operations $+_E$ and $*_E$); m, m1, m2 denote the generic elements of Mat; r, c are integers numbers: e is the generic element of the set E.

- axiom (Get definition)

$(1 \leq i \leq \text{max-row}(m) \wedge 1 \leq j \leq \text{max-col}(m))$

$\Longrightarrow$

$\quad (\text{get}(\text{put}(m,i,j,e),i,j)=e)$

- axiom (Sum definition)

$(\sim m =_m \text{empty-mat} \wedge \sim m1 = \text{empty-mat} \wedge \text{max-row}(m) = \text{max-row}(m1) \wedge \text{max-col}(m) = \text{max-row}(m1)$

$\Longrightarrow$

```
    begin
      m2:=new-mat(max-row(m), max-col(m))
      for i:=1 to max-row(m)
        do
        for j:=1 to max-col(m)
          do
          put(m2,i,j,get(m1,i,j) +E get(m1,i,j))
          od
        od
    end)        m2 =m m +m m1
```

The translation from axioms to Loglan code can be very natural. For example the Loglan code obtained from the second axiom is in the following inserted into the definition of the matrix class:

```
    unit matrix:ring class(n,m:integer):
      var a:arrayof arrayof ring; i:integer;

      unit virtual add:function(x:matrix):matrix;
        var i,j:integer;
        begin
          if max-row=x.max-row andif max-col=x.max-col
          then
          result := new matrix(max-row,max-col);
          for i:=1 to max-row
            do
            for j:=1 to max-col
              do
              result.a(i,j) := a(i,j).add(x.a(i,j))
              od;
            od;
          fi;
        end add;

  ...
      begin (*execution part of class matrix*)
      array a dim (1:n);
      for i:=1 to n
        do
        array a  dim (1:m);
        od;
      end matrix;
```

Let us note that in Loglan the objects are automatically initialized. In the case of previous example, at the definition of a Matrix of Integer, its elements are initialized to 0, so the conditions like $\sim$ m = empty-mat holds for any m $\in$ Mat. Also, we want to note that in the data structure Matrix, which has been implemented in Loglan by translating the related axioms, we have treated the matrix dimensions as attributes of the class Matrix, so, in order to make the notation less cumbersome, the operations get(m,i,j), put(m,i,j,e), max-row(m) and max-col(m), have been identified, respectively, by m(i,j), m(i,j):=e, m.max-row and m.max-col.

4.2. Approximation methods on abstract structures

As a second example of the application of the proposed methodology, let us show the specification of a particular computing method, namely the Hensel construction method. In a way similar to the one followed in the previous example, we can define the classes Polynomial Ring ($P[x]$) and Euclidean Domain, as subclasses of Ring. Then every substructure of Polynomial Ring will inherits also the algorithms defined for $P[x]$ by virtual specification. In this case no further specialized code is necessary.

In fact inheritance allows us to use the code given in $P[x]$, directly in its substructures, without any redefinition.

We know that the Hensel method [Yun],[MiYu] is defined on the Domain $P[x]$: it will be automatically implicit in every substructure (e.g.:$Z[x]$). This is just the case in which the abstraction method allows a specification at a very-high-level, whithout the necessity of further instanciations.

As well known this method gives an iterative mechanism to solve equations of the following type:

$$\Phi(G, H) = 0$$

where

$$\Phi : D[x] \times D[x] \to D[x]$$

being D an abstract Euclidean Domain. The approximate solution G_k, H_k (such that $\Phi(G_k, H_k) \equiv 0 \pmod{I^k}$, for a suitable value of k) of the given equation is obtained starting from an appropriate initial approximation, i.e.: $G_1[x]$ and $H_1[x]$, such that

$$\Phi(G_1, H_1) \equiv 0 \pmod{I}$$

where I is an ideal in $D[x]$.

In the following $+_D, =_D, 0_D$, will indicate respectively the sum operation, the equality relation and the zero element in D. Moreover, the function $EVAL(\Phi(G, H), G_j, H_j)$, computes the value of the function Φ at the point (G_j, H_j); the function $DERIVE$ computes the polynomial derivative function; the function mod_D, given $a \in D$, computes $a \pmod{I}$ and the function $DUPE$ (Diophantine Univariate Polynomial Equation), solves the diophantine equation that is the fundamental step at each iteration of the Hensel algorithm.

In the following figure, we show how the Hensel method can be defined at a very-high-level of abstraction by integrating its definition into the structure $P[x]$. Then every instanciation of $P[x]$ (e.g.: $Z[x]$) automatically inherits this algorithm.

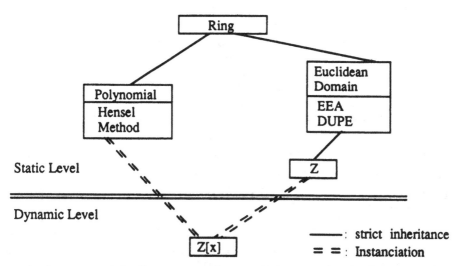

The first part of the figure, as in the previous example, shows a static hierarchy of structures; in this case the Univariate Polynomial structure is enriched by the definition of Hensel method. The second part is related to the dynamic level: at this level the instanciation of objects representing, for example, a Univariate Polynomial over Integers is obtained.

The formal specification of Hensel algorithm is the following:

HENSEL: $\big(\Phi(G,H) \in C^2(G,H) \quad with \ G, H \in D[x]\big)$
$\Longrightarrow$
  begin
    $j := 1;$
    $C := EVAL(\Phi(G,H), G_1, H_1);$
    while $(j < k) \wedge (\sim C =_D 0_D)$
      do
        $A := DERIV(\Phi(G_j, H_j), G);$
        $B := DERIV(\Phi(G_j, H_j), H);$
        $A := mod_D(A, I^k);$
        $B := mod_D(B, I^k);$
        $C := mod_D(C, I^k);$
        $\Delta G_j := 0_D;$
        $\Delta H_j := 0_D;$
        $(\Delta G_j, \Delta H_j) := DUPE(C, A, B);$
        $G_{j+1} := G_j +_D \Delta G_j;$
        $H_{j+1} := H_j +_D \Delta H_j;$
        $C := EVAL(\Phi(G,H), G_{j+1}, H_{j+1});$
        $j := j + 1;$
      od
  end$\big)$ $mod_D(EVAL(\Phi(G,H), G_k, H_k), I^k) =_D 0_D$

We want to underline that this specification refers to previously specified functions $EVAL, DERIVE, DUPE$. As soon as these functions are defined, the translation from the above AL specification to Loglan code is consequent.

References

[CiSa] G. CIONI, A. SALWICKI (Eds): *Advanced Programming Methodologies*, Academic Press (1989).

[Goo] J.W. GOODWIN: *Why Programming Environments Need Dynamic Data Types*, IEEE Trans. on Software Eng. SE-7, 5, (1981).

[Log] W.M. BARTOL et al: *Report on the Programming Language LOGLAN 82*, Polish Scient. Publ. Warsaw (1984).

[Lis] B. LISKOV: *Data Abstraction and Hierarchy*, Proc. OOPSLA '87 (1987).

[Mey] B. MEYER: *Object Oriented Software Construction*, Prentice Hall (1988).

[MiYu] A. MIOLA, D.Y. YUN *Computational Aspects of Hensel Type Univariate Polynomial GCD*, ACM Proc. EUROSAM (1974).

[MiSa] G. MIRKOWSKA, A. SALWICKI: *Algorithmic Logic*, Polish Scient. Publ. Warsaw (1987).

[Sny] A.SNYDER: *Inheritance and the Development of Encapsulated Software Systems*, In "Research Directions in Object Oriented Programming", MIT Press, C.S. Series (1987).

[TeVi] M. TEMPERINI, R. VITALE: *A Formal approach to the specification and manipulation of mathematical objects*, R.251 IASI-CNR Roma (1988).

[ThRE] P. THOMAS, H. ROBINSON-J. EMMS: *Abstract Data Types - Their Specification, Representation, and Use*, Clarendon Press, Oxford (1988).

[Weg] P.WEGNER: *The Object Oriented Classification Paradigm*, In "Research Directions in Object Oriented Programming", MIT Press, C.S. Series (1987).

[Yun] D.Y.Y. YUN: *Algebraic algorithms using P-adic construction*, ACM Proc. SYMSAC (1976).

PROGRAMMING PARADIGMS FOR SYMBOLIC COMPUTATION SYSTEMS
ANALYSIS OF AN EXAMPLE

Uwe Petermann
Department of Informatics, Karl Marx University
Leipzig, 7010, German Democratic Republic

Abstract
The aim of the paper is a discussion of programming paradigms suitable for the design of Symbolic Computation Systems. In a case study the object oriented programming language LOGLAN has been used for the implementation of algorithms for computations in non-commutative polynomial algebras and their quotient skew fields. The discussion is focused at the combination of classical programming paradigms e.g. module nesting with the object oriented programming paradigm.

1. Introduction

1.1. What makes object oriented programming attractive for symbolic computation?

As usual symbolic computation systems are large programs operating on complex data structures. Therefore language constructs for

> (1) data abstraction, data encapsulation and
>
> (2) modularization

are needed. Data structures are often designed by stepwise refinement and simpler data structures are used multiply. Therefore constructs for

> (3) inheritance of capabilities

are necessary. During symbolic computation processes are created many data objects representing intermediate results. Those become useless after some time but consume much memory. Hence, one needs

> (4) dynamic storage management.
>
> (5) The four concepts should fit together.

These five requirements are met more or less by object oriented programming languages. One of them is LOGLAN (cf. [LOG]), the language chosen by the author for an experimental implementation of symbolic computation algorithms[1]. Constructs provided by this language for these purposes will be discussed briefly.

ad 1: The construct for *data encapsulation* is the class notion (cf. 2.1. and 2.3). A class is a syntactic entity combining together data

---

[1] The design of the program has been supported by the Research Project RP I-09 of Polish Ministry of National Education.

(variables), operations (procedures and functions - in a classical terminology, methods - in the object oriented terminology) and other classes. The last point is different to other, more orthodox, object oriented languages where module nesting is not possible (e.g. Smalltalk [GR]) or where nesting of classes is impossible (e.g. Turbo-Pascal 5).

ad 2) Among the *modularization* tools are the classical block oriented tools (best known from, say, Pascal) and coroutines.

ad 3) *Inheritance* of capabilities (variables, operations, classes) is possible by the notion of prefixing (cf. 2.2. and 2.3., 3.1. for applications). This concept known from SIMULA 67 has been freed from restrictions concerning its interaction with module nesting. Overloading of operations is possible due to virtual operations (cf. 3.2.).

ad 4) *Dynamic storage management* is possible by allocation and deallocation of objects of classes.

ad 5) The four concepts are joint together into a unique framework. This mixture of concepts makes the language interesting.

1.2. The example: A program for computation in non-commutative polynomial algebras and their quotient skew fields

LOGLAN has been used in common by J. Apel and the present author for the implementation of sophisticated algorithms for computations in non-commutative polynomial algebras and their quotient skew fields. The algorithms are due to J. Apel and W. Lassner [AL1-2]. The main capabilities offered by the implementation are the following (for the algebraic background see [Bu]):

The user may *define algebraic domains* using the domain constructors: enveloping algebra, quotient skew field and rational numbers. Elements of these domains may be subject to the ring and field operations including the computation of the *canonical representant* of fractions.

The *Buchberger algorithm* (cf. [Bu] for the commutative case) for enveloping algebras may be executed in three versions:

- turning a right to an equivalent left fraction,
- computing a generating system of the syzygy module determined by a right fraction,
- computing for a left ideal $\Im$ given by a generating system

$$f = [f_1, \ldots, f_n]$$

the least element p of a Groebner basis of $\Im$ and the transformation vector s such that

$$p = \mathit{s} \cdot f^T \quad .$$

Two examples should demonstrate the flexibility of the program.
At first the quotient skew field of the algebra SO(3) is considered.
SO(3) is characterized by the following, user defined, parameters.

elements of the vector space basis : x, y, z
commutation rules : $y x = x y - z$
$z x = x z + y$
$z y = y z - x$
coefficient domain : rational numbers
term ordering :   total degree ordering defined by $x < y < z$.

Problem : Multiply the left fractions

$$v_1 = (x y z + 2 y^2 - 2 x^2 + 2)^{-1} (z^2 + 4) \qquad \text{and}$$
$$v_2 = (x^2 + 1)^{-1} (x^2 y + x z) .$$

The product of v_1 and v_2 is

$$v_1 v_2 = (-1/6\ x^5\ y\ z - 1/3\ x^4\ y^2 + 1/3\ x^6 - 5/3\ x^3\ y\ z -$$
$$10/3\ x^2\ y^2 + 3\ x^4 - 3/2\ x\ y\ z - 3\ y^2 - 1/3\ x^2 - 3)^{-1}$$
$$(-1/6\ x^4\ y\ z^2 - 1/6\ x^3\ z^3 + 1/3\ x^5\ z - 7/6\ x^2\ y\ z^2 - 1/2\ x^4\ y$$
$$- 7/6x\ z^3 - x\ y^2\ z + 13/6x^3\ z + y^3 - 7/2\ x^2\ y - 31/6\ x\ z + y)$$

and the canonical representant of the product is

$$v_1 v_2 = (x^2 + 1)^{-1} (x z - y) .$$

In the second example a Groebner-Basis of   an   ideal   in   a   commutative
polynomial ring over rational functions has been computed.
The user defined parameters of the algebraic domain are:

elements of the vector space basis : x, y, z, u
commutation rules :   all commutators vanishing
coefficient domain : rational functions (with   rational   numbers   as
coefficients) in the variables a, b, c, d.
term ordering :   total degree ordering with $x < y < z < u$.

Problem : Compute the Groebner Basis   of   the   ideal   generated   by   the
following polynomials:

(1) $u - (d - b)$

(2) $\quad$ x + y + z + u - (a + c + d)

(3) $\quad$ x z + x u + y z + z u - (a d + a c + c d)

(4) $\quad$ x z u - (a c d)

The Groebner Basis consists of the following five polynomials:

(5) $\quad$ u + (b - d)

(6) $\quad$ x + y + z + u + (- a - c - d)

(7) $\quad$ z^2 + (b - d)x + (-a - c - d)z + (a c + a d + c d)

(8) $\quad$ y z + z^2 + z u + (- a - c - d)z + $\dfrac{- a c d}{b - d}$

(9) $\quad$ y^2 + $\dfrac{a + 2b + c - d}{b - d}$ y z + y u + z u

$\quad$ + $\dfrac{- a b - a c - b c - b d + d^2}{b - d}$ y

$\quad$ + $\dfrac{- a b^2 - a b c + a b d - b^2 c - b^2 d + b c d + 2b d^2 - d^3}{b^2 - 2b d + d^2}$ z

1.3. Related work

The usage of object oriented notions like class notion and prefix notion has been demonstrated for solving logic problems by G. Cioni and A. Kreczmar [CK]. Applications of LOGLAN for algebraic computations first have been studied in a small program implementing symbolic differentiation by D. Szczepanska [Szcz].
A large project using object oriented techniques is the theorem prover of J. Siekmann and his group based on connection graph resolution [Sie]. Because the data structure necessary for this method are rather complicated object oriented techniques seems to be the most adequate.

1.4. Acknowledgments

The program described below has been designed in common by J. Apel and the present author during stays at the Institute of Informatics of Warsaw University. I´d like to thank the colleagues from the LOGLAN group at Warsaw University for their kind support making this programming experiment possible.

2. The object oriented view on abstract data types

2.1. Classes and objects

The central notion of LOGLAN 82 is the notion of class. A *class* is a
syntactical entity grouping together declarations of variables,
procedures and functions as well as classes :

> <u>unit</u> A : <u>class</u> (*formal parameters of A*);
> < *declaration of classes, procedures, functions, variables* >
> <u>begin</u> < *instruction sequence of class A* > <u>end</u>

Using a less programmers like terminology: classes are grouping together
data, operations and notions. The semantical counterpart of a class (say
A) are objects (in other words: instances) which are created at run time
by means of the <u>new</u>-operator:

> x := <u>new</u> A (*actual parameters*);

Creation of an object includes the computation of the value of the
actual parameters and the execution of the instruction sequence of the
class (enabling the initialization of the object). After creation of the
object a reference to it is returned as value of variable x.
Hence, an object of a class is a data structure which may be accessed by
well defined operations (expressed by the procedures and functions of
the class). Classes implement abstract data types.

2.2. Prefixing

A class may be extended by means of *prefixing*. For example:

> <u>unit</u> B : A <u>class</u> (*formal parameters of B*);
> < *declarations of B* >
> <u>begin</u> < *instructions of B* > <u>end</u>;

Objects of class B inherit the features of objects of class A and have
some additional, specific for B, features. By means of prefixing
hierarchies of data types may be defined.

2.3. An application : multiple usage of abstract data types

As an application of the class notion and prefixing will be discussed
the implementation of two-directed lists and their application in two
quit different contexts.

The idea of the list implementation is well known and given by the
following picture. A list consists of a head and the elements joint
together by pointers into a double ring. Heads and elements are objects
of classes HEAD and ELEMENT respectively. Both classes have the common
prefix LINK which provides the pointers.

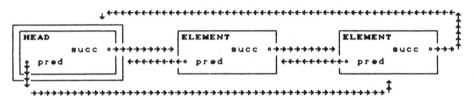

Fig. 1

The declarations of the classes are the following (abbreviated).

```
unit LINK : class; var pred, succ : LINK; end LINK;
unit HEAD : LINK class;
     unit into : procedure (l:ELEMENT);
              < insert the element l into this list > end into;
end LINK;
unit ELEMENT : LINK class;
     unit out : procedure;
     < delete this element from the list it appears in > end out;
end ELEMENT;
```

One application of the notion of lists is the notion of polynomial.
Below a polynomial is defined as a list of monomials. For another
application of the list notion see section 4.

```
unit POLYNOMIAL : HEAD class;
     unit add : function ( p : POLYNOMIAL ) : POLYNOMIAL;
              var m : MONOMIAL, p1 : POLYNOMIAL;
     begin    ...    call p1.into(m)    ...    end add;    ...
end POLYNOMIAL;
unit MONOMIAL : ELEMENT class;
     var coefficient : RING_ELEMENT;         ....
end MONOMIAL;
```

3. Hierarchies of abstract data types

3.1. The type hierarchy defining algebraic domain constructors

The hierarchy of data types defining algebraic domains is presented in the picture below.

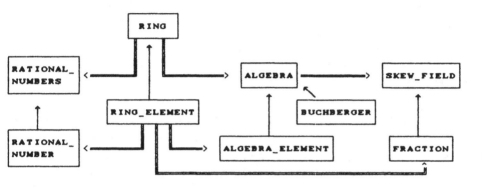

Legend: A ⟶ B means: A is prefix of B
         A ⟶ B means: A is declared within B

Fig.2

Objects of the classes RATIONAL_NUMBERS, ALGEBRA and SKEW_FIELD encode the structure of user defined rings. In the case of polynomial algebras and their skew fields the basis, the term ordering, the coefficient domain and the commutators must be stored. The common ancestor (in the prefix structure) of the mentioned classes is the class RING. There their common features are declared, for instance an operation for the interactive definition of a domain. The implementation of these operation is done within the specialized classes.

3.2. Virtuals

Elements of rings are represented as objects of the classes RATIONAL_NUMBER, ALGEBRA_ELEMENT and FRACTION which are all prefixed by the class RING_ELEMENT. Data encoding the ring structure belong to the syntactic environment of these classes. This combination of prefixing and nesting allows to write the basic algebraic algorithms, e.g. the Buchberger algorithm and the simplification algorithm for fractions, in a quit abstract manner, independent on the actual parameters of the user defined algebraic structures.

Let us discuss a particular consequence of this fact. The Buchberger algorithm is a feature of the considered polynomial algebras. Consequently it is implemented within the class ALGEBRA (cf. the figure 2 above and the declaration below).

```
unit BUCHBERGER : class ;
... Implementation of the Buchberger algorithm ...
      var x, y : RING_ELEMENT , m : MONOMIAL ;
begin
.... x := m.coefficient.add ( y )
   returns the sum of m's coefficient and y as new value of x ....
end BUCHBERGER ;
```

The notion of polynomial as a list of monomials is defined at the same level. Recall from 2.3. that monomials have a coefficient of type RING_ELEMENT. Therefore, at the syntactic level where the Buchberger algorithm is declared the actual nature of the coefficient domain is unpredictable.

For this reason the ring operations are defined as virtual functions of the class RING_ELEMENT which is the common prefix of the classes RATIONAL_NUMBER, ALGEBRA_ELEMENT and FRACTION (cf. the declaration schemes below). The implementation of the ring operations is done in the specialized classes (see the declaration schemes below). The semantics of virtuals makes sure that at run time the call of a ring operation will cause the activation of the operation which is appropriate for the actual ring elements.

```
unit RING_ELEMENT : class ;
    unit virtual add :
        function ( e : RING_ELEMENT ) : RING_ELEMENT ; end ;
end RING_ELEMENT ;
unit RATIONAL_NUMBER : RING_ELEMENT class ;
    unit virtual add :
        function ( r : RATIONAL_NUMBER ) : RATIONAL_NUMBER ;
        ... computation of the sum of rational numbers ...
    end add ;
end RATIONAL_NUMBER ;
unit ALGEBRA_ELEMENT : RING_ELEMENT class ;
    unit virtual add :
        function ( e : ALGEBRA_ELEMENT ) : ALGEBRA_ELEMENT ;
        ... computation of the sum of polynomials ...
    end add ;
end ALGEBRA_ELEMENT ;
```

4. Dynamic storage management

In this chapter we consider dynamic storage management and pointer techniques. The reader is encouraged to recall the following facts about the used realization of the Buchberger algorithm (cf. [AL2]) before trying to understand the figure 3 .
The Buchberger algorithm maintains the following data structure:
- a list g of polynomials, representing the Groebner basis under computation (viewed as a vector),
- a transformation matrix $\mathcal{X}$ such that $g = \mathcal{X} \cdot f^T$ for the ideal basis f being the input for the algorithm,
- the set $\mathcal{P}$ of critical pairs.

In order to speed up the algorithm it has the following capabilities:
- in every loop a subalgorithm tries to reduce the basis g,
- before trying to reduce a critical pair a criterium is applied for finding out whether this effort will be useless.

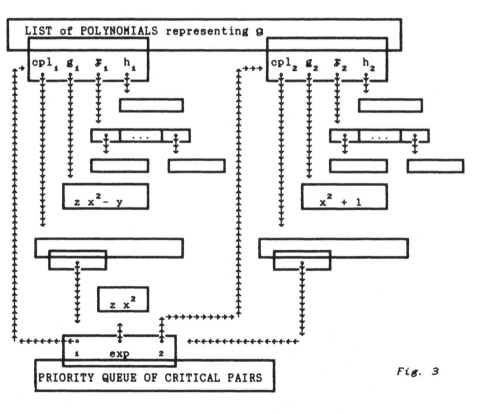

Fig. 3

For the efficient execution of these operations additional information must be kept. Every element g of g is stored together with

- the associated row $\mathcal{Z}$ of $\mathcal{X}$,
- a polynomial h being used in the computation of a left normal form representation,
- a list cpl of the critical pairs g appears in.

Moreover the least upper bound of the exponent vectors of the according leading monomials is adjoined to every critical pair. The set of critical pairs forms a priority queue with respect to this vector.

Pointers are used in order to avoid holding of many copies of objects appearing in several data structure.

The figure 3 above shows a snapshot made during a computation of the Buchberger algorithm. It presents a situation where there exists one critical pair with the polynomials $z\,x - y$ and $x^2 + 1$ (the only elements of the basis under computation) and the power product $z\,x^2$ as the least upper bound of their leading monomials $z\,x$ and x^2.

5. Summary

Experience with the implementation of algebraic algorithms showed the usefulness of several features of an object oriented programming language. After a rather short time a working prototype of the program was available. Deeper inside in the behavior of the algorithms is the main practical result of this effort.

6. References

[AL1] Apel J., Lassner W., Computation of reduced Groebner bases and syzygies in enveloping algebras. SYMSAC 86.
[AL2] Apel J., Lassner W., Computation and simplification in Lie fields. Full paper presented at the EUROCAL 87.
[AP] Apel J., Petermann U., A program for algebraic computation in quotient skew fields of enveloping algebras of Lie algebras - An application of LOGLAN 82. subm. to ISSAC 88 , to app.
[Bu] Buchberger B., History and Basic Features of the Critical-Pair/Completion Procedure, J. of Symbolic Computation, Vol. 3, Nos 1&2, Febr./April 1987, pp. 3-38.
[CK] Cioni G., Kreczmar A., Solving Logic Problems by Object Oriented Languages, Cons. Naz. di Ricerche, Istituto di Analisi dei Systemi ed Informatica, R.158, June 1986.
[GR] Goldberg A., Robson D., SMALLTALK 80: The language and its implementation, Addison Wesley, Reading Mass., 1983.
[LOG] LOGLAN 82 Programming Language, Polish Scientific Publishers, Warsaw 1982.
[Sie] Siekmann, J., Automated deduction and data basis, Report Univ. of Karlsruhe, 1989.
[SIM] Dahl, O., et al., SIMULA 67, Norwegian Comp. Centre, Oslo, 1967.
[Szcz] Szczepanska D., The Progam Differ, in Proc.Summer School on LOGLAN, 1982, to app. Warsaw University.

The computation of Gröbner bases
on a shared memory multiprocessor

Jean-Philippe Vidal
Computer Science Department
Carnegie Mellon University
PITTSBURGH, PA 15213
jpv@CS.CMU.EDU

Abstract

This article presents a system which computes Gröbner bases on a shared memory multiprocessor. The basic idea is that each processor picks an element in the set of unreduced critical pairs, reduces the S-polynomial associated with it and updates the basis and the set of pairs according to the result. The originality of this algorithm relies on the small amount of synchronization it requires among the processes. The details of an implementation on a 16 processors *Encore* machine are given together with results of tests performed with well-known examples of the literature.

1 Introduction

In his Ph.D. [4], Buchberger presented an algorithm which has been studied extensively in the recent years for at least two reasons. The first one is the large list of its applications, including the determination of the membership of a polynomial to an ideal and the solution of systems of algebraic equations. The second one is the apparent contradiction between the simplicity of the algorithm and the difficulty to obtain practical bounds on its complexity.

The definitions and facts that we present here can be found, for example, in Robbiano, [12]. K is a field and $A = K[x_1, \ldots, x_n]$ is the ring of polynomials in $x_1, \ldots, x_n$ over K. It is well-known from Hilbert that any ideal I of A has a finite basis B of polynomials.

An admissible order $\succ$ on the set of power products of $x_1, \ldots, x_n$ (a power product is a monomial with coefficient 1, like $x_1^2 x_2^5$) is a total order such that $T \succ 1$ for every power product T and such that $T_1 \succ T_2$ implies $T_1 T_3 \succ T_2 T_3$ for all power products T_1, T_2, T_3. If P is a polynomial, we call $T(P)$ the leading power product of P with respect to $\succ$ and $C(P)$ the corresponding coefficient. The initial $In(P)$ of P is the product $C(P)\,T(P)$.

For a set of polynomials B and an admissible order $\succ$, we can define a reduction relation $\longrightarrow$. We say that $P \longrightarrow Q$ if and only if there exists in B a polynomial R such that R divides $P - Q$ and $T(R)$ divides $T(P)$. We call $\longrightarrow^*$ the reflexive and transitive closure of $\longrightarrow$. It is immediate that $P \longrightarrow^* 0$ implies that P belongs to the ideal generated by B. On the other hand, if P belongs to I implies that $P \longrightarrow^* 0$, then the basis is called a Gröbner basis or a standard basis of I.

There exist many other characterizations of a Gröbner basis. The one we use to design an algorithm requires to define S-polynomials. First, we call $T(P, Q)$ the least common multiple of the power products $T(P)$ and $T(Q)$. Then, the S-polynomial of two polynomials P and Q is

$$Spol(P,Q) = C(Q)\frac{T(P,Q)}{T(P)}P - C(P)\frac{T(P,Q)}{T(Q)}Q.$$

Buchberger proved that B is a Gröbner basis iff $Spol(P, Q) \longrightarrow^* 0$ for all pairs $\{P, Q\}$ of polynomials of B.

An algorithm can then be designed. Its two main variables are `Basis`, the set of polynomials, which is initially equal to the given basis of I, and `Pairs`, the set of unreduced pairs, which is initially equal to the set of pairs of elements of Basis. Now, the algorithm picks a pair in Pairs and reduces the corresponding S-polynomial w.r.t. $\succ$ and Basis. If the resulting polynomial Q is not equal to 0, then it is added to Basis and all the pairs formed by Q and every other polynomial in Basis are added to Pairs. When, finally. Pairs is empty, Basis is a Gröbner basis of the ideal generated by the input set of polynomials.

This basic algorithm and two criteria used to avoid the reduction of certain pairs are described by Buchberger in [5]. We discuss here the design and implementation of a parallel version of this algorithm.

2 Description of the tools for synchronization

The following concepts appear in many places in the literature. Our source is the book "Operating Systems Principles" by Brinch Hansen, [3], pages 77-116.

A variable v of type T shared among several processes will be noted:

shared T v

Critical regions. Sometimes, a process executing a certain sequence of instructions using the variable v needs that this variable is not modified by another process during this execution. Therefore, at most one process should execute such a sequence involving v at a given time. The object enforcing this policy is called a *critical region associated with* v. We will use the following notation:

region v do *sequence*

Waiting for a condition to hold. A process may need to wait for a shared variable v to have a certain property, i.e. for another process to modify v. The process must test v inside a critical region but it must wait outside this critical region. Otherwise, another process would not be able to modify v. To allow this, we introduce the primitive await. When a process, in a critical region, executes the statement:

await B(v),

it evaluates the Boolean function B(v). If the result is true, it goes on. If it is false, it quits the critical region and joins the waiting queue for this condition. Naturally, when the condition becomes true, only one process of the waiting queue is readmitted in the critical region.

Readers-writers exclusion.

The concept of critical region is somehow limiting. We need a tool allowing an arbitrary number of processes to access v simultaneously, if they do not change v. Such processes will be called *readers* and the processes updating v will be called *writers*. Of course, the same process can be a reader and a writer at different points of time. At any given time, at most one process should be a writer and, if there is such a writer, there should be no reader. Therefore, we introduce the three following notations, in which RWE stands for readers-writers exclusion:

RWE T v
reading_access_to v do *sequence*
writing_access_to v do *sequence*

The first one states that the variable v of type T is protected by the described mechanism. The other two are executed by a process which asks to enter a sequence of statements with reading or writing privileges on v. A reading access is granted if there is no writer and no process waiting to become a writer. A writing access is granted if there is no reader. Therefore, we see that writers have priority over readers.

3   Description of the algorithm

First we state Buchberger's algorithm in order to make clear locations where parallel features can be introduced (Figure 1).

```
Input:   a set B of polynomials, basis of an ideal I.

Basis:= B;
Pairs:= init_pairs(Basis);
while (size(Pairs) ≠ 0) do
  begin
    pair:= choose(Pairs);
    Q:= reduce(spol(pair),Basis);
    if (Q ≠ 0) then
      begin
        Basis:= Basis ∪ {Q};
        Pairs:= update_pairs(Pairs,Basis,Q)
      end;
  end;
```

Figure 1: High-level description of Buchberger's algorithm

If several processors are available, it is possible to reduce several pairs simultaneously. This natural idea was mentioned by Watt in his Ph.D. [16] and by Buchberger [6]. An implementation was done by Ponder [11] and another by Senechaud [13], for Boolean polynomials only. However, these authors treat only the case in which the underlying architecture is a network of processors exchanging messages. Here, we study an architecture in which the different processors share memory. The two main shared variables are Basis and Pairs, the set of pairs waiting to be reduced.

- The variable Pairs is modified each time it is accessed. Therefore, a critical region will protect Pairs efficiently. A process waits for new pairs to arrive in the set Pairs by using an await statement.

- During the reduction of an S-polynomial, a process reads Basis many times but never updates it. As many processes will be simultaneously in this reduction phase, the use of a readers-writers exclusion is justified.

The shared variable nwaiting, whose critical region is equal to the one associated with Pairs, is used to count the number of processes waiting for new pairs to come. If all the processes but one are waiting and if the last one does not bring any new pair to reduce, then the computation is ended. We present the program in Figure 2.

4   Correctness of the algorithm

Owicki introduced correctness proofs for parallel algorithms in [10]. Using her techniques, we present an invariant that gives a strong evidence of the correctness of the algorithm.

Owicki defines *auxiliary variables*. These are variables which appear only in left-hand sides of some assignments and whose only role is to be witnesses of the meaningful components of the state of the program at a given point. We use the auxiliary variables working[i] to tell whether

```
shared list_of_pairs Pairs;
shared integer nwaiting;
RWE list_of_pols Basis;

process worker(i)

  begin
    while (true) do
      begin
        region Pairs do
          begin
            nwaiting = nwaiting + 1;
            if ((nwaiting = ntotalprocesses)
                    and (size(Pairs) = 0)) then
                conclude();
            await (size(Pairs) > 0);
            pair[i]:= choose(Pairs);
            nwaiting = nwaiting - 1;
          end;
        reading_access_to Basis do
          Q[i]:= reduce(spol(pair[i]),Basis);
        if (Q[i] ≠ 0) then
          writing_access_to Basis do
            region Pairs do
              begin
                Basis:= Basis ∪ {Q[i]};
                Pairs:= update_pairs(Pairs,Basis,Q[i]);
              end;
      end;
  end;
```

Figure 2: A first version

a process is working or is waiting for new pairs to come. The completed algorithm is presented in Figure 3.

To prove that it computes a Gröbner basis, we use the second characterization presented in the introduction. B is a Gröbner basis w.r.t. the admissible order $\succ$ iff, for every pair $\{P_1, P_2\}$ of members of B, $Spol(P_1, P_2) \longrightarrow^* 0$.

First, we remark that any change to Basis, Pairs, pair[i] or working[i] is made in a critical region associated with Pairs. Therefore, we introduce the following invariant.
$\mathcal{I}(Pairs,\ Basis,\ pair[1], \ldots, pair[p],\ working[1], \ldots, working[p])$ must be true whenever there is no process in a critical region for Pairs. It says that the S-polynomials of all the pairs of elements of Basis which do not belong to Pairs and on which no process is currently working can be reduced to 0 w.r.t. Basis. Formally stated, the invariant reads as follows:

$$\forall \{P, Q\} \in Basis^2$$
$$\{\{P, Q\} \notin Pairs \wedge$$
$$[\forall i \in \{1, \ldots, p\},\ working[i] = false \vee pair[i] \neq \{P, Q\}]\} \implies$$
$$Spol(P, Q) \longrightarrow^*_{Basis} 0$$

The invariant has to be true before the p workers begin to work. This means that Pairs has been correctly initialized: all the pairs of members of Basis are created and, then, they are filtered by the criteria presented by Buchberger in [5] and refined by Gebauer and Möller in [9]. Likewise, all the variables working[i] are initially false.

A process may change one of the variables mentioned in the invariant only if it is in a critical region for Pairs. Therefore, the fact that $\mathcal{I}$ is really an invariant is proved by checking that if $\mathcal{I}$ holds when a process enters a critical region, then $\mathcal{I}$ still holds when the process leaves it. A listing of the algorithm annotated with assertions can be found in [15].

When a process reaches the statement conclude(), the formula

$$\forall \{P, Q\} \in Basis^2,\ Spol(P, Q) \longrightarrow^*_{Basis} 0$$

holds because Pairs is empty and all the working[i] are false. Therefore, at this point, Basis is a Gröbner basis for the given admissible order.

5 Improvement of the algorithm

A process that computes a lengthy reduction stops all the processes that may want to update Basis and Pairs. This can be circumvented by the following remark. The function reduce (not described here) is just a loop that repeats two distinct operations:

- Find in Basis a polynomial R which can be used to reduce P.

- Use R to reduce P.

There is no need to prevent writers from updating Basis when all the reading processes are already executing the second operation. Therefore, we can shorten the critical region:

```
reading_access_to Basis do
  Q[i]:= reduce(spol(pair[i]),Basis);
```

```
shared list_of_pairs Pairs;
shared integer nwaiting;
RWE list_of_pols Basis;

process worker(i)

  begin
    while (true) do
      begin
        region Pairs do
          begin
            nwaiting = nwaiting + 1;
            if ((nwaiting = ntotalprocesses)
                  and (size(Pairs) = 0)) then
                conclude();
            await (size(Pairs) > 0);
            working[i]:=true;
            pair[i]:= choose(Pairs);
            nwaiting = nwaiting - 1;
          end;
        reading_access_to Basis do
          Q[i]:= reduce(spol(pair[i]),Basis);
        if (Q[i] ≠ 0) then
            writing_access_to Basis do
              region Pairs do
                begin
                  Basis:= Basis ∪ {Q[i]};
                  Pairs:= update_pairs(Pairs,Basis,Q[i]);
                  working[i]:=false;
                end;
        else
            region Pairs do
              working[i]:=false;
      end;
  end;
```

Figure 3: Introducing the auxiliary variables working[i

in the following way:

```
Q[i]:= spol(pair[i]);
reading_access_to Basis do
  red[i]:= choose_to_reduce(Q[i],Basis);
while (red[i]≠0) do
  begin
    Q[i]:= reduce_one_step(Q[i],red[i]);
    reading_access_to Basis do
      red[i]:= choose_to_reduce(Q[i],Basis);
  end;
```

The function `choose_to_reduce(Q,Basis)` returns a polynomial of `Basis` which can be used to reduce `Q`, if there exists such a polynomial. Otherwise, it returns 0.

In this version, processes spend more time in synchronization. Nevertheless, it is more efficient since the constraints imposed on the writers by the readers are smaller, due to the fact that the time spent in actually reducing a polynomial P by a polynomial R is much larger than the time taken by the process to choose R in the basis. This relative time independence between processes seems to be a determining criterion for efficiency.

6 Description of the implementation and experimental results

We implemented the refined version of our algorithm on a 16 processor *Encore* machine. Our program is written in C. A package handling multivariate polynomials over $\mathbb{Z}$ was developed first. A package manipulating integers of arbitrary length was already available: **cmump**, developed at Carnegie-Mellon University by Dwyer, McGeoch, Jacobson and Yee on top of the **mp** package developed at Bell Labs. Computations in $Q[x_1,\ldots,x_n]$ were performed with polynomials in $\mathbb{Z}[x_1,\ldots,x_n]$.

It is unnecessary to reduce all the critical pairs. To eliminate the useless ones from `Pairs`, we used in **update_pairs** the algorithm described by Gebauer and Möller in [9].

The synchronization between the processors uses the **cthread** package developed by Cooper and Draves [8]. It allows parallel programming in C under the MACH operating system, developed by Rich Rashid and al. [1]. **cthread** allowed us to implement easily all the primitives described in section 2.

Our goal is to design a program with all the options that can be found on an implementation of the sequential version of the algorithm, as the AIPI system built by Traverso and Donati and described in [14]: choice among different admissible orders, different levels of trace,... The only option which is not easy to adapt to the refined parallel algorithm is the deletion of redundant elements of the basis during the computation. The solution we propose is not completely satisfactory.

There are also two parameters which are specific to the parallel version of the algorithm. They are the number of processes which are used and the policy followed to allocate memory dynamically. The description of the two possible memory allocation policies can be found in [15].

We tested our implementation on the examples listed in [2] and [14]. We are mostly interested in the speed-up that one can achieve by using several processors. Therefore, we let the number of processors vary and we fix all the other options:

- Three admissible orders are used: lexicographic order, noted L, total order refined by lexicographical order, noted TL, and total order refined by reverse lexicographical order, noted TR. The order chosen among the variables can be found with the complete listing of the examples in [15]. We keep the same order as in [14] when it is possible.

- We do not allow the deletion of redundant elements of the basis to happen during the computation.

- When several members of the basis can be used to reduce a polynomial, we select the one which has been generated first in the basis.

- Critical pairs $\{P, Q\}$ with $T(P, Q)$ of smallest degree are reduced first. Ties are broken in favor of the one with smallest $T(P, Q)$ w.r.t. the admissible order.

- When a new polynomial P enters the basis, the other elements of the basis are not immediately reduced w.r.t. P.

For each computation, we give in Figure 4 the number "#P" of polynomials that enter the basis (including the initial ones), the number "#R" of pairs that are reduced and the time of the computation in seconds. We do not include the time of the final interreduction of the basis. In general, this time is about ten time smaller.

When several processors are used, there is no guarantee that two computations with the same input will give the same statistics, although the resulting reduced bases are identical. This depends on the way the different processors interleave. Results are usually stable, although there are exceptions. We give here the best results.

The speed-ups are encouraging, especially for a small number of processors. When the number of processors becomes larger, there is usually too few pairs to reduce to make all processors busy. The view of gain from parallelization of Buchberger's algorithm is more optimistic than this of Ponder [11]. There are two reasons for this. First, we limited as much as possible the time dependency between the different processes, whereas, in Ponder's algorithms, there is always a serial step where all the processes have to wait for each other. The second reason is that we keep all the refinements of the sequential algorithm, in particular the criteria to filter the useless critical pairs.

7 Conclusion and directions for future research

The essential contribution of this work is the design and the implementation of a parallel version of Buchberger's algorithm on a shared memory multiprocessor. Our tests indicate that the parallelization is efficient when a small number of processors is used. We would like to see if similar results could be obtained on a network architecture. However, the good behaviour of our algorithm is due, on one hand, to the time independence between the processors and, on the other hand, to the filtering of the set of pairs, two techniques that can be difficult to implement on a network.

Acknowledgement
This work was sponsored by the Computer Science Department of Carnegie Mellon University. The author would like to thank Dana Scott for introducing him to the subject and Edmund Clarke for his help and encouragments. My best thanks to Bruno Buchberger who invited me on August 1987 at RISC-Linz and even gave me the listing of an implementation of the sequential algorithm [7]. It is also a pleasure to acknowledge the help I received from Pierre Lescanne who hosted me in Nancy when I wrote the final version of this article.

Name	Order	1 proc		2 proc		5 proc		12 proc	
		#P	#R	#P	#R	#P	#R	#P	#R
Arnborg4	L	12	14	12	14	12	14	12	14
Arnborg5	TL	59	147	59	148	64	159	61	158
Arnborg5	TR	47	106	47	106	50	112	58	129
Butcher	TR	66	159	70	171	74	180	79	199
Katsura4	TL	21	38	22	39	24	41	29	53
Katsura5	TR	26	68	26	68	28	70	29	71
Lazard	TR	35	54	33	54	30	48	31	58
Morgenstern	TR	29	94	29	94	29	94	29	94
Pavelle4	TR	16	32	16	32	16	32	16	35
Robbiano	L	30	91	42	97	36	86	42	107
Rose	TR	22	39	23	40	25	49	26	54
Trinks1	TL	18	27	19	29	19	28	19	30
Trinks2	L	22	28	23	31	22	29	22	29
Valla	TR	80	524	80	524	80	524	90	535

Name	Order	Time (in seconds)			
		1 proc	2 proc	5 proc	12 proc
Arnborg4	L	0.3	0.2	0.2	0.3
Arnborg5	TL	67	33	13	10
Arnborg5	TR	41	21	9	8
Butcher	TR	368	209	77	72
Katsura4	TL	17	10	4	4
Katsura5	TR	1103	551	146	79
Lazard	TR	56	22	2.4	2.1
Morgenstern	TR	45	19	8	8
Pavelle4	TR	4	2.3	1.2	1.1
Robbiano	L	11	7	3.5	3.1
Rose	TR	40	16.7	5	2.7
Trinks1	TL	10	5	1.7	1.9
Trinks2	L	4	2	1	1
Valla	TR	932	482	216	129

Figure 4: Experimental results.

References

[1] M. Accetta, R. Baron, D. Golub, R. Rashid, A. Tevanian, and M. Young. Mach : A New Kernel Foundation For UNIX Development. In *Proceedings Summer 1986 USENIX Technical Conference and Exhibition*, pages 93-112, June 1986.

[2] W. Boege, R. Gebauer, and H. Kredel. Some Examples for Solving Systems of Algebraic Equations by Calculating Gröbner Bases. *Journal of Symbolic Computation*, 1:83-98, 1986.

[3] P. Brinch Hansen. *Operating System Principles*. Prentice-Hall, 1973.

[4] B. Buchberger. *An Algorithm for Finding a Basis for the Residue Class Ring of a Zero-Dimensional Polynomial Ideal.* PhD thesis, Univ. of Innsbruck, 1965.

[5] B. Buchberger. Gröbner Bases : An Algorithmic Method In Polynomial Ideal Theory. In N.K. Bose, editor, *Recent Trends In Multidimensional Systems Theory*, pages 184-232, D.Reidel Publishing Company, 1985.

[6] B. Buchberger. The Parallelization of Critical-Pair/Completion Procedures on the L-Machine. In *Proceedings of the Japanese Symposium on Functional Programming*, pages 54-61, February 1987.

[7] B. Buchberger. *User's Manual for GRÖBNER, a Gröbner Bases Package in muMATH.* Technical Report RISC-Linz 87-38, University of Linz (Austria), 1987.

[8] E.C. Cooper and R.P. Draves. *C Threads.* Technical Report CMU-CS-88-154, Computer Science Department, Carnegie Mellon University, June 1988

[9] R. Gebauer and M. Möller. On an installation of Buchberger's algorithm. *Journal of Symbolic Computation*, 6(2 & 3):275-286, 1988

[10] S. Owicki. *Axiomatic Proof Techniques for Parallel Programs.* PhD thesis, Cornell University, 1975.

[11] C.G. Ponder. *Evaluation of "Performance Enhancements" in Algebraic Manipulation Systems.* Technical report UCB/CSD/ 88/438, Computer Science Division, University of California, Berkeley, August 1988.

[12] L. Robbiano. Gröbner Bases : a foundation for Commutative Algebra. In *Computers and Mathematics*, 1989.

[13] P. Senechaud. Implementation of a parallel algorithm to compute a Gröbner basis on Boolean polynomials. In *Computer Algebra and Parallelism*, pages 159-166, Academic Press, 1989.

[14] C. Traverso and L. Donati. Experimenting the Gröbner basis algorithm with the AIPI system. In *Proceedings ISSAC 1989*, 1989.

[15] J.P. Vidal. *The computation of Gröbner bases on a shared memory multiprocessor.* Technical Report, School of Computer Science, Carnegie Mellon University, to appear.

[16] S. Watt. *Bounded Parallelism in Computer Algebra.* PhD thesis, University of Waterloo Ontario, 1985.

A theory for program and data type specification

Carolyn Talcott
Stanford University
Stanford, CA 94305, USA

1. Introduction

This paper represents the initial stage of a project to develop a wide spectrum formalism which will support not only reasoning about program equivalence, but also specification of programs and data types, and reasoning about properties of computations, operations on programs, and operations on program specifications. In this initial stage a two layered theory of progam equivalence and class membership has been developed. The lower layer is a theory of program equivalence and definedness. Program primitives that can be treated within this theory include functional application and abstraction, conditional, numbers, pairing, and continuation capture and resumption. The upper layer is a theory of class membership with a general comprehension principle for defining classes. Many standard class constructions and data-types can be represented naturally including algebraic abstract data types, list-, record-, and function- type constructions. In addition classes can be constructed satifsying systems of equations such as $[S = A \times G; \quad G = B \to S]$ which are useful in treating programming concepts such as streams and object behaviors. Coroutines can also be classified within this theory.

The general idea of a two-sorted theory of operations and classes is based on the framework developed in [Feferman 75,79,85,87]. The theory presented here, IOCC (Impredicative theory of Operations, Control abstractions, and Classes) is most closely relation to Feferman's IOC_λ (without the ontology axiom). It differs mainly in the choice of primitive constants and axioms for equivalence. The theory of equivalence is based on [Talcott 89] and is essentially the lambda-c theory of [Moggi 89] extended by axioms for primitive data and operations. Models of the full theory can be uniformly constructed from models of the theory of program equivalence using methods of Feferman. Methods have been developed for constructing models of the theory of program equivalence from models of partial algebraic theories called computation theories. This work will be presented in a companion paper. [Talcott 89] contains a fuller development (with proofs) of the equational theory and substantial examples of programming and proving. The papers [Feferman 75,79,82,85,87] also provide many examples developed within a similar framework including peano arithmetic, constructive mathematics, metamathematics,

The remainder of the paper is organized as follows. Section 2 presents the language and basic logic. Section 3 presents the equational theory and develops the theory of control abstractions. Section 4 presents the theory of classes, gives a variety of class definitions and constructions, and illustrates the use of these constructions to specify and prove properties of streams and coroutines. Section 5 concludes with some discussion of related work.

2. The language and logic of IOCC

The language for defining operations (describing computations) is an enrichment of the lambda calculus by constants for primitive data and operations. A class structure is built over the universe of individuals by providing a comprehension mechanism for class formation. For concreteness a specific choice of primitive constants is given. It is easy to abstract from this and give rules for constructing a theory over any given specification of an abstract data type and suitably presented non-algebraic primitive operations.

Standard notation from logic and lambda calculus is used with the following (meta) conventions. Lower case identifiers refer to individuals and identifiers beginning with upper case letters refer to classes. $a, b, c, \ldots x, y, z$ denote individual variables, $e, e_0, \ldots$ are reserved as meta-variables ranging over individual terms, and individual constants are lower case identifiers in this font (for example mt). $A, B, C, \ldots X, Y, Z$ denote class variables, $Cl, Cl_0, \ldots$ are reserved as meta-variables ranging over class terms, and class constants are identifiers beginning with an upper case letter in This font (for example Val). Finally, $\varphi, \varphi_0, \ldots$ denote formulae.

Definition (Terms and formulas): Individual terms are expressions in the underlying programming language. Class terms are built from class variables and constants by comprehension. Atomic formulae express program equivalence, definedness, and class membership. Formulae are built from atomic formulae in the usual way. Individual terms, class terms and formulae are defined inductively as follows.

- Individual terms are those of one of the following forms:

$$\text{individual variable,} \quad \text{individual constant,} \quad e_0(e_1), \quad \lambda x.e.$$

- Class terms are those of one of the following forms:

$$\text{class variable,} \quad \text{class constant ,} \quad \{x \mid \varphi\}.$$

- Formulae are those of one of the following forms:

$$e_0 \cong e_1, \quad e{\downarrow}, \quad e \,\tilde{\in}\, Cl \qquad \neg(\varphi), \quad \varphi_0 \wedge \varphi_1, \quad \forall x.\varphi, \quad \forall X.\varphi.$$

Bound and free variables are determined as usual with λ, $\{\ \mid\ \}$, and $\forall$ being the binding operations. $\lambda x, y.e$ abbreviates $\lambda x.\lambda y.e$ and $f(x, y)$ abbreviates $f(x)(y)$. let is treated as an abbreviation for lambda-application and $f \circ g$ is infix notation for the composition combinator $\lambda f, g.\lambda x.f(g(x))$. The logical connectives ($\vee$, $\Rightarrow$, $\Leftrightarrow$, $\exists$) are treated as syntactic abbreviations in the usual manner. For example, $\varphi_0 \vee \varphi_1 :=: \neg(\neg\varphi_0 \wedge \neg\varphi_1)$.

The logic is essentially a classical logic of partial terms. This means that eliminating (instantiating) universal quantifiers must be restricted to terms that are defined.

Quantifier laws:

(forall.elim) $(\forall x)\varphi \wedge e{\downarrow} \Rightarrow \varphi\{x := e\}$

(forall.intro) $\varphi \Rightarrow (\forall x)\varphi$ % if x does not occur free in any assumptions

3. The equational theory

The lambda axioms are the kernel of the equational theory. They include the usual axioms of equivalence, congruence, and beta-value conversion. The axioms for definedness say that variables and abstractions denote values and that $\cong$ corresponds to strong equality between partial terms. In addition there are the axioms (app), (cmp), and (id) which characterize the basic rearrangements of the structure of an expression that preserve the order of computation and hence give rise to indistinguishable expressions. (A theorem expressing a general class of such rearrangements is given at the end of this section.) The lambda axioms were derived by considering the laws of operational equivalence and extracting key laws adequate for representing computation and rearrangements. They are equivalent to the untyped lambda-c theory of [Moggi 89] if let is treated as an abbreviation. The lambda-c theory was arrived at by considering a class of computational models based on category theoretic concepts.

Lambda axioms:

(equiv) $\cong$ is an equivalence relation.

congruence $\cong$ is a congruence with respect to term formation.

definedness $x{\downarrow}$, $\lambda x.e{\downarrow}m$, and $e_0 \cong e_1 \wedge e_0{\downarrow} \Rightarrow e_1{\downarrow}$

(betav) $(\lambda x.e)(x) \cong e$

(app) $e_0(e_1) \cong \mathtt{let}\{f := e_0\}f(e_1)$

(cmps) $f(g(e)) \cong (f \circ g)(e)$

(id) $(\lambda x.x)(e) \cong e$

3.1. Algebraic primitive constants

The algebraic primitive constants of IOCC are mt, zero, and primitive operations br, iszero, isnat, succ, pred, ispr, pr, fst, and snd. Axioms are given in the full paper. Here only a brief informal interpretation is given.

mt is a distinguished individual that can be recognize among all indiviuals. br is an operation that takes two arguments and produces an operation which when applied to mt returns its second argument and when applied to anything else returns its first argument. if(e_0, e_1, e_2) abbreviates br$(\lambda_-.e_1, \lambda_-.e_2)(e_0)(\mathtt{mt})$ where $_-$ denotes some variable not free in e_1 or e_2. and the usual laws for conditional expressions can be verified.

The primitives $\{\mathtt{zero}, \mathtt{iszero}, \mathtt{succ}, \mathtt{pred}\}$ correspond to the signature of a natural number algebra. isnat is a recognizer for natural numbers. The primitive constants $\{\mathtt{pr}, \mathtt{fst}, \mathtt{snd}\}$ make the value domain a pairing structure and ispr is the recognizer for pairs.

3.2. Control primitives

Control primitives provide mechanisms for altering the flow of control in a computation. Examples include non-local goto, return/escape, exceptions/abort, coroutines, Algol-like labels (cf. [Landin 1965]), Lisp-like catch/throw (cf. [Steele 1984]), and Scheme-like call-with-current-continuation (cf. [Steele and Sussman 75], [Rees, et.al. 1986]). Operational and denotational semantics of control primitives are given in terms of computation states that have a continuation component as well as environment and possibly other components (cf. [Scott and Strachey 1971], [Reynolds 1972]). In [Felleisen 87], [Felleisen, et. al. 87], and [Felleisen and Hieb 89] methods are given for extending lambda-calculus style reduction systems to treat control primitives. [Talcott 89] shows that operational equivalence of programs that include control primitives can be given a first-order semantics. The treatment here is based on that semantics.

The primitive control operation ncc (for "note current continuation") expects a function as an argument and applies that function to a functional abstraction of the current continuation, carrying out this application in a state with empty continuation. In a denotational semantics the denotation of ncc might be written $\lambda f.\lambda k.f(J(k))*$ where $*$ denotes the empty continuation and $J(k) = \lambda v.\lambda k'.k(v)$ is the functional abstraction of the continuation k.

In order to simplify the control axioms the operation top, corresponding to the empty (top-level) contintuation is defined. Continuations are then represented as top composed with an ordinary operations. The control axioms express intrinsic properties of ncc that can be expected to hold in all models: (op) ncc is an operation; (arg) ncc removes its computation context and applies its argument to that context; (id) capturing a context and returning a value to that context is equivalent to simply returning that value; and (cnt) the argument of ncc will be applied to a continuation.

Control axioms:

(top.def) $top \cong \lambda x.ncc(\lambda c.x)$

(op) $ncc \cong \lambda f.ncc(f)$

(arg) $f(ncc(e)) \cong ncc(\lambda c.e(c \circ f))$ % $c \notin Frees(e)$

(id) $ncc(\lambda c.c(x)) \cong x$

(cnt) $ncc(e) \cong ncc(\lambda c.e(top \circ c))$ % $c \notin Frees(e)$

The following lemma gives a sample of consequences of the control axioms.

Lemma (ncc):

(eta) $ncc(e) \cong ncc(\lambda c.e(c))$ % $c \notin Frees(e)$

(esc) $f \circ top \cong top$

(topx) $top(e) \cong ncc(\lambda c.e)$ % $c \notin Frees(e)$

(nc) $ncc(e) \cong ncc(\lambda c.top(e(c)))$

Using ncc many other control primitives can be defined. Examples are given in the full paper. An imporant control abstraction is coroutining. The basic coroutine primitive is resumption. One coroutine resumes another passing zero or more arguments. In addition the control point where the resumer suspended computation is remembered (passed as an additional argument) in order that the resumer may later be resumed. (In the presence of memory the control point can be retained in local memory rather than passed as a parameter to each call.)

Definition (res):   The resumption primitive res is defined by

$$\mathbf{res} \cong \lambda c.\lambda z.\mathrm{ncc}(\lambda k.c(\mathrm{pr}(k,z)))$$

If a coroutine (i.e. one of its resumption points) k is equivalent to an operation that resumes its resumer at a control point represented by $p[x]$ passing $v[x]$, then the resumption of k with x is equivalent to $\mathrm{pr}(\mathrm{top} \circ p[x], v[x])$. This is formalized by the theorem (**res.res**). The proof is given as an illustration of reasoning about control abstractions.

Theorem (res.res):

$$\mathbf{res}(\lambda\mathrm{pr}(c,x).p(\mathbf{res}_1(c,v))) \cong \mathrm{pr}(\mathrm{top} \circ p, v)$$

where c does not occur free in p, v but x may, and $\lambda\mathrm{pr}(c,x).e$ abbreviates $\lambda x.\mathrm{let}\{c := \mathrm{fst}(x)\}\mathrm{let}\{x := \mathrm{snd}(x)\}e$.

Proof (res.res):

$\mathbf{res}(\lambda\mathrm{pr}(c,x).p(\mathbf{res}(c,v)))$

$\cong \mathrm{ncc}(\lambda\mathrm{pr}(c,x).(\mathrm{top} \circ p)(\mathrm{ncc}(\lambda k.c(\mathrm{pr}(k,v)))))$ % defn **res**, (ncc.nc)

$\cong \mathrm{ncc}(\lambda\mathrm{pr}(c,x).\mathrm{ncc}(\lambda k.c(\mathrm{pr}(\mathrm{top} \circ p, v))))$ % (ncc.arg),(ncc.esc)

$\cong \mathrm{ncc}(\lambda\mathrm{pr}(c,x).\mathrm{top}(c(\mathrm{pr}(\mathrm{top} \circ p, v))))$ % (ncc.top)

$\cong \mathrm{pr}(\mathrm{top} \circ p, v)$ % (ncc.id)

□**res.res**

3.3.   Evaluated position contexts

An evaluated position context is an expression with a unique hole in a position that will be evaluated before any other "serious" computation takes place. Thus the result of placing an arbitrary expression (satisfying suitable hygiene conditions) in the hole is equivalent to applying the operation naturally corresponding to the context to that expression. The notion of evaluated position context generalizes the notion of evaluation context (cf. [Felleisen 87]) by looking inside lets, ifs, and ncc applications.

Definition (epcx):   The set of evaluated position contexts and the variables trapped by an evaluated position context are defined as follows. Evaluated position context is the least set closed under the constructions in the first column and $Trap(C)$, the variables trapped by the context C is defined in the second column by induction on context construction.

	C	$Trap(C)$
(mt)	$[\,]$	$\{\}$
(fun)	$C_0(e_1)$	$Trap(C_0)$
(arg)	$x(C_1)$	$Trap(C_1)$
(let)	$\mathrm{let}\{z := x\}C_0$	$\{z\} \cup Trap(C_0)$
(if)	$\mathrm{if}(z, C_1, C_2)$	$Trap(C_1) \cup Trap(C_2)$
(ncc)	$\mathrm{ncc}(\lambda c.C_0)$	$\{c\} \cup Trap(C_0$

$C[\![e]\!]$ is the result of replacing $[\![\ ]\!]$ by e in the first step of the construction of C. Context equality is modulo alpha-conversion as usual with the restriction that a bound variable with a hole in its scope cannot be renamed.

Theorem (epcx):   Let C be an evaluated position context and assume $Frees(e, x, c) \cap Trap(C) = \emptyset$ and $x, c \notin Frees(C)$. Then

(letx) $\qquad \mathtt{let}\{x := e\} C[\![x]\!] \cong C[\![e]\!]$

(let.dist) $\quad C[\![\mathtt{let}\{x := e\} e_0]\!] \cong \mathtt{let}\{x := e\} C[\![e_0]\!]$

(if.dist) $\qquad C[\![\mathtt{if}(e, e_1, e_2)]\!] \cong \mathtt{if}(e, C[\![e_1]\!], C[\![e_2]\!])$

(ncc.dist) $\quad C[\![\mathtt{ncc}(\lambda c.c(e_0))]\!] \cong \mathtt{ncc}(\lambda c.\mathtt{let}\{c := c \circ \lambda x.C[\![x]\!]\} c(e_0))$

4.   The theory of classes and membership

The class axioms express: (eq) that $\cong$ preserves membership; (def) that membership in a class implies definedness; and (ca) that for any formula, the class of elements satisfying that formula can be formed.

Class axioms:

(eq) $\qquad e_0 \cong e_1 \land e_0 \,\tilde{\in}\, Cl \Rightarrow e_1 \,\tilde{\in}\, Cl$

(def) $\qquad e \,\tilde{\in}\, Cl \Rightarrow e\!\downarrow$

(ca) $\qquad x \,\tilde{\in}\, \{x \mid \varphi\} \Leftrightarrow \varphi$

Extensional equality and subset relations on classes are defined in the usual manner.

$$Cl_0 \subseteq Cl_1 \Leftrightarrow (\forall x)(x \,\tilde{\in}\, Cl_0 \Rightarrow x \,\tilde{\in}\, Cl_1)$$

$$Cl_0 \equiv Cl_1 \Leftrightarrow Cl_0 \subseteq Cl_1 \land Cl_1 \subseteq Cl_0$$

4.1.   Basic class operations

We begin by defining several specific classes. $\emptyset$ is the empty class. **Val** is the class of all values. **Mt** is the class containing the single element mt. **Op** is the class of operations—values which satisfy eta conversion. **Cnt** is the class of continuations—operations that escape.

$$\emptyset = \{x \mid x \not\cong x\}; \qquad \mathbf{Val} = \{x \mid x \cong x\}; \qquad \mathbf{Mt} = \{x \mid x \cong \mathtt{mt}\}$$

$$\mathbf{Op} = \{f \mid f \cong \lambda x.f(x)\}; \qquad \mathbf{Cnt} = \{c \mid c \cong \mathtt{top} \circ c\}$$

Class forming operations such as finite set formation ($\{v_1, \ldots, v_n\}$); union ($\cup$); intersection ($\cap$); cartesian product ($\times$); partial and total function space formation ($[\ \overset{p}{\to}\ ]$, $[\ \to\ ]$); and lifting of function application to a class ($f[X]$) are be defined in the usual way. For example

$$Cl_0 \times Cl_1 = \{z \mid (\exists x \,\tilde{\in}\, Cl_0)(\exists y \,\tilde{\in}\, Cl_1)(z \cong \mathtt{pr}(x, y))\}$$

$$Cl_0 \to Cl_1 = \{o \,\tilde{\in}\, \mathbf{Op} \mid (\forall x \,\tilde{\in}\, Cl_0)(o(x) \,\tilde{\in}\, Cl_1)\}$$

$$f[Cl] = \{z \mid (\exists x \,\tilde{\in}\, Cl)f(x) \cong z\}$$

4.2. Fixed points

For any formula $\varphi[X]$, the intersection and union of all classes X satisfying $\varphi[X]$ can be formed.

$$\bigcap_X \varphi[X] = \{x \mid (\forall X)(\varphi[X] \Rightarrow x \,\tilde{\in}\, X)\}; \qquad \bigcup_X \varphi[X] = \{x \mid (\exists X)(\varphi[X] \wedge x \,\tilde{\in}\, X)\}$$

If $\varphi[X]$ is preserved by intersection over non-empty sets of classes and is satisfiable then $\bigcap_X \varphi[X]$ is the smallest class satisfying $\varphi[X]$. Similarly if $\varphi[X]$ is preserved by union over non-empty sets of classes and is satisfiable then $\bigcup_X \varphi[X]$ is the largest class satisfying $\varphi[X]$. These notions are not formalizable in our theory in full generality. However there is an important special case which can be formalized. Namely, formulas representing closure conditions.

A class operator is a class term with a distinguished class variable. We write $T[X]$ making the variable explicit and $T[Cl]$ for the result of replacing the distinguished variable X by Cl (with suitable renaming of bound variables to avoid capture). T is *monotone* if $X \subseteq Y$ implies $T[X] \subseteq T[Y]$. Let $T[X]$ be a monotone operator on classes. The formula $T[X] \subseteq X$ is preserved by intersection over non-empty sets of classes and is satified by **Val**. Hence $\bigcap_X(T[X] \subseteq X)$ is the smallest class X satisfying $T[X] \subseteq X$ and, by monotonicity, it is the minimum fixed point of $T[X]$. Dually, $X \subseteq T[X]$ is preserved by union over non-empty sets of classes and is satisfied by $\emptyset$. Hence $\bigcup_X(X \subseteq T[X])$ is the maximum fixed point of $T[X]$.

Using the minimum fixedpoint construction various forms of inductive generation can be defined and used to define classes such as **Nat**, the class of natural numbers, A^*, the class of sequences from A, and the class of S-expressions. Details are given in the full paper.

4.3. Streams and coroutines

Streams (cf. [Landin 65], [Burge 75], [Abelson and Sussman 85]), and coroutines (cf. [Conway 63]) are generators of potentially infinite lists. They may be empty. A non-empty generator can be accessed to obtain the next element or a generator of the remainder of the list. In the stream case access is by query and in the coroutine case access is by resumption. For many purposes one can identify streams and coroutines of A's with functions from **Nat** to A. In fact such functions are useful for specifying the abstract behavior of a stream or coroutine. Computationally it is important to have a generator representation. One example is pattern matching where you want to generate the matches between a pattern and some object and process them one at a time, quitting when some criteria is met. The possible matches may be finite or infinite. Thus you want them computed 'by need' and streams and coroutines are a natural way of doing this.

For simplicity we focus on infinite streams and coroutines. The class, **Sgen**[A], of streams generating sequences of As consists of operations which, when queried (applied to mt), return a pair consisting of a generator of the remainder of the sequence and the next element of the sequence. Thus **Sgen**[A] is the largest class of operations such that **Sgen**[A] $\equiv$ **Mt** $\to$ [**Sgen**[A] $\times$ A]. This definition reflects the generator view of streams ala Landin and Burge. The Scheme view of streams [Abelson and Sussman 85] as pairs consisting of the first element and a generator of the remainder (of the generated sequence) can be expressed by defining $\mathbf{Str}[A]$ to be the largest class such that $\mathbf{Str}[A] \equiv A \times [\mathbf{Mt} \to \mathbf{Str}[A]]$. The two classes are isomorphic. In the call-by-value world the class defined by $\mathbf{Str}[A] \equiv A \times \mathbf{Str}[A]$ does not contain definable elements. Instead one must have a "lazy" product and interpret the equation as syntactic sugar.

The class $\mathbf{Cgen}[A]$, of coroutines generating sequences of As, consists of operations representing control points which, when resumed, return a pair consisting of the control point generating the remainder of the sequence and the next element of the sequence. Thus $\mathbf{Cgen}[A]$ is the largest class of operations such that (recall $\mathbf{res}(c, z) \cong \mathbf{ncc}(\lambda k.c(\mathbf{pr}(k, z)))$)

$$\mathbf{Cgen}[A] \equiv \{c \,\tilde\in\, \mathbf{Op} \mid \mathbf{res}(c, \emptyset) \,\tilde\in\, \mathbf{top} \circ \mathbf{Cgen}[A] \times A\}.$$

The relation between streams, coroutines, and (infinite) sequences is made explicity by defining operations that map between these classes. $\mathbf{sg2s}$ (for sgen-to-sequence) maps an element s in $\mathbf{Sgen}[A]$ to the A-sequence (element of $\mathbf{Nat} \to A$) generated by s, $\mathbf{cg2s}$ maps an element c in $\mathbf{Cgen}[A]$ to the A-sequence generated by c, $\mathbf{s2sg}$ maps an A-sequence f to a stream generating f, and $\mathbf{s2cg}$ maps an A-sequence f to a coroutine generating f.

Lemma (seq.str.co.iso):

$$f \,\tilde\in\, \mathbf{Nat} \to Z \Rightarrow \mathbf{sg2s}(\mathbf{s2sg}(f)) \cong_{\mathbf{Nat}} \mathbf{cg2s}(\mathbf{s2cg}(f)) \cong_{\mathbf{Nat}} f$$

where the $f \cong_{\mathbf{Nat}} g$ abbreviates $(\forall n \,\tilde\in\, \mathbf{Nat})(f(n) \cong g(n))$.

Thus streams and coroutines can be specified by the sequences they generate. As an example consider the problem of transforming sequences of pairs (of elements from some class) to sequences of elements. (This is an abstraction of an actual piece of network code that uses coroutines. The case of triples to pairs is worked out in detail in [Talcott 85, 89].) The function $\mathbf{f21}$ that carries out the transformation is defined as follows.

$$\mathbf{f21}(in)(2n) = \mathbf{fst}(in(n))$$

$$\mathbf{f21}(in)(2n + 1) = \mathbf{snd}(in(n))$$

For the case when the input and output sequences are generated by streams (coroutines) we specify corresponding transformations $\mathbf{s21}$ ($\mathbf{c21}$) as follows.

$$in \,\tilde\in\, \mathbf{Sgen}[Z \times Z] \Rightarrow \mathbf{sg2s}(\mathbf{s21}(in)) \cong_{\mathbf{Nat}} \mathbf{f21}(\mathbf{sg2s}(in))$$

$$in \,\tilde\in\, \mathbf{Cgen}[Z \times Z] \Rightarrow \mathbf{cg2s}(\mathbf{c21}(in)) \cong_{\mathbf{Nat}} \mathbf{f21}(\mathbf{cg2s}(in))$$

By the theorem (**res.res**), the following definitions meet these specifications.

Definition (s21,c21):

$$\mathbf{s21}(in)(\_) \cong \mathtt{let}\{\mathbf{pr}(in, \mathbf{pr}(x, y)) := in(\mathtt{mt})\}\mathbf{pr}(\lambda\_.\mathbf{pr}(\mathbf{s21}(in), y), x)$$

$$\mathbf{c21}(in)\mathbf{pr}(out, \_) \cong \mathtt{let}\{\mathbf{pr}(in, \mathbf{pr}(x, y)) := \mathbf{res}(in, \mathtt{mt})\}$$
$$\mathtt{let}\{\mathbf{pr}(out, \_) := \mathbf{res}(out, x)\}$$
$$\mathtt{let}\{\mathbf{pr}(out, \_) := \mathbf{res}(out, y)\}$$
$$\mathbf{c21}(in)\mathbf{pr}(out, \_)$$

Abelson, H. and G. J. Sussman [1985] *Structure and interpretation of computer programs*, (The MIT Press, McGraw-Hill Book Company).

Broy, M. and Wirsing, M. [1982] Partial abstract types, *Act Informatica*, **18**, pp. 47–64.

Broy, M., Wirsing, M., and Pepper, P. [1987] On the algebraic definition of programming languages, *ACM TOPLAS*, **9(1)**, pp. 54–99.

Burge, W. H. [1975] Stream processing functions, *IBM journal of research and development*, **19**, pp. 12–25.

Conway, M. [1963] Design of a separable transition-diagram compiler, *Comm. ACM*, **6**, pp. 396–408.

Coppo, M. [1985] A completeness theorem for recursively defined types in: *Automata, languages, and programming, 12th Colloquium*, Brauer, W. (ed.), Lecture Notes in Computer Science Vol. 194, pp.120–129.

Feferman, S. [1975] A language and axioms for explicit mathematics, in: *Algebra and Logic*, Springer Lecture Notes in Mathematics, **450**, pp.87-139.

Feferman, S. [1979] Constructive theories of functions and classes, in *Logic Colloquium '78*, (North-Holland) pp. 159-224.

Feferman, S. [1982] Inductively presented systems and the formalization of meta-mathematics, in: *Logic colloquium 80*, edited by D. van Dalen, D. Lascar, and J. Smiley (North-Holland, Amsterdam) pp. 95–128.

Feferman, S. [1985] A Theory of Variable Types, *Revista Colombiana de Matématicas*, **19** pp. 95–105.

Feferman, S. [1987] Polymorphic typed lambda-calculi in a type-free axiomatic framework, *Proceedings of conference on logic and computation, Carnegie Mellon University*, to appear.

Felleisen, M. [1987] *The calcului of lambda-v-cs conversion: A syntactic theory of control and state in imperative higher-order programming languages*, Ph.D. thesis, Indiana University.

Felleisen,M. Friedman, D. P., Kohlbecker E., and Duba B. [1987] A syntactic theory of sequential control, *Theoretical Computer Science* **52**, pp. 205–237.

Felleisen, M., Hieb, R., [1989] The revised report on the syntactic theories of sequential control and state, Rice COMP TR89-100, Rice University.

Griffin, T. G. [1990] A formulae as types notion of control, *Seventeenth Annual ACM Symposium on Principles of Programmings Languages* pp. 47–58.

Landin, P. J. [1965] A correspondence between Algol 60 and Church's lambda notation, *Comm. ACM*, **8**, pp. 89-101, 158-165.

Moggi, E. [1989] Computational lambda-calculus and monads, *Fourth annual symposium on logic in computer science*, (IEEE).

Plotkin, G. [1975] Call-by-name, call-by-value and the lambda-v-calculus, *Theoretical Computer Science*, **1**, pp. 125–159.

Rees, J., Clinger, W. (eds) [1986] The revised[3] report on the algorithmic language Scheme, *Sigplan Notices*, **21**(12), pp. 37–79.

Reynolds, J. C. [1972] Definitional interpreters for higher-order programming languages, in: *Proceedings, ACM national convention*, pp. 717–740.

Scott, D. and C. Strachey [1971] Towards a mathematical semantics for computer languages, Oxford University Computing Laboratory, Technical Monograph PRG-6.

Steele, G. L. [1984] *Common Lisp: the language* (Digital Press).

Steele, G. L., and G. J. Sussman, [1975] Scheme, an interpreter for extended lambda calculus, Artificial Intelligence Laboratory, Massachusetts Institute of Technology, Technical Report 349.

Talcott, C. L. [1985] The essence of *Rum*: A theory of the intensional and extensional aspects of Lisp-type computation, Ph. D. Thesis, Stanford University.

Talcott, C. L. [1989] *Programming and proving function and control abstractions* Stanford University Computer Science Department Report No. STAN-CS-89-1288.

Talcott, C. L. [1990] *Computational models for theoryis of function and control abstractions* (in preparation)

Talcott, C. L. and Weyhrauch, R. W. [1987] Partial evaluation, higher-order abstractions, and reflection principles as system building tools, in: *IFIP TC2 Working Conference on Partial and Mixed Computation, Ebberup, Denmark, 18-24 October 1987*, Bjorner, D. and Erschov, A. P. (eds.), (North–Holland).

Context Induction: a Proof Principle for Behavioural Abstractions

Rolf Hennicker

Fakultät für Mathematik und Informatik, Universität Passau

Postfach 2540, D-8390 Passau

Abstract

An induction principle, called context induction, is presented which is appropriate for the verification of behavioural properties of abstract data types. The usefulness of the proof principle is documented by several applications: the verification of behavioural theorems over a behavioural specification, the verification of behavioural implementations and the verification of "forget-restrict-identify" implementations.

In particular it is shown that behavioural implementations and "forget-restrict-identify" implementations (under certain assumptions) can be characterized by the same context condition, i.e. (under the given assumptions) both concepts are equivalent. This leads to the suggestion to use context induction as a uniform proof method for correctness proofs of formal implementations.

1 Introduction

Induction proofs play an important role in the verification of properties of programs and data types. Historically, one can distinguish computational and structural induction methods which are based on different paradigms: while computational induction works on an inductively defined set of functions (for proving properties of least fixpoints) structural induction was suggested by [Burstall 69] for proving properties of recursive programs by induction over the (structure of the) arguments. More generally, induction proofs are appropriate for the verification of assertions over any well founded domain (i.e. over any set on which a Noetherian ordering is defined). Particularly important domains are the (finitely generated) models of algebraic specifications where all objects can be denoted by a ground term and hence properties of an abstract data type can be proved by induction on the structure of ground terms (called "term induction", cf. [Pepper et al. 82]) or, more generally, by induction with respect to an arbitrary Noetherian relation on ground terms. Algorithms for proving inductive theorems over data types are implemented, for instance, by Boyer and Moore's theorem prover (cf. [Boyer, Moore 88]) or by the Larch prover (cf. [Garland, Guttag 88]).

This work presents an induction principle, called *context induction*, which is appropriate for proving behavioural properties of data types. In contrast to the classical concepts the principle is not based on the assumption that equations (between terms) denote identities between objects rather interpreting equations as behavioural equivalences of objects as in the behavioural approaches to algebraic specifications proposed by [Reichel 85], [Nivela, Orejas 87] and others. The motivation for this conception is given by the fact that from a software user's point of view internal data representations (of an implementation) are not relevant if they induce the same observable effects, i.e. data objects can be seen equal if they cannot be distinguished by experiments with observable result. In the framework of algebraic specifications such experiments can be formally represented by *contexts* of observable sort over the signature of a specification where a distinguished subset of its sorts is specified as observable. Thus for showing that a certain property is valid for all observable experiments one can formally show this property for all corresponding contexts of observable sort. Since contexts are particular terms (over the signature of the specification) the syntactic subterm ordering defines a Noetherian relation on the set of observable contexts. Hence the proof principle of structural induction induces a proof principle for properties of observable contexts which we call context induction.

After having introduced the principle of context induction (cf. section 3) one main purpose of this paper is to present possible applications for this proof technique. As a first application domain, in section 4 behavioural specifications in the sense of [Reichel 85] and [Nivela, Orejas 87] are considered. In contrast to the classical semantical concepts (initial, terminal, loose semantics) behavioural specifications admit a more abstract view of the semantics of a specification since equations are interpreted as behavioural equivalences. It is shown that for the behavioural analysis of a specification several properties, like membership of an algebra to the behavioural models of a specification or behavioural validity of theorems, can be expressed by corresponding properties on the set of observable contexts such that context induction provides an appropriate verification method. As an example we consider a behavioural specification of a small imperative programming language and prove by context induction a criterion for the behavioural equivalence of programs which can be easily applied for showing particular equivalences.

For the application of formal specifications in the process of program development (e.g. by stepwise refinement) one needs formal implementation notions which describe correct transitions between different abstraction levels. In order to be useful in practice formal implementation concepts should be supplied by proof methods which support the verification of correct program development steps. A major point of this work is adressed to the development of context criteria which allow the verification of implementation relations by context induction:

In section 5, an implementation notion for behavioural specifications is defined which formalizes the intuitive idea that an implementation is correct if it produces correct observable output. Formally, a behavioural specification SP1 is called *behavioural implementation* of SP if all behavioural models of SP1 (after appropriate restriction) are behavioural models of SP as well. It is shown that the behavioural implementation relation can be characterized by a property on the set of observable contexts and hence context induction can be used for the verification of behavioural implementations. As a concrete example an implementation of a specification of states (i.e. environments of a set of identifiers with values in the natural numbers) by a "full-memory" representation of states is proved by context induction.

Section 6 deals with the well-known "forget-restrict-identify" approach to formal implementations (cf. e.g. [Ehrig et al. 82], [Broy et al. 86] and several others). The main step in those concepts is the identification of "concrete" objects which represent the same "abstract" objects e.g. by means of a congruence relation or an abstraction function. Following the approach of [Broy et al. 86] it is shown that also for "forget-restrict-identify" implementations ("FRI-implementations" for short) a context criterion can be formulated and hence context induction provides an appropriate proof method also in this case. (This is not surprising since the identification of concrete representations corresponds to the behavioural equivalence of objects.)

As a consequence of the context criteria we show that under certain conditions FRI-implementations and behavioural implementations are equivalent which leads to the suggestion to use context induction as a uniform proof technique for the verification of implementation relations in the process of formal program development.

2 Basic notions

We assume the reader to be familiar with the basic notions of algebraic specifications (cf. e.g. [Ehrig, Mahr 85]), that are the notions of *signature* $\Sigma = (S, F)$, *total Σ-algebra* $A = ((A_s)_{s \in S}, (f^A)_{f \in F})$, where A_s denote the carrier sets of A and f^A the total operations of A, *Σ-homomorphism* $\phi: A \to B$ between two Σ-algebras A and B, *term algebra* $W_\Sigma(X)$ over an S-sorted family $X = (X_s)_{s \in S}$ of sets of variables, *ground term algebra* W_Σ, *term* $t \in W_\Sigma(X)$, *ground term* $t \in W_\Sigma$, *(ground) substitution* $\sigma: X \to W_\Sigma$, *instantiation* $\sigma(t) = t[\sigma(x_1)/x_1,..., \sigma(x_n)/x_n]$ (i.e. replacement of the variables $x_1,..., x_n \in X$ occurring in t by the terms $\sigma(x_1),..., \sigma(x_n)$), *interpretation* of a term t in a Σ-algebra A with respect to a *valuation* $\alpha: X \to A$ (denoted by t^A if t is ground), *term generated* (or *finitely generated*) Σ-algebra.

Moreover, a total Σ-algebra B is called *Σ-subalgebra* of A if $B_s \subseteq A_s$ for all $s \in S$ and $f^A|_B = f^B$ for all function symbols $f \in F$, where $f^A|_B$ denotes the restriction of f^A to the elements of B. The term generated subalgebra of a Σ-algebra A is denoted by $<A>$.

A signature $\Sigma' = (S', F')$ is called *subsignature* of Σ if $S' \subseteq S$ and $F' \subseteq F$. The *restriction* of a total Σ-algebra A to Σ' is the Σ'-algebra $A|_{\Sigma'} = ((A_s)_{s \in S'}, (f^A)_{f \in F'})$.

3 Context induction

In this section we present the proof principle of *context induction* which has proved to be a powerful tool for the verification of behavioural properties of data structures and their specification. Roughly speaking, behavioural properties are obtained by forgetting unnecessary information of a data type. For example one may derive behavioural identities if one abstracts from particular data representations and identifies all objects which cannot be distinguished by experiments with observable result. In the framework of algebraic specifications such experiments can be formally represented by *contexts* of observable sort over the signature of the specification. Thus for showing that a certain property is valid for all observable experiments one can formally reason about all contexts of observable sort.

3.1 Definition   Let $\Sigma = (S, F)$ be a signature and let $Z = \{z_s \mid s \in S\}$ be an S-sorted set of variables. A term $c \in W_\Sigma(Z)$ is called *context* over Σ (or Σ-context), if c contains exactly one variable $z_s \in Z$. To indicate the variable occurring in c we often write $c[z_s]$ instead of c.
The application of a context $c[z_s]$ to a term $t \in W_\Sigma$ of sort s is defined by the substitution of z_s by t. Instead of $c[t/z_s]$ we also write briefly $c[t]$.   ◊

In the following we consider not all contexts over a given signature but restrict to those contexts which have a result sort belonging to a distinguished subset $S_0 \subseteq S$ of the sorts of the signature. Particularly important examples for the subset S_0 are the set of observable sorts of a behavioural specification or the set of primitive sorts of a hierarchical specification (see next sections). The contexts of observable sort, also called *observable contexts*, represent all possible experiments with observable result.
Formally, let $\Sigma = (S, F)$ be a signature and $S_0 \subseteq S$ be a subset of its sorts. The syntactic subterm ordering defines a Noetherian relation on the set of contexts $c \in W_\Sigma(Z)$ of sort $s \in S_0$. Hence the principle of structural induction (cf. [Burstall 69]) induces a proof principle for properties of contexts of sort $s \in S_0$, called *context induction*.
For showing that a property $P(c)$ is valid for all contexts $c \in W_\Sigma(Z)$ of sort $s \in S_0$ it is sufficient to prove the following conditions:

(0) $P(z_s)$ is valid for all sorts $s \in S_0$.

(1) For all contexts of the form $f(t_1,\ldots, t_{i-1}, c, t_{i+1},\ldots, t_n)$ with
     – a function symbol $f \in F$ with functionality $s_1 x\ldots x s_n \to s$ and result sort $s \in S_0$,
     – terms $t_1,\ldots, t_n \in W_\Sigma$ and
     – a context $c \in W_\Sigma(Z)$ of sort s_i
     holds:
     If $P(c')$ is valid for all subcontexts c' of c with sort $s \in S_0$, then $P(f(t_1,\ldots, t_{i-1}, c, t_{i+1},\ldots, t_n))$ is valid. (In particular, the validity of $P(c)$ can be assumed if the sort s_i of c belongs to S_0.)

3.2 Proposition   *(context induction)*
Let $\Sigma = (S, F)$ be a signature and $S_0 \subseteq S$. A property $P(c)$ is valid for all contexts $c \in W_\Sigma(Z)$ of sort $s \in S_0$ if the conditions (0) and (1) from above are satisfied.

Proof: The proof is a direct consequence of the principle of structural induction. The ordering on the set of contexts is defined by the syntactic subterm ordering.   ◊

4 Behavioural validity

As a first example for an application domain of context induction we consider the theory of behavioural specifications (cf. [Reichel 85] and [Nivela, Orejas 87]). We show that for a given behavioural specification certain properties can be expressed by properties on the set of contexts of observable sort and hence context induction provides an appropriate tool for the behavioural analysis of a specification.
Following the approaches of [Reichel 85] and similarly of [Nivela, Orejas 87] we first briefly summarize the basic notions of behavioural specifications:

A *behavioural specification* $SP = (\Sigma, Obs, E)$ consists of a signature $\Sigma = (S, F)$, a subset $Obs \subseteq S$ of *observable sorts* and a set E of *axioms* (here equations $t = r$ with $t, r \in W_\Sigma(X)$). For example the following behavioural specification STATE describes environments (also called states) of a set of identifiers with values in the natural numbers where the sorts *nat* and *bool* are specified as observable.

spec STATE = enrich BOOL, NAT, ID by
   sorts: state
   obs-sorts: nat, bool
   functs:
      init: $\to$ state
      update: id x nat x state $\to$ state
      lookup: id x state $\to$ nat
      ifstate . then . else . fi: bool x state x state $\to$ state

axioms:
   lookup(x, init) = 0
   lookup(x, update(y, n, s)) =
      ifnat eq-id(x, y) then n else lookup(x, s) fi
   update(x, n, update(y, m, s)) =
      ifstate eq-id(x, y) then update(x, n, s)
      else update(y, m, update(x, n, s)) fi
   ifstate true then s_1 else s_2 fi = s_1
   ifstate false then s_1 else s_2 fi = s_2

(The constant *init* denotes the initial state, the operation *update* assigns a value to an identifier and the operation *lookup* delivers the current value of an identifier. The notation "**enrich...by**" means that STATE is a (syntactic) enrichment of given specifications ID for the identifiers (with equality test *eq-id*), NAT for the natural numbers, and BOOL for the truth values.)

For the definition of the behavioural semantics of a specification [Reichel 85] and [Nivela, Orejas 87] use the notion of *behavioural satisfaction* which is based on the idea that non observable data objects are behaviourally equivalent if they cannot be distinguished by operations with observable result. Formally, given a signature $\Sigma = (S, F)$ and a distinguished subset $Obs \subseteq S$ of observable sorts, a term generated Σ-algebra A *satisfies behaviourally* an equation $t = r$ (written $A \models_{Obs} t = r$) iff for all Σ-contexts $c[z_s]$ (where s is the sort of t) of observable sort, $A \models c[t] = c[r]$ holds w.r.t. the usual satisfaction relation "$\models$". (Here only term generated algebras are considered. Hence the slight difference in the definitions of [Reichel 85] and [Nivela, Orejas 87] is not relevant here.)

The *behaviour class* Beh(SP) of a behavioural specification SP consists of all *behavioural models* of SP, i.e. of all term generated Σ-algebras which behaviourally satisfy all axioms of SP. The *behavioural theory* BTh(SP) of SP consists of all equations $t = r$ which are behaviourally satisfied by all behavioural models of SP. From the definitions follows (see also proposition 2.1.12 in [Nivela, Orejas 87]) that an equation $t = r$ belongs to the behavioural theory BTh(SP) iff for all observable Σ-contexts $c[z_s]$ (where s is the sort of t) and for all ground substitutions $\sigma: X \rightarrow W_\Sigma$, $SP \vdash c[\sigma(t)] = c[\sigma(r)]$ holds (i.e. is deducible from the axioms of SP, cf. [Ehrig, Mahr 85]).

The above discussion shows that in concrete examples the verification of behavioural properties, like behavioural satisfaction, may be a non trivial task since in general one has to reason about infinitely many observable contexts. In particular, we suggest that even the restriction of a behavioural theory to ground equations is (in general) not recursively enumerable. Hence we are interested in proof methods which support the solution e.g. of the following standard problems:

1.) Does a given Σ-algebra A behaviourally satisfy an equation $t = r$?
2.) Is a given Σ-algebra A a behavioural model of a specification ?
3.) Does a given equation $t = r$ belong to the behavioural theory of a specification ?

According to the above definitions and facts each of the three problems can be formally expressed by the validity of a property P(c) for all contexts c of observable sort:

4.1 Definition   Let $SP = (\Sigma, Obs, E)$ be a behavioural specification, let A be a Σ-algebra and let $t, r \in W_\Sigma(X)$ be terms of the same sort. Then for any Σ-context $c[z_s]$ we define:

1.) $P_{A,\ t=r}(c) = true \quad \Leftrightarrow_{def} \quad$ if t is of sort s then $A \models c[t] = c[r]$ holds,
2.) $P_{A,\ SP}(c) = true \quad \Leftrightarrow_{def} \quad$ for all $(t = r) \in E$, if t is of sort s then $A \models c[t] = c[r]$ holds,
3.) $P_{t=r,\ SP}(c) = true \quad \Leftrightarrow_{def} \quad$ if t is of sort s then for all ground substitutions $\sigma: X \rightarrow W_\Sigma$, $SP \vdash c[\sigma(t)] = c[\sigma(r)]$ holds. $\qquad \Diamond$

With this definitions we can formulate the following fact:

4.2 Fact   Let SP, A and t, r be as in definition 4.1.

1.) $A \models_{Obs} t = r$ iff for all Σ-contexts c of observable sort $P_{A,\ t=r}(c)$ is valid.
2.) $A \in Beh(SP)$ iff for all Σ-contexts c of observable sort $P_{A,\ SP}(c)$ is valid.
3.) $(t = r) \in BTh(SP)$ iff for all Σ-contexts c of observable sort $P_{t=r,\ SP}(c)$ is valid. $\qquad \Diamond$

For proving in concrete examples behavioural satisfaction, membership to a behaviour class or membership to a behavioural theory the principle of context induction (cf. proposition 3.2) can be applied.

As an example we consider a behavioural specification PROG of a simple imperative programming language and give a criterion for the behavioural equivalence of programs.

The specification PROG admits usual basic constructs for imperative programs: the empty statement *nop*, the sequential composition ";" of programs, the assignment ": =" of an expression to an identifier, the conditional statement *if . then . else . fi* , and the repetitive statement *for* which repeats a statement n times (for some natural number n). Based on the specification STATE from above the semantics of programs is specified by the state transition function *trans* which determines for a program p and an "old" state s the "new" state after execution of p. The function *value* computes for a given program p and a (result) expression e the evaluation of e under the final state after execution of the program. The results of such evaluations are observable since *nat* is an observable sort (of STATE and hence also of PROG).

```
spec PROG = enrich EXP by                axioms:
   sorts: prog                              trans(nop, s) = s
   functs:                                  trans(p₁; p₂, s) = trans(p₂, trans(p₁, s))
      nop: → prog                           trans(x:= e, s) = update(x, eval(e, s), s)
      . ; .: prog x prog → prog             trans(if e then p₁ else p₂ fi, s) =
      . := .: id x exp → prog                  ifstate (eval(e, s) = 0)
      if . then . else . fi: exp x prog x prog → prog   then trans(p₁, s) else trans(p₂, s) fi
      for: nat x prog → prog                trans(for(n, p), s) =
      trans: prog x state → state              trans(if natexp(n) then nop else p; for(n–1, p) fi, s)
      value: prog x exp → nat            value(p, e) = eval(e, trans(p, init))
where
spec EXP = enrich STATE by
   sorts: exp
   functs:                                axioms:
      natexp: nat → exp                      eval(natexp(n), s) = n
      idexp: id → exp                        eval(idexp(x), s) = lookup(x, s)
      plus: exp x exp → exp                  eval(plus(e₁, e₂), s) = eval(e₁, s) + eval(e₂, s)
      mult: exp x exp → exp                  eval(mult(e₁, e₂), s) = eval(e₁, s) * eval(e₂, s)
      eval : exp x state → nat
```

PROG gives a behavioural specification of our simple imperative programming language where the effects of a program p w.r.t. a (result) expression e can be observed by the evaluation function *value*. Programs p and q have the same behaviour (are behaviourally equivalent) if they induce the same observable effects. Formally this means that the equation p = q belongs to the behavioural theory of PROG. Hence for studying behavioural equivalences of programs we can apply fact 4.2, 3.) which states that two programs p and q are behaviourally equivalent iff the property $P_{p=q,PROG}(c)$ is valid for all contexts over PROG of observable sort *nat* or *bool*. For the verification of $P_{p=q,PROG}(c)$ context induction provides an appropriate proof technique. We will apply this technique for proving a criterion for the behavioural equivalence of programs which can easily be applied for showing particular equivalences.

4.3 Lemma   For all ground terms $p, q \in W_{PROG}$ of sort *prog* holds:
If PROG ⊢ trans(p, st) = trans(q, st) for all ground terms st ∈ W_{PROG} of sort *state*
then $(p = q) \in BTh(PROG)$.
(W_{PROG} denotes the set of ground terms over the signature of PROG.)

Proof by context induction:
Let $p, q \in W_{PROG}$ be arbitrary ground terms of sort *prog* such that PROG ⊢ trans(p, st) = trans(q, st) for all "states" st. By fact 4.2, 3.) we have to show that for all contexts $c[z_s]$ (over the signature of PROG) of observable sort *nat* or *bool* the property $P_{p=q, PROG}$ (c) (for short P(c)) is valid where:

P(c) = true $\Leftrightarrow_{def}$ if s = *prog* then PROG ⊢ c[p] = c[q] holds.

The validity of P(c) is proved by *context induction:*
By proposition 3.2 one has to show that the cases (0) and (1) (of section 3) are satisfied where $S_0 = \{bool, nat\}$.

Case (0):   Let $c \equiv z_{nat}$ or $c \equiv z_{bool}$ be the trivial context consisting of the variable z_{nat} or z_{bool}. Then $P(z_{nat})$ and $P(z_{bool})$ are trivially satisfied.

Case (1):   For the induction step one has to consider all contexts (over the signature of PROG) of the form $f(..., c[z_s],...)$ where f has result sort *bool* or *nat*.
If the context $c[z_s]$ is of sort *bool* or *nat* then the induction step is trivial since in this case from the induction hypothesis PROG ⊢ c[p] = c[q] immediately follows PROG ⊢ f(...,c[p],...) = f(...,c[q],...). Hence it is enough to consider contexts of the form

- eval($c[z_s]$, st), value(p_1, $c[z_s]$) with a context $c[z_s]$ of sort *exp*, a ground term st of sort *state* and a ground term p_1 of sort *prog*,
- lookup(x, $c[z_s]$), eval(e, $c[z_s]$) with a context $c[z_s]$ of sort *state*, a ground term x of sort *id* and a ground term e of sort *exp*,
- value($c[z_s]$, e) with a context $c[z_s]$ of sort *prog* and a ground term e of sort *exp*.

In the first case (contexts of the form eval($c[z_s]$, st), value(p_1, $c[z_s]$)) one can easily show (e.g. again by context induction) that s ≠ *prog* or $c[z_s]$ contains a subcontext of the form natexp($c'[z_s]$) with some context $c'[z_s]$ of sort *nat*. Then we are ready by induction hypothesis.

The second case (contexts of the form lookup(x, $c[z_s]$), eval(e, $c[z_s]$)) can easily be reduced to the case where $c[z_s]$ is of the form trans(c'[z_s], st) with some context c'[z_s] of sort *prog* and some ground term st of sort *state*. Hence it is enough to show that for all contexts $c[z_s]$ of sort *prog* the following (more general) property Q(c) is valid:

Q(c) = true $\Leftrightarrow_{def}$ if s = *prog* then PROG $\vdash$ trans(c[p], st) = trans(c[q], st) holds
for all ground terms st of sort *state*.

The third case (contexts of the form value($c[z_s]$, e)) is also an immediate consequence of Q(c) since PROG $\vdash$ value($c[z_s]$, e) = eval(e, trans($c[z_s]$, init)).

The validity of Q(c) can be shown by a new context induction (over all contexts $c[z_s]$ of sort *prog*) which terminates without needing a further (iterated) context induction. Thereby the case (0) is a direct consequence of the assumption and the induction step can be shown using the induction hypothesis (and for contexts of the form "for(n, $c[z_s]$)" an additional (usual) induction over n). The complete proof is given in [Hennicker 90]. ◊

As it can be seen in the proof often a generalization of the actual assertion is necessary which is sufficient to finish the proof without further (iterated) context induction. This is the case in all standard examples of behavioural theorems and behavioural implementations (see next section) which have been proved by the author, as e.g. the implementation of stacks by arrays with pointers, the implementation of sets by lists, the implementation of states by sequences of pairs, etc..

4.4 Example
The associativity law for the sequential composition of programs is a behavioural theorem of PROG, i.e.
$p_1 ; (p_2 ; p_3) = (p_1 ; p_2) ; p_3 \in$ BTh(PROG).

Proof: It is straightforward to show that for all "states" st,
PROG $\vdash$ trans($p_1 ; (p_2 ; p_3)$, st) = trans(($p_1 ; p_2) ; p_3$, st) holds. Now use lemma 4.3. ◊

5 Behavioural implementations

Formal implementation notions for specifications are a necessary prerequisite for proving the correctness of programs. Hence, in order to be useful in practice formal implementation concepts should be supplied by proof methods which support the verification of correct program development steps. In this section we show that context induction provides a powerful proof technique for the verification of implementations of behavioural specifications.

One main motivation for dealing with behavioural specifications is given by the fact that in general concrete realizations of software systems do not satisfy all properties of a requirement specification but nevertheless are considered to be correct since they produce correct observable output. Hence from the observational point of view a specification should allow to abstract from non observable properties of data structures which in the approaches of [Reichel 85] and [Nivela, Orejas 87] is expressed by constructing the behaviour class of a specification. This more abstract view induces a simple notion of implementation for behavioural specifications which formalizes the intuitive idea that an implementation is correct if it preserves the observable properties of a requirement specification:
A behavioural specification SP1 is a behavioural implementation of SP if the behaviour class of SP1 (after appropriate restriction) is a subclass of the behaviour class of SP.

In order to rule out trivial implementations we assume in the following that each specification contains the specification BOOL of the truth values and restrict the behaviour class of a specification to those algebras which satisfy true $\neq$ false. Then we obtain the following precise definition of behavioural implementations (which is a variant of the implementation concept of [Hennicker 89], adopted to the theory of behavioural specifications as discussed in the last section):

5.1 Definition
Let SP1 = ($\Sigma1$, Obs1, E1) and SP = (Σ, Obs, E) be behavioural specifications such that $\Sigma \subseteq \Sigma1$ and Obs $\subseteq$ Obs1. Moreover, let Beh(SP1) $\neq \emptyset$.
SP1 is called *behavioural implementation* of SP iff for all behavioural models B $\in$ Beh(SP1), $<B|_{\Sigma}> \in$ Beh(SP) holds.

($<B|_{\Sigma}>$ denotes the term generated Σ-algebra which is obtained from B by first *forgetting* all sorts and operations of $\Sigma1$ not belonging to Σ and then *restricting* to those elements which are generated by the operations of Σ (cf. section 2).) ◊

As already mentioned above a crucial point for the usefulness of formal implementation notions is the availability of proof methods which can be applied in practical examples. For behavioural implementations we obtain the following characterization by a context condition which is the basis for implementation proofs by context induction (cf. also [Hennicker 89] for a context criterion for "observational implementations"):

5.2 Proposition   Let $SP1 = (\Sigma 1, Obs1, E1)$ and $SP = (\Sigma, Obs, E)$ be as in definition 5.1. $SP1$ is a behavioural implementation of SP iff for all Σ-contexts $c[z_s]$ of observable sort $s_0 \in Obs$ the following property $P_{SP1, SP}(c)$ is valid:

$$P_{SP1, SP}(c) = true \Leftrightarrow_{def} \text{ for all axioms } (t = r) \in E \text{ and for all ground substitutions } \sigma: X \to W_\Sigma,$$
$$\text{if } t \text{ is of sort } s \text{ then } SP1 \vdash c[\sigma(t)] = c[\sigma(r)] \text{ holds.}$$

Proof: " $\Leftarrow$ ": Let $P_{SP1, SP}(c)$ be valid for all contexts c of observable sort of SP and let $B \in Beh(SP1)$ be an arbitrary behavioural model of SP1. It has to be shown that $<B|_\Sigma> \in Beh(SP)$.
By definition, $<B|_\Sigma> \in Beh(SP)$ iff $<B|_\Sigma> |=_{Obs} t = r$ for all axioms $(t = r) \in E$, i.e. iff for all $(t = r) \in E$ and for all Σ-contexts $c[z_s]$ (where s is the sort of t) of observable sort $s_0 \in Obs$, $<B|_\Sigma> |= c[t] = c[r]$ holds. Since $<B|_\Sigma>$ is term generated over Σ it is enough to consider instantiations $\sigma(t)$ and $\sigma(r)$ by ground substitutions $\sigma: X \to W_\Sigma$.
Now, let $c[z_s]$ be an arbitrary Σ-context of observable sort $s \in S_0$, let $(t = r)$ be an axiom of SP (such that t is of sort s) and let $\sigma: X \to W_\Sigma$ be an arbitrary ground substitution. Then, by assumption, $SP1 \vdash c[\sigma(t)] = c[\sigma(r)]$. Since $Obs \subseteq Obs1$, c is also an observable context of SP1 and hence the equation $c[\sigma(t)] = c[\sigma(r)]$ is (identically) satisfied by all behavioural models of SP1. In particular $B |= c[\sigma(t)] = c[\sigma(r)]$ and hence $<B|_\Sigma> |= c[\sigma(t)] = c[\sigma(r)]$, i.e. $<B|_\Sigma> \in Beh(SP)$.

" $\Rightarrow$ ": Proof by contradiction: Assume that there exists a context $c[z_s]$ of observable sort of SP and an axiom $(t = r) \in E$ (with t, r of sort s) such that $SP1 \nvdash c[\sigma(t)] = c[\sigma(r)]$ for some ground substitution $\sigma: X \to W_\Sigma$. Then the equation $c[\sigma(t)] = c[\sigma(r)]$ is not satisfied by the initial model I of SP1 (in the usual sense) and hence, since c is of observable sort, it is also not behaviourally satisfied by I. Therefore $<I|_\Sigma>$ is not a behavioural model of SP and hence SP1 is not a behavioural implementation of SP. $\Diamond$

Proposition 5.2 characterizes behavioural implementation relations by a property on the set of observable contexts. Hence for proving behavioural implementations in concrete cases the proof technique of context induction can be applied. This will be demonstrated by an example:

5.3 Example   We give a behavioural implementation of the specification STATE (cf. section 4) by a specification HISTORY which implements states by sequences of pairs consisting of an identifier and its associated value (for simplicity we have omitted here all sequence operations which are not necessary for the example). In contrast to the abstract specification of states each sequence stores not only the current value of an identifier x but also all previous values of x. Such implementations of states are particularly useful if one wants to retrieve old states of a system or, more concretely, if one wants to test and to analyze the state transitions performed by the execution of an imperative program.
The specification HISTORY comprises a usual specification NATSEQ of finite sequences of natural numbers. The function *history* computes for a given identifier x and some state s the history of all environments of x, i.e. the sequence of all previous values of x.

```
spec HISTORY = enrich BOOL, NAT, ID, NATSEQ by
    sorts: state
    obs-sorts: nat, bool
    functs:
        init: → state
        <.,.>: id x nat → state
        .o.: state x state → state
        update: id x nat x state → state
        lookup: id x state → nat
        history: id x state → natseq
        ifstate . then . else . fi: bool x state x state → state
```

axioms:
s o init = init o s = s
$(s\ o\ t)\ o\ u = s\ o\ (t\ o\ u)$
$update(x, n, s) = <x, n> o\ s$
$lookup(x, init) = 0$
$lookup(x, <y, n> o\ s)) =$
        ifnat eq-id(x, y) then n else lookup(x, s) fi
$history(x, init) = <0>$
$history(x, <y, n> o\ s)) = ifnatseq\ eq-id(x, y)$
        then $<n> o_{natseq} history(x, s)$ else history(x, s) fi
ifstate true then s_1 else s_2 fi = s_1
ifstate false then s_1 else s_2 fi = s_2

Fact   HISTORY is a behavioural implementation of STATE.

Informally, this fact is clear since using the operations of the signature of STATE the behaviour of states can only be observed via the *lookup*-operation which gives the same current values independently whether a state stores "old" values or not. Formally, the behavioural implementation relation can be proved by *context induction*.

Proof of the fact: By proposition 5.2 one has to show that for all contexts $c[z_s]$ (over the signature of STATE) of observable sort *nat* or *bool* the property $P_{\text{HISTORY, STATE}}$ (c) (for short P(c)) is valid where:

$$P(c) = \text{true} \quad \Leftrightarrow_{\text{def}} \quad \text{for all axioms } t = r \text{ of STATE and for all ground substitutions } \sigma: X \to W_{\text{STATE}},$$
$$\text{if } t \text{ is of sort } s \text{ then HISTORY} \vdash c[\sigma(t)] = c[\sigma(r)] \text{ holds.}$$

The validity of P(c) is proved by **context induction**:

Case (0):   Let $c \equiv z_{\text{nat}}$ or $c \equiv z_{\text{bool}}$ be the trivial context consisting of the variable z_{nat} or z_{bool}. $P(z_{\text{nat}})$ and $P(z_{\text{bool}})$ are are valid since it is obvious that HISTORY satisfies all axioms $t = r$ of STATE with t, r of sort *nat* or *bool*.

Case (1):   For the induction step one has to consider all contexts (over the signature of PROG) of the form $f(\ldots, c[z_s], \ldots)$ where f has result sort *bool* or *nat*. If the context $c[z_s]$ is of sort *bool* or *nat* then the induction step is trivial since in this case from the induction hypothesis HISTORY $\vdash c[\sigma(t)] = c[\sigma(r)]$ immediately follows PROG $\vdash f(\ldots,c[\sigma(t)],\ldots) = f(\ldots,c[\sigma(r)],\ldots)$ for all axioms $t = r$ of STATE (where t is of sort s).
Hence it is enough to consider contexts of the form "lookup(x, $c[z_s]$)" with a context $c[z_s]$ of sort *state* and a ground term x of sort *id*. In this case one has to show that for all contexts $c[z_s]$ of sort *state* the following property Q(c) is valid:

$$Q(c) = \text{true} \quad \Leftrightarrow_{\text{def}} \quad \text{for all axioms } t = r \text{ of STATE and for all ground substitutions } \sigma: X \to W_{\text{STATE}},$$
$$\text{if } t \text{ is of sort } s \text{ then HISTORY} \vdash \text{lookup(x, } c[\sigma(t)]) = \text{lookup(x, } c[\sigma(r)]) \text{ holds.}$$

The validity of Q(c) can be shown by a new context induction (over all contexts $c[z_s]$ of sort *state*) which terminates without needing a further (iterated) context induction. Thereby the proof of case (0) and the induction step are straightforward (using the induction hypothesis and the fact that for all ground terms x, y of sort *id* one can distinguish the cases where HISTORY $\vdash$ eq(x, y) = true, and HISTORY $\vdash$ eq(x, y) = false). The complete proof is given in [Hennicker 90]. ·   ◊

6   FRI-implementations

In the last section we have considered behavioural implementation relations and their verification by context induction. Important alternative approaches to formal implementations are based on the "forget-restrict-identify" concept which requires to connect the model(s) of a "concrete" specification with the model(s) of an "abstract" specification e.g. by means of an abstraction function or a congruence relation (cf. e.g. [Ehrig et al. 82] for the initial semantics approach, [Sannella, Wirsing 82], [Broy et al. 86] for the loose semantics approach). Following the loose approach of [Broy et al. 86] in this section we give a context criterion for "forget-restrict-identify" implementations (for short "FRI-implementations") which implies that context induction is also an appropriate proof method for FRI-implementations. Moreover, as a consequence of the context criterion we obtain that under certain conditions FRI-implementations and behavioural implementations are equivalent. This leads to the suggestion to use context induction as a uniform proof technique for the verification of implementation relations.
We first give the definition of the implementation concept of [Broy et al. 86] (restricted to the case of equational axioms and total algebras and using the terminology "FRI-implementation" instead of "algebraic implementation"). The concept is based on hierarchical specifications.

6.1 Definition ([Broy et al. 86])   Let SP1 = $(\Sigma 1, E1, P)$ and SP = (Σ, E, P) be hierarchical specifications with the same primitive type P such that $\Sigma \subseteq \Sigma 1$. Moreover, let SP1 be consistent, i.e. Mod(SP1) $\neq \emptyset$.
SP1 is called *FRI-implementation* of SP iff for all models B $\in$ Mod(SP1) there exists a model A $\in$ Mod(SP) and a Σ-homomorphism ϕ: $\langle B|_{\Sigma}\rangle \to A$ (cf. definition 5.1 for the notation $\langle B|_{\Sigma}\rangle$).   ◊

As in the case of behavioural implementations also for the applicability of the notion of FRI-implementation in practical examples the availability of appropriate proof methods is important. In the following we show that FRI-implementations can be verified using a modified version of the context condition for behavioural implementations (cf. proposition 5.2) where instead of the observable contexts all contexts of primitive sort are considered.

6.2 Proposition   Let SP1 = $(\Sigma 1, E1, P)$ and SP = (Σ, E, P) be as in definition 6.1 and let S_p be the set of primitive sorts (i.e. sorts of P). SP1 is an FRI-implementation of SP if for all Σ-contexts $c[z_s]$ of primitive sort $s \in S_p$ the property $P_{\text{SP1, SP}}$ (c) defined in proposition 5.2 is valid.

Proof: Let $P_{SP1, SP}$ (c) be satisfied for all Σ-contexts c of primitive sort and let B $\in$ Mod(SP1) be an arbitrary model of SP1. It has to be shown that there exists a model A $\in$ Mod(SP) and a Σ-homomorphism $\phi: <B|_\Sigma> \to A$.

Let A $=_{def} <B|_\Sigma>/\sim$ be the quotient of $<B|_\Sigma>$ w.r.t. the following congruence relation on $<B|_\Sigma>$:

   a $\sim$ b $\Leftrightarrow_{def}$ for all Σ-contexts $c[z_s]$ (where s is the sort of a and b) of primitive sort, $c[a/z_s]^B = c[b/z_s]^B$ holds.

Obviously, $\sim$ is a congruence relation. Then the canonical epimorphism defines a Σ-homomorphism $\phi: <B|_\Sigma> \to A$. Using the assumption it is then straightforward to show that A is a model of SP (see [Hennicker 90] for a more detailed proof). $\Diamond$

Remark   The context condition of proposition 6.2 is not sufficient if FRI-implementations are based on the initial algebra semantics (cf. [Ehrig et al. 82]) since the condition allows the implementation SP1 to be a (consistent) axiomatic enrichment of SP which in the initial algebra approach in general yields not a correct implementation. $\Diamond$

Proposition 6.2 gives a criterion for FRI-implementations by a property on the set of contexts of primitive sort. Hence, as for behavioural implementations, for the verification of FRI-implementations context induction is an appropriate proof technique. For example we can show by the same context induction as in example 5.3 that HISTORY is an FRI-implementation of STATE if the subspecification NAT of the natural numbers is designated as primitive type.

More generally, as a particular consequence of the context characterization of behavioural implementations and of the context criterion for FRI-implementations one obtains that if for two behavioural specifications SP1 and SP a common subspecification can be identified with all sorts observable then SP1 is an FRI-implementation of SP if it is a behavioural implementation of SP.

An interesting question is under which conditions also the reverse direction is true, i.e. when FRI-implementations are behavioural implementations? An answer can be given by means of the following proposition which sharpens the context criterion of proposition 6.2 to a characterization of FRI-implementations:

6.3 Proposition   Let SP1 = ($\Sigma1$, E1, P) and SP = (Σ, E, P) be as in definition 6.1. Moreover, let SP1 be sufficiently complete (cf. e.g. [Broy et al. 86]) and let P be monomorphic (i.e. all models of P are isomorphic). Then the validity of $P_{SP1, SP}$ (c) for all Σ-contexts $c[z_s]$ of primitive sort is a necessary condition for SP1 to be an FRI-implementation of SP.

Proof: The proof is done by contradiction: Assume there exists a context $c[z_s]$ of primitive sort such that $P_{SP1, SP}$ (c) is not valid. Then there exists an axiom (t = r) $\in$ E (of sort s) and a ground substitution $\sigma: X \to W_\Sigma$ such that SP1 $\vdash$ $c[\sigma(t)] = c[\sigma(r)]$. Since SP1 is sufficiently complete an initial model I $\in$ Mod(SP1) exists and, by assumption, I $\not\models$ $c[\sigma(t)] = c[\sigma(r)]$. If SP1 is an FRI-implementation of SP a model A $\in$ Mod(SP) exists and a Σ-homomorphism $\phi: <I|_\Sigma> \to A$. Since P is monomorphic and c is of primitive sort, $\phi(c[\sigma(t)]^I) \neq \phi(c[\sigma(r)]^I)$, i.e. $c[\sigma(t)]^A \neq c[\sigma(r)]^A$. Consequently, A does not satisfy the axiom t = r of E and hence A is not a model of SP (contradiction!). $\Diamond$

Proposition 6.3 and proposition 5.2 use the same context property $P_{SP1, SP}$ (c) for the characterization of FRI-implementations and of behavioural implementations. Hence, under the assumption of proposition 6.3 both implementation concepts are equivalent:

6.4 Corollary   Let SP1 and SP be hierarchical specifications with monomorphic primitive type P and let SP1 be sufficiently complete. Then SP1 is an FRI-implementation of SP iff SP1 is a behavioural implementation of SP where exactly the primitive sorts are specified as observable.

Proof: By proposition 6.3 and proposition 5.2. $\Diamond$

The above result is not surprising since observability concepts are historically founded in concepts considering data type extensions where already abstractions of non primitive values w.r.t. the operations with primitive result were studied (cf. e.g. [Giarratana et al. 76], [Kamin 83]). Behavioural approaches perform the consequent step by giving a more general definition of the semantics of specifications which includes not only the models of a specification but also all behavioural equivalent data structures. This leads to an intuitively clear and simple notion of implementation which was the basis for the development of the context criterion.

7 Concluding remarks

The present study shows that context induction provides an appropriate proof method for the verification of behavioural abstractions, as e.g. the behavioural validity of equations and the correctness of implementations. As a further possible application we can use context induction for proving identities which are valid in the terminal (final) algebra of a specification (cf. [Wand 79]). In contrast to initial algebras, terminal algebras identify as much elements as possible without violating the properties of an underlying primitive data type. Hence terminal validity corresponds to behavioural validity if observable sorts and primitive sorts are identified. A formal characterization of terminal models by contexts of primitive sort is given in [Broy et al. 84] which implies that context induction can also be applied for proving terminal validities.

The context induction proofs in the examples show that many steps of the induction can be carried out schematically. Hence the final aim is the development of algorithms which allow (interactive) context induction proofs by machine. In particular for achieving computer aided verification of the correctness of implementation steps such algorithms are highly desirable. A first attempt for an abstract (semi-)algorithm proving observational implementation relations has been made in [Hennicker 88].

Acknowledgements   I gratefully acknowledge many helpful comments of Martin Wirsing and Peter Padawitz.

References

[Boyer, Moore 88] R. S. Boyer, J. S. Moore: A computational logic handbook. Academic Press (1988).

[Broy et al. 84] M. Broy, C. Pair und M. Wirsing: A systematic study of models of abstract data types. *Theoretical Computer Science* **33**, 139-174, 1984.

[Broy et al. 86] M. Broy, B. Möller, P. Pepper und M. Wirsing: Algebraic implementations preserve program correctness. *Science of Computer Programming* **7**, 1, 35-54, 1986.

[Burstall 69] R. M. Burstall: Proving properties of programs by structural induction. *Comp. Journal* **12**, 41-48, 1969.

[Ehrig, Mahr 85] H. Ehrig, B. Mahr: Fundamentals of algebraic specification 1. EATCS Monographs on Theor. Comp. Science, Vol. 6, Springer Verlag, 1985.

[Ehrig et al. 82] H. Ehrig, H.J. Kreowski, B. Mahr und P. Padawitz: Algebraic implementation of abstract data types. *Theoretical Computer Science* **20**, 209-263, 1982.

[Garland, Guttag 88] S. J. Garland, J. V. Guttag: Inductive methods for reasoning about abstract data types. *Proc.* POPL'88, 219-228, 1988.

[Giarratana et al. 76] V. Giarratana, F. Gimona und U. Montanari: Observability concepts in abstract data type specification. In: A. Mazurkiewicz (ed.): *Proc.* MFCS'76, *5th Internat. Symp. on Mathematical Foundations of Comp. Science.* Springer Lecture Notes in Computer Science **45**, 576-587, 1976.

[Hennicker 88] R. Hennicker: Beobachtungsorientierte Spezifikationen. Dissertation, Fakultät für Mathematik und Informatik, Universität Passau, 1988.

[Hennicker 89] R. Hennicker: Observational implementations. In: B. Monien, R. Cori (eds.): *Proc.* STACS'89, *6th Annual Symposium on Theoretical Aspects of Computer Science.* Springer Lecture Notes in Computer Science **349**, 59-71, 1989.

[Hennicker 90] R. Hennicker: Context induction: a proof principle for behavioural abstractions (long version). Techn. Berichte, Fakultät für Math. und Informatik, Universität Passau, MIP-9001, 1990.

[Kamin 83] S. Kamin: Final data types and their specification. ACM TOPLASS **5**, 1, 97-121, 1983.

[Nivela, Orejas 87] Mª P. Nivela, F. Orejas: Initial behaviour semantics for algebraic specifications. In: D.T. Sannella, A. Tarlecki (eds.): *Proc. 5th Workshop on Algebraic Specifications of Abstract Data Types.* Springer Lecture Notes in Computer Science **332**, 184-207, 1987.

[Pepper et al. 82] P. Pepper, M. Broy, F. L. Bauer, H. Partsch, W. Dosch, M. Wirsing: Abstrakte Daten typen: Die algebraische Spezifikation von Rechenstrukturen. *Informatik-Spektrum* **5**, 107-119, 1982.

[Reichel 85] H. Reichel: Initial restrictions of behaviour. IFIP *Working Conference*, The Role of Abstract Models in Information Processing, 1985.

[Sannella, Wirsing 82] D.T. Sannella, M. Wirsing: Implementation of parameterized specifications. In: M.Nielsen, E.M. Schmidt (eds.): *Proc.* ICALP'82, *9th Coll. on Automata, Languages and Programming.* Springer Lecture Notes in Computer Science **140**, 473-488, 1982.

[Wand 79] M. Wand: Final algebra semantics and data type extensions. *Journal of Computer and System Sciences* **19**, 27-44, 1979.

Completion modulo Associativity, Commutativity and Identity (AC1) *

Jean-Pierre Jouannaud   **Claude Marché**
LRI, Bat. 490
Université de Paris-Sud – Centre d'Orsay
91405 ORSAY CEDEX
FRANCE

Abstract: Rewriting with associativity, commutativity and identity has been an open problem for a long time. In a recent paper [BPW89], Baird, Peterson and Wilkerson introduced the notion of constrained rewriting, to avoid the problem of non-termination inherent to the use of identities. We build up on this idea in two ways: by giving a complete set of rules for completion modulo these axioms; by showing how to build appropriate orderings for proving termination of constrained rewriting modulo associativity, commutativity and identity.

Key words: Class rewriting, Constrained rewriting, Termination, Completion modulo AC1, Constrained completion, Rewrite orderings.

1   Introduction

Equations are ubiquitous in mathematics and sciences. Among the most common equations are associativity, commutativity and identity (existence of a neutral element). Rewriting is an efficient way of reasoning with equations, introduced by Knuth and Bendix [KB70]. When rewriting, equations are used in one direction chosen once and for all. Unfortunately, Orientation alone is not a complete inference rule: given a set of equational axioms E, there may be equal terms (in the theory of the axioms) which cannot be rewritten to a same term once the axioms are oriented into rules. Knuth and Bendix showed how to recover completeness by adding another inference rule, called "critical pairs computation", which adds new equationnal consequences by unifying left hand sides of rules. A basic assumption of this technique is that rewriting terminates for any input term. In case of associativity and commutativity (hereafter denoted by AC) however, this assumption cannot be fullfilled. Peterson and Stickel (see also Lankford and Ballantyne [LB77]) have shown how to solve this case by building associativity and commutativity in the rewriting process, as well as in the computation of critical pairs [PS81]. This has been further generalized to an arbitrary finitary[1] theory E whose congruence classes are finite [JK86], excluding therefore the

---

*This work was partly supported by the "Greco de programmation du CNRS"

[1] i.e., any equation in the theory possesses a finite complete set of most general unifiers.

case of associativity, commutativity and identity (hereafter denoted by AC1). The latter theory is of keen interest for two reasons: the identity axiom comes along with associativity in most practical examples; for a given equation, associative-commutative unification yields in general many more most general solutions than AC1 unification, as shown by Bürkert [BHK*88].

Unfortunately, AC1-rewriting is non-terminating in most practical cases. For example, in the theory of Abelian groups, we get the following infinite derivation (using the rule $-(x + y) \rightarrow (-x) + (-y)$ for computing the inverse of a sum):

$$
\begin{aligned}
-0 \quad &=_{AC1} \quad -(0 + 0) \rightarrow \quad (-0) + (-0) \\
&=_{AC1} \quad -(0 + 0) + (-0) \rightarrow \quad (-0) + (-0) + (-0) \\
&etc \dots
\end{aligned}
$$

Since this phenomenon is simply related to the existence of a subterm $x + y$ in the left hand side of a rule, which collapses when either x or y is instantiated to 0, it may happen quite often. A consequence is that AC1-rewrite orderings cannot really exist. Peterson, Wilkerson and Baird introduced "constrained" rewriting as a mean to avoid non-terminating computations. The basic idea is to forbid instantiating a variable by a identity in case this may lead to non-termination. We show in the next section how constrained rewriting allows to solve the problem of non-termination. In particular, we show how to obtain an ordering for proving termination of constrained AC1-rewriting from an almost arbitrary AC-rewrite ordering. Section 3 then describes a class of AC1-completion procedures by a set of non-deterministic inference rules, together with its correctness and completeness proof. The latter is based on the technique of "proof algebras", originally introduced in [BDH86], whose principle is to code the inference rules as rewrite rules on proofs. The completeness proof of AC1-completion, however, is not a trivial application of this technique, since one inference rule may yield several rewrite rules on proofs. This makes it doubtful that such a proof could be carried out without this powerful technique.

Our notations and definitions are consistant with [DJ90]. We assume them known. Complete proofs of our results can be found in [Mar89]

2   Constrained AC1-rewriting

We start with a few elementary definitions.

Definition 2.1 *Let $F = L \cup A \cup Z$ be a set of function symbols, where $L = \{f_0, f_1, \dots\}$ is the set of free symbols, $A = \{+_0, +_1, \dots\}$ is the set of AC1 symbols, and $Z = \{0_0, 0_1, \dots\}$ is the set of zeros, 0_i being the identity of $+_i$. We also use $+$ and $*$ to denote two particular AC1-symbols with respective identities 0 and 1.*

An F-algebra $\mathcal{A}$ is an AC1-algebra if it validates the set of AC1 equations:

$$
\forall + \in A, 0 = zero(+) \left\{ \begin{aligned} (x + y) + z &= x + (y + z) \\ x + y &= y + x \\ x + 0 &= x \end{aligned} \right.
$$

Definition 2.2 *In the following, we denote by $s!$ the normal form of s for the following canonical rewriting system:*

$$
\forall + \in A, 0 = zero(+) \left\{ \begin{aligned} x + 0 &\rightarrow x \\ 0 + x &\rightarrow x \end{aligned} \right.
$$

Definition 2.3 *Two terms s and t are unifiable modulo AC1 if there exists a substitution σ such that $s\sigma =_{AC1} t\sigma$. We denote $CSU_{AC1}(s, t)$ a complete set of unifiers of s and t, i.e.:*

$$
\left\{ \begin{aligned} &\forall \theta \in CSU_{AC1}(s, t) \; s\theta =_{AC1} t\theta \\ &\forall \sigma \; s\sigma =_{AC1} t\sigma \implies \exists \theta \in CSU_{AC1}(s, t), \sigma =_{AC1} \theta\sigma' \end{aligned} \right.
$$

The definition of unification is modified to obtain the definition of *matching* by requiring that one term only, say s, can be instantiated by σ.

For any two terms s and t, $CSU_{AC1}(s,t)$ is finite as a consequence of the combination method described in [BJS88] and the elementary case (with F reduced to a set of constant symbols) described in [LS76].

The interesting property of AC1-unification is that in many cases, $CSU_{AC1}(s,t)$ is much smaller than $CSU_{AC}(s,t)$: for example, if x, u, v, w, t are variables, then $x + x + x$ and $u + v + w + t$ have a unique most general AC1-unifier while there are 1044569 most general AC-unifiers [BHK*88]. Matching enjoys similar properties. We think that this property would make the AC1-completion faster than AC-completion. In [BPW89], examples are given which confirm this hope.

2.1 Constrained rewriting

The idea of Baird, Peterson and Wilkerson is to forbid the instantiations of variables by zeros, when they cause termination problems. For example, the computation of the inverse of a sum in Abelian groups becomes:

$$(x \neq 0) \wedge (y \neq 0) \mid -(x + y) \rightarrow (-x) + (-y)$$

Definition 2.4 *A constrained rule (for our purpose) is a triple written out as $\Phi \mid l \rightarrow r$, where Φ is a quantifier-free formula built up with the logical connectives $\wedge$ and $\vee$, from atoms of the form $x \neq 0$ where $x \in Var(l)$ and $0 \in Z$.*

Definition 2.5 (satisfiability of a constraint) *By $\Phi\sigma \neq False$ we mean that the formula $\Phi\sigma$ is satisfiable when the symbol $=$ is interpreted as $=_{AC1}$*

For instance, $x \mapsto 0 + 0$ doesn't satisfy $x \neq 0$. Notice that satisfiability of a constraint can be easily checked: since $x\sigma \neq_{AC1} 0$ is equivalent to $(x\sigma)! \neq 0$ syntactically, $\Phi\sigma \neq False$ is equivalent to $\Phi(\sigma!)$ satisfiable when $=$ is syntactic equality.

Constrained rewriting checks whether an instance of the rule satisfies the constraint. As usual, we have three different notions of rewriting, without equations, in the quotient algebra, or with extensions "à la Peterson-Stickel" [PS81]. All of them are used in the completion process. We do not recall the corresponding notions for the AC-case (without constraints), which can be readily inferred from the definitions below by taking the constraints out and replacing $AC1$ by AC.

Definition 2.6 *s rewrites to t by $\Phi \mid l \rightarrow r$ at position p (written out as $s \xrightarrow[\Phi \mid l \rightarrow r]{p} t$) if:*

$$p \in \mathcal{F}Pos(s) \text{ and } \exists \sigma \text{ substitution s.t. } \begin{cases} s|_p = l\sigma \\ t = s[r\sigma]_p \\ \Phi\sigma \neq False \end{cases}$$

Written out as $s \xrightarrow[\Phi \mid l \rightarrow r / AC1]{} t$, constrained rewriting modulo AC1 must satisfy:

$$\exists s', t', p \text{ and } \sigma \text{ s.t. } \begin{cases} s =_{AC1} s' \\ t =_{AC1} t' \\ s' \xrightarrow[\Phi \mid l \rightarrow r]{p} t' \end{cases}$$

Written out as $s \xrightarrow[AC1 \backslash \Phi \mid l \rightarrow r]{p} t$, constrained extended AC1-rewriting must satisfy:

$$p \in \mathcal{F}Pos(s) \text{ and } \exists \sigma \text{ substitution s.t. } \begin{cases} s|_p =_{AC1} l\sigma \\ t = s[r\sigma]_p \\ \Phi\sigma \neq False \end{cases}$$

Note that /AC1-rewriting actually rewrites AC1-equivalence classes, while AC1\-rewriting uses AC1-matching, hence applies a restricted form of $=_{AC1}$ between s and $s[l\sigma]_p$.

2.2 AC1-rewrite orderings

Given a set R of rules, the non-deterministic computation of a normal form of a term requires that there are no infinite chains in the rewrite graph, a property called *termination*. Proving termination can be simply achieved by comparing for each rule $l \to r \in R$ its left hand side l with its righthand side r in some appropriate rewrite ordering:

Definition 2.7 *Given a set E of equational axioms, an E-rewrite ordering is a quasi-ordering $\geq_E$ satisfying the following properties:*

- *E-compatibility: its associated equivalence contains $=_E$,*
- *termination: its strict part does not admit infinite chains,*
- *closure under context application: $s \geq_E t \implies u[s] \geq_E u[t]$ for any context $u[.]$,*
- *closure under instantiation: $s \geq_E t \implies s\sigma \geq_E t\sigma$ for any substitution σ.*

Moreover, $\geq_E$ is called an E-simplification ordering in case it satisfies the subterm property, *i.e., a term is greater (or equivalent) to any of its subterms.*

To prove AC1-termination of a rewriting system R, we need a rewrite ordering compatible with AC1. Assume that such an ordering compares $s+x$ and s, that is $s+x \succ s$. Then $(s+x)\sigma \succ s\sigma$ for any substitution σ. Taking $\sigma = \{x \mapsto 0\}$ yields $s\sigma \succ s\sigma$ since $(s+x)\sigma =_{AC1} s$, a contradiction since $\succ$ must be terminating. We show in the following that AC1-rewriting orderings need not be closed by arbitrary instantiations, but by those instantiations only allowed in constrained AC1-rewriting.

Let us consider the following constrained rule to avoid non-termination in the example of Abelian groups:

$$(x \neq 0) \wedge (y \neq 0) \mid -(x+y) \to (-x) + (-y)$$

One question is whether we can check termination of this constrained rule by showing that the left hand side is greater than the right hand side in some rewrite ordering ? In other words, we want an ordering closed by all substitutions σ which satisfy the above constraint, but not necessarily by the other substitutions. Another question is how to compute the constraint of a rule when the ordering is given? The answer of this second question is simple, already suggested by Baird, Peterson and Wilkerson: for each substitution σ which assigns a identity to a variable, we must check whether the left hand side is greater than the right hand side in the ordering. If this is not the case, then the identity rule must have applied to the instantiated left hand side. This suggest that the ordering should satisfy the following property:

Definition 2.8 $\succ$ *is closed under non-zero instantiation if*

$$(P) \quad \begin{cases} s \succ t \\ (s!)(\sigma!) = (s\sigma)! \end{cases} \implies s\sigma \succ t\sigma$$

Lemma 2.1 *Assume that $\succ$ satisfies (P). Then $\forall s \succ t, \forall x \in \mathcal{V}ar(s), \forall \sigma, \forall 0 \in Z, x\sigma \neq_{AC1} 0 \implies s\sigma \succ t\sigma$*

Proof: by contradiction: $(s!)(\sigma!) \neq (s\sigma)!$ implies that σ instantiates some variable to zero, because $(s!)(\sigma!)$ contains a redex $x + 0$ or $0 + x$. □

We now assume known an ordering $\succ$ satisfying (P). Given this ordering, our goal is to compute a constraint which eliminates the non-terminating chains from the graph of the rewrite relation. Given a finite set X of variables, let

$$S_{AC1}(X) = \{\rho = (x_1 \mapsto 0_1, \ldots, x_k \mapsto 0_k) | k \geq 0, x_1, \ldots, x_k \in X, 0_1, \ldots, 0_k \in Z\}$$

be the finite set of all possible instantiations of some variables in X by an arbitrary identity. Our goal is to compute for all pairs (l, r) a formula $\Phi = \Phi(l, r)$ satisfying:

> (Q) $\forall \rho \in S_{AC1}(\mathcal{V}ar(l))$ $\Phi\rho \neq$ False $\implies l\rho \succ r\rho$

Φ is actually any condition on ρ such that $l\rho \succ r\rho$. It can of course be computed by checking all possible cases of instantiation of a variable by a identity. Before to see how to compute an optimized Φ, we show the adequacy of this approach.

Notations: Given a pair (l, r) of terms, let $C_{AC1}(l, r)$ be a logical formula satisfying (Q), and $\Theta_{AC1}(l, r) = \{\rho \in S_{AC1}(\mathcal{V}ar(l)) | C_{AC1}(l, r)\rho =$ False$\}$. Note that $\Theta_{AC1}(l, r)$ is redundant as defined here. Only those substitutions which are maximal in the subsumption ordering are necessary. For example, if $C_{AC1}(l, r) = (x \neq 0) \wedge (y \neq 0)$ then the substitution $\{x \mapsto 0, y \mapsto 0\}$ is not necessary, hence we can take $\Theta_{AC1}(l, r) = \{\{x \mapsto 0\}, \{y \mapsto 0\}\}$.

The following theorem shows that the termination problem is solved provided an ordering satisfying (P) is given together with an algorithm computing a constraint satisfying (Q).

Theorem 2.1 (Adequacy of properties (P) and (Q)) *Let l and r be two terms and $\Phi = C_{AC1}(l, r)$. For an arbitrary substitution σ:*

$$\begin{cases} \text{if } \Phi\sigma \neq \text{False then } l\sigma \succ r\sigma \\ \text{if } \Phi\sigma = \text{False then } \exists \rho \in \Theta_{AC1}(l, r), \exists \lambda \text{ s.t. } \sigma = \rho\lambda \end{cases}$$

Proof: write σ as $\rho\lambda$ where $\rho = \sigma|_X$, $X = \{x | x\sigma =_{AC1} 0, 0 \in Z\}$. □

We now give an algorithm for computing a formula satisfying (Q). Given an AC1-ordering $\succ$ satisfying (P), let

$$
\begin{array}{l}
\varphi(l, r) = \psi(l!, r!) \\
\text{where } \psi(l, r) = \quad \text{if} \quad l \succ r \\
\qquad\qquad\qquad\qquad \text{then} \quad \bigwedge_{\substack{(x,0) \in I(l) \\ \sigma = \{x \mapsto 0\}}} (x \neq 0 \vee \varphi(l\sigma, r\sigma)) \\
\qquad\qquad\qquad\qquad\qquad \text{where } I(l) = \{(x, 0) \in \mathcal{V}ar(l) \times Z | \exists p, s \; l|_p = x + s \text{ or } s + x\} \\
\qquad\qquad\qquad\quad \text{else} \quad \text{False}
\end{array}
$$

Lemma 2.2 ((Q) is satisfied) *Let $\Phi = \varphi(l, r)$. Then*

$$\forall \rho \in S_{AC1}(\mathcal{V}ar(l)), \; \Phi\rho \neq \text{False} \implies l\rho \succ r\rho$$

Proof: by induction on $|\mathcal{V}ar(l)|$, and by case introspection. □

We are left with the problem of finding an ordering satisfying (P). We show now that any AC-simplification ordering can be made into an AC1-ordering satisfying (P). For a particular AC-simplification ordering, we may choose the associative path ordering [BP85].

Definition 2.9 *Given an AC-simplification ordering $\geq$, let*

$$s \succeq t \ \textit{if} \ s \downarrow \ \geq t \downarrow$$

Note that $s \geq s!$ since applying an identity equation transforms a redex into one of its subterms.

Proposition 2.1 $\succeq$ *is an AC1-quasi-ordering satisfying (P), whose strict part is terminating. Furthermore, if all identities are minimal for $\geq$, then $\succeq$ is closed under context application.*

Proof: the last statement is based on the following technical lemma, which is a consequence of (P):

Lemma 2.3 *Let s be a term such that $\forall 0 \in Z \ s \neq_{AC1} 0$. Then $(u[s]_p)! = (u!)[s!]_q$ where $q \in Pos(u!)$ depends upon u and p only (not on s).*

Using the lemma, since identities are minimal and $s \succ t$, then s is not a identity. Hence, $(u[s]_p)! = (u!)[s!]_q > (u!)[t!]_q$ since $>$ is closed under context and $s \succ t \Longrightarrow s! > t!$. But $(u!)[t!]_q \geq ((u!)[t!]_q)! = (u[t]_q)!$, hence $u[s]_p \succ u[t]_p$ by definition of the ordering, which proves closure by context application. □

We conclude this section with two remarks:

- This result shows that (P) is the appropriate property replacing the closure by instantiation. In the following, we assume that *AC1-rewrite orderings* satisfy (P) instead of the full closure by instantiation.

- The last hypothesis that identities are minimal is quite natural, since otherwise the AC1-ordering cannot be well-founded: $0 \succ s =_{AC1} s + 0 \succ s + s =_{AC1}$ etc...

3 AC1-completion

As now customary, we describe the completion process by a set of inference rules which mimics the inference rules for AC-completion. The main difference is the computation of constraints when a rule is added, and the use of the constraints when rules or equations are reduced. The problem of soundness of the rules is then addressed before to deal with the most difficult part, completeness.

3.1 Inference rules for AC1-completion

In the following, $\succ$ is an AC1-rewrite ordering, E is the set of equations, N is the set of non-protected rules, P is the set of protected rules (i.e. the extensions), and $R = N \cup P$.

Orient

$$E \cup \{l = r\}; N; P \ \vdash \ E \cup \{l\rho = r\rho | \rho \in \Theta_{AC1}(l,r)\}; N \cup \{\Phi \mid l \rightarrow r\}; P \ \text{if} \ \begin{cases} l \succ r \\ \Phi = C_{AC1}(l,r) \end{cases}$$

Orient turns an equation into a rule, and computes its constraint. The "forbidden" instantiations of the equations are left as equations.

Extend

$$E; N; P \ \vdash \ E; N; P \cup \{\Psi \mid g\theta \to d\theta[r\theta]_q\} \text{ if } \begin{cases} \Phi \mid l \to r \in R \\ g = d \in AC1 \\ q \in \mathcal{F}Pos(d) \text{ with } q \neq \Lambda \\ \theta \in CSU_{AC1}(d|_q, l) \\ \Psi = C_{AC1}(g\theta, d\theta[r\theta]_q) \end{cases}$$

Extend adds an extension as a protected rule, and computes the associated constraint. Actually, in the AC1 case, the same constraint could be kept here, but we left this form for generality.

Deduce

$$E; N; P \ \vdash \ E \cup \{r\theta = l\theta[d\theta]_q\}; N; P \text{ if } \begin{cases} \Phi \mid l \to r \in R \\ \Psi \mid g \to d \in R \\ q \in \mathcal{F}Pos(l) \\ \theta \in CSU_{AC1}(l|_q, g) \end{cases}$$

Deduce adds *AC*1-critical pairs as new equations.

Delete

$$E \cup \{l = r\}; N; P \ \vdash \ E; N; P \text{ if } l =_{AC1} r$$

Delete removes trivial equations.

Compose rule

$$E; N \cup \{\Phi \mid l \to r\}; P \ \vdash \ E; N \cup \{\Phi' \mid l \to r'\} \cup \{\Phi\rho \mid l\rho \to r\rho | \rho \in \Theta_{AC1}(g\theta, d\theta), \Phi\rho \neq \text{False}\}; P$$

$$\text{if } \begin{cases} \Psi \mid g \to d \in R \\ r \xrightarrow[\Psi|g\to d/AC1]{\theta} r' \\ \Phi' = C_{AC1}(l, r') \end{cases}$$

Compose rule reduces the right-hand side of rules, and recomputes the constraint. Here, it is important (for efficiency) to compute the new constraint which can improve over the previous one (it may be empty for example).

Compose extension

$$E; N; P \cup \{\Phi \mid l \to r\} \ \vdash \ E; N; P \cup \{\Phi' \mid l \to r'\} \cup \{\Phi\rho \mid l\rho \to r\rho | \rho \in \Theta_{AC1}(g\theta, d\theta), \Phi\rho \neq \text{False}\}$$

$$\text{if } \begin{cases} \Psi \mid g \to d \in R \\ r \xrightarrow[\Psi|g\to d/AC1]{\theta} r' \\ \Phi' = C_{AC1}(l, r') \end{cases}$$

Compose extension is the analogous rule for extensions.

Simplify

$$E \cup \{l = r\}; N; P \ \vdash \ E \cup \{l' = r\} \cup \{l\rho = r\rho | \rho \in \Theta_{AC1}(g\theta, d\theta)\}; N; P$$

$$\text{if } \begin{cases} \Psi \mid g \to d \in R \\ l \xrightarrow[\Psi|g\to d/AC1]{\theta} l' \end{cases}$$

Simplify reduces equations as usual.

Collapse

$$E; N \cup \{\Phi \mid l \to r\}; P \;\vdash\; E \cup \{l' = r\}; N \cup \{\Phi\rho \mid l\rho \to r\rho \mid \rho \in \Theta_{AC1}(g\theta, d\theta), \Phi\rho \neq \text{False}\}; P$$

$$\text{if} \begin{cases} \Psi \mid g \to d \in R \\ l \xrightarrow[\Psi\mid g \to d/AC1]{\theta} l' \\ (l, r) \succ (g, d) \end{cases}$$

Collapse reduces the left-hand side of constrained rules resulting in new (unconstrained) equations. The ordering $\succ$ is $(\rhd, \succ)_{lex}$ (in fact, all terminating ordering will be convenient) where $\rhd$ is defined as follows : $l \rhd g$ iff $|l!| >_{\mathbb{N}} |g!|$ (or simply $|l| >_{\mathbb{N}} |g|$ if we assume that all rules are normalized). It is terminating. ($|s|$ is the size of s, i.e. cardinal of $Pos(s)$).

Lemma 3.1 *Assume that the equation $l = r$ is valid in $E \cup R \cup AC1$ for all $\Phi \mid l \to r \in R$. Then*

$$E; N; P \;\vdash\; E'; N'; P' \Longrightarrow =_{E \cup R \cup AC1} \;\equiv\; =_{E' \cup R' \cup AC1}$$

hence $l = r$ is valid in $E' \cup R' \cup AC1$ for all $\Phi \mid l \to r \in R'$.

Proof: $=_{E \cup R \cup AC1} \;\subseteq\; =_{E' \cup R' \cup AC1}$ is clear. $=_{E' \cup R' \cup AC1} \;\subseteq\; =_{E \cup R \cup AC1}$ follows from the hypothesis. $\square$

3.2 Correctness

Definition 3.1 *An AC1-completion algorithm is an algorithm which takes for input a set of equations E_0 and an AC1-rewrite ordering $\succ$ and produces a (finite or infinite) sequence $(E_n; N_n; P_n)$ where $R_0 = \phi$ and for all i, $E_i; N_i; P_i \;\vdash\; E_{i+1}; N_{i+1}; P_{i+1}$. Let:*

$$\begin{cases} E_\infty = \bigcup_{n=0}^{\infty} \left(\bigcap_{i=n}^{\infty} E_i \right) \;,\; N_\infty = \bigcup_{n=0}^{\infty} \left(\bigcap_{i=n}^{\infty} N_i \right) \\ P_\infty = \bigcup_{n=0}^{\infty} \left(\bigcap_{i=n}^{\infty} P_i \right) \;,\; R_\infty = \bigcup_{n=0}^{\infty} \left(\bigcap_{i=n}^{\infty} R_i \right) = N_\infty \cup P_\infty \end{cases}$$

E_∞ and R_∞ are respectively the sets of persisting equations and the set of persisting rules. We say that the algorithm fails if E_∞ is not empty, diverges if R_∞ is infinite, and succeeds otherwise.

Theorem 3.1 (Correctness)

$$\text{If completion does not fail,} \quad =_{E_0 \cup AC1} \;\equiv\; =_{R_\infty \cup AC1} .$$

This result follows from the previous lemma, but we must assume that the starting set of rules does not contain any constrained rule. This is true in practice since we usually start from an empty R_0. So, this method does not permit to handle fields' theory, for which we would want to start with the constrained rule $x \neq 0 \mid x * x^{-1} \to 1$.

3.3 Fairness and Completeness

Definition 3.2 *A derivation $E_0; N_0; P_0 \;\vdash\; E_1; N_1; P_1 \;\vdash\; \dots$ is fair if all persisting critical pairs and extensions are computed, i.e.*

$$\begin{cases} CP_{AC1}(R_\infty) \subset \bigcup_{i=0}^{\infty} E_i \\ Ext_{AC1}(R_\infty) \subset \bigcup_{i=0}^{\infty} R_i \end{cases}$$

An AC1-completion algorithm is fair if all sequences that it produces is fair.

Fairness is fundamental in completion procedures, it expresses completeness of the search strategy. In practice, we also like that the simplification rules are used as much as possible. This yields sets of rules which are inter-reduced, an important property as far as the uniqueness of the completion result is concerned.

We will prove in 3.5 that as in AC-completion, extensions of extensions are redundant. This will prove that in the rule *Extend* we can consider only $\Phi \mid l \rightarrow r \in N$, and the second condition for fairness can be transformed to:

$$Ext_{AC1}(N_\infty) \subset \bigcup_{i=0}^{\infty} R_i$$

Theorem 3.2 (Completeness) *Assume that the completion is fair and succeeds. Then,*

$$\forall s, t \quad s =_{E_0 \cup AC1} t \Longrightarrow \exists u, v \quad {}_{AC1 \backslash R_\infty}\!\!\!\overset{\displaystyle s}{\searchrow} \qquad \overset{\displaystyle t}{\nearrow}{}_{AC1 \backslash R_\infty}$$
$$u =_{AC1} v$$

Proof (sketch): The proof is a variant of the general method described in [BD89]. It consists in five steps:
- Formal definition of the AC1-proofs algebra.
- Definition of a rewriting system on AC1-proofs. Rules are derived from peaks and cliffs commutation lemmas, and from AC1-completion inference rules, where the rules *Orient, Compose, Simplify and Collapse* each produces two rewrite rules (the first or the second applies whether the constraint is satisfied or not).
- Proof of correctness of this system.
- Proof of termination of this system. The proof ordering is similar to those of [BD89].
- Conclusion. □

3.4 Remarks

- In practice, extended rewriting is used instead of rewriting modulo. Actually, implementations use flattened terms, which gives a mixture of both relations.

- To get a R_∞ more inter-reduced, the rule *Collapse* can be improved: if extensions of the collapsed rule $l \rightarrow r$ had already been calculated, they can be removed. This preserves correctness since extensions are equational consequences of the rule and the theory AC1, and it preserves completeness because a rewrite proof with an extension can be transformed to a proof using AC1-steps and an equationnal step $l' = r$, and a rewrite step with $g \rightarrow d$. It means that in an implementation, extensions of a rule must be joined to the rule in some way (labeling, numbering,...).

- An example of a fair completion procedure is described in [JK86].

3.5 Redundancy of extensions of extensions

Lemme 3.1 *The only extensions needed are extensions of rules of the form $\Phi \mid l_1 + l_2 \rightarrow r$, which are extended in $\Phi \mid (x + l_1) + l_2 \rightarrow x + r$ and $\Phi \mid l_1 + (l_2 + x) \rightarrow r + x$ $(x \notin Var(l))$.*

Corollary 3.1 *Extensions of extensions are redondant.*

Now the inference rule *Extend* can be replaced by

$$E; N; P \vdash E; N; P \cup \{\Phi \mid (x + l_1) + l_2 \rightarrow x + r, \Phi \mid l_1 + (l_2 + x) \rightarrow r + x\}$$
$$\text{if } \Phi \mid l_1 + l_2 \rightarrow r \in N \text{ and } x \notin Var(l_1 + l_2)$$

4 Conclusion

Based on Baird, Peterson and Wilkerson's idea of constrained rewriting, we have given a complete set of rules for AC1-completion together with its correctness and completeness proofs. Moreover, we have shown how to construct rewrite orderings for checking termination of constrained AC1-rewriting. One may ask whether the techniques described here extend to other similar cases, for example to ACI-rewriting (I=idempotency). The answer is negative: in ACI-rewriting, not only the substitutions but also contexts must be constrained, a much harder task.

Acknowledgements We thank Leo Bachmair who pointed out an error well hidden in a previous version of this work.

References

[BD89]   Leo Bachmair and Nachum Dershowitz. Completion for rewriting modulo a congruence. *Theoretical Computer Science*, 67(2&3):173–201, October 1989.

[BDH86]   L. Bachmair, N. Dershowitz, and J. Hsiang. Orderings for equational proofs. In *Proc. 1st IEEE Symp. Logic in Computer Science, Cambridge, Mass.*, pages 346–357, June 1986.

[BHK*88] Hans-Jurgen Bürckert, Alexander Herold, Deepak Kapur, Jorg H. Siekmann, Mark E. Stickel, Michael Tepp, and Hantao Zhang. Opening the AC-unification race. *J. Automated Reasoning*, 4(4):465–474, December 1988.

[BJS88]   A. Boudet, J.-P. Jouannaud, and M. Schmidt-Schauß. Unification in free extensions of Boolean rings and Abelian groups. In *Proc. 3rd IEEE Symp. Logic in Computer Science, Edinburgh*, July 1988.

[BP85]   Leo Bachmair and David A. Plaisted. Termination orderings for associative-commutative rewriting systems. *J. Symbolic Computation*, 1(4):329–349, December 1985.

[BPW89]   T. Baird, G. Peterson, and R. Wilkerson. Complete sets of reductions modulo Associativity, Commutativity and Identity. In *Proc. Rewriting Techniques and Applications 89, Chapel Hill, LNCS 355*, pages 29–44, Springer-Verlag, April 1989.

[DJ90]   Nachum Dershowitz and Jean-Pierre Jouannaud. *Handbook of Theoretical Computer Science*, chapter Rewrite Systems. Volume B, North-Holland, 1990. (to appear).

[JK86]   J.-P. Jouannaud and H. Kirchner. Completion of a set of rules modulo a set of equations. *SIAM Journal on Computing*, 15(4), 1986.

[KB70]   D. E. Knuth and P. B. Bendix. Simple word problems in universal algebras. In J. Leech, editor, *Computational Problems in Abstract Algebra*, pages 263–297, Pergamon Press, 1970.

[LB77]   Dallas S. Lankford and A. M. Ballantyne. *Decision procedures for simple equationnal theories with commutative-associative axioms: Complete sets of commutative-associative reductions*. Research Report Memo ATP-39, Department of Mathematics and Computer Sciences, University of Texas, Austin, Texas, USA, August 1977.

[LS76]   M. Livesey and J. Siekmann. *Unification of Bags and Sets*. Research Report, Institut fur Informatik I, Universität Karlsruhe, West Germany, 1976.

[Mar89]   Claude Marché. *Complétion modulo Associativité, Commutativité et élément neutre*. Research Report 513, Laboratoire de Recherche en Informatique, Université de Paris-Sud, Orsay, France, Septembre 1989.

[PS81]   Gerald E. Peterson and Mark E. Stickel. Complete sets of reductions for some equationnal theories. *Journal of the ACM*, 28(2):233–264, April 1981.

Polymorphic Type Checking with Subtypes in Prolog

Thom W. Frühwirth[*]
Department of Computer Science, SUNY at Stony Brook
Long Island, NY 11794-4400, USA

Abstract

In this paper, we give an executable specification of a state-of-the-art polymorphic type checking system with subtypes in Prolog. We show that the implementation reduces to modifying simple well-known meta-interpreters into type meta-interpreters and applying the so-called generate-and-test approach to programming in Prolog. This study emphasizes that Prolog is suitable as a language for defining executable specifications and that Prolog can be augmented with a simple but powerful type system. The type language augmenting Prolog programs with type definitions and type declarations is a subset of Prolog itself. Therefore it is possible to use types explicitly in a program.

Prolog	Meta-Interpreter	Executable Specification	Partial Evaluation
Type Checking	Type Languages	Subtypes	Polymorphism

1 Introduction: Types for Prolog

It is generally agreed that type information supports debugging by detecting type inconsistencies as in [Mycroft/O'Keefe], program verification [Kanamori/Horiuchi], program documentation [Bruynooghe] and optimized compiling [Xu/Warren]. [Mycroft/O'Keefe] introduced *type checking* in Prolog, based on the work of [Milner] for the functional language ML. In such *declaration based systems*, the user adds *typings* for function and predicate symbols to the program. The typings are considered as *presuppositions* on the meaning of a predicate, they do not necessarily cover the denotation of the predicate. This is a very useful feature, as Prolog predicates tend to be 'under-specified' for the sake of simplicity and flexibility.

In the following example of our type checking system *type definitions* for functions are given as clauses for the distinguished binary predicate ':'.*Type declarations* for predicates are considered as type definitions for the distinguished type 'pred'. The complete program for append(L1,L2,L3), which succeeds when the list L3 is the result of appending the list L2 to list L1 is given as:

```
[]:list(A).
[X|L]:list(A):- X:A, L:list(A).
append(X,Y,Z):pred:- X:list(A), Y:list(A), Z:list(A).
append([],L,L).
append([X|L1],L2,[X|L3]):- append(L1,L2,L3).
```

The predicate append/3 is declared as accepting arguments of type list(A). The type clauses for the polymorphic type list(A) state that the empty list [] is of type list(A) and that the term [X|L] is of type list(A) if X is of type A and L is of type list(A). This means that all elements of the list have a type A, which is left unspecified as a *type parameter*.

The possibility to define such parameterized types is called *parametric polymorphism*. Polymorphism refers to the fact that a variable, a function symbol or a predicate symbol is associated with multiple types [Wegner/Cardelli 85]. *Inclusion polymorphism* allows the specification of subtypes, and *additive polymorphism* makes it possible to define a type as union of other types. Only some recent proposals deal with all three kinds of polymorphism [Dietrich/Hagl 88]. Polymorphism can significantly reduce the loss of flexibility due to enforcing a type discipline in type-free languages. Generally speaking, parametric polymorphism is more easier handled in type checking systems, while inclusion and additive polymorphism is a natural option in type inference systems.

A program can be checked to see if it is *well-typed* with respect to the type declaration. [Mycroft/O'Keefe] adopted the slogan of [Milner] that "well-typed programs do not go wrong". The notion of "wrong" is independent of success, failure or looping of a query. For example, the query append([X],[Y],[Z]) is well-typed but fails, the query append([],a,a) is ill-typed but succeeds, the query append([X|L1],L2,L1) is well-typed but loops. The usefulness of the notion of well-typing stems from the fact that if a program and a query are well-typed, then variables in the query can be instantiated only to terms allowed by their types. This follows from the theorem proven in [Mycroft/O'Keefe], that one step of

---

[*] Current Address: Technical University of Vienna, Comp. Science, Paniglgasse 16/E181B, A-1040 Wien, Austria
Research was partially supported by a grant from the Austrian Fulbright Commission and by a grant from the Austrian Bundeskammer der Gewerblichen Wirtschaft

SLD-resolution will take a well-typed resolvent into a new well-typed resolvent. Thus run-time type checking is unnecessary. Unfortunately, this theorem does not hold in general anymore when subtypes are added, as we will do later. For an in-depth discussion of this topic see [Dietrich/Hagl].

In the rest of the paper, we define a polymorphic type language for Prolog, introduce three basic meta-interpreters, show how meta-predicates can be well-typed, answer type queries with type meta-interpreters, check the consistency of type answers, type-check programs by well-typing their clauses and discuss related work. Some familiarity with the practical [Sterling/Shapiro] and theoretical [Lloyd] aspects of Prolog is assumed.

2 A Polymorphic Type Language for Prolog

When adding a type system to a (logic) programming language, it is desirable not to destroy the semantics of the language, i.e. the type system should fit into the semantics. By using a type language equal or similar to the programming language to be extended, a consistent embedding can be supported. In addition, this makes it easier to deduce, reason about and utilize type information. Hence in our case, the type language is a subset of Prolog itself[1].

Terminology Types are defined by a binary predicate with the distinguished predicate symbol ':'[2], which is written as infix operator. The *type atom* t:p means that the term t *has type* p. We also say that the *type of* t is p. A *type clause* is a clause whose head is a type atom and whose body is a type goal. A *type goal* is either a type atom, a conjunction of type atoms or a disjunction of type atoms. A type clause with head t:p is called clause *for type p typing t*. A *type* p is defined by the finite set of clauses for type p. A *type term* is the term denoting type p. A *type term* is either a type parameter or a type constructor of arity n applied to n type terms as arguments. A *type parameter* A is a variable. A *typed term* is the term t in a type atom t:p. A typed term is either a type argument or a function symbol of arity n applied to n typed terms as arguments. A *type argument* X is a variable. Type parameters and type arguments are taken from disjoint sets of variables. A *general type term* is a type constructor of arity n applied to n type parameters as arguments. A *typed logic program* is a logic program augmented with type clauses.

Now we can define type definitions for function symbols and type declarations for predicate symbols.

Definition A *type definition* for a function symbol f/n is a type clause typing f/n. It relates the type of f/n to the type of its n arguments:

$$f(X_1,X_2,\ldots X_n):p:- X_1:p_1, X_2:p_2,\ldots X_n:p_n.$$

where p is a general type term, each p_i is a type parameter or a general type term, each X_i is a type argument and $n \geq 0$. If n=0 then the type clause is a fact defining the type of a constant. There are no local type parameters, that is, each type parameter occurring in a body of a type clause also occurres in its head. There is no principal problem with allowing local type parameters, but they would make type-checking less precise as they hide type information. For example, if the type of the elements of a list is local, there is no way to (type-)check if two lists operate on elements of the same type.

We require that each symbol is typed by exactly one type clause. In this way, our type systems disallows *overloading*. If the same function symbol should be shared by different types, subtypes can be used.

Through subtypes we now introduce additive and inclusion polymorphism. A type is either defined by a finite set of type definitions or by a single subtype definition. In practice, this restriction can be relaxed, as types violating it can be automatically transformed to a subtype definition by introducing new subtypes.

Definition A *subtype definitions* for a type p is a type clause defining p as the union of subtypes p_i:

$$X:p:- X:p_1; X:p_2;\ldots X:p_n.$$

where ';' is an infix operator denoting disjunction, p and each p_i are general type terms, X is a type argument and n>0. If n=1 then type term p is called an *alias* for type term p_1. We call each p_i a *direct subtype* of p. A type q is a *subtype* of a type p if q is a direct subtype of p or q is a direct subtype of q_1 and q_1 is a subtype of p. In other words, the subtype relation is the transitive closure of the direct subtype relation. In order to avoid circular definitions, i.e. that a type (or an instance of it) is defined as subtype of itself, and overlapping subtypes, i.e. that subtypes have intersecting domains, we require that p and its subtypes p_i are pairwise nonunifiable.

Definition A *type declaration* for a predicate symbol p/n is a type clause for the distinguished *predicate type* 'pred':

$$p(X_1,X_2,\ldots X_n):pred:- X_1:p_1, X_2:p_2,\ldots X_n:p_n.$$

where each p_i is an arbitrary type term and each X_i is a type argument. Notice that type declarations are similar to type definitions. This makes it particularly easy to give types for meta-programs, i.e. programs which manipulate other programs as data. We will show at the end of the next section.

In the following we define two basic operations on types we will need for type-checking - namely intersection and union. For a more detailed discussion see [Frühwirth-3].

---

[1] Originally [Frühwirth-2] the type predicates were defined by an extension of Prolog called HiLog [Chen/Kifer/Warren].

[2] Of course this could be any other predicate symbol as well provided it is not used otherwise.

Definition Given a set of types for the same typed term. We define the *intersection* of types to be the set of *common subtypes* which includes for each pair of types
  a) the result of their successful unification[3] whenever possible
  b) the intersection of their direct subtypes otherwise.

The set of *minimal subtypes* of types is the minimal subset of the intersection of types such that each type in the intersection of types, i.e. each common subtype, is either
  a) contained in the subset or
  b) one of its supertypes is contained in the subset.

Definition Given a set of terms and their types. Then the *union* of types is the set of common superytypes includes for each pair of types
  a) the result of their successful unification whenever possible
  b) the common supertypes of their direct supertypes otherwise.

The set of *minimal supertypes* of types is the minimal subset of the union of types such that each common supertype is either
  a) contained in the subset or
  b) one of its subtypes is contained in the subset.

In the following we assume, without loss of generality, that for each two types defined, there is at most one minimal subtype and minimal supertype. We call such a type system *deterministic*, because every term and atom respectively has at most one type[4].

3 Meta-Interpreter

In this section we define three basic meta-interpreters which will be of use later when typing terms, atoms and conjunctions. Because there is no distinction between program and data in logic programming, it is quite easy to write so-called *meta-programs* which manipulate other programs. *Meta-predicates* are predicates which are defined over goals. A meta-program which interprets programs is called a *meta-interpreter*.

The 'plain-vanilla' Meta-Interpreter is a beloved part of the Prolog folklore:

```
prove(true).
prove((A,B)):- prove(A), prove(B).
prove(A):- clause((A:-B)), prove(B).
```

where the predicate clause/1 unifies with a program clause. As usual in Prolog implementations, we assume that facts are represented as rules with the body 'true'. This special predefined predicate 'true' is handled in the first clause of the meta-interpreter, while the second clause recursively traverses conjunctions. The third clause performs an actual derivation step by choosing a clause with clause/1 and further proving its body. Note that unification still is implicitly handled by the underlying Prolog system, while resolution is made explicit.

This meta-interpreter behaves exactly like the underlying Prolog system. Unfortunately it also shares a unpleasant property of Prolog implementations: The danger of infinite computations due to endless recursion. A query like (:-append([X|L1],L2,L1)) looks pretty harmless and we would expect it to fail, but instead it loops producing an infinite sequence of resolvents (:-append([X|L3],L2,L3), :-append([X|L4],L2,L4),...). There is no general way to decide if a recursion will loop or not, because this would imply solving the Halting Problem. But we can make certain provisions. One idea is to limit the number of derivation steps. Another idea is to stop computation by not unfolding certain atoms.

A depth-bound Meta-Interpreter The first idea can be implemented by adding a counter to the plain vanilla meta-interpreter, which is decremented at every derivation step. If the counter is zero, no more unfolding is possible. This method is called *iterative deepening* and a compromise between efficient depth-first evaluation and avoidance of infinite computations. We will use natural numbers $(0,s(0),s(s(0)),...)$ for counting to keep things simple and in pure logic.

A meta-interpreter which limits the maximum number of derivation steps can be defined as:

```
plimit(true,N).
plimit((A,B),N):- plimit(A,N), plimit(B,N).
plimit(A,s(N)):- clause((A:-B)), plimit(B,N).
```

In the first clause, which terminates the meta-interpreter successfully, we do not care about the value of the counter N. In the second clause, N is passed to the two conjuncts. There is no need to decrement N here, because the number of atoms in a conjunction is finite, so there is no danger of some infinite computation. But in the third clause, which actually does one derivation step by unfolding an atom A, we decrement the counter by one. Once the counter is zero, it cannot unify with s(N) anymore, so the third clause cannot be selected anymore and the meta-interpreter will terminate.

---

[3] As [Mycroft/O'Keefe] point out, unification *with* occur-check is a must.
[4] A term (atom) has no type if a function or predicate symbol occurring in th term or literal is not defined by a type.

A Partial Evaluator Now consider the second idea. Suppose that from a query (:-g) we have derived a non-empty resolvent (:-g$_1$,...g$_n$). Then the clause (g:-g$_1$,...g$_n$) is a *conditional answer* to the initial query [Cheng et al],[van Emden]. Such a incomplete computation of an answer is called *partial evaluation* [Venken],[Takeuchi/Furukawa].

The set of all conditional answers for a given query and program is called a *residue* of the initial query and the program. The meta-interpreter is accordingly extended in such a way that in each derivation step, either the selected goal is unfolded or returned as part of the residue depending. A partial evaluator can be derived from the plain meta-interpreter. An additional clause to deal with residual goals and an additional argument returning the residual goals is added:

```
peval(true,true).
peval((A,B),(C,D)):- peval(A,C), peval(B,D).
peval(A,A):- residual(A).
peval(A,C):- not_residual(A), clause((A:-B)), peval(B,C).
```

where the predicates residual/1 and not_residual/1 respectively determine if a selected goal is to be returned or unfolded.

Type Declarations for Meta-Predicates In the following we illustrate the suitability of our type language to type meta-predicates. This issue is not addressed in most other works on types and Prolog. We consider the control-predicates for conjunction, disjunction etc. as meta-predicates and declare:

```
true:pred.
(X,Y):pred:- X:pred,Y:pred.
(X;Y):pred:- X:pred,Y:pred.
```

The meta-call predicate call/1 of Prolog can be easily typed as:

```
call(X):pred:- X:pred.
```

We can concisely type built-in meta-predicates like bagof/3

```
bagof(X,Y,Z):pred:- X:A, Y:pred, Z:list(A).
```

and our predicates for meta-interpreters:

```
prove(X):pred:- X:pred.
plimit(X,N):pred:- X:pred, N:nat.
peval(X,Y):pred:- X:pred, Y:pred.
```

This examples should suffice to show the ease of typing meta-predicates in our versatile type system.

4 Answering Type Queries with a Type Meta-Interpreter

In the following we give a specification-like implementation for our typing algorithm. Our main concern is not efficiency gained by tricky coding, but a readable and essentially pure Prolog program.

Answering Type Queries... Consider a type query (:-t:p). The query will either succeed possibly instantiating p and t or fail. The successful answer means that t has type p provided the type parameters and type arguments are instantiated as given by the answer. To illustrate this, assume an additional type 'const' with two facts a:const and b:const in addition to the type for lists. Consider the following examples:

```
:-  []:A.
    A=list(B).        % [] has type 'list(B)'
:-  [a|b]:list(A).
    no.               % [a|b] is not a valid list
:-  [a,b]:list(const).
    yes.              % [a,b] is of type list(const)
:-  X:list(const).
    X=[];             % multiple answers generated by backtracking
    X=[a];
    X=[a,a];
    ...
    X=[a,...a];
    ...
```

Clearly, such an infinite enumeration of answers is not very instructive. In the above example, we can get no idea that the type list(const) also includes lists with elements 'b'. Such lists are produced on backtracking after the infinitely many lists of a's, so we have no chance getting to a list with b's. Remembering the meta-interpreter for iterative deepening, we can overcome this trouble and submit the query as follows:

```
:-  plimit(X:list(const),s(s(s(0)))).
    X=[];
    X=[a];
    X=[a,a];
    X=[a,b];
    X=[b];
    X=[b,a];
    X=[b,b].
```

...with a Type Meta-Interpreter Using plimit/2 is nice, but note that each successful answer will always bind t to a ground term. We can prove this proposition by induction in showing that (1) type clauses with empty body (facts) have a constant (which is a ground term) in the head term by definition and (2) type clauses with non-empty body (rules) produce a ground head term as each variable in the head term is typed by a type goal in the body by definition and each type goal produces a ground term by the induction hypothesis.

We are rather interested in the type of the term as it is, with all its variables. Instead of a partial enumeration with plimit/2, we would like an answer stating, for example, that the term [X] is of type list(A) if the variable X is of type A. This is an conditional answer. Hence we can try to use our partial evaluator peval/2. In order to avoid the instantiation of variables, we return the current type goal whenever the term to be typed is a type argument. To check if a term is an unbound variable, we use the built-in predicate var/1, to check that a term is non-variable term, we use not_var/1. We modify the meta-interpreter according to our needs into ptype/2[5]:

```
ptype(true,true).
ptype((A,B),(C,D)):- ptype(A,C), ptype(B,D).
ptype(X:A,X:A):- var(X).
ptype(X:A,C):- not_var(X), clause((X:A:-B)), ptype(B,C).
```
Some examples[6] show the behavior of the type meta-interpreter ptype/2:
```
:- ptype([X]:list(A),C).
   C=X:A.
:- ptype([b,X,a]:A,C).
   A=list(const), C=X:const.
```
As ptype/2 has a clause for conjunction, we can also answer conjunctions of type queries:
```
:- ptype(([a]:A,[X]:list(A)),C).
   A=list(const), C=X:list(const).
```
Since type declarations have the same syntax as type definitions, we can also type atoms:
```
:- ptype(append([a],X,[Y]):pred,C).
   C=(X:list(const),Y:const).
```
Type Answers with Subtypes To illustrate the behavior of ptype/2 with subtypes, consider the following definitions:
```
sue:woman.
joe:man.
X:human:- X:woman.
X:human:- X:man.
```
With subtypes, a term may have more than one type:
```
:- ptype(sue:A,C).
   A=woman, C=true;
   A=human, C=true.
```
If we assume that in the Prolog program, the type clauses defining the subtypes come before the type clauses defining the supertypes, the first answer will always be the most specific type. A type query to find the common type of 'sue' and 'joe' will produce:
```
:- ptype((joe:A,sue:A), C).
   A=human, C=true.
```
The first answer is the minimal supertype. According to the definition of the type language, there is at most one minimal supertype. In general backtracking may produce additional common supertypes. Concluding, if we add subtypes, it is important to keep in mind that only the first answer of ptype/2 is the most general one.

Consistent Type Answers As the result of a type query, multiple types for the same variable may be returned as answer:
```
:- ptype((X:woman,X:man),C).
   C=(X:woman,X:man).
:- ptype(append([],[L],L):pred,C).
   C=(L:A,L:list(A)).
```
Clearly, we would expect a type error in both cases. In the first example, because the intersection of the types 'woman' and 'man' is empty. In the second example, the variable L cannot be of type A and a list with elements of type A at the same time. In other words, multiple types for the same variable have to be *consistent* and they are whenever their intersection is non-empty. We are also interested in the result of the intersection, i.e. the minimal subtype of a variable with multiple types. According to the definition of the type language, there is at most one minimal subtype.

---
[5] In the following we assume that each subtype clause of the form (H:-B1;...Bn) is unfolded into n clauses (H:-Bi).
[6] In the examples, redundand parantheses and 'true' atoms are removed from the actual answers to enhance readability.

We implement the consistency check and intersection of types by a generate-and-test approach:

```
check_types(A,B):-
    subtypes(A,B),      % generate subtypes
    factor(B),          % test them by factoring
    !.                  % cut avoids backtracking
```

The predicate factor/1 is a test which *factors*[7] type goals, i.e. intersects types for the same variable by unifying them. It cannot deal with subtypes. Instead the predicate subtypes/2 generates smaller and smaller guesses for the result of the intersections by replacing types in the residue of ptype/2 with its subtypes. The cut '!' is necessary to avoid further backtracking once a consistent set of subtypes is found. Otherwise additional solutions with smaller types may be returned.

The predicate subtypes/2 takes a type goal, and indeterministically replaces some of its type atoms with a subtype:

```
subtypes(true,true).
subtypes((A,B),(C,D)):- subtypes(A,C), subtypes(B,D).
subtypes(X:A,X:A).
subtypes(X:A,X:C):- not_var(A), clause((Y:A:-B)), var(Y), subtypes(B,X:C).
```

Note that subtypes/2 is very similar to ptype/2 and is just another partial evaluator[8]. The check for a non-variable type, not_var(A), avoids unnecessary binding of type parameters. A subtype clause is recognized by the fact that it has exactly one subgoal and that the type argument of the head is a variable. The recursive call to subtype/2 ensures that all (not only direct) subtypes of a given type are produced on backtracking.

The predicate factor/1 takes a type goal, looks at each possible pair of its type atoms and intersects them, if necessary. The predicate uses a divide-and-conquer strategy. First it factors the conjuncts of a conjunction independently and then factors types of common type arguments from the conjuncts by applying factor/2. The predicate factor/2 pairwise unifies the type goals of its arguments, taking one type goal from the first and the other from the second argument:

```
factor(true).
factor(X:A).
factor((A,B)):- factor(A), factor(B), factor(A,B).
factor(true,B).
factor(X:A,true).
factor(X:A,Y:B):- not_same_var(X,Y).
factor(X:A,Y:B):- same_var(X,Y), unify(A,B).
factor(X:A,(B,C)):- factor(X:A,B), factor(X:A,C).
factor((A,B),C):- factor(A,C), factor(B,C).
```

where same_var(X,Y) succeeds if X and Y are identical unbound variables and unify/2 unifies its arguments. For example, assume the following type definitions:

```
mother(X,Y):pred:- X:woman, Y:human.
father(X,Y):pred:- X:man, Y:human.
```

and the type queries

```
:- ptype((father(X,Y),father(Y,Z)):pred,C), check_types(C,D).
   C=(X:man,Y:human,Y:man,Z:human), D=(X:man,Y:man,Y:man,Z:human).
:- ptype((X:woman,father(X,Y):pred),C), check_types(C,D).
   no.
```

5 Type-Checking

In this context the aim of (static) type checking is to establish that a program is indeed well-typed. Type-checking a program means to determine if each clause in the program is well-typed. Well-typing a clause consists of two steps. First we type the clause by typing its body and deriving the type of the arguments of the head. Then this *derived type* is compared to the given, *declared type* of the corresponding predicate.

Typing Clauses To type a clause (H:-B) we cannot use simply a conjunction (:- ptype(H:pred,TH), ptype(B:pred,TB)), because that would not produce a derived type for the arguments of the head. The reason is that the call (:-ptype(H:pred,TH)) would already type the clause head H according to its type declaration. The subsequent comparison with the declared type would be useless and not reveal any type error. For the derived type, we are interested in the type of the arguments of the head without reference to the declared type. The type of an argument is determined by the function symbols and variables occurring in that argument. Therefore we assume that each argument is initially typed by a type parameter (instead of being typed by the declared type as given in the type declaration). The predicate make_type_param/2 replaces each type in the type declaration HD by a type parameter and that is how we can compute the derived type TH.

---

[7] The unification of types needed for intersection of types is referred to as *factoring* in [van Emden] in the context of type inference for lambda expressions.

[8] Indeed, in an earlier version of this paper, instead of a new predicate subtypes/2 a single clause was added to ptype/2, but this was both inefficient *and* tricky coding.

```
type_clause((H:-B),(TH,TB),HD,H1):-
        clause((H:pred:-HD)),            % get declared type of head
        make_type_param(HD,H1),          % generate type parameters from it
        ptype(H1,TH),                    % type the clause head
        ptype(B:pred,TB),                % type the clause body
        !.                               % cut avoids backtracking
    make_type_param(true,true).
    make_type_param(X:A,X:B).            % B is a new type argument
    make_type_param((A,B),(C,D)):-
        make_type_param(A,C),
        make_type_param(B,D).
```

The predicate type_clause/4 takes a clause and returns the types of its variables, the declared and derived type as its answer. The subgoal clause/1 lets us find the declared type HD of the clause. The subgoal make_type_param/2 generates a conjunction of type parameters H1 from the declared type by replacing each type argument with a new distinct type parameter. This conjunction and the body of the clause is then typed by ptype/2. Again we are only interested in the first solution, as solutions found on backtracking would contain non-minimal types. Hence a cut is present at the end of the clause.

Checking the Declared Type against the Derived Type From the well-typing rules for the type system with parametric polymorphism alone [Mycroft/O'Keefe] we know that a clause is well-typed if the declared type is an *instance* of the derived type[9]. To find out how to handle subtypes, first consider the following example:

```
parent(X,Y):pred:- X:human, Y:human.
parent(X,Y):- mother(X,Y).
parent(X,Y):- father(X,Y).
```

The predicate parent/2 has either type man or woman for the first argument. The declared type of the first argument, human, covers the union of the (derived) types woman and man. This is equivalent to the condition that the declared type covers the derived type of each clause. To verify this requirement, the predicate check_decl/2 uses the same generate-and-test approach as check_type/2. The declared type covers the derived type if we can replace the types in the declared type by subtypes such that the resulting type is an instance of the derived type. We use subtypes/2 for this purpose again. Finally, the predicate instance(A,B) checks if A is an instance of B. Note that the presence of the cut, which prevents further backtracking, is important. Otherwise we could generate smaller and smaller guesses for HD1 to fulfill the instance/2 check. The effect would be that the type checker would only check if the derived type and the declared type intersect.

```
check_decl(HD,H1):-
        subtypes(HD,HD1),                % generate subtypes of declared type
        instance(HD1,H1),                % compare declared to derived type
        !.                               % cut avoids backtracking
```

Well-Typing Clauses Now we can state that a clause[10] is well-typed if:

```
well_typed((H:-B)):-
        type_clause((H:-B),THB,HD,H1)    % type the clause
        check_type(THB,THB1),            % make types consistent
        check_decl(HD,H1).               % check derived against declared type
```

The clause is typed by type_clause/4, the resulting residue THB made consistent with check_type/2 and the derived type H1 is checked against the declared type HD with check_decl/2. Some examples for type_clause/4 illustrate the behavior of this type-checker. First we well-type append/3:

```
:- type_clause((append([],L,L):-true),THB,HD,H1).
   THB=(L:B,L:C),
   HD=([]:list(D),L:list(D),L:list(D)),
   H1=([]:list(A),L:B,L:C).
```

The subgoal check_type/2 will unify B and C. Then check_decl/2 will succeed as HD is an instance of H1.

```
:- type_clause((append([X|L1],L2,[X|L3]):-append(L1,L2,L3)),HB,HD,H1).
   THB=(X:A,L1:list(A),L2:E,X:C,L3:list(C),L1:list(A),L2:list(A),L3:list(A)),
   HD=([X|L1]:list(D),L2:list(D),[X|L3]:list(D)),
   H1=([X|L1]:list(A),L2:E,[X|L3]:list(C)).
```

The subgoal check_type/2 will unify A and C as well as E and list(A). Then check_decl/2 will succeed as HD is an instance of H1.

---

[9] This is equivalent to the original rule where the head atom is first also typed by the declaration and the result must be a variant of the declaration. We do not type the head atom with the declared type to be able to deal with subtypes.

[10] Facts are considered to be clauses with the body 'true', queries are considered to be clauses with the head 'true'.

An example for a predicate with subtypes is presented next:

```
:- type_clause((parent(X,Y):- mother(X,Y)),THB,HD,H1).
    THB=(X:A,Y:B,X:woman,Y:human),
    HD=(X:human,Y:human),
    H1=(X:A,Y:B).
```

First A is bound to woman and B to human. Then check_decl/2 succeeds as there is a subtype replacement for HD, (X:woman,Y:human), such that HD is an instance of H1. Analogously the second clause of parent/2 is well-typed.

6 Related Work

Our type system is based on the [Mycroft/O'Keefe] approach to type checking. The main difference is that we add inclusion and additive polymorphism, i.e. subtypes, to our type-checking system. Instead of using an extra-logical functional type language, we use a type language based on Prolog itself. Thus type definitions have a clear semantics as binary predicates. They can also be used freely in the program itself.

Well-typing is defined as a fixpoint-operator for a type system with monomorphic types in [Yardeni/Shapiro]. Their approach is based on the sets of ground terms which can occur as arguments of predicates. They use a BNF-style notation to define their types. The absence of polymorphism enforces rather general types, as in the example of append/3:

```
Any_list => [] ; [Any|Any_list].
type append(Any_list,Any_list,Any_list).
```

Consider the following example taken from their paper to define typings for a merge-sort program:

```
Natural => 0 ; s(Natural).
Nat_list => [] ; [Natural|Nat_list].
Special_list => [] ; [[Natural]|Special_list].
List_of_Nat_list => [] ; [Nat_list|List_of_Nat_list].
type mergesort(Nat_list,Nat_list).
type convert(Nat_list,Special_list).
type msort(List_of_nat_lists,List_of_nat_lists).
...
mergesort(Xs,Ys):- convert(Xs,Xs1), msort(Xs1,[Ys]).
...
```

With monomorphic types one needs more type definitions than in a polymorphic type checking system like ours:

```
0:nat.                      s(N):nat:- N:nat.
[]:list(A).                 [X|L]:list(A):- X:list(A), L:list(A).
mergesort(X,Y):pred:- X:list(nat), Y:list(nat).
convert(X,Y):pred:- X:list(nat), Y:list(list(nat)).
msort(X,Y):pred:- X:list(list(nat)), Y:list(list(nat)).
```

Note that the type of the second argument of convert/2 can be given more precise in [Yardeni/Shapiro]. Indeed, any more general type declaration, i.e. List_of_Nat_list, would result in an ill-typed program, as in that case the set of ground terms inferred relative to the type declaration is always smaller than the type declaration itself. This stems from the fact that the semantics of the type system is based on the notion of sets of ground terms, while our type checking system checks equivalency of types on the type-level. In other words, the former is a *value-based* and the latter is a *name-based* type system [Wegner/Cardelli].

[Xu/Warren] integrate type checking and type inference into a uniform type system and give a clear semantics for type declarations. This is not possible in our type system, as it is not defined on the ground terms of the Herbrand universe, but rather treats free variables different from terms. We believe that this allows more useful typings. Their system is concentrates on type inference, while our concern is solely type checking.

[Hanus] proposes a more general type language and definition of well-typing than that of [Mycroft/O'Keefe], which allows a more natural treatment of high-order predicates, but may require runtime type checking. We do not deal with typings for higher-order predicates in this paper, this is the topic of current research.

[Dietrich/Hagl] add inclusion polymorphism to the approach of [Mycroft/O'Keefe]. In contrast to our work, their elaborate well-typing algorithm deals explicitly with the problem of runtime type checking, but requires mode information to be present.

In [Cardelli-2] a powerful type language for applicative languages is proposed. There is also a notion of sets of types, based on the concept of so-called power types. The paper gives a semantic account of sets of types as types of types, while we consider type sets as a purely syntactical means.

[Jacobs] presents a type language for algebraic database programming languages. Our type language is less powerful but has a simple and decidable type checking procedure, while [Jacobs] gives type checking rules but does not deal with their efficient implementation.

An approach in the same spirit as our meta-interpreter implementation technique was taken in [van Emden] to derive conditional answers for polymorphic type inference of lambda expressions. He also uses factoring to intersect types.

[Smolka] modified order-sorted logic, which models inclusion polymorphism naturally, to parametrically order-sorted logic (POS) in order to handle parametric polymorphism. Though this elaborate approach is rather different to ours and relies on notions of generalized constraint languages, partial algebras and rewriting systems, the actual implementation, as far as it is described, employs an algorithm similar to ours. But contrary to our work, [Smolka] notes that he can "only give an incomplete algorithm" whose success depends on the order of subgoals.

7 Conclusions

We have implemented a prototype of a state-of-the-art polymorphic type checking system with subtypes for Prolog in Prolog with Prolog. Therefore the type system is naturally embedded into typeless Prolog. In other words, *Prolog is the typed language is the type language is the type system implementation language*. We gave a meta-interpreter based specification of a type checking system. In this way, the problem of implementing was reduced mainly to modifying a set of standard meta-interpreters. By considering typings for predicates as special case of type definitions, it is as easy in the type system to type meta-predicates as it is to use them in Prolog. Therefore meta-programs like meta-interpreter can be typed concisely in our type system, an issue not addressed fully in previous work.

Further work will tackle the open problems associated with typing higher-order constructs such as apply/n. Other goals are to annotate the type checker with error-messages in a methodic way and to derive an efficient Prolog implementation from its specification in Prolog.

Acknowledgements

We are grateful to You-Chin Fuh, Michael Kifer, Patreek Mishra and David Warren (in alphabetical order) for enlightening discussions and anonymous referees for comments.

References

[Bruynooghe] Bruynooghe M, Adding Redundancy to Obtain More Reliable and More Readable Prolog Programs, 1st Int Conference on Logic Programming, Marseille France, 1982

[Cardelli-1] Cardelli L, Basic Polymorphic Type Checking, Draft, AT&T Bell Laboratories, Murray Hill New Jersey, ≥ 1984

[Cardelli-2] Cardelli L, Structural Subtyping and the Notion of Power Type, 15th ACM Symposium on Principles of Programming Languages, San Diego California, ACM Press, January 1988

[Chen/Kifer/Warren] Chen W, Kifer M and Warren D, HiLog: A First-Order Semantics for Higher-Order Logic Programming Constructs, SUNY at Stony Brook, accepted at the North American Conference on Logic Programming, USA, 1989

[Cheng et al] Cheng M H M, van Emden M H and Strooper P A, Complete Sets of Frontiers in Logic-based Program Transformation, Meta 88 Workshop, Bristol England, July 1988

[Dietrich/Hagl] Dietrich R and Hagl F, A Polymorphic Type System with Subtypes for Prolog, 2nd European Symposium on Programming, Nancy France, 1988

[Frühwirth-1] Frühwirth Thom W, Type Inference by Program Transformation and Partial Evaluation, Meta-Programming in Logic Programming, Abramson H and Rogers M H (eds), MIT Press, Cambridge Massachusetts, 1989

[Frühwirth-2] Frühwirth Thom W, A Polymorphic Type Checking System for Prolog in HiLog, 6th Israel Conference on Artificial Intelligence and Computer Vision, Ramat Gan Israel, December 1989

[Frühwirth-3] Frühwirth Thom W, Types in Logic Programming, Ph.D. Thesis, Technical University Vienna, Computer Science Department E181B, Vienna Austria, March 1990

[Hanus] Hanus M, Horn Clause Programs with Polymorphic Types: Semantics and Resolution, TAPSOFT '89, Lecture Notes in Computer Science 351, Goos G and Hartmanis J (eds), Springer, New York New York, 1989

[Jacobs] Jacobs D, A Type System for Algebraic Database Programming Languages, 2nd International Workshop on Database Programming Languages, Gleneden Beach Oregon, June 1989

[Kanamori/Horiuchi] Kanamori T and Horiuchi K, Polymorphic Type Inference in Prolog by Abstract Interpretation, Logic Programming '87 6th Conf., Lecture Notes in Computer Science 315, Goos G and Hartmanis J (eds), Springer, New York New York, 1987

[Lloyd] Lloyd J W, Foundations of Logic Programming, Second, extended Edition, Springer Verlag, Berlin Germany, 1987

[Milner] Milner R, A Theory of Type Polymorphism in Programming, Journal on Computer and System Sciences Vol 17 No 3, 1978, pp 348-375

[Mycroft/O'Keefe] Mycroft A and O'Keefe R A, A Polymorphic Type System for Prolog, Artificial Intelligence, Vol 23, No 3, August 1984, pp 295-307

[Smolka] Smolka G, Logic Programming with Polymorphically Order-Sorted Types, Lilog-Report 55, IBM Deutschland GmbH, Germany, October 1988

[Sterling/Shapiro] Sterling L and Shapiro E, The Art of Prolog, MIT Press, Cambridge Massachusetts, 1986

[Takeuchi/Furukawa] Takeuchi A and Furukawa K, Partial Evaluation of Prolog Programs and its Application to Meta Programming, Information Processing 86, 415-420, North Holland, 1986

[van Emden] van Emden M H, Conditonal Answers for Polymorphic Type Inference, in 5th Int Logic programming Conference and 5th Int Symposium on Logic programming, Kowalski R A and Bowen K A (eds), MIT Press, Cambridge Massachusetts, 1988

[Venken] Venken R, A Prolog Meta-Interpreter for Partial Evaluation and its Application to Source to Source Transformation and Query-Optimization, in T.O'Shea (ed), Advances in Artificial Intelligence, ECCAI, Elsevier Science Publisher, Holland, 1985

[Wegner/Cardelli] Wegner P and Cardelli L, On Understanding Types, Data Abstraction, and Polymorphism, Computing Surveys, Vol 17, No 4, December 1985

[Xu/Warren] Xu J and Warren D S, A Theory of Types and Type Inference in Logic Programming Languages, Ph.D. Thesis, State University of New York at Stony Brook, Department of Computer Science, Stony Brook New York, July 1989

[Yardeni/Shapiro] Yardeni E and Shapiro E, A Type System for Logic Programs, in Concurrent Prolog: Collected papers, Shapiro E (ed), Vol 2, MIT Press, Cambridge Massachusetts, 1987, pp 211-244

On the Power of Subsumption and Context Checks

Roland N. Bol[1]

Krzysztof R. Apt[1,2]

Jan Willem Klop[1,3]

Abstract

Loop checking is a mechanism used to prune infinite SLD-derivations. Here we study two classes of loop checking mechanisms - subsumption checks and context checks. We analyze their soundness, completeness relative strength and related concepts. We prove their soundness (no computed answer substitution to a goal is missed) and demonstrate their completeness (all resulting derivations are finite) for some classes of logic programs. The completeness theorems for the subsumption checks make use of a simple version of Kruskal's Tree Theorem [K], called Higman's Lemma [H].

This paper is a sequel to Apt, Bol and Klop [ABK] where a formal framework for studying loop checking mechanisms was introduced and where so-called equality checks were studied.

1. Introduction

Logic programming is advocated as a formalism for writing executable specifications. However, even when these specifications are correct in the logical sense, their execution by means of a PROLOG interpreter may lead to divergence. This problem motivated the study of loop checking mechanisms which are used to discover some form of looping in SLD-derivations (see [B], [BW], [C], [PG], [SGG], [SI], [V]).

The use of a PROLOG interpreter augmented with a loop check allows us to use a larger class of logic programs as correct *executable* specifications. Which class it is depends on the selected loop check. To study such problems in a rigorous way, we introduced in our previous paper Apt, Bol and Klop [ABK] a number of natural concepts like soundness, completeness and relative strength of loop checks. We also introduced there the concept of a *simple loop check* arising when the loop checking mechanism does not depend on the analyzed logic program and showed that no sound and complete simple loop check exists, not even for programs without function symbols. Then we analyzed a number of natural simple loop checks based on the *equality* between goals, respectively resultants, of the derivations. Finally we introduced a class of logic programs, called *restricted programs*, in which a restricted form of recursion is allowed, and established the completeness of these loop checks for restricted programs without function symbols.

In this paper we study a more powerful class of simple loop checks based on the *inclusion* between goals, respectively resultants, of the derivations. We call these loop checks *subsumption checks*. Subsumption checks are stronger than the corresponding equality checks and therefore they prune SLD-derivations earlier than their counterparts. This makes it more difficult to establish their soundness but opens a possibility for completeness for a larger class of programs than restricted ones. We show that subsumption checks are complete for three natural classes of logic programs without function symbols. These completeness theorems make use of a simple version of Kruskal's Tree Theorem, called Higman's Lemma ([H]). While the use of this theorem to establish termination of term rewriting systems is well-known (see e.g. [D] or [K]), we have not encountered any applications of this theorem in the area of logic programming.

Finally we study a simple loop check introduced by Besnard [B], which we call a *context check*. As for the equality and subsumption checks, some variations on this context check can be made. It appears that the context checks are sound and complete for restricted programs without function symbols.

---

[1] Centre for Mathematics and Computer Science
P.O.Box 4079, 1009 AB Amsterdam, The Netherlands

[2] Department of Computer Sciences, University of Texas at Austin,
Austin, Texas 78712-1188, USA

[3] Department of Computer Sciences, Free University of Amsterdam
De Boelelaan 1081, 1081 HV Amsterdam, The Netherlands
This research was partly supported by Esprit BRA-project 3020 Integration.

For reasons of space, most proofs are omitted.

2. Basic notions

In this section we recall some basic concepts presented in [ABK]. Throughout this paper we assume familiarity with the basic concepts and notations of logic programming as described in [L]. For two substitutions σ and τ, we write $\sigma \leq \tau$ when σ is more general than τ and for two expressions E and F, we write $E \leq F$ when F is an instance of E. We then say that F is *less general* than E. An SLD-derivation step from a goal G, using a clause C and an idempotent mgu θ, to a goal H is denoted as $G \Rightarrow_{C,\theta} H$. By an SLD-derivation we mean an SLD-derivation in the sense of [L] *or an initial fragment (subderivation) of it*.

2.1 Loop checks

The purpose of a loop check is to prune every infinite SLD-tree to a finite subtree of it containing the root. We define a loop check as a set of SLD-derivations (depending on the program): the derivations that are pruned exactly at their last node. Such a set of SLD-derivations L(P) can be extended in a canonical way to a function $f_{L(P)}$ from SLD-trees to SLD-trees by pruning in an SLD-tree the nodes in { G | the SLD-derivation from the root to G is in L(P) }. We shall usually make this conversion implicitly.

In this paper, we shall restrict ourselves to an even more restricted form of a loop check, called simple loop check, in which the set of pruned derivations is independent of the program P. This leads us to the following definitions.

DEFINITION 2.1.
Let L be a set of SLD-derivations.
$RemSub(L) = \{ D \in L \mid L$ does not contain a proper subderivation of D $\}$.
L is *subderivation free* if L = RemSub(L). □

In order to render the intuitive meaning of a loop check L: 'every derivation $D \in L$ is pruned *exactly* at its last node', we need that L is subderivation free. Note that RemSub(RemSub(L)) = RemSub(L).

In the following definition, by a *variant* of a derivation D we mean a derivation D' in which in every derivation step, atoms in the same positions are selected and the same program clauses are used. D' may differ from D in the renaming that is applied to these program clauses for reasons of standardizing apart and in the mgu used. It has been shown that in this case every goal in D' is a variant of the corresponding goal in D (see [LS]). Thus any variant of an SLD-refutation is also an SLD-refutation and yields the same computed answer substitution up to a renaming.

DEFINITION 2.2.
A *simple loop check* is a computable set L of finite SLD-derivations such that
- for every derivation D: if $D \in L$ then for every variant D' of D: $D' \in L$;
- L is subderivation free. □

DEFINITION 2.3.
A *loop check* is a computable function L from programs to sets of SLD-derivations such that for every program P, L(P) is a simple loop check. □

DEFINITION 2.4.
Let L be a loop check. An SLD-derivation D of $P \cup \{G\}$ is *pruned by L* if L(P) contains a subderivation D' of D. □

EXAMPLE 2.5 (see also [B] and [vG]).
We define the *Variant of Atom (VA)* check as:
$VA = RemSub(\{ D \mid D = (G_0 \Rightarrow_{C_1,\theta_1} G_1 \Rightarrow ... \Rightarrow G_{k-1} \Rightarrow_{C_k,\theta_k} G_k)$ such that for some i and j, $0 \leq i \leq j < k$,
G_k contains an atom A that is - a variant of an atom A' in G_i and
                              - introduced while resolving $A'\theta_{i+1}...\theta_j$, the further instantiated version of A', that is selected in G_j)}. □

2.2 Soundness and completeness

The most important property of a loop check is definitely that using it does not result in a loss of success. Even the loss of solutions is undesirable. Finally, we would like to retain only shorter derivations and prune the longer ones that give the same result. This leads to the following definitions, where for a derivation D, $|D|$ stands for its length, i.e. the number of goals in it.

DEFINITION 2.6.

i) A loop check L is *weakly sound* if for every program P and goal G, and SLD-tree T of $P \cup \{G\}$: if T contains a successful branch, then $f_{L(P)}(T)$ contains a successful branch.

ii) A loop check L is *sound* if for every program P and goal G, and SLD-tree T of $P \cup \{G\}$: if T contains a successful branch with a computed answer substitution σ, then $f_{L(P)}(T)$ contains a successful branch with a computed answer substitution σ' such that $\sigma' \leq \sigma$.

iii) A loop check L is *shortening* if for every program P and goal G, and SLD-tree T of $P \cup \{G\}$: if T contains a successful branch D with a computed answer substitution σ, then either $f_{L(P)}(T)$ contains D or $f_{L(P)}(T)$ contains a successful branch D' with a computed answer substitution σ' such that $\sigma' \leq \sigma$ and $|D'| < |D|$. □

Obviously, a shortening loop check is sound, and a sound loop check is weakly sound. In [ABK] it is shown that the VA check of Example 2.5, although intuitively appealing, is not even weakly sound.

The purpose of a loop check is to reduce the search space for top-down interpreters. We would like to end up with a finite search space. This is the case when every infinite derivation is pruned.

DEFINITION 2.7.

A loop check L is *complete (w.r.t. a selection rule R)* if every infinite SLD-derivation (via **R**) is pruned by L. □

In general, comparing loop checks is difficult. The following relation comparing loop checks is not very general: most loop check will be incomparable with respect to it. Nevertheless it turns out to be very useful.

DEFINITION 2.8.

Let L_1 and L_2 be loop checks.
L_1 is *stronger than L_2* if for every program P and goal G, every SLD-derivation $D_2 \in L_2(P)$ of $P \cup \{G\}$ contains a subderivation $D_1 \in L_1(P)$. □

In other words, L_1 is stronger than L_2 if every SLD-derivation that is pruned by L_2 is also pruned by L_1. Note that the definition implies that every loop check is stronger than itself. The following theorem will enable us to obtain soundness and completeness results for loop checks which are related by the 'stronger than' relation, by proving soundness and completeness for only one of them.

THEOREM 2.9 (Relative Strength). *Let L_1 and L_2 be loop checks, and let L_1 be stronger than L_2.*
  i)   If L_1 is weakly sound, then L_2 is weakly sound.
  ii) If L_1 is sound, then L_2 is sound.
  iii) If L_1 is shortening, then L_2 is shortening.
  iv) If L_2 is complete then L_1 is complete.
PROOF. Straightforward. □

2.3 The existence of sound and complete loop checks

The undecidability of the halting problem implies that there cannot be a sound and complete loop check for logic programs in general, as logic programming has the full power of recursion theory. So our first step is to rule out programs that compute over an infinite domain. We shall do so by restricting our attention to programs without function symbols, so called *function-free* programs.

So our question can be reformulated as: is there a sound and complete loop check for function-free programs? In this paper, we shall only address this question for simple loop checks.

THEOREM 2.10. *There is no weakly sound and complete simple loop check for function-free programs.*
PROOF. Let L be a simple loop check that is complete for function-free programs. Consider the following infinite SLD-derivation D, obtained by repeatedly using the clause $A(x) \leftarrow A(y), S(y,x)$ (using the leftmost selection rule): $D = \leftarrow A(x_0), B(x_0) \Rightarrow \leftarrow A(x_1), S(x_1, x_0), B(x_0) \Rightarrow \leftarrow A(x_2), S(x_2, x_1), S(x_1, x_0), B(x_0) \Rightarrow \ldots$.

Since L is a complete loop check, D is pruned by L and since L is simple, the goal at which pruning takes place is independent of the program used for this derivation. Suppose that D is pruned by L at the goal $\leftarrow A(x_n), S(x_n, x_{n-1}), \ldots, S(x_1, x_0), B(x_0)$.

Now let $P = \{ S(i, i+1) \leftarrow \mid 0 \leq i < n \} \cup \{ A(0) \leftarrow, A(x) \leftarrow A(y), S(y, x), B(n) \leftarrow \}$. Extending D to an SLD-tree of $P \cup \{G\}$ (still using the leftmost selection rule), we see that the only successful branch of this SLD-tree of $P \cup \{G\}$ goes via the goal that is pruned by L. Hence L is not weakly sound. □

3. Equality checks

In this section, we introduce some simple loop checks. For each of them, there exist two versions: the first one is weakly sound, the second one shortening. The second, shortening version is obtained by adding an additional condition to the first one. By this construction, the first version is always stronger than the corresponding second version.

Starting with the Variant of Atom check, we can make three independent modifications of it.

1. Adding this additional condition, dealing with the computed answer substitution 'generated so far'. A neat formulation of this condition can be obtained by the use of *resultants* instead of goals in SLD-derivations. When considering a derivation $G_0 \Rightarrow_{C_1, \theta_1} G_1 \Rightarrow \ldots$, to every goal $G_i = \leftarrow S_i$ there corresponds the resultant $R_i = S_0 \theta_1 \ldots \theta_i \leftarrow S_i$. Resultants were introduced in [LS].

2. Replace *variant* by *instance*. This yields the *Instance of Atom (IA)* check. This check is still unsound: it is even stronger than the VA check. Besnard [B] has introduced a weakly sound version of this loop check. This check and related ones (derived from VA; shortening versions) are discussed in section 5. We shall refer to these checks as the *context checks*.

3. Replace *atom* by *goal*. This yields the *Equals Variant of Goal (EVG)* check. Informally, this loop check prunes a derivation as soon as a *goal* occurs that is a variant of an earlier goal. Replacing 'variant' by 'instance' again yields the *Equals Instance of Goal (EIG)* check. The shortening versions are called *Equals Variant of Resultant (EVR)* and *Equals Instance of Resultant (EIR)*.

   Taking goals instead of atoms as a basis for a loop check yields two independent choices again.

3a. Whereas equality between atoms is unambiguous, equality between goals is much less clear. In SLD-derivations, we regard goals as lists, so both the number and the order of occurrences of atoms is important. However, we may also regard them as multisets, where the order of the occurrences is unimportant.

   So we shall consider *two* EVG checks: EVG_L (for list) and EVG_M (for multiset). The same holds for EIG, EVR and EIR. We shall refer to these eight loop checks as the *equality* checks. These checks are discussed in the remainder of this section.

3b. Finally, we may replace 'G_2 is a variant/instance of G_1' by 'G_2 is *subsumed by* a variant/instance of G_1'. We define 'G_1 subsumes G_2' as '$G_1 \subseteq G_2$'. Thus we can make a distinction between 'subsumed by a variant' and 'subsumed by an instance'. Usually in literature, 'subsumed by a variant' is not considered, 'subsumed by an instance' is simply called 'subsumed' (see e.g. [CL]). Subsumption can also be defined for resolvents.

   This yields the *subsumption* check. Since this modification is again independent of the others, there are also eight subsumption checks. These checks are discussed in section 4.

The equality checks are studied in detail in [ABK]. In the rest of this section we recall the basic definitions and results. In fact, we should give a definition for each equality check. This would yield eight almost identical definitions. Therefore we compress them into two definitions, trusting that the reader is willing to understand our notation. The equality relation between goals regarded as lists is denoted by $=_L$; similarly $=_M$ for multisets.

DEFINITION 3.1.

For Type $\in \{L, M\}$, the *Equals Variant/Instance of Goal$_{Type}$* check is the set of SLD-derivations

$$EVG/EIG_{Type} = RemSub(\{ D \mid D = (G_0 \Rightarrow_{C_1, \theta_1} G_1 \Rightarrow \ldots \Rightarrow_{C_k, \theta_k} G_k) \text{ such that for some } i,$$
$$0 \leq i < k, \text{ there is a renaming/substitution } \tau \text{ such that } G_k =_{Type} G_i \tau \}). \ \square$$

DEFINITION 3.2.

For Type $\in \{L,M\}$, the *Equals Variant/Instance of Resultant$_{Type}$* check is the set of SLD-derivations

$EVR/EIR_{Type} = RemSub(\{ D \mid D = (G_0 \Rightarrow_{C_1,\theta_1} G_1 \Rightarrow ... \Rightarrow G_{k-1} \Rightarrow_{C_k,\theta_k} G_k)$ such that for some i,

$0 \le i < k$, there is a renaming/substitution τ such that $G_k =_{Type} G_i\tau$ and

$G_0\theta_1...\theta_k = G_0\theta_1...\theta_i\tau \})$. □

Usually, once a loop check is defined, we shall present two kinds of results. First, we prove it soundness (in fact, the loop checks we present are either weakly sound or shortening). After that, we define one or more classes of programs, for which we then prove that the loop check is complete.

THEOREM 3.3 (Equality Soundness).

 i) All equality checks based on resultants are shortening. A fortiori they are sound.

 ii) All equality checks based on goals are weakly sound.

PROOF. See [ABK]. □

DEFINITION 3.4.

The *dependency graph D_P* of a program P is a directed graph whose nodes are the predicate symbols of P and

$(p,q) \in D_P$ iff there is a clause in P using p in its head and q in its body.

D_P^* is the reflexive, transitive closure of D_P. When $(p,q) \in D_P^*$, we say that p *depends on* q.

For a predicate symbol p, the *class of p* is the set of predicate symbols p 'mutually depends' on:

$clp(p) = \{ q \mid (p,q) \in D_P^* \text{ and } (q,p) \in D_P^* \}$. □

DEFINITION 3.5.

Given an atom A, let *rel(A)* denote its predicate symbol. Let P be a program.

A clause $A_0 \leftarrow A_1,...,A_n$ (n≥0) is called *restricted w.r.t. P* if for $i = 1,...,n-1$, $rel(A_i)$ does not depend on $rel(A_0)$ in P. The atoms $A_1,...,A_{n-1}$ are called *non-recursive* atoms of the clause $A_0 \leftarrow A_1,...,A_n$.

A program P is called *restricted* if every clause in P is restricted w.r.t. P. □

THEOREM 3.6 (Equality Completeness).

 All equality checks are complete w.r.t. the leftmost selection rule for function-free restricted programs.

PROOF. See [ABK]. □

4. Subsumption checks

As already stated, there are eight subsumption checks. We define them by means of two parametrized definitions, again trusting that the reader is willing to understand our notation. The inclusion relation between goals regarded as lists is denoted by $\subseteq_L$; similarly $\subseteq_M$ for multisets. Note: $L_1 \subseteq_L L_2$ if all elements of L_1 occur in the same order in L_2; they need not to occur on adjacent positions. For example, $(a,c) \subseteq_L (a,b,c)$.

DEFINITION 4.1.

For Type $\in \{L,M\}$, the *Subsumes Variant/Instance of Goal$_{Type}$* check is the set of SLD-derivations

$SVG/SIG_{Type} = RemSub(\{ D \mid D = (G_0 \Rightarrow_{C_1,\theta_1} G_1 \Rightarrow ... \Rightarrow G_{k-1} \Rightarrow_{C_k,\theta_k} G_k)$ such that for some i,

$0 \le i < k$, there is a renaming/substitution τ with $G_k \supseteq_{Type} G_i\tau \})$. □

DEFINITION 4.2.

For Type $\in \{L,M\}$, the *Subsumes Variant/Instance of Resultant$_{Type}$* check is the set of SLD-derivations

$SVR/SIR_{Type} = RemSub(\{ D \mid D = (G_0 \Rightarrow_{C_1,\theta_1} G_1 \Rightarrow ... \Rightarrow G_{k-1} \Rightarrow_{C_k,\theta_k} G_k)$ such that for some i,

$0 \le i < k$, there is a renaming/substitution τ with $G_k \supseteq_{Type} G_i\tau$ and

$G_0\theta_1...\theta_k = G_0\theta_1...\theta_i\tau \})$. □

LEMMA 4.3. *All subsumption checks are simple loop checks.*

PROOF. Straightforward. □

The following example shows the differences between the behaviour of various subsumption checks and the equality checks.

EXAMPLE 4.4.

Let P = { A(y) ← A(0),C(y)   (C1),
          A(0) ←   (C2),
          B(1) ←   (C3),
          C(z) ← B(z),A(w)   (C4) },
and let G = ←A(x).

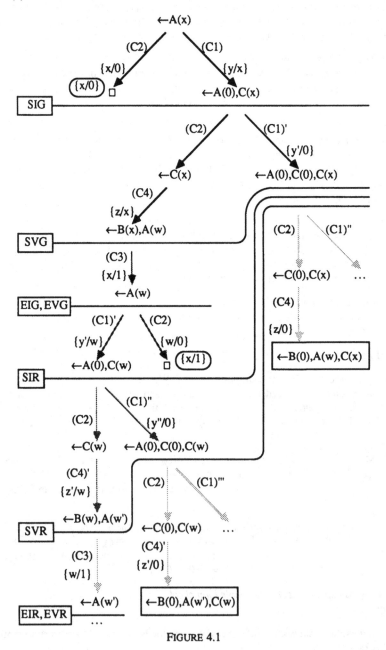

FIGURE 4.1

Figure 4.1 shows an SLD-tree of P∪{G} using the leftmost selection rule. It also shows how this tree is
pruned by different loop checks. First we explain the behaviour of the loop checks with respect to this tree.

Then we shall make some generalizing comments on this behaviour. In this example, the distinction between list versus multiset based loop checks does not play a role.

Starting at the root, the first loop check that prunes the tree is the SIG check. It prunes the goal $\leftarrow A(0),C(x)$, because it contains $A(0)$, an instance of $A(x)$. Following the leftmost infinite branch two steps down, the SVG check prunes the goal $\leftarrow B(x),A(w)$, because it contains $A(w)$, a variant of $A(x)$. One step later, the atom $B(x)$ is resolved, so the EIG and EVG checks prune the goal $\leftarrow A(w)$ for the same reason.

However, the loop checks based on resultants do not yet prune the tree. The computed answer substitution built up so far maps x to x after the first three steps and to 1 later on. This clearly differs from the substitutions $\{x/0\}$ and $\{x/w\}$, which are used to show that $A(0)$ resp. $A(w)$ are an instance resp. a variant of $A(x)$.

Now the derivation repeats itself, but with x replaced by w. Therefore the loop checks based on resultants prune the tree during this second phase, exactly there where the corresponding loop checks based on goals pruned during the first phase. The side branch that is obtained by repeatedly applying the first clause (and corresponding side branches later on) is pruned by the subsumption checks at the goal $\leftarrow A(0),C(0),C(x)$. This goal contains the previous goal $\leftarrow A(0),C(x)$. Therefore both the resultant based and the goal based loop checks prune this goal. In contrast, the equality checks do not prune this infinite branch because the goals in it become longer every derivation step.

The loop checks based on goals all prune out the solution $\{x/1\}$, so they are not sound. Among these loop checks, the SIG check prunes as soon as possible for a weakly sound loop check. Conversely, the SIR check prunes this tree as soon as possible for a shortening loop check. □

We have the following soundness results.

THEOREM 4.5 (Subsumption Soundness).
   i) All subsumption checks based on resultants are shortening. A fortiori they are sound.
   ii) All subsumption checks based on goals are weakly sound. □

We now shift our attention to the completeness issues. From the results of the previous section and the fact that subsumption checks are stronger than the corresponding equality checks we deduce the following result.

COROLLARY 4.6 (Subsumption Completeness 1). *All subsumption checks are complete w.r.t. the leftmost selection rule for function-free restricted programs.*
PROOF. By the Equality Completeness Theorem 3.6 and the Relative Strength Theorem 2.9. □

However, since the subsumption checks are stronger than the corresponding equality checks, we can try to find other classes of programs for which the subsumption checks are complete. We know that the subsumption checks are not complete for all programs, not even in the absence of function symbols. For P = $\{A(x)\leftarrow A(y),S(y,x)\}$, a derivation of $P\cup\{\leftarrow A(x),B(x)\}$ is not pruned by any of the subsumption checks, as was shown in Theorem 2.10.

A close analysis of the proof of this theorem shows that the problem is caused by three 'events' occurring simultaneously, namely:
1. A new variable, y, is introduced by a 'recursive' atom, $A(y)$.
2. There is a relation between this new variable, y, and an old variable, x, namely via the atom $S(y,x)$.
3. The 'recursive' atom $A(y)$ is selected before the 'relating' atom $S(y,x)$.

It appears that, in order to obtain the completeness of the subsumption checks, it is enough to prevent any of these events. Clearly, the use of restricted programs and the leftmost selection rule prevents the third event. We shall now introduce two new classes of programs, preventing the first and the second event, respectively.

DEFINITION 4.7.
A clause C is *non-variable introducing* (in short *nvi*) if every variable that appears in the body of C also appears in the head of C. A program P is *nvi* if every clause in P is nvi. □

DEFINITION 4.8.
A clause C has the *single variable occurrence* property (in short *is svo*) if in the body of C, no variable occurs more than once. A program P is *svo* if every clause in P is svo. □

Clearly, in nvi programs the first event cannot occur, whereas in svo programs the second event is prevented. We now prove that the weakest of the subsumption checks, the SVR_L check, is complete for function-free nvi programs. To this end we use the following (weakened) version of Kruskal's Tree Theorem, called Higman's Lemma. (See [H]; for a formulation of the full version of Kruskal's Tree Theorem, see [D] or [K].) We also need a specialized formalization of the 'being a variant of' relation.

LEMMA 4.9 (Higman's Lemma). *Let* $w_0, w_1, w_2, \ldots$ *be an infinite sequence of (finite) words over a finite alphabet* Σ. *Then for some* i *and* $k > i$, $w_i \sqsubseteq_L w_k$. □

DEFINITION 4.10.
Let X be a set of variables. We define the relation $\sim_X$ on resultants as $R_1 \sim_X R_2$ if for some renaming ρ, $R_1 \rho = R_2$ and for every $x \in X$, $x\rho = x$. Now let G be a goal and let $k \geq 1$. Then the relation $\sim_{X,G,k}$ stands for the restriction of the relation $\sim_X$ to resultants $G_1 \leftarrow G_2$ such that G_1 is an instance of G and $|G_2| \leq k$. □

LEMMA 4.11. *Suppose that the language L has no function symbols and finitely many predicate symbols and constants. Then for every finite set of variables X, every goal G and* $k \geq 1$, *the relation* $\sim_{X,G,k}$ *is an equivalence relation with only finitely many equivalence classes.*
PROOF. The proof is straightforward. □

For a resultant R, the equivalence class of R w.r.t. the relation $\sim_{X,G,k}$ will be denoted as $[R]_{X,G,k}$, or just $[R]$ whenever X, G and k are clear from the context. In order to prove that the SVR_L check is complete for nvi programs, we prove that infinite derivations in which no new variables are introduced are pruned by the SVR_L check. We omit the proof that every derivation of an nvi program (and an arbitrary goal) has a variant that indeed does not introduce new variables.

DEFINITION 4.12.
An SLD-derivation $D = (G_0 \Rightarrow_{C_1,\theta_1} G_1 \Rightarrow \ldots)$ is *non-variable introducing* (in short *nvi*) if $\text{var}(G_0) \supseteq \text{var}(G_1) \supseteq \text{var}(G_2) \supseteq \ldots$. □

LEMMA 4.13. *In the absence of function symbols, every infinite nvi SLD-derivation is pruned by* SVR_L.
PROOF. Let $D = (G_0 \Rightarrow_{C_1,\theta_1} G_1 \Rightarrow \ldots)$ be an infinite nvi SLD-derivation.
We take for Σ the set of equivalence classes of $\sim_{\text{var}(G_0),G_0,1}$ as defined in Definition 4.10. By Lemma 4.11, Σ is finite. To apply Higman's Lemma 4.9 we represent for $j \geq 0$ a goal $G_j = \leftarrow A_{1j}, \ldots, A_{n_jj}$ (or rather the corresponding resultant $G_0 \theta_1 \ldots \theta_j \leftarrow G_j$) as the word $[G_0 \theta_1 \ldots \theta_j \leftarrow A_{1j}], \ldots, [G_0 \theta_1 \ldots \theta_j \leftarrow A_{n_jj}]$ over Σ. The sequence of representations of $G_0, G_1, G_2, \ldots$ yields an infinite sequence of words $w_0, w_1, w_2, \ldots$ over Σ.
Now by Higman's Lemma 4.9, for some j and $k > j$: $[G_0 \theta_1 \ldots \theta_j \leftarrow A_{1j}], \ldots, [G_0 \theta_1 \ldots \theta_j \leftarrow A_{n_jj}] \sqsubseteq_L [G_0 \theta_1 \ldots \theta_k \leftarrow A_{1k}], \ldots, [G_0 \theta_1 \ldots \theta_k \leftarrow A_{n_kk}]$. So by the definition of $\sim_{\text{var}(G_0),G_0,1}$, there exist renamings $\rho_1, \ldots, \rho_{n_j}$ which do not act on the variables in G_0, such that $(G_0 \theta_1 \ldots \theta_j \leftarrow A_{1j})\rho_1, \ldots, (G_0 \theta_1 \ldots \theta_j \leftarrow A_{n_jj})\rho_{n_j} \sqsubseteq_L (G_0 \theta_1 \ldots \theta_k \leftarrow A_{1k}), \ldots, (G_0 \theta_1 \ldots \theta_k \leftarrow A_{n_kk})$.
However, D is nvi, so $\text{var}(G_j) \subseteq \text{var}(G_0)$ and therefore the renamings ρ_h do not act on the atoms A_{ij} of G_j ($1 \leq h, i \leq n_j$). Thus $G_j = G_j \rho_1 \sqsubseteq_L G_k$ and $G_0 \theta_1 \ldots \theta_j \rho_1 = G_0 \theta_1 \ldots \theta_k$. So D is pruned by SVR_L. □

LEMMA 4.14. *Let P be a function-free nvi program and let* G_0 *be a goal in* L_P. *Let D be an infinite SLD-derivation of* $P \cup \{G_0\}$. *Then a variant D' of D is an infinite nvi derivation.* □

Now we have the following completeness results.

THEOREM 4.15. *The* SVR_L *loop check is complete for function-free nvi programs.*
PROOF. By Lemma 4.3, 4.13 and 4.14. □

COROLLARY 4.16 (Subsumption Completeness 2).
    All subsumption checks are complete for function-free nvi programs.
PROOF. By Theorem 4.15 and the Relative Strength Theorem 2.9. □

THEOREM 4.17 (Subsumption Completeness 3).
    All subsumption checks are complete for function-free svo programs.
PROOF. The proof resembles the proof of Lemma 4.13. □

5. Context checks

The problem with the Instance of Atom check is that it does not take into account the context of the atom. This is incorrect: whereas solving ←A(x) or ←A(y) makes no difference, solving ←A(x),B(x) is essentially more difficult than solving ←A(y),B(x). To remedy this problem we should keep track of the links between the variables in the atom and those in the rest of the goal.

Roughly speaking, the IA check prunes a derivation as soon as a goal G_k occurs that contains an instance $A\tau$ of an atom A that occurred in an earlier goal G_i. But when a variable occurs both inside and outside of A in G_i, we should not prune the derivation if this link has been altered. Such a variable x in G_i is substituted by $x\theta_{i+1}\dots\theta_k$ when G_k is reached. Therefore τ and $\theta_{i+1}\dots\theta_k$ should agree on x. This leads us to a loop check introduced by Besnard [B].

DEFINITION 5.1.
The *Variant/Instance Context check on Goals* is the set of SLD-derivations

CVG/CIG = RemSub({ D | D = $(G_0 \Rightarrow_{C_1,\theta_1} G_1 \Rightarrow \dots \Rightarrow G_{k-1} \Rightarrow_{C_k,\theta_k} G_k)$ such that for some i and j,
$0 \le i \le j < k$, there is a renaming / substitution τ such that for some atom A in G_i:
$A\tau$ appears in G_k as the result of resolving $A\theta_{i+1}\dots\theta_j$ in G_j and for every variable
x that occurs both inside and outside of A in G_i, $x\theta_{i+1}\dots\theta_k = x\tau$ }).   □

Besnard describes the condition on the substitutions as follows: 'When $A\tau$ is substituted for $A\theta_{i+1}\dots\theta_k$ in $G_i\theta_{i+1}\dots\theta_k$, this should give an instance of G_i.' We show that this formulation is equivalent to ours. Let $G_i = \leftarrow(A,S)$, that is A occurs in G_i and S is the list of other atoms in G_i. Then $(A\tau,S\theta_{i+1}\dots\theta_k)$ should be an instance of (A,S), say $(A\sigma,S\sigma)$.

Clearly, $x\sigma = - x\tau$ for $x \in var(A)$,
        $- x\theta_{i+1}\dots\theta_k$ for $x \in var(S)$,
so for $x \in var(A) \cap var(S)$, we have $x\tau = x\theta_{i+1}\dots\theta_k$.
The following example clarifies the use of the context checks.

EXAMPLE 5.2.
Let P = { A(0) ←   (C1),
        B(1) ←   (C2),
        A(x) ← A(y)   (C3),
        C ← A(x),B(x)   (C4) },
let G = ← C.
We apply the CIG check on two SLD-trees of P∪{G}, via the leftmost and rightmost selection rule, respectively. This yields the trees in Figure 5.1.

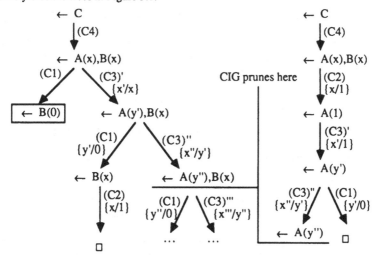

FIGURE 5.1

The goal $G_3 = \leftarrow A(y')$ in the rightmost tree, that was incorrectly pruned by the VA check, is not pruned by the CIG check. Certainly, $A(y')$ is the result of resolving $A(1)$ in G_2, the further instantiated version of $A(x)$ in G_1. But replacing $A(x)\theta_2\theta_3$ by $A(y')$ in $G_1\theta_2\theta_3$ yields $\leftarrow A(y'),B(1)$: *not* an instance of $\leftarrow A(x),B(x)$. □

In Example 4.4, the context checks act exactly in the same way as the corresponding subsumption checks. This shows that CVG and CIG are not sound. Again we can obtain sound, even shortening, versions by using resultants instead of goals.

DEFINITION 5.3.
The *Variant/Instance Context check on Resultants* is the set of SLD-derivations

$\quad$ CVR/CIR = RemSub({ $D \mid D = (G_0 \Rightarrow_{C_1,\theta_1} G_1 \Rightarrow ... \Rightarrow G_{k-1} \Rightarrow_{C_k,\theta_k} G_k)$ such that for some i and j,
$\quad\quad 0 \leq i \leq j < k$, there is a renaming/substitution τ such that $G_0\theta_1...\theta_k = G_0\theta_1...\theta_i\tau$ and for
$\quad\quad$ some atom A in G_i: $A\tau$ appears in G_k as the result of resolving $A\theta_{i+1}...\theta_j$ in G_j and for
$\quad\quad$ every variable x that occurs both inside and outside of A in G_i: $x\theta_{i+1}...\theta_k = x\tau$ }). □

Using Besnard's phrasing, the conditions on the substitutions can be summarized as: 'When $A\tau$ is substituted for $A\theta_{i+1}...\theta_k$ in the resultant $R_i\theta_{i+1}...\theta_k$, this should give an instance of R_i.'

The following theorems state the soundness and completeness results for the context checks.

THEOREM 5.4 (Context Soundness).
i) The context checks based on resultants are shortening. A fortiori they are sound.
ii) The context checks based on goals are weakly sound. □

THEOREM 5.5 (Context Completeness 1).
All context checks are complete w.r.t. the leftmost selection rule for function-free restricted programs.
PROOF. The proof resembles the proof for the equality checks as presented in [ABK], but is more complex. □

THEOREM 5.6 (Context Completeness 2). *All context checks are complete for function-free nvi programs.*
PROOF. The proof resembles the proof of Lemma 4.13, but is more complex. Then Lemma 4.14 can be used. □

References

[ABK] K.R. APT, R.N. BOL and J.W. KLOP, *On the Safe Termination of PROLOG Programs*, in: Proceedings of the Sixth International Conference on Logic Programming, (G. Levi and M. Martelli eds.), MIT Press, Cambridge Massachusetts, 1989, 353-368.

[B] Ph. BESNARD, *On Infinite Loops in Logic Programming*, Internal Report 488, IRISA, Rennes, 1989.

[BW] D.R. BROUGH and A. WALKER, *Some Practical Properties of Logic Programming Interpreters*, in: Proceedings of the International Conference on Fifth Generation Computer Systems, (ICOT eds), 1984, 149-156.

[C] M.A. COVINGTON, *Eliminating Unwanted Loops in PROLOG*, SIGPLAN Notices, Vol. 20, No. 1, 1985, 20-26.

[CL] C.L. CHANG and R.C. LEE, *Symbolic Logic and Mechanical Theorem Proving*, Academic Press, New York, 1973.

[D] N. DERSHOWITZ, *A note on Simplification Orderings*, Information Processing Letters 9, 1979, 212-215.

[vG] A. VAN GELDER, *Efficient Loop Detection in PROLOG using the Tortoise-and-Hare Technique*, J. Logic Programming 4, 1987, 23-31.

[H] G. HIGMAN, *Ordering by divisibility in abstract algebra's*, Proceedings of the London Mathematical Society (3) 2 (7), 1952, 215-221.

[K] J.B. KRUSKAL, *Well-Quasi-Ordering, the Tree Theorem, and Vazsonyi's Conjecture*, Transactions of the AMS 95, 1960, 210-225.

[L] J.W. LLOYD, *Foundations of Logic Programming*, Second Edition, Springer-Verlag, Berlin, 1987.

[LS] J.W. LLOYD and J.C. SHEPHERDSON, *Partial Evaluation in Logic Programming*, Technical Report CS-87-09, Dept. of Computer Science, University of Bristol, 1987.

[PG] D. POOLE and R. GOEBEL, *On Eliminating Loops in PROLOG*, SIGPLAN Notices, Vol. 20, No. 8, 1985, 38-40.

[SGG] D.E. SMITH, M.R. GENESERETH and M.L. GINSBERG, *Controlling Recursive Inference*, Artificial Intelligence 30, 1986, 343-389.

[SI] H. SEKI and H. ITOH, *A Query Evaluation Method for Stratified Programs under the Extended CWA*, in: Proceedings of the Fifth International Conference on Logic Programming, MIT Press, Cambridge Massachusetts, 1988, 195-211.

[V] L. VIEILLE, *Recursive Query Processing: The Power of Logic*, Theoretical Computer Science 68, No. 2, 1989.

Putting Algebraic Components Together:
A Dependent Type Approach (*)

Jean-Claude Reynaud

Laboratoire d'Informatique Fondamentale et d'Intelligence Artificielle
IMAG-CNRS
46, avenue Félix Viallet
38031 GRENOBLE (FRANCE)
e-mail: reynaud@lifia.imag.fr

Abstract

We define a framework based on dependent types for putting algebraic components together. It is defined with freely generated categories. In order to preserve initial, loose and constrained semantics of components, we introduce the notion of SPEC-categories which look like specific finitely co-complete categories. A constructive approach which includes parametrization techniques is used to define new components from basic predefined ones. The problem of the internal coding of external signature symbols is introduced.

0 - Introduction

Nowadays, specification languages are studied, both theoretically and practically. They describe programs at an abstract stage without anticipating (as far as possible) the technical implementation choices. ACTONE [EM85], OBJ2 [FGJM85], PLUSS [Gau84] and LPG [BE86, Re87] designed and implemented at LIFIA, are (among others) such languages. In the early work on algebraic specification, abstract data types were specified by a presentation, i.e. a signature together with a set of axioms. Such an approach is adequate for small specifications, but to build large and complex specifications it is more convenient to put together small specifications in a structured way. In this paper, structuring concepts are put in a unified framework which allows us to deal with them in a coherent syntactic and semantic way.

Recently, Bergstra, Heering and Klint [BHK88] have proposed a Module Algebra which works for algebra based languages such as ASL [Wi86]. Our approach is different in that it follows a category theoretic treatment in the context of initial/free algebra semantics. Moreover, parametrization is handled. Our view of components has been influenced by the work of the "Berlin school" on module specifications [EW86, PP88], but has been modified to take into account interesting aspects of LPG which combine specification and programming features[BR88]. The definition of components constitutes the algebraic level of a specification in LPG. Their combination defines the meta-level of a specification.

Expressions are terms built with components and operators on components. Moreover, a formula like SPEC1=SPEC2 where SPEC1 and SPEC2 are meta-terms must make sense (it may for instance compare two development plans). The defined calculus has to agree with algebraic and meta-level semantics (i.e. meta-terms must define algebraic components according to their free, loose or constrained semantics) and operates in **freely generated categories**. Our approach is in a certain sense very similar to the characterization of the typed λ-calculus by cartesian closed categories [LS86]. But instead of these categories, we use specific finitely co-complete categories. These categories will be called **SPEC-categories**.

It is well known that categories with all finite co-limits provide a natural framework for syntactic aspects of specifications, independently of the underlying used logic [GB85]. To define categories with

----

(*) *Work supported in part by ESPRIT Project 1598 (Replay) and PRC Greco-Programmation*

finite co-limits, we use the dependent types approach suggested by Cartmell [Car78] and called **generalized algebraic logic** in [Poi85]. However, when a loose or constrained semantics is used (i.e. properties in LPG), the power of the generalized algebraic logic is not sufficient to completely define the meta-level system. To deal with interesting models inside the generalized algebraic logic, we introduce the notion of **SPEC-categories**. These categories look rather like **dual** categories of the **Network categories** previously introduced by Cartmell [Cart78]. Semantic properties are introduced at morphism level.

We conclude by giving the analogy between concepts used for components and concepts used for the meta-level. Morphisms will be seen to play a central role in algebraic specification languages, at least from the modularity point of view. Constructions to denote explicitly them must be provided by these languages in order to reach effective modular specifications.

1 - Background and basic ideas

First, let us briefly review the basic notions, definitions, and facts concerning the algebraic formalism and let us fix the notations used in the rest of this paper.

A **signature** S is a triple $<S, \Omega, P>$ where S is a set of sort names, Ω is an indexed (on S^*xS) family of sets $\{\Omega_{us}\}$ $u \in S^*$, $s \in S$ (operator symbols) and P is an S^*-indexed family of sets (predicate symbols).

A **signature morphism** φ: $<S, \Omega, P> \rightarrow <S', \Omega', P'>$ is a triple $<f, g1, g2>$ where f is an application $S \rightarrow S'$, g1 is a family of mappings $g1_{us}$: $\Omega_{us} \rightarrow \Omega' f^*(u)f(s)$
where $f^*(s1, ..., sn)$ denotes $f(s1),...,f(sn)$ and g2 is an S^*-indexed family of functions $g2_u$: $P_u \rightarrow P'f^*(u)$.

To define the notion of **specification**, we have to give the form of the allowed axioms, i.e. to define the underlying logic. For simplicity, these notions will be expressed in the case of equational logic. The generalization to other logics is straightforward and has been done, specially in [BG85].
- Let Σ be an algebraic signature, an equational specification is a pair $SP=<\Sigma,E>$ where E is a set of equations. When E is finite, we say that the specification is finite. In LPG, we consider only finite specifications. A Σ-model A satisfies the specification SP if A satisfies each equation in E.
- Let $SP=<\Sigma,E>$ be a specification. Let E^* be the class of the models which satisfy E and E^{**} the set of equations satisfied by all models in E^*. Then the pair $T=<\Sigma,E^{**}>$ is the equational **theory** specified by SP.

Now, let us define the notion of theory morphism and its restriction to specification morphism as used in LPG:
- A **theory morphism** φ_T: T -> T' is a signature morphism φ: $\Sigma \rightarrow \Sigma'$ such that the forgetful functor $U\varphi$: $Alg_{\Sigma'} \rightarrow Alg_{\Sigma}$ maps each T'-model on a T-model and each T'-morphism on a T-morphism.
The category of theories has theories as objects and theory morphisms as morphisms. This category is denoted Theo. Semantic properties are defined by construction in this category because it is independent of operational properties (i.e. of deductive systems).

Practically, this semantic definition must be converted into an equivalent syntactic one by equations transformations. Let $e=<X,t1,t2>$ be a Σ-equation with the set X of variables. The translated Σ'-equation $\varphi\#(e)=<X^\#,\varphi\#(t1),\varphi\#(t2)>$ is defined as follows:

(a) $X^\#$ variables w.r.t. Σ' defined by $X^\#_{s'}=\cup\varphi(s)=s' X_s$ for all s' in S'

(b) $\varphi\#$ is the unique extension of m: $X \rightarrow U\varphi(T\Sigma'(X^\#))$, i.e. $\varphi\#$: $T\Sigma(X) \rightarrow U\varphi(T\Sigma'(X^\#))$
If open formulae are used, the translation is more complex, see [ST84].

The following theorem gives a necessary and sufficient condition such that a signature morphism associated to a pair of specifications can be extended to a theory morphism:
Theorem: Let $\varphi: \Sigma \rightarrow \Sigma'$ be a signature morphism and $SP=<\Sigma,E>$, $SP'=<\Sigma',E'>$ be specifications. Then φT: $<\Sigma,E^{**}> \rightarrow <\Sigma',E'^{**}>$ is a theory morphism if and only if for all $e \in E$, $\varphi\#(e) \in E'^{**}$.
For the equivalence of the two definitions, see [GB85]. In the rest of this paper , we use the word **specification** for **theory** or **closed presentation**, keeping in mind that LPG works operationally with finite specifications.

LPG works with three levels of logic: equational logic, positive conditional logic, Horn clause logic with equality. Clearly, the meta-level system must abstract from any kind of logic as much as possible. Some answers are given by the theory of the institutions [GB85]. More precisely, the only hypothesis made here is the existence of free functors underlying specification morphisms. In other words, we assume to work in the framework of "liberal institutions" as introduced by Tarlecki [Tar85].

Let I be an institution and $SPEC_I$ its associate category of specifications. The following result holds[GB85]:

***Result1**: $SPEC_I$ has all finite co-limits (is finitely co-complete).*

Intuitively, this result can be interpreted as the possibility to perform syntactic transformations on given specifications to get a new one. These transformations include:
- renaming of signature symbols so that all symbols are distinct.
- introduction of new symbols which denote equivalence classes of distinct symbols.
- translation of equations according to new symbol definitions and specification morphisms.

In this framework, given specifications and morphisms, we can generate new specifications and morphisms in a regular way. In fact, most of operations on components can be defined as specific co-limits. The main operations(in LPG) are: (a) Enrichment and Extension, (b) Hiding (or forgetting), (c) Union, (d) Product, (e) Parametrization and Instantiation, (f) Specific operations on properties (Inherits, Satisfies, Combines). See [BR88].

Let Δ_0 be the category of basic predefined types. Some new specifications are in the closure of Δ_0 by all finite co-limits. Let $Colim(\Delta_0)$ denotes this closure. Intuitively, $Colim(\Delta_0)$ is the smallest co-complete category whose objects include the objects of Δ_0 and whose morphisms include the morphisms of Δ_0. The important point here is that $Colim(\Delta_0)$ is a category freely generated by some co-limit constructors on the category Δ_0. Here, we just give the construction of $Colim(\Delta_0)$. Its justification is developed in the section 2. A+B and Coeq(f,g) denote respectively the co-product of A and B and the co-equalizer of morphisms f and g. i1 and i2 are injections in the co-product and h the co-equalizer morphism.

(1) All objects of Δ_0 are objects (of $Colim(\Delta_0)$).
(2) All morphisms of Δ_0 are morphisms.
(3) If A and B are objects, so is A+B.
(4) For all objects A and B,
      i1(A,B): A->A+B, i2(A,B): B->A+B are morphisms.
(5) For all objects A and B and morphisms f,g: A->B,
     Coeq(f,g) is an object and h: B->Coeq(f,g) is a morphism.
(6) Close morphisms by composition rules in a category.
(7) Impose all equations between morphisms which have to hold in any finitely co-complete category. The equivalence classes of morphisms are morphisms of $Colim(\Delta_0)$.
(8) There are no other objects and morphisms.

Obviously, $Colim(\Delta_0)$ is a subcategory of $SPEC_I$ by the result1. The operations with result in $Colim(\Delta_0)$ are: Union, Product, Instantiation, Combines. This is very similar to compute reachable elements in an algebra by means of composition of operators. From this point of view, these operations can be seen as derived operations w.r.t. co-limit constructors.

The result of the others operations are not in $Colim(\Delta_0)$. The reason is that we define a new specification by adding pieces of syntax (in Enrichments or Extensions) or deleting some syntax (in Hidding). This kind of syntax cannot be reached by colimits computation from Δ_0. Clearly, with these last operations, we move from $Colim(\Delta_0)$ to a new subcategory of $SPEC_I$, say $Colim(\Delta_1)$. This is very similar to non reachable elements in an algebra.

2 - Categories with finite co-limits as free structures

In section 1, we have shown that some operations on specifications can be abstracted as operations in categories with all finite co-limits. In order to define the co-limit constructors, we use the following theorem:

Theorem[McL72]; If a category C has an initial object, co-equalizers for all pairs of morphisms f,g: A->B, and all co-products for all pair of objects, then C has all finite co-limits.

To formalize category theory, we use a dependent type approach suggested by Cartmell [Car78] and called generalized algebraic logic. In a sense, this logic is equal to the essentially algebraic logic previously introduced by Freyd [Frey72] as long as a Set-based model is used in the interpretation. However, the Cartmell paper introduces explicitly the types on the level of the specifications by using a dependent type discipline. This type discipline makes the specifications easier to track. It is known that these logics can be interpreted in categories with finite limits. This result insures that initial/free models always exist and thus an initial/free semantics can be given for the meta-level system. Roughly, generalized algebraic logic works as follow:

• expressions are built from an alphabet which includes a distinguished set of variables. Rules are of the form:

$$\frac{x_1:T1, \dots , x_n:Tn}{C}$$

where x_i are variables. Four kinds of rules are to be distinguished according to the form of the conclusion C:

(T)	T	"T is a type"
(:)	t:T	"t is a term of type T"
(T=)	T1=T2	"the types T1 and T2 are equal"
(=:)	t1=t2 :T	"t1 and t2 are equal as terms of type T"

• theories are specified by a set S of sort symbols and a set Ω of operator symbols such that for each sort and operator symbol there is an introduction rule of the form:

$$\frac{x_1:T1, \dots , x_n:Tn}{s(x1, \dots,x_n)} \qquad \frac{x_1:T1, \dots , x_n:Tn}{\omega(x1, \dots,x_n):T}$$

and by a set of axioms which are either T= or =: rules. The premises $x_1:T1, ..., x_n:Tn$ of a rule must be well-formed. For instance, the variable x_i only occurs in the expressions Tj with $i<j$. Well-formed premises are called contexts.

The definition starts with one sort (or type) SPEC (for the specifications) and types Hom(A,B) for the morphisms from A to B. There exists a type Hom(A,B) for every ordered pair A,B of specifications. This is defined by the two following introduction rules:

[1] $\dfrac{}{\overline{SPEC}}$ [2] $\dfrac{A,B:SPEC}{Hom(A,B)}$

Then, composition and identities are introduced:

[3] $\dfrac{A:SPEC}{id(A):Hom(A,A)}$ [4] $\dfrac{A,B,C:SPEC,\ f:Hom(A,B),\ g:Hom(B,C)}{f{\bullet}g:Hom(A,C)}$

Axioms are defined by =: -rules:

[5] $\dfrac{A,B:SPEC,\ f:Hom(A,B)}{id(A){\bullet}f=f :Hom(A,B)}$ [6] $\dfrac{A,B:SPEC,\ f:Hom(A,B)}{f{\bullet}id(B)=f :Hom(A,B)}$

[7] $\dfrac{A,B,C,D:SPEC,\ f:Hom(A,B),\ g:Hom(B,C),\ h:Hom(C,D)}{(f{\bullet}(g{\bullet}h))=((f{\bullet}g){\bullet}h) :Hom(A,D)}$

The interpretation as a Set-based model consists of a set M_{SPEC} and a family of sets $M_{<x,y>}$ indexed by x,y $\in M_{SPEC}$. The operators are interpreted as morphisms:

$\bullet M : M_{<x,y>} \times M_{<y,z>} \to M_{<x,z>}$ $x,y,z \in M_{SPEC}$

$id(x)^M : 1 \to M_{<x,x>}$

which have to satisfy the axioms. Models are small categories.

Following this approach, we can define initial object, co-products and co-equalizers. This gives us categories with all finite co-limits. Then, specific co-limits like pushouts can be defined as derived operators. For more details, see [Re89].

If one enriches or extends a type, a new object (say O_1) and a new morphism (say m_1) are introduced. This object is non reachable by finite co-limit computation. This is very similar to adding a constant in a signature and equations to define this constant, i.e. we move to another theory. We show that previously computed terms are compatible with extension and enrichment.

Let G_1 be the underlying of Δ_1. Let G_2 be obtained by adding the vertex O_1 and the arrow m_1 to G_1. With respect to finite co-limits, G_i freely generates $Colim(\Delta_i)$, $i=1,2$. The aim is to define a canonical finitely co-continuous functor $h^\$: Colim(\Delta_1) \to Colim(\Delta_2)$ which is intended to determine uniquely this extension. Let AFL be the category of finitely co-complete categories and U be the obvious forgetful functor which considers a category as a graph.

Theorem: *Let $h:G_1 \to G_2$ be an inclusion graph morphism. There exist a unique inclusion graph morphism which extends h w.r.t. the categorical structure and $h=U(h^\$)$.*

Proof: Follows from an adjoint situation. []

3 - Abstracting operations on components

From now on, we suppose that the underlying logic (of the axiomatizations) provides a liberal institution for the specifications in the sense of Tarlecki [Tar85]. The following result holds:

Result2: For every specification morphism φ, there is a functor φ^* (the free functor) left adjoint to the forgetful functor U_φ.

Specifications with loose and constrained semantics are introduced by properties and parameterized components. In these cases, the ordinary categorical framework is too weak to bind the algebraic and meta-level semantics. Therefore we introduce semantic properties in the categorical stucture. The examples developed below enable problems to be pinpointed.

Typically, consider a pushout construction associated to a parameterized data type:

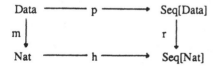

The free functor p* must be persistent, but m* is not persistent in general. This means that some meta-terms are not well-formed w.r.t. algebraic and meta-level semantics, and the operator Push, for instance, must be a partial operator on morphisms. Well-formed terms w.r.t. parameterized data type must be of the form Push(f,g) where f has an underlying free functor.

Moreover, all such pushouts do not agree with practical parametrization. Consider a parameterized data type (say Seq[Data]) enriched by a total order (say <) on Data and with Nat as parameter. We get the following diagram:

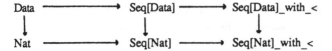

If we instantiate Seq[Data]_with_< with Nat, we want the same result as:
 (1) to instantiate Seq[Data] with Nat
 (2) to enrich Seq[Nat] by the total order < on Nat.
This is exactly a generic enrichment in the LPG language. Let p1 and p2 denote respectively the left and right parametrization. We require:
 (p1*p2)(Nat) =p2(p1(Nat)).
This result is called compatibility of composition with evaluation.

Let Seq[Data]_with_<_= be an enrichment of Seq[Data]_with_<, and let p3 be the obvious associated parametrization. We want:
 (p1*p2*p3)(Nat) = ((p1*p2)*p3)(Nat) = (p1*(p2*p3))(Nat),
i.e. associativity of parametrization.

On the other hand, some data constraints [GB85] must be considered as in the following example (in an LPG-like syntax).
 property EQ **import** BOOL **sorts** t **operators** =:(t,t) -> bool **equations** ...
 end EQ
Clearly, BOOL is used inside the property. The wished assumption is that the carrier "bool" really has two elements:{true, false}. So, the models of the property must be restricted to algebras which have the boolean algebra as a sub-algebra. Now, using EQ, the property partial-order:PO can be defined as:
 property PO **import** BOOL **sorts** t **operators** =, <= :(t,t) -> bool **equations** ...
 satisfies EQ[t **operators** =] **end** PO
Obviously, BOOL must also be preserved in PO. This means that morphisms
 f1: BOOL -> EQ and f2: BOOL -> PO
support data constraints (more precisely TS constraints as defined in [BR88]).
Let g: EQ -> PO be the morphism induced by the clause **satisfies**, we have f2=g*f1 and g propagates the TS constraints.

An essential question is: can such requirements be defined in a categorical framework inside generalized algebraic logic? First note that morphisms are not labelled by a semantic information. To do this, we must introduce sub-types of Hom(A,B):
 -Hom^T(A,B) where morphisms do support a TS constraint.
 -Hom^{-T}(A,B) where morphisms do not support a TS constraint.
 -Hom$^+$(A,B), a sub-type of Hom^T(A,B), where morphisms must have an underlying free persistent functor.
 At first, note that a TS constraint is nothing else than the semantic definition of a theory morphism(possibly in higher order logic, but it is not the matter). Composition of such constraints follows morphisms composition. So, the crucial semantic distinction is between morphisms which have underlying free persistent functors and morphisms which have not them.
 Let Hom$^-$(A,B) be morphisms which do not support these functors. The properties of these sub-types are:
 Hom$^+$(A,B) and Hom$^-$(A,B) must be disjoint, i.e. the diagram:

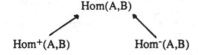

must be interpreted as a co-product in Set-based models. Obviously, this is outside the scope of generalized algebraic logic (remenber that generalized algebraic logic is interpreted in categories with finite limits) and free structures are lost. Such an interpretation is not necessary if we are able to internalize this disjunction (like in order-sorted algebras) i.e.: given an element t in Hom(A,B), we can compute by calculus on the given axioms if t is in Hom$^+$(A,B) or in Hom$^-$(A,B).

But this is not possible. Consider the composition operator, $f \cdot g$, where f is in Hom$^+$ and g in Hom$^-$. $f \cdot g$ may be in Hom$^+$ or in Hom$^-$ and this cannot be decided at the syntactic level because it depends on specific models under consideration. To deal with free structures, we adopt a more restricted point of view. For instance, we do not consider all persistent morphisms, but only those which can be built by composition of persistent morphisms. This seems reasonable because persistent morphisms are used to link data types and for parameterized types (where pushouts are used).

3.1 - SPEC-categories

We introduce the concept of **SPEC-categories**. This concept is influenced by the "Network categories" used by Cartmell [Cart85] as a first step toward a categorical treatment of the type theory of Martin-Löf. Of course, our context is different. Furthermore, dual notions are used and distinguished morphisms are closed by compositions. First, we define D-categories:

Definition: A D-category C consists of a category C and a set of **distinguished morphisms** of C called the D-morphisms with the condition: if f and g are D-morphisms such that dom(f)=codom(g), then h=f·g is a D-morphism.

The closure of distinguished morphisms by composition modelizes closure of persistent morphisms. We denote h$^+$ a distinguished morphism h of C and we define specific pushouts called **D-pushouts**.

Definition: If h:A -> B is a morphism and f$^+$:A -> G is a D-morphism in a D-category C, then a D-pushout consists of an object T of C, a D-morphism f'$^+$: B -> T and a morphism g:G -> T such that the diagram:

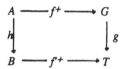

is a pushout square in C.

Intuitively, a "SPEC-category" is a D-category which is finitely co-complete and having consistent specified D-pushouts. Here is the precise definition:

Definition: A "SPEC-category" is a D-category C, finitely co-complete and for every D-morphism f$^+$ and for every morphism h whose domain coincides with that of f$^+$, a D-pushout

A ——————— f$^+$ ————→ B

h $\downarrow$ $\quad\quad\quad$ $\downarrow$ &$^+$1(f$^+$,h)

B ——— &$^+$2(f$^+$,h) ——→ Push$^+$(f,g)   such that the following "coherence" conditions hold:

(a) the pushout of a D-morphism f$^+$ with the identity morphism id(A) is the trivial pushout:

A ——————— f$^+$ ————→ B

id(A) $\downarrow$ $\quad\quad\quad$ $\downarrow$ id(B)

A ——————— f$^+$ ————→ B

b) the specified pushouts fit together as follows. If f$^+$:A -> G , g$^+$:G -> G' are D-morphisms, h:A -> B is a morphism in C, then the pushout

$$A \xrightarrow{\quad f^+ \bullet g^+ \quad} G'$$

$$h \downarrow \qquad\qquad \downarrow \&^+1(f^+\bullet g^+,h) \qquad \textit{is exactly the pushout diagram that results}$$

$$B \xrightarrow{\&^+2(f^+\bullet g^+,h)} Push^+(f^+\bullet g^+,h) \qquad \textit{from fitting together the individual pushouts:}$$

$$A \xrightarrow{\quad f^+ \quad} G \qquad\qquad G \xrightarrow{\quad g^+ \quad} G'$$

$$h \downarrow \quad \downarrow \&^+1(f^+,h) \qquad \&^+1(f^+,h) \qquad\qquad \downarrow \&^+1(g^+,\&1(f^+,h))$$

$$B \xrightarrow{\&^+2(f^+,h)} Push^+(f^+,h) \qquad Push^+(f^+,h) \xrightarrow{\&^+2(g^+,\&1(f+,h))} Push^+(g^+,\&1(f^+,h))$$

Push$^+$, $\&^+1$, $\&^+2$ are operators in SPEC-category structures. Let G_Δ be a graph with a distinguished set of arrows. Clearly, G_Δ freely generates a D-category Δ. This category freely generates a SPEC-category Δ_{SPEC}. These operations can be described in generalized algebraic logic as follows. Distinguished morphisms are represented by the sub-types Hom$^+$(A,B) of Hom(A,B). Distinguished pushouts are built with operators $\&^+1$, $\&^+2$ and Push$^+$. They are defined like in the section 2 (but with sub-types Hom$^+$) and the following rules which define the coherence conditions have to be added:

$$\frac{A,B:SPEC,\ f^+:Hom^+(A,B)}{}$$
Push$^+$(f$^+$,id(A))=B :SPEC,
$\&^+1$(f$^+$,id(A))=id(B) :Hom$^+$(B,B),
$\&^+2$(f$^+$,id(A))=f$^+$:Hom$^+$(A,B)

$$\underline{A,B,G,G':SPEC,\ h:Hom(A,B),\ f^+:Hom^+(A,G),\ g^+:Hom^+(G,G')}$$
Push$^+$(f$^+$.g$^+$,h)=Push$^+$(g$^+$,$\&^+1$(f$^+$,h)) :SPEC,
$\&^+1$(f$^+$.g$^+$,h)=$\&^+1$(g$^+$,$\&^+1$(f$^+$,h))   :Hom(G',Push$^+$(f$^+$.g$^+$,h)),
$\&^+2$(f$^+$.g$^+$,h)=$\&^+2$(f$^+$,h).$\&^+2$(g$^+$,$\&^+1$(f$^+$,h)) :Hom$^+$(B,Push$^+$(f$^+$.g$^+$,h))

Obviously, distinguished pushouts are introduced to modelize parameterized data types. But what do the coherence conditions mean? From a specification point of view, condition (a) modelizes extensions and enrichments of data types which are degenerated cases of parametrization. The coherence condition (b) modelizes the associativity of parametrization and its compatibility with evaluation. SPEC-categories provide a natural framework to deal with operations on algebraic components when a loose semantics is used.

3.2 - Models of SPEC-categories

Let SPEC$_I$ be the category of specifications in a given liberal institution I. We have:

Theorem: SPEC$_I$ is a SPEC-category.

Proof: Take injective morphisms in SPEC$_I$ which have strongly free persistent functors as distinguished morphisms and assume the construction in [EM85] for distinguished pushouts.

In ΔSPEC, objects are (names of) specifications and morphisms are (names of) specification morphisms. All are freely generated by G_Δ. The subcategories of SPEC$_I$ closed by SPEC operations and isomorphic to Δ_{SPEC} (as SPEC-categories) are the semantic domains for a given liberal institution I.

However, a model of Δ_{SPEC} must be a real environment for a given user, i.e. for each object of Δ_{SPEC}, we assign an effective specification and for each morphism an effective specification morphism in SPEC$_I$ so that the categorical structure is preserved. Here, we define the notion of model in a given liberal institution I.

Definition: *Let I be a given liberal institution. A model of Δ_{SPEC} in I is an **injective structure-preserving functor** J_I: Δ_{SPEC} -> $SPEC_I$.*

By a structure-preserving functor, we mean a functor which preserves co-limits, maps distinguished morphisms in Δ_{SPEC} on strongly persistent morphisms in $SPEC_I$ and distinguished pushouts on distinguished pushouts in $SPEC_I$. The injectivity of J_I means that a semantic object is denoted by only one syntactic object.

We also define model morphisms by:

Definition: *Let J_I and J_I' be models. A morphism between J_I and J_I' is a natural transformation μ: J_I => J_I' .*

Model morphisms characterize environment morphisms in $SPEC_I$. The situation is as follow:

(1) Let J(1) and J(2) be two naturally isomorphic models. From a meta-level point of view, we cannot distinguished between the two environments. So, from a practical point of view, we must define canonical environments (i.e. the active environments effectively in the system)

(2) There is a morphism μ: J(1) -> J(2). Intuitively, from the definition of a natural transformation, we have a "regular translation" from the environment defined by J(1) to the environment defined by J(2) and preserving the distinguished structure. Clearly, theorems in J(1) can be used in J(2) (translated by the components of the natural transformation). Types enrichments, relations between properties induce such morphisms.

(3) There is no morphism between J(1) and J(2). This means that there is no general relation between the two environments (except the meta-structure).

Isomorphic models can be identically represented if canonical models exist. From a practical point of view, the problem is to transform external user symbols into internal concrete symbols in a given environment, so that such canonical models can be defined. This includes the problem of what is really shared by two given components. Due to lack of space, we cannot deal with this problem here. But the key point is to use meta-terms to denote internal concrete symbols.

4 - Conclusion

The reader has probably noticed that the key point —as in algebraic programming— is the use of free structures. Here, we give some analogies between algebraic specifications and meta-level specifications.

	Algebraic level	**Meta-level**
Logic	-equational logic -positive conditional logic	-generalized algebraic logic
Models	-algebras	-SPEC-categories
Morphisms	-homomorphisms of algebras	-structure preserving functors between SPEC-categories.
Constants (0-ary constructors)	-constants in algebraic signatures	-Specification and morphism names in libraries
n-ary constructors	-constructor operators	-co-products, co-equalizers -constructors for distinguished pushouts.
Formulae	-equational axioms -conditional axioms	-axioms in generalized algebraic logic
Initial semantics	-freely generated algebras	-freely generated SPEC-categories

Loose semantics   -potential realization   -potential environments

    In a constructive logic framework, basic components play a role similar to basic types in typed λ-calculus where terms (or proofs) are derived by freely generating a cartesian closed category. But in this case, we freely generate a SPEC-category. Note that the types (of components and morphisms) are derived by using a dependent type discipline (à la Martin-Löf) which probably allows us to use existing type systems for these constructions. As in the usual Curry-Howard isomorphism, a meta-term can be viewed as a proof that some specification has been derived. An important point is that specification of components (description of the semantic behaviour) and programming with components (constructive calculus) are well distinguished by this two level approach.

References

[BE86] D. Bert, R. Echahed, *Design and implementation of a generic, logic and functional programming language*, LNCS 213, pp.119-132 (1986).

[BHK88] Bergstra and al., *Module Algebra*, Report P8823. University of Amsterdam, (Nov. 1988).

[BR88] D.Bert, J.C. Reynaud, *Primitives for Algebraic Components*,
    Esprit Project 1598, Replay/T2.3/I (July 1988).

[Cart78] J. Cartmell, *Generalized Algebraic Theories and Contextual Categories*,
    PhD. Thesis, Oxford (1978).

[Cart85] J. Cartmell, *Formalizing the Network and Hierarchical Data Models. An Application of categorical logic.* Symposium on Category Theory and Computer Science, LNCS 283

[EM85] H. Ehrig, B. Mahr, *Fundamentals of algebraic specification 1 : Equations and initial semantics*,
    Springer, (1985).

[EW86] H. Ehrig, H. Weber, *Programming in the large with algebraic module specifications*,
    IFIP-Congress (1986)

[FGJM85] K.Futatsugi, J.A. Goguen, J.P.Jouannaud, J. Meseguer, *Principles of OBJ2*,
    Proc. of the 12th ACM Symposium on Principles of Programming Languages, pp.52-66 (1985)

[Frey72] P. Freyd, *Aspects of Topoi*, Bull. Austral. Math. Soc. 7,1972.

[Gau84] M.C. Gaudel, *A first introduction to PLUSS*. Université Paris Sud, Orsay Techn. Rep., 1984.

[GB85] J.A. Goguen, R.M.Burstall, *Introducing institutions*,
    Proc. Logics of Programming Workshop LNCS 164, pp.221-256 (1984).

[LS86] J. Lambek, P.J. Scott, *Introduction to higher order categorical logic*,
    Cambridge University Press 1986.

[McL72] S. MacLane, *Categories for the working mathematician*,
    Springer 1972.

[Poi85] A.Poigne, *Algebra Categorically*,
    Symposium on Category Theory and Computer Science, LNCS 283, pp.76-102.

[PP88] F.Parisi-Presicce, *Product and iteration of module specifications*,
    CAAP'88, LNCS 299 (1988)

[Re87] J.C. Reynaud, *Semantique de LPG*,
    RR 651 IMAG, 56 LIFIA (1987)

[Re89] J.C. Reynaud, *A calculus for putting Algebraic Components Together.*
    REPLAY/T2.3/F, ESPRIT Project 1598(REPLAY), Sept. 1989.

[ST84] D.T. Sannella, A. Tarlecki, *Building specifications in an arbitrary institution*,
    Proc. of the Intl. Symp. on Semantics of Data Types, LNCS 173, Springer(1984).

[Tar85] A. Tarlecki, *On the existence of free models in abstract algebraic institutions*,
    TCS 37 (1985) pp.269-304.

[Wi86] M. Wirsing, *Structured algebraic specifications: a kernel language.*
    TCS 42, 1986, 123-249.

The Use of Proof Plans in Formal Methods

Alan Bundy
Department of Artificial Intelligence,
University of Edimburg, Scotland

1. Introduction

Proof plans is a new AI technique for controlling the search that arises in automatic theorem proving. We have applied it to the satisfaction of the proof obligations arising from the use of formal methods in software engineering. We first describe the particular formal methods technique we have adopted as a vehicle and then describe how proof plans are used within this technique.

2. Program Synthesis using Theorem Proving

We are concerned with the synthesis of logic/functional programs in the Nuprl style, [Constable et al 86]. The basic idea is to start with a logical specification, *spec(Inputs, Output)* between the inputs to and outputs from a program, and then prove a conjecture of the form:

$$\forall\ Inputs,\ \exists\ Output.spec(Input,Output)$$

in a constructive logic. Because a constructive logic is used, any proof of this conjecture must implicity encode a program, prog(Inputs), which obeys the specifications, i.e. for which:

$$\forall\ Inputs.spec(Input,prog(Input))$$

Nuprl uses a logic based on Martin Lof Intuitionist Type Theory, [Martin-Lof 79]. This makes trivial the extraction of prog from the proof, since each rule of inference of the logic has an associated program construction step. The program is, thus, built as a side effect of constructing the proof. There is a direct relation between each proof step and the corresponding part of the program, for instance, proofs by mathematical induction create recursive programs. We are, therefore, particularly interested in inductive proofs. The program is a logic/functional program in the Type Theory logic. As a programming language, this logic is higher order with very flexible types. Type checking is done at synthesis time.

Naturally the theorem proving required to do this synthesis is combinatorially explosive - in fact, the Type Theory is more badly behaved in this respect than resolution theorem provers. For instance, it has a potentially infinite set of rules of inference, some of which have infinite branching rates. It is an open question as to whether this bad behaviour can be tamed with throwing away the benefits of the logic from a program synthesis point of view. The Nuprl solution to this problem is to control the search by a combination of user interaction and built-in simplification routines. The latter are implemented as tactics: ML programs which call various rules of inference when executed, cf. LCF. The user can also use custom built tactics to encode a sequence of rule applications.

We have built our own version of Nuprl, which we call Oyster, [Horn 88]. It differs from Nuprl in being implemented in Prolog rather than Lisp, being considerably smaller and cheaper to run, and using Prolog rather than ML as the tactic language. We have found that the pattern directed invocation of Prolog makes the writing of tactics much simpler and clearer than with ML.

3. Proof Plans to Control Search

Our work has been to try to automate the search process to a much greater extent than in Nuprl or similar systems. We have adapted the inductive proof heuristics of Boyer and Moore, [Boyer & Moore 79], to the Oyster system, and implemented them as tactics. These tactics have been successfully tested on a number of standard theorems from the literature, [Bundy et al 89a].

In Boyer and Moore's system, their heuristics are applied in a fixed order. This makes their system brittle. We have been developing a technique, called proof plans, for applying the tactics in a more flexible manner. Each tactic is partially specified in a method. Our Clam plan formation program, [van Harmelen 89], is then used to build a proof plan especially adapted to the current conjecture. This has give our system improved performance over the Boyer-Moore system.

We have also analysed the Boyer-Moore heuristics and rationally reconstructed the reasoning behind their design and order. This analysis has been captured in a tactic, the induction strategy, which is at a higher level of abstraction than any of their heurisitcs, and is extremely successful in proving theorems. the analysis has also enabled us to generalise some of the heuristics and add new ones, extending the power of the system. For instance we can now prove existential theorems (Boyer and Moore are restricted to universal quantification) and use inductive schenmnata that are not suggested by recursions in the original conjecture, [Bundy et al 89b].

References

[Boyer & Moore 79] R.S. Boyer and J.S. Moore. A Computational Logic. Academic Press, 1979.ACM monograph series.

[Bundy et al 89a] A. Bundy, F. van Harmelen, J. Hesketh, and A. Smaill. Experiments with proof plans for induction. Journal of Automated Reasoning, 1989. In press. Earlier version available from Edinburgh as Research Paper No 413.

[Bundy et al 89b] A. Bundy, F. van Harmelen, J. Hesketh, A. Smaill, and A. Stevens. A rational reconstruction and extension of recursion analysis. In N.S. Sridharan, editor, Proceedings of the Eleventh International Joint Conference on Artificial Intelligence, pages 359-365, Morgan Kaufmann, 1989. Available from Edinburgh as Research Paper 419.

[Constable et al 86] R.L. Constable, S.F. Allen, H.M. Bromley, et al. Implementing Mathematics with the Nuprl Proof Development System., Prentice Hall, 1986.

[Horn 88] C.Horn. The Nuprl Proof Development System. Working Edinburgh version of Nuprl has been renamed Oyster.

[Martin-Lof 79] Per Martin-Lof. Constructive mathematics and computer programming. In 6th International Congress for Logic, Methodology and Philosophy of Science, pages 153-175, Hanover, August 1979. Published by North Holland, Amsterdam. 1982.

[van Harmelen 89] F. van Harmelen. The CLAM Proof Planner, User Manual and Programmer Manual. Technical Paper TP-4, Dept. of Artificial Intelligence, Edinburgh, 1989.

A Prolog Technology Theorem Prover:
A New Exposition and Implementation in Prolog[1]

Mark E. Stickel
Artificial Intelligence Center
SRI International
Menlo Park, California 94025

Abstract

A Prolog technology theorem prover (PTTP) is an extension of Prolog that is complete for the full first-order predicate calculus. It differs from Prolog in its use of unification with the occurs check for soundness, depth-first iterative-deepening search instead of unbounded depth-first search to make the search strategy complete, and the model elimination reduction rule that is added to Prolog inferences to make the inference system complete. This paper describes a new Prolog-based implementation of PTTP. It uses three compile-time transformations to translate formulas into Prolog clauses that directly execute, with the support of a few run-time predicates, the model elimination procedure with depth-first iterative-deepening search and unification with the occurs check. Its high performance exceeds that of Prolog-based PTTP interpreters, and it is more concise and readable than the earlier Lisp-based compiler, which makes it superior for expository purposes. Examples of inputs and outputs of the compile-time transformations provide an easy and quite precise way to explain how PTTP works. This Prolog-based version makes it easier to incorporate PTTP theorem-proving ideas into Prolog programs. Some suggestions are made on extensions to Prolog that could be used to improve PTTP's performance.

1 Introduction

A Prolog technology theorem prover (PTTP)[2] is an extension of Prolog that is complete for the full first-order predicate calculus [17]. We present here a new exposition and implementation of PTTP that uses Prolog to explain and implement PTTP.

PTTP is characterized by the use of sound unification with the occurs check where necessary, the complete model elimination inference procedure rather than just Prolog inference, and the depth-first iterative-deepening search procedure rather than unbounded depth-first search. These particular inference and search methods are used instead of other complete methods because they can be implemented using basically the same implementation ideas, including compilation, that enable Prolog's very high inference rate. Other inference systems and search methods may explore radically different and smaller search spaces than PTTP, but PTTP's design enables it to come closer to matching Prolog's inference rate.

Several PTTP-like systems have been implemented:

- A Lisp-based interpreter [15].

- A Lisp-based compiler [17].

---

[1]This research was supported by the National Science Foundation under Grant CCR-8611116. The views and conclusions contained herein are those of the author and should not be interpreted as necessarily representing the official policies, either expressed or implied, of the National Science Foundation or the United States government.

[2]The name connotes two things: PTTP employs highly efficient *Prolog technology* in its implementation. It is also a *technology theorem prover* in the same way that TECH was a *technology chess program* [5], i.e., it is a "brute force" theorem prover that relies less on detailed analysis than on high-speed execution of small logical steps and whose capabilities will increase as Prolog machine technology progresses.

- F-Prolog, a Prolog-based interpreter [20].

- Expert Thinker, a commercial version of F-Prolog [13].

- Parthenon [3] and METEOR [2], parallel implementations based on the Warren abstract machine and SRI model for OR-parallel execution of Prolog.

- SETHEO and PARTHEO, sequential and parallel Warren abstract machine implementations inspired by the connection method with input-formula preprocessing and additional inference and search strategy options [8].

Several other deduction systems developed in recent years also use features associated with PTTP, such as compiled inference operations for the full first-order predicate calculus, especially for linear strategies, and the use of depth-first iterative-deepening search in deduction.

We present here a new implementation of Prolog using a Prolog-based compiler. First-order predicate calculus formulas are translated by the PTTP compiler, written in Prolog, to Prolog clauses that are compiled by the Prolog compiler and will then directly execute the PTTP inference and search procedure.

The new implementation has several advantages. First, its performance is high, although still not equal to that of the Lisp-based compiler implementation.

Second, the Prolog-based PTTP should generally produce much shorter object code than our Lisp-based compiler and compilation speed should also be improved. The Prolog clauses produced by the PTTP compiler typically will be compiled by the Prolog compiler to a concise abstract-machine target language. Our Lisp-based PTTP compiled its input to Lisp code that was then compiled to machine code rather than a Prolog abstract-machine language, so object code could be quite large and compilation time long.

The code for the Prolog-based version is also shorter and more perspicuous than that for the Lisp-based version. Modifiability is enhanced. Elements of PTTP, like logical variables and backtracking, that are basic features of Prolog had to be explicitly handled in the Lisp version of the PTTP compiler. In effect, we had to write a PTTP-to-Prolog compiler *and* a Prolog-to-Lisp compiler for the Lisp version; for this Prolog-based version, only the former is necessary.

The Prolog-based version is also more readily usable by those who would like to incorporate PTTP reasoning for some tasks into larger logic programs written in Prolog. Since the output of this PTTP-to-Prolog compiler is pure Prolog code, it is easy to achieve parallel execution of PTTP inference by simply executing the code on any parallel implementation of standard, sequential Prolog.

Finally, we feel that this version of PTTP in Prolog has pedagogical value. This description, and the code for the PTTP-to-Prolog compiler, explain clearly and precisely the principles of a Prolog technology theorem prover. Example inputs and outputs of the transformations used by PTTP clearly describe PTTP's operation.

We illustrate by example PTTP's recipe for transforming first-order predicate calculus formulas to Prolog clauses that, when executed, perform the complete model elimination theorem-proving procedure on the formulas.

First, first-order predicate calculus formulas are translated to Prolog clauses and their contra-positives.

The recipe then specifies application of

- A compile-time transformation for sound unification that linearizes clause heads and moves unification operations that require the occurs check into the body of the clause where they are performed by a new predicate that performs sound unification with the occurs check.

- A compile-time transformation for complete depth-bounded search that adds extra arguments for the input and output depth bounds to each predicate and adds depth-bound test and decrement operations to the clause bodies.

- A compile-time transformation for complete model elimination inference that adds an extra argument for the list of ancestor goals to each predicate and adds ancestor-list update operations to the clause bodies; additional clauses are added to perform the model elimination pruning and reduction operations.

The recipe also requires run-time support in the form of

- The unify predicate that unifies its arguments soundly with the occurs check.

- The search predicate that controls iterative-deepening search's sequence of bounded depth-first searches.

- The identical_member and unifiable_member predicates that determine if a literal is identical to or unifiable with members of the ancestor list.

A technical report contains full source code and sample output for PTTP in Prolog [18].

2 Sound Unification

The first obstacle to general-purpose theorem proving that must be overcome is Prolog's use of unification without the occurs check. For reasons of efficiency, many implementations of Prolog do not check whether a variable is being bound to a term that contains that same variable. This can result in unsound or even nonterminating unification. The following Prolog programs "prove" that there is a number that is less than itself and that in a group $a \circ z = z$ for some z.[3]

```
X<(X+1).                          p(X,Y,f(X,Y)).
:- Y<Y.                           :- p(a,Z,Z).
```

The invalid results rely upon the creation of circular bindings for variables during unification.

Although applying the occurs check in logic programming can be quite costly, it is less likely to be too expensive in theorem proving, since the huge terms sometimes generated in logic programming are less likely to appear in theorem proving.

Although it is easy to write a Prolog predicate unify that performs sound unification with the occurs check [11,14], the trick is to invoke this unification algorithm instead of Prolog's whenever necessary during the unification of a goal and the head of a clause.

It has often been noted that one case in which the occurs check is certain to be unnecessary is in the unification of a pair of terms with no variables in common (as is the case of Prolog goals and clause heads) provided at least one of the terms has no repeated variables (terms without repeated variables are called *linear*).

Based on the existence of a Prolog predicate unify that performs sound unification with the occurs check and the observation that the occurs check is unnecessary if the clause head is linear, there is an elegant method of transforming clauses to isolate parts that may require unification with the occurs check [11,12]. Repeated occurrences of variables are replaced by new variables to make the clause head linear. Unifying the clause head with a goal can then proceed without the occurs check and will not create any circular bindings. The new variables in the transformed clause head are then unified with the original variables by sound unification with the occurs check in the transformed clause body.

In the examples above, the clauses

```
X<(X+1).                          p(X,Y,f(X,Y)).
```

---

[3]The literal p(X,Y,Z) denotes $x \circ y = z$, where o is the group multiplication operation. The literal p(X,Y,f(X,Y)) states that every X and Y have a product f(X,Y).

are replaced by the clauses

```
X<(X1+1) :-                             p(X,Y,f(X1,Y1)) :-
    unify(X,X1).                            unify(X,X1),
                                            unify(Y,Y1).
```

in which the occurs check needs to be performed only during the calls to unify in the body.

3 Complete Search Strategy

Even for Horn clauses, Prolog is unsatisfactory as a theorem prover because many theorem-proving problems cannot be solved using Prolog's unbounded depth-first search strategy.

A simple solution to this problem is to replace Prolog's unbounded depth-first search strategy with bounded depth-first search. Backtracking when reaching the depth bound would cause the entire search space, up to a specified depth, to be searched completely. A complete search strategy could perform a sequence of bounded depth-first searches: first one tries to find a proof with depth 1, then depth 2, and so on, until a proof is found. This is called *depth-first iterative-deepening search* [6]. The effect is similar to breadth-first search except that results from earlier levels are recomputed rather than stored. The lower storage requirements and greater efficiency of the stack-based representation for derived clauses used in depth-first search compensate for the recomputation cost.

Because the size of the search space grows exponentially as the depth bound is increased, the number of recomputed results is not excessive. In particular, depth-first iterative-deepening search performs only about $\frac{b}{b-1}$ times as many operations as breadth-first search, where b is the branching factor [19] (for $b = 1$, when there is no branching, breadth-first search is $O(n)$ and depth-first iterative-deepening search is $O(n^2)$, where n is the depth). Korf [6] has shown that depth-first iterative-deepening search is asymptotically optimal among brute-force search strategies in terms of solution length, space, and time: it always finds a shortest solution; the amount of space required is proportional to the depth; and, although the amount of time required is exponential, this is the case for all brute-force search strategies; in general, it is still only a constant factor more expensive than breadth-first search.

Consider the following fragment of a set of axioms of group theory:

```
p(e,X,X).                               % left identity
p(U,Z,W) :- p(X,Y,U), p(Y,Z,V), p(X,V,W).  % associativity clause (1 of 2)
```

Use of these clauses can be controlled during depth-first iterative-deepening search by adding extra arguments for the depth bound before and after the literal is proved. The depth bound is reduced by the size of the clause body at each inference step and the computation is allowed to proceed only if the depth bound remains nonnegative. The transformed clauses are:

```
p(e,X,X,Depth,Depth).
p(U,Z,W,DepthIn,DepthOut) :-
    DepthIn >= 3, Depth1 is DepthIn - 3,
    p(X,Y,U,Depth1,Depth2), p(Y,Z,V,Depth2,Depth3), p(X,V,W,Depth3,DepthOut).
```

A "driver" predicate search can be written easily to try to prove its goal argument with progressively greater depth bounds within specified limits. The execution of search(Goal,Max,Min, Inc) attempts to solve Goal by a sequence of bounded depth-first searches that allow at least Min and at most Max subgoals, incrementing by Inc between searches. Max can be specified to bound the total search effort. It can also be reduced by specifying Min when it is known that no solution can be found with fewer than Min subgoals. When the branching factor is small and there are few new inferences for each additional level of search, total search effort may be reduced by skipping some levels by specifying an Inc value greater than one.

The **search** predicate succeeds for each solution it discovers. Backtracking into **search** continues the search for additional solutions. When only a single solution (proof) is needed, the **search** call can be followed by a cut operation to terminate further attempts to find a solution.

4 Complete Inference System

Prolog's inference system is often described in terms of the reduction of the initial list of literals in the query to the empty list by a sequence of Prolog inference steps. Each step matches the leftmost literal in the list with the head of a clause, eliminates the leftmost literal, and adds the body of the clause to the beginning of the list. If the list of literals is :- q1,...,qn then the lists

```
:- q2,...,qn
:- p1,...,pm,q2,...,qn
```

can be derived by resolution with the clauses q1 and q1 :- p1,...,pm.

Prolog's incompleteness for non-Horn clauses can be demonstrated by its failure to prove Q from $P \vee Q$ and $\neg P \vee Q$. All the contrapositive clauses of $P \vee Q$ and $\neg P \vee Q$[4]

```
q :- not_p.
p :- not_q.
q :- p.
not_p :- not_q.
```

are insufficient to reduce :- q to the empty list of literals.

Prolog employs the *input* restriction of resolution; derived clauses are allowed to be resolved only with input clauses. Although input resolution is complete for Horn clauses, it is incomplete in general. However, the *linear* restriction of resolution, in which derived clauses can be resolved with their own ancestor clauses or with input clauses, is complete in general.

The *model elimination (ME)* procedure [9,10] can be viewed as very convenient and efficient way to implement linear resolution. It is a complete inference system for non-Horn as well as Horn sets of clauses.[5] The model elimination procedure does not eliminate the leftmost literal in the resulting list of literals as Prolog does, but instead retains it as a *framed literal*:

```
:- [q1],q2,...,qn
:- p1,...,pm,[q1],q2,...,qn
```

The literal q1 is framed (and shown as [q1] to signify its framed status); the literals p1,...,pm are unframed; the literals q2,...,qn are framed or unframed as they were in :- q1,...,qn. Leftmost framed literals are removed immediately.

The *ME reduction* inference rule uses framed literals to eliminate complementary literals:

```
:- q2,...,qn
```

can be derived from :- q1,...,[qi],...,qn if q1 is complementary to some framed literal qi.

This inference rule makes it possible to prove Q from $P \vee Q$ and $\neg P \vee Q$:

---

[4]The complement of literal p is not_p. Rather than use a negation operator, we use pairs of predicate names p and not_p, q and not_q, etc.

[5]The *SL resolution* procedure [7] is similar; the principal difference is its need for an additional factoring operation. Prolog's inference system is often referred to as *SLD resolution* (SL resolution for definite, i.e., Horn, clauses).

```
:- q                    % initial goal
:- p,[q]                % resolve with q :- p
:- not_q,[p],[q]        % resolve with p :- not_q
:- [p],[q]              % use ME reduction rule
:-                      % delete leftmost framed literals
```

The ME reduction rule employs reasoning by contradiction. If, as in the above proof, in trying to prove Q, we discover that Q is true if P is true and also that P is true if $\neg Q$ is true, then Q must be true. The rationale is that Q is either true or false; if we assume that Q is false, then P must be true, and hence Q must also be true, which is a contradiction; therefore, the hypothesis that Q is false must be wrong and Q must be true.

The list of framed literals to the right of a literal is just the list of that goal's ancestors. The list of ancestor literals can be passed in an extra argument position; the current goal can be added to the front of the list and the new list passed to subgoals in nonunit clause bodies.

The clauses

```
p(e,X,X).
p(U,Z,W) :- p(X,Y,U), p(Y,Z,V), p(X,V,W).
```

can be transformed to

```
p(e,X,X,Ancestors).
p(U,Z,W,Ancestors) :-
    NewAncestors = [p(U,Z,W) | Ancestors],
    p(X,Y,U,NewAncestors), p(Y,Z,V,NewAncestors), p(X,V,W,NewAncestors).
```

An extra clause that performs the ME reduction operation is included in each transformed procedure:

```
p(X,Y,Z,Ancestors) :- unifiable_member(not_p(X,Y,Z),Ancestors).
```

This clause succeeds each time the literal p(X,Y,Z) can be made complementary to an ancestor literal. The unifiable_member predicate is a membership-testing predicate that uses sound unification with the occurs check.

In addition, an extra clause at the beginning of each procedure that eliminates some cases of looping has been found to be cost-effective. The model elimination procedure remains complete with this search-space pruning by identical ancestor operation.

```
p(X,Y,Z,Ancestors) :- identical_member(p(X,Y,Z),Ancestors), !, fail.
```

The identical_member predicate tests whether a literal is identical (by using the == predicate) to a literal in the list.

5 Evaluation

The cost of PTTP compared to Prolog in terms of size of the input can be determined by

- A Prolog clause is required for each literal (all contrapositives are required).

- Two clauses are added to each procedure: one for the model elimination reduction operation and one for the identical-ancestor pruning operation.

- An extra unify literal is added to the body of a clause for each repeated occurrence of a variable in the head of the clause.

Example	Number of Clauses	Depth of Proof	Lisp Implementation		Prolog Implementation	
			Number of Inferences	Run Time (sec)	Number of Inferences	Run Time (sec)
1	5	4	5	0.002	5	0.005
2	7	10	1,589	0.373	1,938	0.637
3	5	10	206	0.046	264	0.095
4	5	7	26	0.005	32	0.010
5	9	4	4	0.001	4	0.002
6	9	7	26	0.005	32	0.010
7	7	6	24	0.004	24	0.006
8	9	13	3,104	0.652	3,830	2.522
9	8	10	163	0.027	191	0.135
Total			5,147	1.115	6,320	3.422

Table 1: PTTP Performance on Chang and Lee Examples

- Three extra literals are added to the body of each nonunit clause: one to test the depth bound, one to decrement it, and one to save the head on the list of ancestor goals.

- Two extra arguments are added to each literal for the input and output depth bounds.

- One (or more—our implementation uses two) extra argument is added to each literal for the list of ancestor goals.

- Additional arguments and literals may optionally be added to compute the information needed to print the proof after it is found.

Table 1 gives results for the examples that appear in Chang and Lee [4], pp. 298–305, for both the Lisp implementation [17] and this Prolog implementation of PTTP running on a Symbolics 3600 with IFU. The Prolog implementation performs one thousand to three thousand model elimination inferences per second. This is a high inference rate for a theorem prover, although it is low for Prolog. The Lisp implementation of PTTP is somewhat more efficient.

We examine here some sources of inefficiency in this Prolog implementation of PTTP. Because many of these are inherent limitations of Prolog, this discussion can be taken as identifying some problems with Prolog that inhibit the development of the highest possible performance PTTP in Prolog and arguing for particular extensions to Prolog. Similar extensions exist in some Prolog implementations. In particular, there have been many proposed schemes for destructive assignment operations on data structures or global variables, though none has become standard or widely available.

5.1 Inefficiency of Sound Unification

The sound unification procedure with the occurs check is written in Prolog. For Prolog implementations that allow predicates programmed in lower-level languages, it should be possible to substantially speed up the unification done by unify calls introduced by the sound-unification transformation and unifiable_member calls introduced by the complete-search transformation. Ideally, Prolog systems should provide an efficient unify predicate.

The principal reason for the Lisp implementation of PTTP performing fewer inferences than the Prolog implementation is that the Lisp implementation performs a cut operation if the head of a unit clause subsumes rather than merely unifies with the goal. For example, no alternatives need be tried, and a cut operation can be performed if the goal p(e,a,a) is solved by the unit clause p(e,X,X), since the goal has been solved without instantiation. But if the goal p(e,Y,a) is solved with this clause, alternatives that do not match Y and a must still be considered. A cut operation can likewise be performed in the ME reduction operation if a goal is identical to the complement of an ancestor goal, not merely unifiable with it.

Determining whether to cut is done at very little cost in the Lisp implementation of PTTP by checking whether the unification operation added any entries to the trail. It would be desirable if this could be done equally cheaply in Prolog. Unification with the clause head would be constrained so that the substitution would instantiate only the head if possible, and the user would be able to determine if subsumption occurred. This eliminates the need to perform both unification and subsumption tests.

5.2 Inefficiency of Complete Search

We see the possibility of only relatively small improvements of the basic method of incorporating iterative-deepening search. The extra operations appear to be quite efficient.

However, there is an occasionally useful optimization of the iterative-deepening search strategy that is expensive to implement in Prolog. Suppose that, in an exhaustive depth-bounded search, every time a goal fails due to the depth-bound test, the number of subgoals in the clause exceeds the depth bound by more than one. Then incrementing the depth bound by only one for the next search will surely lead to failure again. To ensure the possibility of finding a new proof in the next search, the depth bound should be increased by the minimum amount by which the number of subgoals exceeds the depth bound. Adding the extra in-line code or procedure for this in Prolog would probably be ineffective. The only way of saving this minimum in Prolog is with database assertions, which makes accessing and especially updating the minimum quite expensive. The extra time required would be noticeable; only rarely would search levels be skipped in compensation.

Another example of inefficiency is the extremely high cost of optionally counting the number of inferences so that the total can be printed at the end of each bounded depth-first search and when a proof is found. Because inferences on success and failure branches must both be counted, the count can be saved only with database assertions. Assignable global variables would be much more efficient for keeping track of the inference count and the minimum amount by which the number of subgoals exceeds the depth bound.

5.3 Inefficiency of Complete Inference

The retention and access of ancestor goals in lists is quite inefficient. This inefficiency is difficult to remedy in Prolog.

There are two major problems. The first is that in the transformed clause

```
p(U,Z,W,Ancestors) :-
    NewAncestors = [p(U,Z,W) | Ancestors],
    p(X,Y,U,NewAncestors), p(Y,Z,V,NewAncestors), p(X,V,W,NewAncestors).
```

the goal that matches p(U,Z,W) is reconstructed and added to the front of Ancestors to form NewAncestors. This is quite wasteful since the goal (or rather its arguments) is already stored in its choice point on the stack. Making the ancestor goal directly available to the user as a term could eliminate the need for reconstructing it to add it to the ancestor list.

The second problem is the retention of the goals in an unindexed linear list. Even indexing on just the sign and predicate symbol, as in the Lisp implementation of PTTP, appreciably reduces the number of attempted matches in the model elimination reduction and pruning operations.

Although looking up a goal in a linear list is expensive, using a more complex data structure may be even more costly because clause heads are added to the ancestor list frequently (whenever solving the body of nonunit clauses) and their addition must be temporary (the head of a clause must be in the ancestor list only for the duration of the solution of the body).

A separate linear list could be used for each signed predicate, but this could result in a very large number (twice the number of predicates in the problem) of extra arguments to each predicate.[6] Separate lists are used in the Lisp implementation of PTTP, but instead of being passed as extra arguments, they are maintained in global variables that can be dynamically rebound.

Adding global variables that can be dynamically rebound like the special variables of Lisp would likewise provide an efficient mechanism for Prolog to access this information without the cost of passing the information through extra argument positions. Global variables, if they can be dynamically rebound, can be very useful even without destructive assignment operations. They could be a "conservative extension" of Prolog that promotes efficiency without adding side-effects that would damage or conceal the logical, nonprocedural interpretation of logic programs.

6 Conclusion

We have described and demonstrated by example the extension of Prolog to full first-order predicate calculus theorem proving, with sound unification, a complete search strategy, and a complete inference system, by means of three simple compiler transformations. The result is an implementation of a Prolog technology theorem prover (PTTP) in which transformed Prolog clauses perform PTTP-style theorem proving at a rate of thousands of inferences per second. We have also suggested some extensions to Prolog that would enable higher performance.

Writing the transformations in Prolog and transforming first-order predicate calculus formulas to Prolog clauses minimizes the effort necessary to implement a PTTP, makes PTTP-style theorem proving readily available in Prolog, and makes it easy to explain how PTTP theorem proving works.

PTTP's high inference rate is achieved at the cost of not allowing more flexible search strategies or elimination of redundancy in the search space by subsumption. Although PTTP is one of the fastest theorem provers in existence when evaluated by its inference rate and performance on easy problems and it has been used to solve reasoning problems in planning and natural-language-understanding systems effectively (we think it represents a local optimum in the space of theorem-proving performance), its high inference rate can be overwhelmed by its exponential search space and it is unsuitable for many difficult theorems for which conventional theorem provers have demonstrated some success. Besides being used as a stand-alone theorem prover, PTTP can play a useful subordinate role in the proof of difficult theorems by executing the theory resolution [16] or linked inference principle [21] procedures, or by performing fast refutation checks on newly derived clauses [1].

A technical report contains full source code and sample output for PTTP in Prolog [18].

Acknowledgements

I would like to thank Fernando Pereira and Mabry Tyson for their useful comments on the text of this paper and to thank Fernando for giving me feedback on the Prolog code in the technical report as well.

References

[1] Antoniou, G. and H.J. Ohlbach. Terminator. *Proceedings of the Eighth International Joint Conference on Artificial Intelligence*, Karlsruhe, West Germany, August 1983, 916–919.

[2] Astrachan, O. METEOR: model elimination theorem prover for efficient OR-parallelism. Unpublished, 1989.

---

[6]Actually, our implementation uses two extra arguments for ancestors—one for positive-literal ancestors and one for negative-literal ancestors—instead of the single list described here.

[3] Bose, S., E.M. Clarke, D.E. Long, and S. Michaylov. Parthenon: a parallel theorem prover for non-Horn clauses. *Proceedings of the Fourth IEEE Symposium on Logic in Computer Science*, Asilomar, California, June 1989.

[4] Chang, C.L. and R.C.T. Lee. *Symbolic Logic and Mechanical Theorem Proving*. Academic Press, New York, New York, 1973.

[5] Gillogly, J.J. The technology chess program. *Artificial Intelligence 3*, 3 (Fall 1972), 145–163.

[6] Korf, R.E. Depth-first iterative-deepening: an optimal admissible tree search. *Artificial Intelligence 27*, 1 (September 1985), 97–109.

[7] Kowalski, R. and D. Kuehner. Linear resolution with selection function. *Artificial Intelligence 2* (1971), 227–260.

[8] Letz, R., J. Schumann, S. Bayerl, and W. Bibel. SETHEO: a high-performance theorem prover. To appear in *Journal of Automated Reasoning*.

[9] Loveland, D.W. A simplified format for the model elimination procedure. *Journal of the ACM 16*, 3 (July 1969), 349–363.

[10] Loveland, D.W. *Automated Theorem Proving: A Logical Basis*. North-Holland, Amsterdam, the Netherlands, 1978.

[11] O'Keefe, R.A. Programming meta-logical operations in Prolog. DAI Working Paper No. 142, Department of Artificial Intelligence, University of Edinburgh, June 1983.

[12] Plaisted, D.A. Non-Horn clause logic programming without contrapositives. *Journal of Automated Reasoning 4*, 3 (September 1988), 287–325.

[13] Satz, R.W. *Expert Thinker* software package. Transpower Corporation, Parkerford, Pennsylvania, 1988.

[14] Sterling, L. and E. Shapiro. *The Art of Prolog*. MIT Press, Cambridge, Massachusetts, 1986.

[15] Stickel, M.E. A Prolog technology theorem prover. *New Generation Computing 2*, 4 (1984), 371–383.

[16] Stickel, M.E. Automated deduction by theory resolution. *Journal of Automated Reasoning 1*, 4 (1985), 333–355.

[17] Stickel, M.E. A Prolog technology theorem prover: implementation by an extended Prolog compiler. *Journal of Automated Reasoning 4*, 4 (December 1988), 353–380.

[18] Stickel, M.E. A Prolog technology theorem prover: a new exposition and implementation in Prolog. Technical Note 464, Artificial Intelligence Center, SRI International, Menlo Park, California, June 1989.

[19] Stickel, M.E. and W.M. Tyson. An analysis of consecutively bounded depth-first search with applications in automated deduction. *Proceedings of the Ninth International Joint Conference on Artificial Intelligence*, Los Angeles, California, August 1985, 1073–1075.

[20] Umrigar, Z.D. and V. Pitchumani. An experiment in programming with full first-order logic. *Proceedings of the 1985 Symposium on Logic Programming*, Boston, Massachusetts, July 1985, 40–47.

[21] Wos, L., R. Veroff, B. Smith, and W. McCune. The linked inference principle, II: the user's viewpoint. *Proceedings of the 7th International Conference on Automated Deduction*, Napa, California, May 1984, 316–332.

Parametric queries, linear constraints and variable elimination

Jean-Louis Lassez

IBM T.J. Watson Research Center

P.O.Box 704

Yorktown Heights, NY 10598

jll@ibm.com

Abstract

Various forms of declarative linear arithmetic are introduced in a number of languages from CLP($\Re$) to Mathematica. In order to find canonical representations of constraints, to handle delays of non-linear constraints, to resolve guards in committed choice languages and other related problems, we need to answer a new and more powerful type of queries: *parametric linear queries*. We propose here a simple mathematical formalism to address that problem. In a first part we show that Fourier's variable elimination procedure and associated elementary theorems allow us to derive directly from their specification a number of interesting sets. For instance we obtain the subsumption cone, which characterizes the set of all linear constraints implied by a set of linear constraints, the convex hull of a collection of polyhedral sets, the separability set which characterizes the hyperplanes separating two given polyhedral sets, and of course the set of answers to a given parametric query. If Fourier's variable elimination is a very powerful conceptual tool telling us what problems we can solve trivially in principle via variable elimination, it is in general hopelessly impractical as it generates for each variable eliminated an exponentially growing set of mostly redundant constraints. In a second part we use a method for variable elimination which rests on a generalization of the notion of objective function in linear programming. It is more efficient than Fourier's procedure as it bypasses all the costly intermediate steps and generates far less redundancy. In a third part we apply that method to solve more efficiently the problem of implicit equalities which is a key component in the computation of canonical representations of linear constraints. In the concluding remarks we mention that such techniques could be used as a basis for a symbolic computation system in the linear case. The main problem faced here is that the size of the output may be exponential. To (partially) overcome this problem we propose a technique to generate very efficiently approximations of the output. These approximations have a small size, they represent spheres rather than polyhedral sets.

1   Introduction

Various forms of declarative linear arithmetic are built in languages of the CLP class [J&L] such as CLP($\Re$), CHIP, CAL, Prolog III, BNR-Prolog. Declarative arithmetic has also been introduced in languages not related to Logic Programming such as Mathematica and Trilogy, and in principle at least could be introduced in the paradigms Functional and Object Oriented Programming.

Let S be the set of constraints in store. What type of information do we want to extract from S, during execution or at output time? First examples are, does $S \Rightarrow Q$? where Q is of the types: $z = 3$, $z + y - z = z - y + 3z \leq 4$. For such queries a simple yes/no answer is required and can be obtained by showing that the constraint $S \wedge \neg Q$ is not solvable. This is the standard technique for subsumption in Theorem Proving.

n Logic Programming one goes a level higher: we do not merely ask for a yes/no answer, unless the query s ground (that is has no variables). For a general query, we obtain as a side effect of the solvability test, a set f substitutions which form a finite representation of the set of answers. So the examples of queries we just gave orrespond to ground queries in a Logic Program, despite the presence of variables. A trivial case of a type of uery that would correspond to the more powerful queries in Logic Programs is: do the constraints in store imply hat the variable z has a fixed value? More formally: $\exists \alpha \forall z : S \Rightarrow z = \alpha$? Clearly here we not only want to know rhether z has a fixed value, but if so we want to know its value.

More generally linear relationships between the program variables may be implied by the constraints in store. This information is essential for representing constraints in a canonical form, for output standardization, constraint propagation, the elimination of redundancy in parallel (see [L&H&M], [L&Mc88], [L&Mc89] for details). In CLP($\Re$), a non-linear expression such as $z = log(z - y)$ is delayed. The knowledge that $z - y$ has a fixed value r for some α will resolve the delay.

Let us consider now inequality queries. In CLP($\Re$) the output should represent the relationships between the nput variables only. However the constraints in store contain auxiliary variables introduced during the execution f the rules in the program. For example, let z, y be the input variables and u, v be the auxiliary variables in $r = \{z + 2y + u \le 1, -y - u + v \le 2, z + u - v \le 0\}$. After eliminating u and v we obtain $\{z - y \le 2\}$ as the utput. A related situation occurs in order to resolve guards in committed choice languages [M], [S]. The guards ontain existential queries, and their execution leads to a similar problem of variable (or quantifier) elimination.

These problems can be formalized as answering *parameterized queries* of the form:
$\alpha, \beta, \gamma, ... \forall z, y, ... : S \Rightarrow \alpha z + \beta y + ... \le$ (or =) γ and $R(\alpha, \beta, ..., \gamma)$? where $R(\alpha, \beta, ..., \gamma)$ is a set of linear relations n the parameters such as $\alpha = 0$, $\beta \le 2\gamma$. What we request is a finite representation of the set of answers. The ovelty and the apparent technical difficulty come from the fact that we quantify over coefficients of an arithmetic xpression, not over its variables.

n the next section we show that Fourier's variable elimination procedure and associated elementary theorems llow us to derive directly from their specification a number of interesting sets. For instance we obtain the subsumption cone of S, which characterizes the set of all constraints implied by a set S of linear constraints. From the absumption cone we can also derive information about the set of hyperplanes cutting S or the set of supporting yperplanes of S. We can also obtain executable specifications for the convex hull of a collection of polyhedral sets, he separability set which characterizes the hyperplanes separating two given polyhedral sets, and of course the set f answers to a given parametric query. We see here that variable elimination is a very simple and powerful tool o reason about linear constraints. Unfortunately Fourier's procedure which is of great significance for historical nd theoretical reasons in Linear Programming [D&E] is essentially not meaningful practically. It generates incrementally sets of constraints of exponentially growing size. Furthermore these constraints are mostly redundant [L&H&M]. So in the third section we propose another method for variable elimination. We present the problem of ariable elimination as a problem of answering a particular parametric query. The minimal set of generators of the et of answers to the query represents the set of constraints resulting from variable elimination. The formulation f the problem is a simple and natural generalization of the classical linear programming problem. This method is more efficient than Fourier's as it bypasses the costly intermediate steps, and generates far less redundancy.

In the fourth section we consider the case of parametric equality queries. It essentially reduces to the problem of finding implicit equalities among the constraints in the set. This problem is simple and has been addressed in the literature (see eg [L&Mc88], [L&Mc89]), [F&R&T]). However the existing methods carry an overhead that is significant in practice. What is of interest here is to determine whether implicit equalities exist before paying the price of computing them systematically.

Using the preceding framework and a recent extension to Fourier's theorem [L&M], we provide a formulation which is a variant of Duality Theory in Linear Programming. From this we can derive algorithms to determine the existence of answers to the equality query as a side effect of solvability without the overhead inherent in other methods.

We conclude with a few remarks concerning implementation issues and the possibility of extending the techniques presented in this paper to related problems, for instance the determination of causes of unsolvability. Also we mention how one can efficiently provide approximations to the answers in the hard case where the answers have an exponential or otherwise unmanageable size.

2 Executable Specifications

Let us first say a few words about Fourier's elimination procedure and solvability algorithm [F]. Despite its simplicity, its historical and theoretical importance, it is not well known and for sake of being self contained it is described here informally: Let S be a set of inequality constraints $ax + by + ... \leq c$. We first select a variable say x, and consider all possible pairs of constraints from S where x appears with coefficients of opposite signs. this set is empty, that is if x appears with coefficients of the same sign in all constraints, these constraints are deleted. If the set of pairs is not empty, from each pair we generate a new constraint which does not contain x by computing an appropriate linear combination of the two constraints. These new constraints replace in S the constraints that contained x, giving a set $S1$. Now S is solvable if and only if $S1$ is solvable. In geometric terms $S1$ represents the projection wrt to the x-axis of the polyhedral set associated to S. So variable elimination is a projection operation. The process is repeated until all variables have been eliminated. Fourier's theorem tells us that S is not solvable if and only if a contradiction $0 \leq c$ (where c is a negative number) has been generated in the process.

As we mentioned previously, Fourier's result can be used to establish in a straightforward manner fundamental theorems in Linear Programming. Not surprisingly, as variable elimination is a powerful tool, we will have the same benefit in our context. As a first illustration consider the problem of computing the convex hull of a set of points directly from its specification: A point P is in the convex hull of points $P_1, ..., P_n$ iff $\exists \lambda_1, ..., \lambda_n, \lambda_i \geq 0$ and $\sum \lambda_i = 1$ such that $P = \sum \lambda_i P_i$.

Let (x,y,..) be the coordinates of P. If we eliminate the λ's from this specification we obtain a relationship between solely the coordinates (x,y,...) which is solvable if and only if the initial relationship is. It therefore represents the desired convex hull.

Example: let $P_1 = (1,0,0)$, $P_2 = (0,1,0)$, $P_3 = (0,0,1)$ and $P = (x,y,z)$. We have $x = \lambda_1, y = \lambda_2, z = \lambda_3, \lambda_1 + \lambda_2$

$s = 1, \lambda_1 \geq 0, \lambda_2 \geq 0, \lambda_3 \geq 0$. We trivially obtain a representation of the convex hull by eliminating the λ's: $+ y + z = 1, x \geq 0, y \geq 0, z \geq 0$. So variable elimination provides us with a systematic way of characterizing interesting sets of constraints directly from an existential specification.

We address now the problem of obtaining existential specifications for sets of constraints implied by a set S of inequality constraints. A constraint C is a *quasi-linear combination* of constraints of $S = \{C_1, ..., C_n\}$ iff C is obtained by adding a positive number to the right hand side of a non-negative linear combination of constraints of S. The following theorem is a direct corollary to Fourier's theorem. It is very rarely mentioned, does not seem to have been used in that form at least, but is in fact equivalent to the fundamental Duality Theorem in Linear Programming [A]. It provides a simple characterization of the set of constraints implied by S, and forms the basis of our approach. (For sake of simplicity we will use the word combination for non-negative combination unless specifically stated).

Theorem 1 (Subsumption Theorem [A]) *A constraint C is implied by a set of constraints S iff C is a quasi-linear combination of constraints of S.*

Now we can specify that a constraint $C = \alpha x + \beta y + ... \leq \gamma$ is implied by S: Let the constraints in S be $\{a_1 x + b_1 y + ... \leq c_1, a_2 x + b_2 y + ... \leq c_2, ...\}$. C is implied by S iff $\exists \lambda_1 \geq 0, \lambda_2 \geq 0...$, and $q \geq 0$ such that

$$\sum \lambda_i a_i = \alpha$$

$$\sum \lambda_i b_i = \beta$$

$$\vdots$$

$$\sum \lambda_i c_i + q = \gamma$$

Define the *subsumption cone* of S, denoted $SC(S)$ as the polyhedral set obtained by elimination of the λ's and q from the above specification. By Fourier's elimination we have

Proposition 1 *Let S be a set of linear inequalities, a constraint $\alpha x + \beta y + ... \leq \gamma$ is implied by S iff the point $(\alpha, \beta, ..., \gamma)$ belongs to the subsumption cone of S.*

Example: $S = -x \leq 0, -y \leq 0, x + y \leq 1$ we have $\alpha = -\lambda_1 + \lambda_3, \beta = -\lambda_2 + \lambda_3, \gamma = \lambda_3 + q, \lambda_1 \geq 0, \lambda_2 \geq 0, \lambda_3 \geq 0, q \geq 0$. From which we derive $SC(S) = \{-\alpha + \gamma \geq 0, -\beta + \gamma \geq 0, \gamma \geq 0\}$. We use the word cone in the definition because as no constant appears in the specification, the resulting set of inequalities is always an homogeneous system defining a cone.

This notion of subsumption cone is useful when we have to test repeatedly for implication. Using S requires running a linear program, using $SC(S)$ requires a simple evaluation of the constraints. $SC(S)$ also gives us information about cutting and supporting hyperplanes. The points in $SC(S)$ characterize the implied constraints. Dually the constraints which are incompatible with S are characterized by the open cone symmetric to $SC(S)$ with respect to the origin. Consequently the constraints which are not implied and are not incompatible correspond to points in the complement of the two cones, which is straightforward to check. The faces of these constraints are the hyperplanes which cut S. The supporting hyperplanes of S correspond to points on the facets of $SC(S)$ as they are both implied by S and at the limit of cutting.

Clearly two sets of constraints that have the same implications, that is the same subsumption cone, are equivalent: they define the same polyhedral set. So a subsumption cone uniquely determines a polyhedral set. Now a subsumption cone may be pointed or not. When pointed, it is the convex closure of its extreme rays. The other case is a little bit too involved to be addressed here. Let us just mention that these two cases correspond to the fact that S may or may not be full dimensional. The complete treatment requires the use of the canonical form [L&Mc88] and results about the structure of polyhedral cones [G&T].

Proposition 2 *Let S be a set of linear inequalities. The set of constraints derived from the set of extreme rays of the subsumption cone of S is a set of constraints equivalent to S (under assumption of full dimensionality).*

Consider the previous example. Each of the constraints $-\alpha + \gamma \geq 0, -\beta + \gamma \geq 0, \gamma \geq 0$ defines a facet of the subsumption cone. To obtain the extreme rays of the cone we intersect the constraints in all possible pairs of adjacent hyperplanes supporting the facets. That is we solve the systems: $\{-\alpha + \gamma = 0, -\beta + \gamma = 0, \gamma \geq 0\}$ $\{-\alpha + \gamma = 0, \gamma = 0, -\beta + \gamma \geq 0\}$, $\{-\beta + \gamma = 0, \gamma = 0, -\alpha + \gamma \geq 0\}$ Simplifying we obtain : $\alpha = \beta = \gamma, \gamma \geq$ which gives the constraint $\gamma x + \gamma y \leq \gamma$ equivalent to $x + y \leq 1$, while $\alpha = \gamma = 0, \beta \leq 0$ is equivalent to $-y \leq 0$ and $\beta = \gamma = 0, \alpha \leq 0$ is equivalent to $-x \leq 0$.

Using this technique we can find an executable specification for the convex hull $CH(P_i, 1 \leq i \leq n)$ of a collection of polyhedral sets P_i.

Proposition 3 $CH(P_i, 1 \leq i \leq n) = $ *extreme rays* $\{\bigcap_i^n SC(P_i)\}$ *(under assumption of full dimensionality).*

Indeed a constraint is implied by the convex hull iff it is implied by all P_i's. Consequently the subsumption cone of the convex hull is equal to the intersection of the subsumption cones of the P_i's. The extreme ray extraction gives us a set of constraints defining the affine hull. Algorithmically we can compute in parallel the $SC(P_i)$ by variable elimination, the intersection is trivial as we just collect all the sets of constraints together, finally computing extreme rays is a classical problem. The general case will be discussed in the full paper.

So we have found two methods to answer parametric queries, one consists in first computing the subsumption cone and adding to it the relations that the parameters must satisfy in the query. Else we can express directly using theorem 1 that the constraint in the query is implied by the system, and eliminate variables. The subsumption cone is therefore a new tool to reason about sets of constraints with interesting computational properties. It corresponds naturally to the least model in logic programming, as variable elimination corresponds to resolution constraints to clauses and parameters to logic variables. Other sets can be defined similarly, for instance we can express that a parametric constraint is implied by a system $S1$, while its opposite is implied by a system $S2$. Eliminating the appropriate variables will give us a relation which characterizes the set of hyperplanes separating $S1$ and $S2$. A simple variant would be to characterize pairs of parallel hyperplanes at a fixed distance d from each other and which separate $S1$ and $S2$. Another interesting application of variable elimination is the computation of the image of the polyhedral set by a linear application. One needs only eliminate the source variables in the specification. The image is given by the resulting constraints. We will now propose an alternative to Fourier' method for variable elimination which leads to a more practical system.

3 Variable elimination via extreme points

Assume we want to eliminate given variables from a set of constraints S. Consider the parametric query when the existentially quantified variables are the variables from S that we want to keep. $\exists \alpha, \beta, \gamma, \ldots \forall x, y, \ldots : S = \alpha x + \beta y + \ldots \leq \gamma$? The set of answers to this query represents the set of constraints implied by the projection of S in the (x, y, ...) space. It is easy to see that we can in fact restrict ourselves to linear combinations, rather than the quasi-linear. So the projection we want to compute will be a minimal set of generators for the set of linear combinations which are answers to the query. We express now that the constraint in the query is a linear ombination of the constraints in S. Let the constraints in S be $\{a_1 z + b_1 y + ... \leq c_1, a_2 z + b_2 y + ... \leq c_2, ...\}$ we hen have the relations:

$$\text{(I)} \quad \begin{aligned} \sum \lambda_i a_i &= \alpha \\ \sum \lambda_i b_i &= \beta \\ &\vdots \\ \sum \lambda_i c_i &= \gamma \\ \sum \lambda_i d_i &= 0 \\ &\vdots \\ \sum \lambda_i &= 1 \\ \lambda_i &\geq 0 \end{aligned}$$

here the equalities whose right-hand-side is zero correspond to eliminated variables. We have normalized the oefficients of the linear combination so that their sum is equal to one, without loss of generality. This is in fact ore than syntactic convenience. One sees easily that the set of solutions to (I) is closed for normalized linear ombinations. In geometrical terms it means that the set of points whose coordinates are the coefficients of the near combinations is a convex set. A classical theorem states that the set of points in a polytope is the convex losure of a finite set of extreme points. So if we can show that our convex set has a finite set of extreme points E e will have a characterization of the set of answers which is a specialization of the subsumption theorem: (where is the set of constraints which correspond to E).

Theorem 2 *A constraint C is an answer to the query Q iff it is a quasi-linear combination of the finite set of onstraints in G.*

n order to establish this result and provide a way of computing G we generalize the optimization function in inear Programming in the following way.

n (I) the set of constraints that are not parameterized represents, but for the lack of objective function, a near programming problem in standard form. An objective function Φ is a mapping of R^n into R. Let Δ be the olyhedral set associated with the constraints. $\Phi(\Delta)$ is an interval in R, and the linear programming problem is o determine its maximum or minimum (when they exist). That is we have to compute one or the other of the xtreme points of the image of a polyhedral set. What we also know is that the value of the maximum or minimum obtained as an image of an extreme point of Δ. We generalize this picture by taking as objective function a unction Φ, from R^n to R^m this time, defined by the parametric constraints in (I), and by considering the set of xtreme points of $\Phi(\Delta)$ instead of a minimum or maximum. We have again the fact that the extreme points in (\Delta)$ are images of the extreme points of Δ, and as Δ is a polytope, $\Phi(\Delta)$ has a finite number of extreme points. his provides an informal proof for the result we needed:

Theorem 3 *Let P be the generalized linear program:*

$$extr(\Phi(\Delta))$$

$$\Phi = \begin{cases} \sum \lambda_i a_i = \alpha \\ \sum \lambda_i b_i = \beta \\ \vdots \\ \sum \lambda_i c_i = \gamma \end{cases}$$

$$\Delta = \begin{cases} \sum \lambda_i d_i = 0 \\ \vdots \\ \sum \lambda_i = 1 \\ \lambda_i \geq 0 \end{cases}$$

The solutions to that program determine a finite set of constraints which defines the projection of S.

However, the finite set of constraints should be minimized by redundancy elimination to obtain a better represen tation of the projection of S on the (x, y, ...) space. As there are algorithms to compute sets of extreme poin [M&R] we can effectively obtain G. Implementation issues are not trivial and will be mentioned briefly in the la section.

4   Existence of implicit equalities

As we mentioned previously, much is known about the handling of equality queries. In a set of inequality co straints, those which can be replaced by an equality constraint by simply replacing $\leq$ by $=$ without changing tl semantics are called *implicit equalities*. This set of constraints plays a role analogous to the set G in the previou section. There are a number of methods to compute them, a standard one being to run a linear program fo each constraint in the set. This is not very efficient, particularly in the case where there are no implicit equaliti present, which occurs frequently for a large class of problems. In the case of CLP($\Re$) where backtracking ma occur, all this work is wasted. There are far more sophisticated ways of computing implicit equalities by usir a single linear program [F&R&T]. However in these methods the size of the problem is substantially increase as well as the number of variables. In logic based programming languages, we would rather want to reduce tl number of variables than increase it. So these algorithms also lead to a substantial overhead in our setting.

What we need here is an efficient algorithm that answers the existential query first, so that we pay the pri of generating the answers only when we have a guarantee that they exist. Recently, it was found that Fourier algorithm for solvability of inequality constraints has this property [L&M]. It was established in [L&M] th implicit equalities exist if and only if Fourier's algorithm generates a tautology $0 \leq 0$. So we have "for free" tl information we request as a side effect of solvability.

We will use the results of the previous section to provide an efficient method of determining the existence implicit equalities as a side effect of a simple and efficient solvability test, and to separately generate them whe required. The results from [L&M] are also used to establish correctness. Essentially we formulate the solvabili problem in a variant of duality in linear programming. It is a variant in that first we view the dual space as space of linear combinations and not according to its usual economic or geometrical interpretation. So we a justified in adding a normalization constraint which would not be meaningful otherwise. And also of course is extended so as to take care of implicit equalities. Let S be the set of constraints, its quasi-dual formulati D expresses that we have normalized linear combinations of constraints in S that eliminate all variables. It therefore an application of Theorem 1 in a particular case. The objective function is obtained as in the case of linear programming but its use will be adapted to our purpose. We have now the theorem:

Theorem 4 *1. If the quasi-dual linear program D is not solvable then S is solvable and contains no implicit equalities.*

    2. If the quasi-dual linear program D is solvable then:

        (a) If the objective function has a strictly positive minimum then S is solvable and does not contain any implicit equality.

        (b) If the objective function has zero as a minimum then S is solvable and contains implicit equalities.

        (c) If in the process of minimizing the objective function a negative value is obtained, then S is not solvable.

    3. When implicit equalities exist they can be obtained by generating the set of extreme points of D with the objective constraint set to zero.

The proof of this theorem is obtained as a consequence of [L&M] and the arguments in the previous section. It is important to note that we have not given an algorithm here strictly speaking, but rather a different formulation of the problem. Any solving algorithm can be used with this formulation for parts 1 and 2 in the above theorem. As for part 3 any algorithm which generates all extreme points can be applied, or more efficient incremental methods warranted.

Concluding Remarks

As with other problems in linear programming it is not necessarily so that algorithms with great theoretical complexity cannot be quite efficient in practice. Here we know that the problems we address have substantial theoretical complexity, but they are so recent that we have only partial evidence about practical suitability in our context.

Concerning the implementation in the inequality case several problems need to be addressed. First, in principle the number of extreme points can be so large as to be unmanageable. In the practical problems we encountered it has not been the case yet. One reason is that for very small or very sparse systems variants of Fourier's algorithm that include simple forms of redundancy elimination can perform quite well. For systems that are nearly square, that is where the number of variables and the number of constraints are similar, the extreme point method works quite well. These cases are those met most frequently in current implementations. Ultimately we would rather keep the initial representation than attempt to output an exponential number of constraints. Nevertheless this problem is being investigated thoroughly, we will come back to it later, for a different type of applications. Elimination of redundancy is a key issue from a practical point of view. Even for simple problems significant amounts of redundant constraints can be generated. Furthermore, in a projection we deal with constraints that are tangent to the set we construct, consequently round-off errors can seriously interfere with redundancy elimination. The many algorithms [M&R] to generate extreme points essentially avoid the issue of degeneracy. These techniques are not suitable in our case. We are currently investigating a promising method due to Kruse [K].

In the case of equality constraints, the situation is simpler. The techniques from linear programming can be easily adapted. Also we know that we can have at most n implicit equalities in a set of n constraints. In practice there will be far less, and each extreme point gives several answers. So we will not face an explosion in the number of extreme points to be computed.

Other problems can be addressed using techniques introduced in this paper. For instance, constraints being expressed as linear combinations of constraints in S, we could find the causes of redundancy or causes of unsolvability. Techniques of intelligent backtracking could then be applied. A comparison, evaluation and integration of various algorithms is in progress and will be reported in [H&L].

It has also been recently proposed in an important paper [KKR] to use constraints in the context of logic databases. An interesting point is that the approach is a bottom up evaluation rather than the traditional top down of logic programs. A consequence is that the number of variables is fixed during execution rather than unbounded. Therefore methods based on variable elimination might be more successful in that setting. Here, we are applying variable elimination to a restricted type of constraints. One could consider an extension to a symbolic computation system for the full linear case. A major problem to be faced is that even in our simple case, the size of the output may be exponential. There is little need to consider an extension if we cannot solve this problem. The only way out that we can see is to settle for an approximation. Let us propose a simple one, whose implementation and properties will be evaluated in the full paper. We will therefore remain informal here. Beringer [B] has proved the very interesting fact that, assuming the constraints normalised, then the objective function in the quasi dual gives the radius of the largest sphere included in the associated polyhedral set. (If the quasi dual is not solvable then the radius is not bounded). We can use this fact to obtain an approximation of the set of answers. Geometrically we have a polyhedral set whose projection has a large number of facets, in fact so large that it makes no sense to attempt to compute it. We want an approximation of the projection that has a simple (small) syntactic representation. Assume that the polyhedral set is such that the spheres it contains have a bounded radius. We can compute via the objective function of the quasi dual the radius of the largest sphere(s) included in the set, (Beringer's theorem). is then simple to obtain the locus of the centers of the spheres by a simple translation of the constraints. This locus is itself a polyhedral set. The approximation we propose is the projection of this family of spheres. The radius of a projected sphere remains the same, so one simplex is sufficient. If the locus is too costly to project we can either take a subset or repeat the process by approximating the locus. So this approximation gives us a somewhat central subset of solutions. We can obtain approximations of other areas of the set of solutions by considering subpolyhedra obtained by translations of the constraints. This technique is used in the case where the polyhedral set admits subspheres of unbounded radius. Finally, It may be worth mentioning that a number of important properties of linear constraints related to efficient implementations of negation and canonical representations in querying system have their counterparts in other domains of computation (term algebras, convex geometry, etc.). An axiomatisation of this phenomenon has been reported in [LMc90].

References

[A]   S. Achmanov, *Programmation Linéaire*, Editions Mir, Moscou 1984.

[B]   H. Beringer (personal communication, publication forthcoming)

[D&E]   G.B. Dantzig and B.C. Eaves, Fourier-Motzkin Elimination and Its Dual, *Journal of Combinatory Theory Ser. A*, 14 (1973) 288-297.

[F]   J.B.J. Fourier, reported in: Analyse des travaux de l'Académie Royale des Sciences, pendant l'année 1824, Partie mathématique, *Histoire de l'Académie Royale des Sciences de l'Institut de France* (1827) xlvii-lv. (Partial English translation in: D.A. Kohler, Translation of a Report by Fourier of his work on Linear Inequalities, *Opsearch* 10(1973) 38-42.)

[F&R&T] R.M. Freund, R. Roundy and M.J. Todd, Identifying the Set of Always-Active Constraints in a System of Linear Inequalities by a Single Linear Program, Technical Report, Sloan School of Management, Massachusetts Institute of Technology, October 1985.

[G&T] A.J. Goldman and A.W. Tucker, Polyhedral Convex Cones in Linear Inequalities and Related Systems. *Kuhn-Tucker Ed. Annals of Mathematical Studies 38. Princeton University Press 1956.*

[H&L] T. Huynh and J-L. Lassez, Design and Implementation of Algorithms for Variable Elimination in Linear Arithmetic Constraints.

[J&L] J. Jaffar and J-L. Lassez, Constraint Logic Programming, *POPL 87*, 111-119.

[J&M&S&Y] J. Jaffar, S. Michaylov, P. Stuckey and R. Yap, The CLP($\Re$) Language and System, IBM Research Report, T.J. Watson Research Center, forthcoming.

[KKR] P. Kanellakis, G. Kuper and P. Revesz, Constraint Query Languages, *PODS 90.* Nashville.

[K] H.J. Kruse, Degeneracy graphs and the neighborhood problem. Springer Verlag Lecture Notes in Economics and Mathematical Systems No 260, 1986.

[LMc90] J-L Lassez, K. McAloon, A Constraint Sequent Calculus *LICS 90.* Philadelphia.

[L&H&M] J-L. Lassez, T. Huynh and K. McAloon, Simplification and Elimination of Redundant Arithmetic Constraints, *Proceedings of NACLP 89*, MIT Press.

[L&M] J-L. Lassez and M.J. Maher, On Fourier's Algorithm for Linear Arithmetic Constraints, IBM Research Report, T.J. Watson Research Center, 1988.

[L&Mc88] J-L. Lassez and K. McAloon, Applications of a Canonical Form for Generalized Linear Constraints, *Proceedings of the FGCS Conference*, Tokyo, December 1988, 703-710.

[L&Mc89] J-L. Lassez and K. McAloon, Independence of Negative Constraints, *TAPSOFT 89*, Advanced Seminar on Foundations of Innovative Software Development, LNCS 351 Springer Verlag 89.

[M] M. Maher, A Logic Semantics for a class of Committed Choice Languages, *Proceedings of ICLP4*, MIT Press 87.

[M&R] T.H. Matheiss and D.S. Rubin, A Survey of Comparison of Methods for Finding All Vertices of Convex Polyhedral Sets, *Mathematics of Operations Research*, 5 (1980) 167-185.

[S] V. Saraswat, Concurrent Constraint Logic Programming, Ph.D. Dissertation, Carnegie Mellon University 1989.

AC-Unification Race:
The System Solving Approach And Its Implementation [*]

Mohamed Adi　　　　**Claude Kirchner**

INRIA Lorraine & CRIN
BP 239
54506 Vandœuvre-Les-Nancy Cedex
France
E-mail: {adi, ckirchner}@loria.crin.fr

Abstract

This paper presents an algorithm and an implementation in C language of the Associative-Commutative unification based on solving *systems* of equations. Benchmarks are proposed for evaluating the performances of this algorithm and its implementation.

1　Introduction

Associative-commutative unification (in short AC-unification) is solving equations in the term algebra when a finite set of functions symbols $(+_i)_{i \in I}$ are associative and commutative, that is satisfy $AC(+_i)$: $(x +_i y) +_i z = x +_i (y +_i z)$ and $x +_i y = y +_i x$.

This unification problem has been the most intensively studied after the unification problem in the empty theory for at least two reasons. The first one is that the associative and commutative identities are associated to many algebraic structures of interest for theorem proving or algebraic specifications. The second and more technical one is that, in term rewriting applications, one cannot dissociate associativity from commutativity [22] because the rewriting relation associated with (left or right) associativity modulo commutativity is not terminating. Thus one should rewrite modulo associativity and commutativity, both as identities.

But solving associative-commutative equations is a difficult problem unlike for commutativity only. Difficulties are firstly in the discovery of complete AC-unification procedures, secondly in the proof of their termination, thirdly in managing the algorithmic complexity of the problem which is known to be NP-complete [14].

The first AC-unification algorithms were independently discovered by Livesey and J. Siekmann [21] and M. Stickel [26,25]. They differ mainly in the way generalization is handled: M. Stickel generalizes using variables and thus transforms an AC-equation into a homogeneous linear Diophantine equation, while Livesey and J. Siekmann consider certain variables as constants, so that an AC-equation is transformed into an inhomogeneous linear Diophantine equation. The termination of Stickel's algorithm in the presence of free symbols was proved by F. Fages [9] almost ten years after its discovery. An extensive description of Stickel's algorithm, together with the use of constraints allowing to squeeze the search space are given by J.-M. Hullot [13].

---

[*]This work has been partly supported by the GRECO de programmation of CNRS (France)

A. Herold and J. Siekmann gave later an improvement of Livesey-Siekmann's algorithm based on solving homogeneous and inhomogeneous linear Diophantine equations and on computing AC-unifiers from AC1-unifiers (AC1 denotes AC with an identity). A different approach to AC-unification based on solving systems of equations and on three main operations decomposition, merging and AC-mutation has been proposed by C. Kirchner [17,15]. This allows one to unify in particular in the presence of several AC and free function symbols as an instance of a general approach to unification-algorithm combination [16]. A. Boudet [2] gives a precise description of the control on transformations to be applied in order to solve a system efficiently.

All these algorithms use linear (in)homogeneous Diophantine equation-solving which has been studied in particular by Fortenbacher [10], Clausen and Fortenbacher [5], G. Huet [12], M. Lambert [18] and D. Lankford [19]. C. Kirchner's approach needs to solve systems of linear homogeneous Diophantine equations. These systems are studied by J.-F. Romeuf [23] and by E. Contejean and H. Devie [8] who give a very nice generalization of Fortenbacher's algorithm.

Using a different point of view, J. Christian and P. Lincoln [20] gave a new AC unification algorithm using a matrix with constraints which avoids solving linear Diophantine equations when the initial AC-problem consists only in linear equations.

Because of its practical importance, particularly in theorem proving, a set of benchmarks was given in [3], in order to compare implementations and to stimulate the design and implementation of efficient AC-unification algorithms. This presents the implementation in the language C of the AC-unification algorithm based on solving systems of equations and first presented in [16,15]. In order to demonstrate the validity of our approach, we compare its results with the benchmarks proposed in [3] and we give new benchmarks illuminating the behavior of the implementation on *systems* of AC-equations. Some of these benchmarks are given below, the full results can be found in [1]. For example given an $AC(f)$ symbol and variables x, u, v, w, y, the system:

$$S = \begin{cases} f(x,x,x) =^? f(u,v,w,y) \\ f(u,u,u) =^? f(x,v,w,y) \\ f(v,v,v) =^? f(u,x,w,y) \\ f(w,w,w) =^? f(u,v,x,y) \\ f(y,y,y) =^? f(u,v,w,x) \end{cases}$$

requires 0.12 seconds to be solved while the sequential method requires 639.64 seconds only to solve the first equation using Kapur and Zhang's implementation [3].

The program, written in C, has been designed in a modular and integrable way in order to be easily incorporated into large softwares like theorem prover or programming languages. It is freely distributed.

2 AC-unification

Before presenting the AC-unification algorithm working on systems [16,15], we first recall some of the basic definitions of unification. Given a set X of variables and a set F of function symbols, the algebra $T(F, X)$ is the set of terms built over F and X. A substitution is an endomorphism on $T(F, X)$ denoted by $(x_1 \mapsto t_1), \cdots, (x_n \mapsto t_n)$. The theory A is the smallest congruence on $T(F, X)$ defined by a set of axioms. A multiequation is a nonempty multiset of terms, a system of multiequations is a multiset of multiequations and a disjunction system is a multiset of systems of multiequations.

A substitution σ is a solution of : 1) a multiequation e if $\sigma(t_1) = \sigma(t_2)$ for all t_1 and t_2 in e, 2) a system of multiequations S if σ is a solution of each multiequation in S, 3) a disjunction system U if σ is solution of at least one system in U. A multiequation $e = \{t_1, \cdots, t_m\}$ is also denoted by $t_1 =^? \cdots =^? t_m$.

In this paper, we are interested in associative commutative theories which comprise the following axioms: $(x + y) + z = x + (y + z)$ and $x + y = y + x$.

We consider that $F = F_d \cup F_{AC}$ where F_d is a set of free symbols and F_{AC} the set of AC function symbols. In order to solve a system of multiequations, we introduce three processes: decomposition, which when possible, simplifies multiequations without considering axioms, merging, which groups together the constraints on the same variables, and mutation, which transforms certain systems into disjunctions of systems using AC identities.

2.1 Decomposition and merging

Decomposition and merging are defined as usual by the following transformation rules.

Decomposition	$f(t_1,\cdots,t_n)=^?g(t'_1,\cdots,t'_n)$	$\Longrightarrow$	$(t_1=^?t'_1) \wedge \cdots \wedge (t_n=^?t'_n)$ if $f = g \in F_d$
Clash	$f(t_1,\cdots,t_n)=^?g(t'_1,\cdots,t'_n)$	$\Longrightarrow$	$fail$ if $f \neq g$
Merging	$x=^?t_1=^?\cdots=^?t_m \wedge x=^?t'_1=^?\cdots=^?t'_n$	$\Longrightarrow$	$x=^?t_1\cdots=^?t_m=^?t'_1\cdots=^?t'_n$ if $x \in X$.

In particular, this allows one to postpone replacement until it is needed, as we will see later.

2.2 Mutation

If there is no failure by rule **Clash**, decomposition and merging processes yield three kinds of multiequations:

1. $x_1=^?\cdots=^?x_n$.

2. $x_1=^?\cdots=^?x_n=^?g(t_1,\cdots t_m)$ such that $g \in F$.

3. $x_1=^?\cdots=^?x_n=^?t^1_1 + t^1_2=^?\cdots=^?t^m_1 + t^m_2$ such that $m \geq 2$ and $+ \in F_{AC}$.

Where the $x_i \in X$ and $t_j, t^k_1, t^k_2 \in T(F, X)$. A system consisting of multiequations of type (1) and (2) is called a **fully decomposed system**. Since AC theories are strict (or simple) [16,4], it is easy to solve such a system. The problem is to transform a system of type 3 multiequations into an equivalent disjunction of fully decomposed systems (if such exists). This transformation is called AC mutation.

It is important to be able to treat theories with several AC and free symbols. Based on previous work on combining of unification algorithms [16,11,24,27], one can build a mutation operation for a combination of AC theories from the mutation operations of the elementary subtheories. In the present case, let $A_{+_1},\cdots,A_{+_n}$ be n AC (elementary) theories and $F_{AC} = \{+_i|1 \leq i \leq n\}$. The problem is to build an AC unification algorithm for the theory $A = A_{+_1} \cup \cdots \cup A_{+_n}$ when unification algorithms are given for each AC theory A_{+_i} $(i = 1,\cdots n)$. This is achieved by extracting from a system S built over $T(F_d \cup F_{AC}, X)$ all pure subsystems:
S_{+_i} $(1 \leq i \leq n)$ such that S_{+_i} is a submultiset of S built over $+_i$ and variables.
Let us give an example:

Example 1 *Let $n = 2$, $+_1 = +$ and $+_2 = *$.*

The system : $\begin{cases} x*y=^?a*(z+u) \\ x+y=^?v+a \\ v \quad =^?a+b \end{cases}$ *is generalized in the following system:* $S = \begin{cases} x*y =^?x_1 * x_2 \\ x_1 \quad =^?a \\ x_2 \quad =^?z+u \\ x+y=^?v+x_1 \\ v \quad =^?x_1 + x_3 \\ x_3 \quad =^?b \end{cases}$

With $S_+ = \{x_2=^?z+u, x+y=^?v+x_1, v=^?x_1+x_3\}$ *and* $S_* = \{x*y=^?x_1 * x_2\}$.

Given an AC mutation procedure for each AC theory A_{+_i} $(i = 1, \cdots, n)$, the procedure FULL-DEC described below proposes a control to transform a system into a fully decomposed disjunction system in the AC theory $A = A_{+_1} \cup \cdots \cup A_{+_n}$.

DEC-COMP $(S :$ a system of $T(F_d \cup F_{AC}, X))$
    transform S into a system S' by **Decomposition** and **Merging** rules.
    if it fails by the **Clash** rule
    then returns(fail).
    else Let S_{+_i} be a nonfully decomposed subsystem of S.
        if such a system does not exist
        then returns(S).
        else if $x =^? x_1 =^? \cdots =^? x_n =^? t_1 =^? \cdots =^? t_m \in S$ **then** replace all occurrences of each variable
$$x_j \ (j = 1, \cdots, n) \text{ in } S_{+_i} \text{ by the variable } x.$$
        $[R_j]_{j \in J} \leftarrow$ AC mutation(S_{+_i}) $([R_j]_{j \in J}$ is a disjunction of R_j equivalent to S_{+_i}).
        $R'_j \leftarrow (S - S_{+_i}) \cup R_j$ for all $j \in J$ (i.e S_{+_i} is replaced by its equivalent R_j).
        [return(DEC-COMP $(R'_j))]_{j \in J}$.
END DEC-COMP

We will carry out the following example along the paper.

Example 2 *Let* $+, *$ *be in* F_{AC}, *f in F_d and S the system to be solved:* $S = \begin{cases} r & =^? f(x + y, z * w) \\ r & =^? f(u + v, t * q) \\ x + v =^? u + u \end{cases}$

By merging and decomposition rules, the subsystem : $\begin{cases} r =^? f(x + y, z * w), \\ r =^? f(u + v, t * q) \end{cases}$

is transformed into an equivalent system: $\begin{cases} r & =^? f(x + y, z * w) \\ x + y =^? u + v \\ z * w =^? t * q \end{cases}$

S is then transformed into : $S' = \begin{cases} r & =^? f(x + y, z * w) \\ x + y =^? u + v \\ x + v =^? u + u \\ z * w =^? t * q \end{cases}$

with $S_+ = \begin{cases} x + y =^? u + v \\ x + v =^? u + u \end{cases}$ *and* $S_* = \{ z * w =^? t * q \}$

In the next section, we show how to solve S_+ and S_* but for the moment we suppose having two disjunctions of fulled decomposed systems $S_1, \cdots, S_k$ and $R_1, \cdots, R_l$ which are equivalents respectively at S_+ and S_*. Since there are no shared variables, the disjunction of systems: $[\{r =^? f(x + y, z * w)\} \cup S_i \cup R_j]_{i=1 \cdots k, \ j=1 \cdots l}$ is equivalent to the initial system.

3   AC mutation

As we have already seen, it is sufficient to know how to compute the mutation operation for a pure AC-system, that is a system built over variables and only one AC-operator. We summarize in this section how this mutation is performed in our implementation.

We consider systems, called AC-systems, of the form: $(t_1^k + t_2^k =^? r_1^k + r_2^k)_{k=1 \cdots q}$ in $T(\{+\}, X)$ where $+$ is an AC-function symbol. First, the AC-system is flattened and transformed into another type of system called a system of homogeneous linear Diophantine equations (in short Diophantine system) which we know how to solve. Then, the minimal solutions of the initial AC-system are computed by combining the Diophantine system minimal solutions.

Firstly the flattened form is computed. It is defined for a term t in $T(\{+\}, X)$ as $x_1 \star x_2 \star \cdots \star x_n$ where $x_i (i \in [1, n])$ are variables and the set of terms $T(\{+\}, X)$ with the operation denoted by

$\star$, is a free commutative monoid. The product $x_1 \star x_2 \star \cdots \star x_n$ is obtained by eliminating all the occurrences of the symbol $+$ in t. For example, $x \star y \star z \star w$ is the flattened form of $x + ((y + z) + w)$.

After flattening all the equations of the AC-system, we simplify each equation by eliminating variables which appear in both its left and right hand side and then computing coefficients as follows. Let S be an AC-system flattened and simplified: $S = (x_1 \star \ldots \star x_m =^? y_1 \star \ldots \star y_p)_{k \in [1..q]}$ where the x_i, y_j are variables from X.

Since $\star$ is associative-commutative, S can also be written:

$$S = (a_1^k x_1 \star \ldots \star a_m^k x_m =^? b_1^k y_1 \star \ldots \star b_p^k y_p)_{k \in [1..q]}$$

where $a_i^j x$ stands for $\underbrace{x \star \ldots \star x}_{a_i^j \ times}$ and for all $k \in [1..q]$, the coefficients $(a_i^k)_{i \in [1..m]}$ and $(b_j^k)_{j \in [1..p]}$ are natural numbers.

In [17,16] it has been shown that solving such AC-systems can be reduced to solving systems of homogeneous linear Diophantine equation (called Diophantine system) whose coefficients are $(a_i^k)_{i \in [1..m]}$ and $(-b_j^k)_{j \in [1..p]}$ and then combining solutions. In other words, solving linear Diophantine systems of equations is only one part of the problem. The second important one is to properly combine its solutions. Here, we just show the transformation by the following example:

Example 3 *Let us consider the AC-system S_+ given before:* $\begin{cases} x + y =^? u + v \\ x + v =^? u + u \end{cases}$

Then the flattened and simplified AC-system with coefficients is: $\begin{cases} 1x \star 1y =^? 1u \star 1v \\ 1x \star 1v =^? 2u \end{cases}$

and the Diophantine system can easily be deduced from the previous system.

$$\begin{cases} 1x_{nat} + 1y_{nat} - 1u_{nat} - 1v_{nat} = 0 \\ 1x_{nat} - 2u_{nat} + 1v_{nat} = 0 \end{cases}$$

where variables $x_{nat}, y_{nat}, u_{nat}, v_{nat}$ range over **N**.

4 Solving systems of homogeneous and linear Diophantine equations

We solve the Diophantine system as in real or rational vector spaces using the Gaussian elimination method. Very recently, direct solving of systems of two Diophantine equations [23] or of an arbitrary number of Diophantine equations [8], have been proposed. We are currently investigating the gain of efficiency that they allow.

We make clear in this section how our implementation is currently working.

Let $AX = 0$ be the Diophantine system to be solved such that $A = (a_{ij})_{i=1\cdots m}^{j=1\cdots n}$ is an $m \times n$ integer matrix and $X = (x_i)_{i=1\cdots n}$ are the distinct variables of the system.

The first step consists of triangulating the matrix A which depends on the values of m and n. In other words, after applying the following algorithm on the matrix:

```
for i = 1 to m − 1
    for k = i + 1 to m
        for   j = i + 1 to n
            a_kj = a_ii.a_kj − a_ki.a_ij
        end for
    end for
end for
```

we get a matrix of the form: $M = \begin{cases} \begin{array}{l} b_{11}x_1 + b_{12}x_2 + b_{13}x_3 + \cdots + b_{1n}x_n = 0 \quad (1) \\ 0 \;\;+ b_{22}x_2 + b_{23}x_3 + \cdots + b_{2n}x_n = 0 \quad (2) \\ \cdots \end{array} \\ if\ m \geq n \begin{cases} b_{nn}x_n = 0 \quad (n) \\ \cdots \\ b_{mn}x_n = 0 \quad (m) \end{cases} \\ if\ m < n\ \ b_m x_m + \cdots + b_n x_n = 0 \qquad (m) \end{cases}$

It is easy to check that the system associated to the matrix M has not a nontrivial positive solution for $m \geq n$ and at least $b_{in} \neq 0$ $(i = n, \cdots, m)$. But if $b_{nn}, \cdots, b_{mn}$ are null, the system is reduced to $n-1$ equations by eliminating the $m-n+1$ last equations.

Henceforth, we suppose that $m < n$ and start to solve the last equation (m), which is the simplest. In order to solve this equation, the variables with negative coefficients are transferred to the other side of the equation to obtain a Diophantine equation. If there is no minimal solution to this equation, the process is stopped with no solutions to the system.

Let $s_1, \cdots, s_k \in N^{n-m+1}$ be the minimal solutions of the Diophantine equation. A solution has the general form: $(x_m, \cdots, x_n) = \sum_{j=1}^{k} y_j s_j$ where $y_j \in N$.

Hence the ith element of the vector $(x_m, \cdots x_n)$ can be written:

$$x_i = (\sum_{j=1}^{k} y_j s_j)_{i-m+1} = \sum_{j=1}^{k} y_j (s_j)_{i-m+1} \qquad i = m, \cdots, n$$

Elsewhere, we have for each equation l $(l = 1, \cdots, m-1)$:

$$\sum_{i=l}^{m-1} b_{li}x_i = -\sum_{i=m}^{n} b_{li}x_i$$
$$= -\sum_{i=m}^{n} b_{li}(\sum_{j=1}^{k} y_j (s_j)_{i-m+1}) = -\sum_{i=m}^{n} b_{li} \sum_{j=1}^{k}(y_j (s_j)_{i-m+1})$$
$$= -\sum_{i=m}^{n} \sum_{j=1}^{k} b_{li}.(y_j (s_j)_{i-m+1}) = -\sum_{i=m}^{n} \sum_{j=1}^{k} y_j.(b_{li}.(s_j)_{i-m+1})$$
$$= -\sum_{j=1}^{k} \sum_{i=m}^{n} y_j.(b_{li}.(s_j)_{i-m+1}) = -\sum_{j=1}^{k} y_j(\sum_{i=m}^{n} b_{li}.(s_j)_{i-m+1})$$

We get a system with $m-1$ equations and $m+k-1$ variables $(x_1, \cdots x_{m-1}, y_1, \cdots y_k)$ whose matrix is already triangulated. Then we immediately solve the last Diophantine equation:

$$b_{m-1,m-1}x_{m-1} + \sum_{j=1}^{k} y_j(\sum_{i=m}^{n} b_{mi}.(s_j)_{i-m+1}) = 0.$$

The process is performed until all equations are exhausted and then solutions can be easily deduced from variables $y_1, \cdots y_k$ by the relation $(x_m, \cdots, x_n) = \sum_{j=1}^{k} y_j s_j$ and $x_1, \cdots, x_{m-1}$ from $x_m, \cdots, x_n$ by the triangulated matrix. Using this process, the set of solutions obtained is not minimal. Thus, at the end of the process, all non minimal solutions are eliminated to get the minimal solution set. A full example is given in [1].

5 Combining solutions of Diophantine systems

Combining solutions is the other expensive part of the AC-unification algorithm. It requires in combining solutions of a Diophantine system to obtain a strictly positive one which may correspond to a set of AC-unifiers of the AC-system.

Let $s_1, s_2, \cdots, s_k$ be the minimal solutions of the Diophantine system such that $s_i = (s_i^1, \cdots, s_1^n)$ where n corresponds to terms $t_1, t_2, \cdots, t_n$ of the AC-system. New variables $z_1, z_2, \cdots, z_k$ are associated to $s_1, s_2, \cdots, s_k$.

Example 4

	x_1	x_2	x_3	x_4	
s_1	5	2	4	0	z_1
s_2	0	6	2	5	z_2
s_3	1	4	2	3	z_3

where $t_i = x_i$ $(i = 1, 2, 3, 4)$. Then s_3 is a strictly positive solution and corresponds to the system:

$$\begin{cases} x_1 =^? z_3 \\ x_2 =^? z_3 + z_3 + z_3 + z_3 \\ x_3 =^? z_3 + z_3 \\ x_4 =^? z_3 + z_3 + z_3 \end{cases}$$

But s_1 is not strictly positive solution. Hence, $x_4 = \lambda$ where λ is an empty term such that $\lambda + t = t + \lambda = t$ which is not allowed in AC-unification. This case brings us to combine such solution with others solutions without repetition.

We can then check that there are 2^k possibilities of combination using a word of k bits $w_1, w_2, \cdots, w_k$. Now for every possibility, we are testing if $w_1.s_1 + \cdots + w_k s_k$ is a strictly positive vector. If it is the case, we form the AC-system: $(t_i = w_1.s_1^i.z_1 + \cdots + w_k s_k^i.z_k)_{i=1..n}$

where $+$ is an AC function symbol and: $w_j s_j^i.z_j = \begin{cases} \underbrace{z_j + \cdots + z_j}_{s_j^i \ times} & if \quad w_j = 1. \\ \wedge & if \quad w_j = 0. \end{cases}$

The system $(t_i = w_1.s_1^i.z_1 + \cdots + w_k s_k^i.z_k)_{i=1..n}$ is decomposed, merged and AC-mutated again until we have a disjunction of fully decomposed system (which may be empty). Finally, the set of substitutions associated with all fully decomposed systems is the set of AC-unifiers (in general, it is the minimal set).

6 Implementation

Our C program implements AC-unification, based on the approach sketched above. This approach is proved sound and complete in [15]. The C program handles systems of equations in the term algebra in the presence of AC-function symbols and returns the set of all most general AC unifiers (unifiers are indeed constructed). A system of equations whose terms have the same top symbol is solved at one time since it can be reduced to a system of linear Diophantine equations solving. In contrast, Stickel's implementation requires to sequentially solve each equation in the AC-system. We also implemented a Diophantine system solving by using the gaussian elimination method as described above. This still requires an algorithm to solve one linear Diophantine equation and this is performed using an implementation of Clausen and Fortenbacher's algorithm based on transformation to a graph problem. Since AC theories are strict, the detection of cycles is done on fully decomposed systems as follows: we first test if there are no variables occurring both in the left and right hand side of the system (which is often the case), otherwise we use the standard method described, for example, in [17].

To compare this implementation, we have chosen to implement the recent algorithm of Christian and Lincoln [20] which obviates the need to solve homogeneous linear Diophantine equations.

7 Discussion

We have implemented the unification algorithms for the AC theory proposed by Christian-Lincoln and Claude Kirchner. We have also proposed benchmarks for testing unification of *systems* of AC-equations.

Considering the result of benchmarks and of our experiments, what are the advantages of the system-solving approach over previously proposed equation-based approaches?

The first very big improvement concerns the efficiency of non-trivial AC-systems solving. Let us extract some examples from the benchmark tables (Appendix A). Our system requires 0.12 seconds for computing a complete solution set of acunisys-32, while the sequential method requires, for solving the first equation, 639.640 seconds (for Kapur's and Zhang's [3] ac-time which seems to be the fastest), and the remaining equations are still to be solved. Now if we consider the acunisys-33 and acunisys-34 examples which take respectively 0.08 and 0.14 seconds, a sequential method will start to solve the first equation which is proved by E. Domenjoud [7] to have 34359607481 minimal unifiers, and thus the resulting system is clearly untractable using today's computers.

The second advantage is that the (minimal) solutions of a system are computed directly. In a sequential approach, intermediate terms have to be built and are only used to compute the solutions of a derived equation. They are after that thrown away, implying the need for memory management and garbage collection.

Our conclusion is that the system-solving approach is more efficient because it allows one to group more constraints on variables together. But this is not the whole story since the last sentence is only true in the case of systems the equations in which share variables. For equations with no or few shared variables, the matrix of minimal solutions of the associated Diophantine system is spare. It is then very costly to perform combinations in order to built AC-solutions. We therefore have to improve the combination algorithm in such a way that it detects, as much as possible, the unnecessary combinations. This can be solved using the technique of [6] or by more specific implementation techniques.

Acknowledgments: We gratefully acknowledge Alexandre Boudet, Nachum Dershowitz, Eric Domenjoud, Hélène Kirchner, Pierre Lescanne, Denis Lugiez and René Schott for many interesting and fruitful discussions or comments about this paper.

References

[1] M. Adi and C. Kirchner. *AC-Unification Race: the System Solving Approach, Implementation and Benchmarks.* Research Report 89-R-169, CRIN, Nancy (France), 1989.

[2] A. Boudet. *A new Combination Technique for AC Unification.* Internal Report 494, LRI, Orsay (France), June 1989.

[3] H-J. Bürckert, A. Herold, D. Kapur, J. Siekmann, M. Stickel, M. Tepp, and H. Zhang. Opening the AC-unification race. *Journal of Automated Reasoning*, 4(1):465–474, 1988.

[4] H-J. Bürckert, A. Herold, and M. Schmidt-Schauß. On equational theories, unification and decidability. *Journal of Symbolic Computation*, 8(1 & 2):3–50, 1989. Special issue on unification. Part two.

[5] M Clausen and A. Fortenbacher. Efficient solution of linear diophantine equations. *Journal of Symbolic Computation*, 8(1 & 2):201–216, 1989. Special issue on unification. Part two.

[6] E. Domenjoud. AC unification through order-sorted AC1 unification. In H-J. Bürckert and W. Nutt, editors, *Proceedings of UNIF'89, third international workshop on unification*, Lambrecht (FR Germany), June 1989. Also in CRIN Reseach Report 89-R-67.

[7] E. Domenjoud. *Number of Minimal Unifiers of the Equation $\alpha x_1 + \cdots + \alpha x_p \doteq_{AC} \beta y_1 + \cdots + \beta y_q$.* Research Report 89-R-2, CRIN, Nancy (France), 1989. To appear in the Journal of Automated Reasoning (1990).

[8] H. Devie E. Contejean. Solving systems of linear diophantine equations. In H-J. Bürckert and W. Nutt, editors, *Proceedings of UNIF'89, third international workshop on unification*, Lambrecht (FR Germany), June 1989.

[9] F. Fages and G. Huet. Complete sets of unifiers and matchers in equational theories. *Theoretical Computer Science*, 43(1):189–200, 1986.

[10] A Fortenbacher. Algebraische unifikation. 1983. Diplomarbeit, Institut für Informatik, Universität Karlsruhe.

[11] A. Herold. *Combination of Unification Algorithms in Equational Theories.* PhD thesis, Universität Kaiserslautern, 1987.

[12] G. Huet. An algorithm to generate the basis of solutions to homogenous linear diophantine equations. *Information Processing Letters*, 7(3):144–147, 1978.

[13] J-M. Hullot. Compilation de formes canoniques dans les théories équationelles. Thèse de 3ième cycle, Université de Paris Sud, Orsay, France, 1980.

[14] D. Kapur and P. Narendran. NP-completeness of the set unification and matching problems. In J. Siekmann, editor, *Proceedings 8th Conference on Automated Deduction*, Springer-Verlag, 1986.

[15] C. Kirchner. From unification in combination of equational theories to a new AC-unification algorithm. In H. Aït-Kaci and M. Nivat, editors, *Resolution of Equations in Algebraic Structures*, pages 171–210, Academic Press, New-York, 1989.

[16] C. Kirchner. Méthodes et outils de conception systématique d'algorithmes d'unification dans les théories équationnelles. Thèse d'état de l'Université de Nancy I, 1985.

[17] C. Kirchner. Methods and tools for equational unification. In *Proceedings of the Colloquium on Resolution of Equations in Algebraic Structures*, Austin (Texas), May 1987.

[18] J.-L. Lambert. Une borne pour les générateurs des solutions entières positives d'une équation diophantienne linéaire. *Compte-rendu de L'Académie des Sciences de Paris*, 305(1):39–40, 1987.

[19] D. Lankford. *Non-negative integer basis algorithms for linear equations with integer coefficients*. Technical Report, Louisiana Tech University, Ruston, LA 71272, 1987.

[20] P. Lincoln and J. Christian. Adventures in associative-commutative unification. *Journal of Symbolic Computation*, 8(1 & 2):217–240, 1989. Special issue on unification. Part two.

[21] M. Livesey and J. Siekmann. *Unification of Bags and Sets*. Technical Report, Institut fur Informatik I, Universität Karlsruhe, 1976.

[22] G. Peterson and M. Stickel. Complete sets of reductions for some equational theories. *Journal of the Association for Computing Machinery*, 28:233–264, 1981.

[23] J.-F. Romeuf. *A polynomial algorithm for solving systems of two linear diophantine equations*. Technical Report, Laboratoire d'Informatique de Rouen (France) and LITP, 1989.

[24] M. Schmidt-Schauss. Combination of unification algorithms. *Journal of Symbolic Computation*, 8(1 & 2):51–100, 1989. Special issue on unification. Part two.

[25] M.E. Stickel. A unification algorithm for associative-commutative functions. *Journal of the Association for Computing Machinery*, 28:423–434, 1981.

[26] M.E. Stickel. *Unification Algorithms for Artificial Intelligence Languages*. PhD thesis, Carnegie-mellon University, 1976.

[27] K. Yelick. Combining unification algorithm for confined equational theories. In J.-P. Jouannaud, editor, *Proceedings of the 1st Conference on Rewriting Techniques and Applications*, pages 301–324, Springer-Verlag, Dijon (France), May 1985.

A Benchmarks

The following tables are extracted from [1] that gives a large set of examples. They present performances of our implementation of Christian and Lincoln's algorithm [20] (column CL) and C. Kirchner's algorithm [17,16] (column CK). Terms are in flattened form (f and g are AC function symbols, $x, y, z, u, v, w, t, p, r, s$ are variables and a, b, c, d, e are constants). The # column precises the cardinality of the complete set of AC-unifiers that is obtained. Certain systems require one to combine a very large number of minimal solutions of the Diophantine system. For example acunisys-22 has 291 Diophantine solutions and therefore 2^{291} combinations have to be tested. In this case we only give the number of minimal solutions of the Diophantine system and the time indicated corresponds to the construction of the Diophantine system and the computation of its solutions. The algorithms are implemented in C. Times are given in seconds on a Sun 3/260.

Example	Problem	#	CK	CL
acuni − 1	$f(x, a, b) == f(u, v, c, d)$	12	0.080	0.0200
acuni − 2	$f(x, a, b) == f(u, v, w, c)$	30	0.300	0.1400
acuni − 3	$f(x, a, b) == f(u, v, w, t)$	56	1.120	0.6200
acuni − 4	$f(x, y, a) == f(u, v, w, c)$	204	1.080	0.9000
acuni − 5	$f(x, y, a) == f(u, v, w, t)$	416	1.480	1.9200
acuni − 6	$f(x, y, z) == f(u, v, w, c)$	870	2.240	3.5600
acuni − 7	$f(x, y, z) == f(u, v, w, t)$	2161	3.920	9.0400
acunisys − 1	$f(x, y, z) == f(u, v, w, t)$ $f(x, y, a) == f(u, u, u, u)$	# dio − solutions : 234	1.3600	− − − − −
acunisys − 2	$f(x, y, z) == f(u, v, w, t)$ $f(x, y, z) == f(u, v, w, c)$	870	3.3200	− − − − −
acunisys − 3	$f(x, y, z) == f(u, v, w, t)$ $f(x, y, z) == f(u, u, v, w)$	2901	7.9600	− − − − −
acunisys − 4	$f(x, y, z) == f(u, v, w, t)$ $f(x, y, z) == f(u, u, u, u)$	# dio − solutions : 150	0.8600	− − − − −
acunisys − 5	$f(x, y, z) == f(u, v, w, t)$ $f(x, x, a) == f(u, c, c, d)$	1052	17.0000	− − − − −
acunisys − 6	$f(x, y, z) == f(u, v, w, t)$ $f(x, x, a) == f(u, c, c, c)$	1052	10.7800	− − − − −
acunisys − 7	$f(x, y, z) == f(u, v, w, t)$ $f(x, x, a) == f(u, u, c, c)$	0	0.1200	− − − − −
acunisys − 8	$f(x, y, z) == f(u, v, w, t)$ $f(x, x, a) == f(u, u, v, c)$	68	0.6400	− − − − −
acunisys − 9	$f(x, y, z) == f(u, v, w, t)$ $f(x, x, a) == f(u, u, u, c)$	966	8.2200	− − − − −
acunisys − 10	$f(x, y, z) == f(u, v, w, t)$ $f(x, x, y) == f(u, c, c, c)$	# dio − solutions : 282	1.2000	− − − − −
acunisys − 11	$f(x, y, z) == f(u, v, w, t)$ $f(x, x, y) == f(u, v, w, t)$	13703	26.5600	− − − − −
acunisys − 12	$f(x, y, z) == f(u, v, w, t)$ $f(x, x, y) == f(u, u, c, d)$	366	4.1600	− − − − −
acunisys − 13	$f(x, y, z) == f(u, v, w, t)$ $f(x, x, y) == f(u, u, v, w)$	1365	2.6200	− − − − −
acunisys − 14	$f(x, y, z) == f(u, v, w, t)$ $f(x, x, y) == f(u, u, v, v)$	103	0.2400	− − − − −
acunisys − 15	$f(x, y, z) == f(u, v, w, t)$ $f(x, x, y) == f(u, u, u, c)$	# dio − solutions : 120	0.5000	− − − − −
acunisys − 16	$f(x, y, z) == f(u, v, w, t)$ $f(x, x, x) == f(u, c, c, d)$	428	3.4800	− − − − −

Heuristical Criteria in Refutational Theorem Proving

Siva Anantharaman
LIFO, Dépt. Math-Info.
Université d'Orléans
45067 Orléans Cedex 02
FRANCE
E-mail: siva@univ-orleans.fr

Nirina Andrianarivelo
LIFO, Dépt. Math-Info.
Université d'Orléans
45067 Orléans Cedex 02
FRANCE
E-mail: andria@univ-orleans.fr

1 Introduction

Several attempts of automated deduction have been made via the well-known Unfailing Knuth-Bendix approach in the recent past([HR-87], [Ru-87], [Bac-87], [AH-89]). It appeared to us from these, that the practical efficiency of this approach can probably be increased: (i) if a target-oriented strategy can be employed for selecting or generating the 'next' rule from the current list, (ii) if there is some way of telling if a rule is more 'useful' than the others in the proof-process. On the other hand, this approach needs, theoretically, to work with a reduction ordering *total on ground classes*, and arrives at the final proof by 'simplification alone'. While this is often not the most efficient way in practice, it *is* a cumbersome point to surmount when one generalizes *UKB* to axiomatic rewriting ([AM-89]).

In our present work, we have tried to find some solutions for all these problems. First, in a preliminary section, we show that we can drop the above hypothesis on the underlying reduction ordering, provided some limited paramodulation is done on the inequalities (*'order-saturation strategy'*; see also [AH-89]).

The second part builds a systematic method for (partially) tackling the first 2 questions. It is based on a concept called *measure*, which helps in the construction of a target-oriented strategy on the sets of rules. A final section gives examples, where the software $SBR3$, implementing these new ideas, has been able to shorten considerably all our earlier proofs ([AH-89]).

Acknowledgement. We are indebted to Jieh HSIANG for his interest in this work, and his valuable advices.

2 Overview of the UKB-Inference Rules in Refutational Theorem-Proving

We give here a quick review of an inference system, applicable to the context of refutational theorem-proving via the Unfailing Knuth-Bendix Completion approach. We begin with a few remarks concerning our terminology and notation, which we have tried to keep as standard as possible, say as employed in [Bac-87]. The symbol > will designate (as usual) a fixed reduction ordering on terms. We will employ the word 'rule' to mean indifferently an oriented rule *or* an unoriented equation, both covered - for us - by the notation $l \doteq r$. *The symbol '=' will, for us, exclusively signify syntactic equality.* The notation $l \rightarrow r$ will designate (as usual) an explicitly oriented rule. The notions of reduction or simplification (resp. overlaps) are extended as in [HR-87], [Bac-87] to cover the case of unoriented 'rules'. The smallest reduction ordering containing simplifications by the 'rules' in a system S, will be denoted (as in [AM-89]) by $\Rightarrow_S$. (Note the difference in notation here with [Bac-87]).

We will employ some more unusual notation: Let $\mathcal{E}$ be a system of rules, s, t be terms, $l \doteq r$ a rule in $\mathcal{E}$, p an occurrence in s, and σ a substitution such that: $s/p = \sigma l, s[p \to \sigma r] = t$. If $s > t$ in the (given) ordering, this will be denoted by: $s \hookrightarrow_{\mathcal{E}} t$, or $t \hookleftarrow_{\mathcal{E}} s$; while if s and t are *uncomparable* in the ordering, we will write $s =_{\mathcal{E}} t$. (Obviously the relation $\leftrightarrow_{\mathcal{E}}$ contains $\Rightarrow_{\mathcal{E}}$). When the context is unambiguous, $\mathcal{E}$ will often be omitted in the subscripts.

We assume for the rest of the paper that the ordering $>$ is *coherent* in the following sense: If s, u are ground terms and p an occurrence in s such that, $s > s[p \leftarrow u]$, then *for all occurrences q, disjoint with p in s and all ground v*, we have necessarily: $s[q \leftarrow v] > s[q \leftarrow v, p \leftarrow u]$.

N.B. This property of coherence is easily established for all usual orderings (like the rpo, lpo, and the polynomial ordering). On the other hand, *we do not make any hypothesis of totality of the given ordering* on (the congruence classes of) ground terms.

The inference system, that we will call $\mathcal{URC}$ (Unfailing Refutational Completion), consists of the following set of inference rules:

> E is the set of unoriented equations
> R is the set of oriented rules
> NE is the set of inequalities (all supposed ground).
> $>$ is a reduction ordering on terms, containing R.

A binary operator denoted $\neq$, not appearing in the rules of E, R, is assumed to be the top operator of all the inequalities in the set NE. The given ordering $>$ is extended to the inequalities in the obvious way.

1) Orienting an equation

$$\frac{(E \cup \{s \doteq t\}, R, NE)}{(E, R \cup \{s \to t\}, NE)} \qquad \text{if } s > t$$

2) Right Simplification of an oriented rule

$$\frac{(E, R \cup \{s \to t\}, NE)}{(E, R \cup \{s \to t'\}, NE)} \qquad \text{if } t \Rightarrow_{E \cup R} t'.$$

3) Left-simplification of an oriented rule

$$\frac{(E, R \cup \{s \to t\}, NE)}{(E \cup \{s' \doteq t\}, R, NE)} \qquad$$
if $s \Rightarrow_{R \cup E} s'$ at a position not at the top, or by $l \doteq r$ with $s \rhd l$ ($\rhd$ is the proper subsumption relation)

4) Simplifying an equation

$$\frac{(E \cup \{s \doteq t\}, R, NE)}{(E \cup \{s' \doteq t\}, R, NE)} \qquad \text{if } s \Rightarrow_{R \cup E} s' \text{ not at the top}$$

5) Simplifying an inequation

$$\frac{(E, R, NE \cup \{s \neq t\})}{(E, R, NE \cup \{s' \neq t\})} \qquad \text{if } s \Rightarrow_{R \cup E} s'$$

6) Adding an equational consequence

$$\frac{(E, R, NE)}{(E \cup \{s \doteq t\}, R, NE)} \qquad$$
if $s \doteq t$ is obtained by a non-variable overlap between two rules from $R \cup E$

7) Adding an inequational consequence: <u>order-saturation</u>

$$\frac{(E, R, NE)}{(E, R, NE \cup \{A' \neq B'\})}$$

if $A' \neq B'$ is an overlap between an existing inequality $A \neq B$ in NE and a rule $l \doteq r$ from E such that $A \neq B \not\leq A' \neq B'$

8) Deleting a trivial equation

$$\frac{(E \cup \{s \doteq s\}, R, NE)}{(E, R, NE)}$$

9) Subsumption of an equation

$$\frac{(E \cup \{u \doteq v\} \cup \{s[\sigma u] \doteq s[\sigma v]\}, R, NE)}{(E \cup \{u \doteq v\}, R, NE)}$$

Note that if $NE = \emptyset$ the above inference system corresponds essentially to the usual unfailing completion.

We will be considering, in what follows, any (arbitrarily) given sequence $\{(E_i, R_i, NE_i)\}, i \geq 0$, where: i) E_0 is the set of user input initial equations, $R_0 = \emptyset$, and NE_0 is the set of user input initial inequalities, ii) And the triple $(E_{i+1}, R_{i+1}, NE_{i+1})$ is obtained from the triple (E_i, R_i, NE_i) by the application of one or more of the above inference rules, for any i.

For any i, the system $E_i \cup R_i$, will be denoted henceforth 'more simply' by $\mathcal{E}_i$.

We also assume explicitly that this sequence of derivations is fair in the following sense:

(a) Any (extended or usual) critical pair between any two 'persisting' rules is in some $\mathcal{E}_i$,

(b) Any inequality obtainable from an element of an NE_j by order-saturation, or by simplification, w.r.t. a 'persisting' rule, is in some NE_i, $i \geq j$.

Let us recall that, conventionally, if $s =_E t$ is the equational theorem to be proved (in the equational theory defined be E), the initial inequality set NE_0 just contains its skolemised negation, $\bar{s} \neq \bar{t}$, where all the variables (assumed free) have been replaced by corresponding skolem constants.

2.1 $\mathcal{URC}$ is Refutationally Complete

Definition 1 *Let $\mathcal{E}$ be a given set of rules, and $\mathcal{P}$ a given chain of ground terms:*

$$s = s_0 \leftrightarrow_{\mathcal{E}} s_1 \leftrightarrow_{\mathcal{E}} \ldots \leftrightarrow_{\mathcal{E}} s_{r-1} \leftrightarrow_{\mathcal{E}} s_r \leftrightarrow_{\mathcal{E}} \ldots \leftrightarrow_{\mathcal{E}} s_n = t.$$

i) A subchain $s_{r-1} \leftrightarrow_{\mathcal{E}} s_r \leftrightarrow_{\mathcal{E}} s_{r+1}$ of length 2 is said to define a left-peak at index r (or at s_r) in $\mathcal{P}$ iff $s_r > s_{r-1}$, and $s_r \not< s_{r+1}$. The two occurrences p, q in s_r where the two rules of $\mathcal{E}$ are applied to the left and to the right, will be called the occurrences at the left-peak. A right-peak in $\mathcal{P}$ is defined in a similar manner. A 2-sided peak is both a left- and a right-peak.

ii) A subchain $\mathcal{Q}$ of $\mathcal{P}$ is said to define a g-peak of width m in $\mathcal{P}$ iff:

- it is of the form $s_{r-1} \leftrightarrow_{\mathcal{E}} s_r \rightleftharpoons_{\mathcal{E}} \ldots \rightleftharpoons_{\mathcal{E}} s_{r+m} \leftrightarrow_{\mathcal{E}} s_{r+m+1}$, of length $m + 2$,

- it has exactly one left-peak at s_r and one right-peak at s_{r+m}, all the other successive intermediary terms being uncomparable.

iii) $\mathcal{P}$ is said to be monotonous decreasing (resp. increasing) iff we have, for all $0 \leq r < n$: either $s_r \hookrightarrow_{\mathcal{E}} s_{r+1}$ or $s_r \rightleftharpoons_{\mathcal{E}} s_{r+1}$ (resp. either $s_r \hookleftarrow_{\mathcal{E}} s_{r+1}$ or $s_r \rightleftharpoons_{\mathcal{E}} s_{r+1}$). $\mathcal{P}$ is said to be monotonous iff it is either monotonous decreasing or monotonous increasing.

iv) The chain $\mathcal{P}$ is said to be semi-monotonous iff it has no g-peak (or equivalently: iff exists an index $0 \leq n_1 \leq n$ such that $\{s_0, \ldots, s_{n_1}\}$ is monotonous decreasing, while $\{s_{n_1}, \ldots s_n\}$ is monotonous increasing).

(For instance, any 'classical peak' is a 2-sided peak; any 2-sided peak is a g-peak of width 0; and any 'classical valley' is semi-monotonous).

Lemma 1 *Let s and t be any two ground terms, such that $s \leftrightarrow^*_\mathcal{E} t$, that for some j, the set NE_j contains $s \neq t$, and that there exists a semi-monotonous $\mathcal{E}_j$-proof-chain P going from s to t. Then there exists an $i \geq j$ such that NE_i contains an instance of the inequality $x \neq x$.*

The refutational completeness of $\mathcal{URC}$ can thus established if we show that an entire $\mathcal{E}_0$-proof-chain, corresponding to a 'valid' inequality $s \neq t$ in NE_0, can be replaced by a semi-monotonous $\mathcal{E}_i$-chain, for some later i. For that we will need the following

Definition 2 *Let $\mathcal{E}$ be a system of rules, and P any $\mathcal{E}$-chain of ground terms.*

i) The $\mathcal{E}$-complexity of P is defined as the ordered pair (M, n), denoted $c_\mathcal{E}(P)$, where: M is the multiset of the terms in P, and n is the number of g-peaks in P.

ii) Let $\ll$ denote the multiset extension of the given reduction ordering. Then a strict partial ordering $\prec$ on such ordered pairs is defined as the lexicographic combination of $\ll$ on the first component, with the usual $<$ on integers.

(Note that a chain P is semi-monotonous iff its complexity is of the form $(M, 0)$). We now generalize the classical peak-reduction lemma.

Theorem 1 *Let s and t be any two ground terms, such that $s \leftrightarrow^*_\mathcal{E} t$. Suppose that for some j, we have an $\mathcal{E}_j$-chain P from s to t, whose number of g-peaks is > 0. Then there exists an index $i \geq j$, and an $\mathcal{E}_i$-chain P' from s to t, such that: $c_{\mathcal{E}_i}(P') \prec c_{\mathcal{E}_j}(P)$.*

Corollary 1 *The inference system $\mathcal{URC}$ is refutationally complete (under the assumed fairness hypotheses).*

3 The Notion of Measure

Definition 3 *A measure on the algebra of terms $T(\mathcal{F}, \mathcal{X})$, is a map from $\mathcal{F} \times T(\mathcal{F}, \mathcal{X})$ into the set N of non-negative integers, verifying the following conditions:*

1. *for all $op \in \mathcal{F}$, not appearing in a term t , $m(op, t) = 0$.*

2. *(Stability): for all $op \in \mathcal{F}$, substitution σ, and term u,*

$$m(op, \sigma u) \geq m(op, u)$$

3. *(Subterm-Property): for all $op \in \mathcal{F}$, and terms t, u,*

$$m(op, u[t]) \geq m(op, t)$$

Examples of measure:

1. For any operator op, and any term t, set $m(op, t)$ to be equal to:

   - 0, if op does not occur in t (or if op is varyadic),
   - the number of times op occurs in the tree representation of t if the arity of op is $\neq 0$,
   - 1 otherwise.

   This will be called the 'coarse' measure, and denoted m_c. It can be refined in several ways to suit our purposes. The following refinement, that we label the 'semi-coarse' measure, will be denoted by m_0.

2. $m_0(op, t)$ is defined recursively as follows: If op is varyadic, or if op does not figure in t, then $m_0(op, t)$ is set to be 0. Otherwise write $t = f(t_1, \ldots, t_n)$; then

$$m_0(op, t) = \begin{cases} Max\{m_0(op, t_i) \mid i = 1, \ldots n\} & \text{if } f \text{ is varyadic,} \\ 1 + \sum_{i=1}^{n} m_0(op, t_i) & \text{if } f = op, \\ \sum_{i=1}^{n} m_0(op, t_i) & \text{otherwise} \end{cases}$$

3. Let t be any term, and f be any function symbol. Then define a binary function, denoted by $m_1(f, t)$, recursively as follows: If f does not appear in t, then $m_1(f, t) = 0$. Otherwise write $t = g(t_1, \ldots, t_n)$; then

$$m_1(f, t) = \begin{cases} 1 + \sum_{i=1}^{n} m_1(f, t_i) & \text{if } f = g, \\ Max\{m_1(f, t_i) \mid i = 1, \ldots, n\} & \text{otherwise} \end{cases}$$

Such a binary function gives a still finer example of measure. (In [AH-89], some heuristics based on this m_1 were employed).

It is worth noting that for any measure m, and any fixed function symbol op, $m(op, -)$ viewed as a unary function on the second variable, defines a quasi-ordering on terms.

3.1 Extension of a measure to Rules and Inequalities

We assume from now onwards, for the rest of the paper, that we are working in the context of refutational theorem proving, as described in Section 2.

Definition 4 *Let m be any given measure on $T(\mathcal{F}, \mathcal{X})$. Then, for any function symbol $op \in \mathcal{F}$, and any rule $l \doteq r$ in E or R, and any inequality $A \neq B$ in NE, we set:*

$$m(op, l \doteq r) = inf\{m(op, l), m(op, r)\}$$

$$m(op, A \neq B) = max\{m(op, A), m(op, B)\}$$

And finally, for any op in $\mathcal{F}$, we set:

$$m(op, NE) = max_{A \neq B \in NE}\{m(op, A \neq B)\}$$

Notation. For any term t, the set of function symbols appearing in t will be denoted by $F(t)$. If $\mathcal{E}$ is any set of rules, $F(\mathcal{E})$ is the set of all function symbols appearing in the rules of $\mathcal{E}$. And finally for any set of (ground) inequalities NE, $F(NE)$ will denote the set of function symbols other than $\neq$, appearing in the ground terms of NE.

We now introduce some new notions. These are destinated to help us localize, among the rules generated during a proof-process, those which are 'less crucial' for the obtention of the proof.

Definition 5 *Let m be any given measure, $>$ a given reduction ordering on $T(\mathcal{F}, \mathcal{X})$, op any given function symbol, $\mathcal{G}$ a fixed set of ground terms, and S any given set of rules. Then m is said to be compatible with $>$, on op, w.r.t. S and $\mathcal{G}$, iff:*

- for any rule $l \doteq r$ in S and substitution σ such that σl be a subterm of an element in $\mathcal{G}$

  and $\sigma l > \sigma r$, we have $m(op, \sigma l) \geq m(op, \sigma r)$.

(The above definition says that $>$ and the quasi-ordering $m(op, -)$, are not in conflict on the matches of the rules in S onto the subterms of elements in $\mathcal{G}$).

Definition 6 *Let $\{(E_i, R_i, NE_i)\}$ be an arbitrarily given sequence of URC- derivations as described in Section 2, and m a given measure on terms. Then for any $i \geq 0$, we define $\overline{F}_i$ as the set of all function symbols $op \in F(\mathcal{E}_i)$ satisfying all the following conditions:*

- the measure m is compatible with the reduction ordering '$>$' on op, w.r.t. $\mathcal{E}_i$ and NE_i.

- *if $op \notin F(NE_i)$, and if there exists a rule $l \doteq r$ in $\mathcal{E}_i$ such that $m(op, l) \neq m(op, r)$, then there also exists a rule $g \doteq d \in \mathcal{E}_i$ with either $m(op, g) = 0$ or $m(op, d) = 0$.*

The set $\overline{F}_i \bigcap F(NE_i)$ will be denoted by F_i.

(Note that at least F_0 and $\overline{F}_0$ can be explicitly calculated manually).

Let us give a few examples here to illustrate these definitions.

Example 3.1.1. Consider for instance the initial system $\mathcal{E}_0$:

$$(x * x) * y \doteq y, \quad (x * y) * z \doteq (y * z) * x$$

and the initial inequality: $(a * b) * c \neq a * (b * c)$.

Consider the measure m on terms defined by the binary function m_1 described above. Then m is compatible with the ordering $rpos$ on '$*$', w.r.t. $\mathcal{E}_0$ and NE_0. In fact, it can be verified that for any $\mathcal{URC}$-derivation chain obtained from this initial system, m remains compatible with $rpos$ on '$*$' w.r.t. $\mathcal{E}_i$ and NE_i for any i. Here we have $F_i = \overline{F}_i = \{*\}$, for all i.

Remark 1. It happens, in many interesting practical cases, that there exists an index i_0, such that $\overline{F} = \bigcap_{j \geq i_0} \overline{F}_j \neq \emptyset$. If this is the case, we will say that the $\mathcal{URC}$-derivation chain is *m-controllable* on the set of function symbols $\overline{F}$ (w.r.t. the given reduction ordering).

Example 3.1.2. Consider the initial set of equations:

$$f(a, f(x, y)) \doteq f(b, f(x, y)), \quad f(a, f(a, y)) \doteq a, \quad f(b, f(x, b)) \doteq b$$

And the inequality: $a \neq b$.

Then for the measure defined by m_1, any $\mathcal{URC}$ derivation chain is m_1-controllable on the set of function symbols $\{f, a, b\}$.

Consider now, for any rule $l \doteq r$ in $\mathcal{E}_i$ the following property:

there exists an $op \in F_i$, such that :
(HC$_i$) $\quad \inf \{m(op, l), m(op, r)\} > m(op, NE_i)$

(We will occasionally need to say more explicitly: $l \doteq r$ has the property **(HC$_i$)** w.r.t. the function symbol $op \in F_i$).

This property, qualifiable as 'the Heuristical Condition at Level i', is destinated to give us partial information on the 'uselessness' for the proof process (at least in some special cases), of any new rule $l \doteq r$ generated by the inference system $\mathcal{URC}$.

This is made clearer in the following propositions. Please observe that, when the Simplification-first Strategy accompanies $\mathcal{URC}$, the above property is in effect to be satisfied by the new rule in its normalised form.

Proposition 1 *If a rule $l \doteq r$ in $\mathcal{E}_i$ has the property* **(HC$_i$)**, *then it can neither simplify nor order-saturate any of the inequalities in NE_i.*

We are going to show that, *in some special cases*, rules having **(HC$_i$)** are useless for the proof-process. For that we need the following result whose proof needs to work with the coarse or the semi-coarse measure (it is inadaptable for other measures, for the present). And in order to be able to work with the semi-coarse measure in non-trivial cases, we have first to refine the way one counts the number of occurrences of variables in terms.

Definition 7 *Let t be any term, and x a given variable. Then we call the s-number of occurrences of x in t the integer $snum(x, t)$ defined recursively as follows: If x does not occur at all in t, then $snum(x, t) = 0$. Otherwise write $t = f(t_1, \ldots, t_n)$; then*

$$snum(x, t) = \begin{cases} Max\{snum(x, t_i) \mid i = 1, \ldots n\} & \text{if } f \text{ is varyadic,} \\ \sum_{i=1}^{n} snum(x, t_i) & \text{otherwise} \end{cases}$$

Proposition 2 *Consider a URC-derivation chain $\{(E_i, R_i, NE_i)\}$, and suppose that for a given i, the following conditions hold:*

- *for any rule $l \doteq r$ in $\mathcal{E}_i$, the s-number of occurrences of any variable x is the same on l and r. (We will call such rules strongly regular).*

- *F_0 is a non-empty subset of $F(NE_i)$ such that for any $op \in F_0$ and any rule $l \doteq r$ in $\mathcal{E}_i$, we have $m_0(op, l) = m_0(op, r)$. (We will say that the rules are non-contracting on F_0).*

Then for any $j > i$, we have $F_0 \subset F(NE_j)$ and the above conditions also hold for the rules in $\mathcal{E}_j$ (with respect to the same measure m_0).

And the following theorem is now immediate.

Theorem 2 *Let $\{(E_i, R_i, NE_i)\}$ be a URC-derivation chain such that, for some given i, and some $\emptyset \neq F_0 \subset F(NE_i)$ the rules of $\mathcal{E}_i$ are strongly regular and non-contracting on F_0. Let $l \doteq r$ be any rule having the property (HC_i), w.r.t. a function symbol in F_0. Then any rule obtained from $l \doteq r$ by simplification, or by superposition, has the property (HC_j), for every $j > i$ (and w.r.t. the same function symbol). In other words, such rules can be 'deleted' from $\mathcal{E}_j$ for every $j \geq i$).*

We give a non-trivial illustrative example for the above theorem, from the theory of Alternative Rings.

Example 3.1.3. Consider the Initial System :

$$g(x + y) \doteq g(x) + g(y), \quad g(g(x)) \doteq x$$
$$x * (y + z) \doteq (x * y) + (x * z), \quad (x + y) * z \doteq (x * z) + (y * z)$$
$$(x * y) * y \doteq x * (y * y), \quad (x * x) * y \doteq x * (x * y)$$
$$g(x) * y \doteq g(x * y), \quad x * g(y) \doteq g(x * y).$$

And the Inequality $(cx * cy) * cx \neq cx * (cy * cx)$ ('The Middle Law').

The operator '+' is declared AC, with two-sided cancellability. The measure we work with is m_0 (which coincides with m_1 on these systems). The set F_0 under consideration is evidently $\{*\}$. Thus, in the proof-process, we may delete all new rules generated with measures strictly higher than 2 w.r.t. '*' .See also [AH-89].

Remark 2. It must be noted that the semi-coarse measure m_0 is not fine enough to help us identify *all* the useless rules in a proof-process, via the above criterion, even for derivation chains satisfying the conditions of the above Theorem.

Remark 3. It is not true that rules having the property (HC_i) can be deleted from the proof-process in *all* cases, without any hypotheses.

Remark 4. Though we have not been able to prove it so far, it seems likely that, w.r.t. arbitrary measures m, deletion of rules can be justified completely (in the sense of the above theorem), if we replace the condition (HC_i) by the following much stronger condition:

$$(\overline{\text{HC}_i}) \qquad \begin{array}{l} \text{for } every \ op \in \overline{F}_i, \text{ we have :} \\ \{m(op, l) = m(op, r)\} > m(op, NE_i). \end{array}$$

These remarks allow us to consider henceforth the deletion problem as secondary, and fix as our primary objective the obtention of a reasonable target-oriented selection strategy on rules. We propose to build such strategies on a comparative study of the measures of the various rules w.r.t. the function symbols in the set $\overline{F}_i$. This is the object of our next section.

4 The filtration-sorting strategy on rules. Examples

As above, let $\{(E_i, R_i, NE_i)\}$ be any URC-derivation chain, and m any given measure. (Recall that for any i, $\mathcal{E}_i$ denotes the set $E_i \cup R_i$). Let *Sort* be any given sorting strategy on lists. Applying this strategy for choosing the next rule on every $\mathcal{E}_i$ for performing simplifications and/or overlaps is of course not incorrect, but turns out to be far more inefficient in practice, compared to its refinements that we define below.

Definition 8 *i) Let $\mathcal{E}$ be any given set of rules. A unary function γ from $\mathcal{E}$ to the set $\mathbf{N}$ of non-negative integers is called an index function on $\mathcal{E}$.*

ii) Let γ be any given index function on $\mathcal{E}$. For any integer j, let $\mathcal{E}_j$ be the subset of $\mathcal{E}$ consisting of those of the rules rr with $\gamma(rr) \le j$. We will say that $\bigcup_j \mathcal{E}_j$ is the filtration defined on $\mathcal{E}$ by γ. The elements of $\mathcal{E}_j$ are said to have a filtration index $\le j$, w.r.t. γ.

iii) To every given index function γ on $\mathcal{E}$, we may associate a new sorting strategy γ-Sort as the lexicographic combination of the quasi-orderings defined by γ and Sort on $\mathcal{E}$.

iv) We may similarly define Sort-γ as the inverse lexicographic combination of these two quasi-orderings.

Examples of indices. Let $\mathcal{E}$ be any system of rules.

1) The usual size function on $\mathcal{E}$ can be viewed as an index function on $\mathcal{E}$, and the corresponding sorting strategy is the 'classical' sorting on lists of rewrite-rules.

2) This classical size function can be refined into a new function size1, by setting size1(rr) as the size of the left hand side of rr if the rule rr is oriented, and as size(rr) otherwise. The corresponding sorting strategy (which essentially gives priority to oriented rules), has already been used, with profit, in the proofs of the Moufang Identities in [AH-89].

3) We now give an example of an index function based on measures. Let $\mathcal{E}$ be a system of rules, F a given set of function symbols, and m a given measure on terms. For any rule $rr \in \mathcal{E}$, define $\mathrm{Ind}(rr) = Max\{m(op, rr) \mid op \in F\}$; this will be called the filtration-index of the given rule w.r.t. m, and the set of function symbols F.

The corresponding sorting strategies (defined as above) will be called the *filtration-sorting strategies* associated to m, the set of function symbols F, and *Sort*.

These filtration-sorting strategies dependent on m, will in practice be used on the sets E_i, R_i, NE_i, for every i, and with respect to the set of function symbols $\overline{F}_i$ as defined in the previous Section. In case the derivation chain is m-controllable (see the definition above) on a set of function symbols $\overline{F}$, this latter can replace all the F_i.

4.1 Examples

We give below several examples to illustrate the gain in efficiency in UKB-based theorem proving attempts, due to the order-saturation and/or the filtration-sorting. The software used is SBR3, an extension of SbReve2 ([AMH-89]), incorporating all the ideas presented in this paper. The implementation (in CLU) was done by the authors, at LIFO - Université d'ORLEANS (France), in September 1989.

Example 4.1.1. Consider the initial system: $(x * x) * y \doteq y$, $(x * y) * z \doteq (y * z) * x$

and the initial inequality: $(a * b) * c \neq a * (b * c)$.

Here is an extract from a script file of a quick proof for the associativity of '*' (obtained in 1 sec.) where we have set $a > b > c$. We do not know of any quick proof with a total ordering on ground terms.

```
The equation or Rule:    [0] ((a * b) * c) =/= (a * (b * c)) -> 1
     was reduced to:     [4] ((b * c) * a) =/= (a * (b * c)) -> 1
New Rule (or Ineqn.):: [14] z * x == (x * (x1 * x1)) * z
     From: (x * y) * z == (y * z) * x, and  (x * x) * y -> y
New Rule (or Ineqn.):: [17] ((b * c) * a) =/= ((b * c) * a) -> 1
     From:[14] z * x == (x * (x1 * x1)) * z
```

and [4] $((b * c) * a) =/= (a * (b * c))$ -> 1
*** Proved ***
Knuth-Bendix runtime: Total: 1 second.
Computed 10 critical pairs and ordered 4 equations into rules.

Example 4.1.2. Consider the Initial System:

$$0 + x \doteq x, \quad 0 * x \doteq 0, \quad x * 0 \doteq 0$$
$$g(x) + x \doteq 0, \quad g(x + y) \doteq g(x) + g(y), \quad g(g(x)) \doteq x$$
$$x * (y + z) \doteq (x * y) + (x * z), \quad (x + y) * z \doteq (x * z) + (y * z)$$
$$(x * y) * y \doteq x * (y * y), \quad (x * x) * y \doteq x * (x * y)$$
$$g(x) * y \doteq g(x * y), \quad x * g(y) \doteq g(x * y)$$

And the initial Inequality NE:
 $((cx * cy) * cx) =/= (cx * (cy * cx))$ -> 1

. . . . .
Equational theory: AC: +
Cancellation Law holds now for the AC-Operator: '+'.
New Rule (or Ineqn.)::
 [32] $((x * y1) * y) + ((y1 * x) * y) \rightarrow (x * (y1 * y)) + (y1 * (x * y))$
 From: $(x * x) * y \rightarrow x * (x * y)$, and $(x + y) * z \rightarrow (x * z) + (y * z)$
New Rule (or Ineqn.)::
 [34] $(x * (x * y)) * y \rightarrow x * (x * (y * y))$
 From: $(x * x) * y \rightarrow x * (x * y)$, and $(x * y) * y \rightarrow x * (y * y)$
New Rule (or Ineqn.)::
 [39] $(x * (y1 * y)) + (y1 * (x * y)) + g((y1 * x) * y) == (x * y1) * y$
 From: [32], and $g(x) + x \rightarrow 0$
New Rule (or Ineqn.):: [40] $(cx * (cy * cx)) =/= (cx * (cy * cx))$ -> 1
 From: [39], and $((cx * cy) * cx) =/= (cx * (cy * cx))$ -> 1
 *** Proved ***
Knuth-Bendix runtime: Total: 13 seconds.
Computed 100 critical pairs and ordered 19 equations into rules.

Remark. The measure used is the one defined by m_1 in Section 3. The derivation chain is m_1-controllable on '*'. The underlying sorting strategy on rules is according to their size. But that alone would have chosen rule [34] prior to rule [32] for overlaps. Now [34] has filtration-index 3, while that of [32] is 2. So [32] is chosen first.... Thus the deletion problem has indeed become secondary.

Example 4.1.3. We will just indicate here that all of the sophisticated proofs, obtained in [AH-89] for the Moufang Identities in Alternative Rings, have been shortened considerably by the present refinements. (Recall that these proofs already used order-saturation, and heuristics for deletion). By using the measure m_1 above, and employing the associated filtration-sorting, in a lexicographic combination with size, we have been able to prove each of them in less than 30 mts. as compared to 2 to 3 hrs. in the earlier attempt.

Example 4.1.4. Here is an example from Propositional Calculus, related to the so-called Lukasiewics Logic. Consider the Initial System:

$$\text{true} \Rightarrow x \doteq x$$
$$(x \Rightarrow y) \Rightarrow ((y \Rightarrow z) \Rightarrow (x \Rightarrow z)) \doteq \text{true}$$
$$(not(x) \Rightarrow not(y)) \Rightarrow (y \Rightarrow x) \doteq \text{true}$$
$$((x \Rightarrow y) \Rightarrow y) \doteq ((y \Rightarrow x) \Rightarrow x)$$

Then it can be proved (as has been done automatically, and quickly, by SBR3) that the binary function 'OR' defined by OR(x, y)= $(not(x) \Rightarrow y)$, is commutatif and associatif. And then it can be established (via AC-UKB) that *for any x, y, we have either $x \Rightarrow y$ or $y \Rightarrow x$.* (Automated proof obtained in 24 minutes by SBR3 on a SUN 3/260).

This is the so-called Conjecture of Lukasiewjcz, which took several years of manual work to get proved. (See [AB-89] for the details).

5 Conclusion

We hope to have convinced the reader by now, that the extra time spent on the calculations of the measures of the various rules is not wasted, but serves instead as the key factor in the reduction of the size of the search-space. It would seem however that there exists no index function γ, and no sorting strategy *Sort*, such that γ-*Sort* (or *Sort*-γ) be uniformly efficient in all cases. This is the main reason why the software SBR3 has opted for a lexicographic combination of more than one filtration-sorting, giving an appreciable overall efficiency.

Perhaps some future theoretical work will throw more light on this point, as well as on the deletion problem evoked in the previous Section.

References

[AH-89] S. ANANTHARAMAN, J. HSIANG, Automated Proofs of the Moufang Identities in Alternative Rings, *To appear in the J. Automated Reasoning, 1989*

[AM-88] S. ANANTHARAMAN, J. MZALI, Unfailing Completion Modulo a set of Equations, *Research Report, no. 470, LRI-Orsay (Fr.), 1989*

[AHM-88] S. ANANTHARAMAN, J. HSIANG, J. MZALI, SbReve2: A term Rewriting Laboratory with (AC-)Unfailing Completion, *RTA (1989)*

[AB-89] S. ANANTHARAMAN, M-P. BONACINA, Automated Proofs in the Logic of Lukasiewicz, *Research Report no. 89-11, LIFO - Orléans.*

[Bac-87] L. BACHMAIR, Proof Methods for Equational Theories, *Ph.D. Thesis, University of Illinois at Urbana-Champaign, Urbana, Illinois, USA, 1987*

[De-87] N. DERSHOWITZ, Termination of Rewriting, *J. Symbolic Computation, Vol 3, pp 59-116, 1987*

[DJ-90] N. DERSHOWITZ, J.-P. JOUANNAUD, Rewrite Systems, *Handbook of Theoretical Computer Science, Vol B, North-Holland, 1990*

[HR-87] J. HSIANG, M. RUSINOWITCH, On word problems in equational theories, *Proc. of the 14th ICALP, Springer-Verlag LNCS, Vol 267, pp 54-71, 1987*

[KB-70] D. E. KNUTH, P. B. BENDIX, Simple Word Problems in Universal Algebras, *Computational Problems in Abstract Algebras, Ed. J. Leech, Pergamon Press, pp 263-297, 1970*

[Ru-87] M. RUSINOWITCH, Démonstration Automatique par des Téchniques de Réécriture, *Thèse d'Etat, Université de Nancy I, 1987*

Requirements for Standards in Knowledge Base Systems

Giuseppe Attardi
Dipartimento di Informatica
Universita' di Pisa, Italy

Since the knowledge base component is usually a small portion of an overall application, it is essential that such component can be easily integrated with the rest of a system. One approach to this problem is to adopt a series of standards that facilitate the interfacing and to exploit object-oriented programming to provide the necessary glue. We sketch a layering of standards, from the resource level, through a network, library, up to an object oriented toolkit level.

A well understood Knowledge Base Model is essential in this framework, and we suggest some requirements that it should fullfill.

Finally, to allow specialized programming languages to coexist, we illustrate a solution to the problem of language interoperability which has been successfully experimented.

Reconciling Symbolic and Numeric Computation in a Practical Setting

M. C. Dewar
School of Mathematical Sciences
University of Bath
Claverton Down
Bath BA2 7AY
United Kingdom

M. G. Richardson
Numerical Algorithms Group Ltd.
Wilkinson House
Jordan Hill Rd.
Oxford OX2 8DR
United Kingdom

1 Introduction

Since the advent of the electronic computer, one of its major applications has been numerical analysis. Over the years, collections of "packaged" subprograms have been developed, to enable users to choose a thoroughly tested, high quality implementation of an algorithm "off the shelf", rather than have to write their own "bespoke" version.

A well known general purpose library is the **NAG** Fortran Library, [NAG LTD. 1988] which contains implementations of algorithms in many fields such as quadrature, optimisation, differential equations, linear algebra and statistics. This library has, over the years, earned a reputation for quality and reliability, and now (at Mark 14) contains nearly nine hundred user-callable Fortran subroutines and functions. These are intended to be called directly from the user's own program; control over the operation of the algorithm is maintained via various special parameters, which the user sets.

An alternative approach to mathematical problem solving is found in computer algebra systems, one of the best known examples of which is **REDUCE** [Hearn 1987]. **REDUCE** is an interactive, Lisp based program, whose commands use a mathematical form of syntax. Solutions produced by symbolic systems such as **REDUCE** are exact, whereas numerical solutions, such as those produced by **NAG** Library routines, are often approximations due to numerical techniques and machine arithmetic. **REDUCE** is much easier to use, since it "understands" problems in virtually the same terms in which the user does, namely mathematically. Moreover the details of the various algorithms it uses are hidden from the user, giving a clean and simple interface. Thus, although its operation may often be slower, it can be quicker to use in practice, since it requires no lengthy coding or debugging stages.

Both approaches have their advantages and disadvantages in different contexts: some problems can be solved easily by one and only with great difficulty, or not at all, by the other. Simple examples are inverting an ill-conditioned matrix, which is not recommended by numerical analysts, and solving non-factoring algebraic equations of degree 5 or more, which is impossible by analytic methods.

Thus, it would be advantageous to have a system which combines both problem solving methodologies and has the friendly user interface of a computer algebra system. Such a system is **IRENA** [Dewar 1989], which is an interface to the **NAG** Library built on top of **REDUCE**. In this paper we will discuss some of the main differences between the two paradigms and the solutions we adopted to resolve them.

Some of the main features of **IRENA** can be seen in the following example. Suppose we wish to find:

$$\min \left((x_1 + 10x_2)^2 + 5(x_3 - x_4)^2 + (x_2 - 2x_3)^4 + 10(x_1 - x_4)^4 \right)$$

subject to the conditions:

$$1 \leq x_1 \leq 3, \ -2 \leq x_2 \leq 0, \ 1 \leq x_4 \leq 3$$

starting from the initial guess $(3, -1, 0, 1)$. We have decided to use routine E04JAF which uses a quasi-Newton algorithm, and is designed to be used with continuous functions with continuous first and second derivatives. The session with **IRENA** is in figure 1. The user has provided three parameters: the constraints as a rectangle named *bounds*, the initial guess as a vector *x*, and the function to be minimised as a function *funct1*. The parameters are provided by a sequence of keys separated by commas. The order is unimportant and, as we shall see later, the number of parameters used in a particular call may vary. The **NAG** routine actually takes eleven parameters plus the function, which must be coded as a Fortran subroutine. **IRENA** returns a list of the names of the parameters which contain the results, in this case *f* is the minimum obtained at the point *x*. For this example it also issues a warning that the result may not be correct.

```
4: e04jaf(bounds=rec[ 1:3, -2:0, *:*, 1:3],
4:     vec x {3,-1,0,1},
4:     funct1(x1,x2,x3,x4)=(x1 + 10*x2)^2 + 5*(x3 - x4)^2
4:                                 + (x2 - 2*x3)^4 + 10*(x1 - x4)^4);
** ABNORMAL EXIT from NAG Library routine E04JAF: IFAIL =    5
** NAG soft failure - control returned
```

There is some doubt about whether the point X found by //E04JAF// is a
minimum. The degree of confidence in the result decreases as IFAIL
increases. Thus, when IFAIL = 5 it is probable that the final X gives a
good estimate of the position of a minimum, but when IFAIL = 8 it is
very unlikely that the routine has found a minimum.
{X F}

```
93: x;
[           1         ]
[                     ]
[ - 0.0852325899880082]
[                     ]
[   .40930359107539   ]
[                     ]
[           1         ]

94: f;
2.433787512120732
```

Figure 1: A session with **IRENA**

2   The Need for an Enhanced Numeric Interface

REDUCE is, essentially, a package for symbolic mathematical manipulation and so, rightly, does not concern itself
with complicated numerical objects. In addition, parameters to **NAG** Fortran Library routines are not always ideal
from the users' point of view. There are a number of reasons for this involving the structure of Fortran, practicalities
of its use and the historical development of the Library.

2.1   Fortran

Fortran 77 does not require that arrays carry information about their dimensions with them . Thus, when a Fortran
routine is required to process an array of variable size, parameters specifying both the array name and the dimensions
(other than the last) are required. (In many **NAG** routines, all the dimensions are required: this was mandatory
in Fortran IV and is still useful for compilers with array checking.) In defining a user interface for **IRENA** ,
we have made vectors and matrices carry with them complete dimensional information, accessible to Fortran via the
IRENA "defaults" system defined in section 5.

There is no means of dynamically allocating memory in Fortran 77, so routines which have a variable requirement for
workspace must be given a sufficiently large array (and, usually, its dimensions) as parameters. **IRENA** automatically
provides appropriate parameters, which need not concern the user.

Fortran 77 has no facility for defining additional data types and its only "higher-level" data types are arrays
and character strings. The draft Fortran 8x Standard describes an array as "a set of data, all of the same type ...
arranged in a rectangular pattern" [ANSI 1989]. Thus, many natural mathematical objects have no Fortran equivalent.
Examples are various special matrix types, such as triangular, band and sparse matrices, intervals, rectangular regions
and their higher dimensional analogues and hierarchical data sets (*samplesets* in **IRENA**). The flexibility of Lisp lists
allows such types of objects to be defined for **IRENA**: they are translated into appropriate **NAG** routine parameters
by *jazz*, an **IRENA** subsystem, described in section 4, which is used to "reorganise" Fortran parameters in various
ways, producing a more "mathematical" interface.

In a call to a Fortran subroutine, the user must specify all output parameter names in addition to the input
parameters. It may be the case that only some of the output parameters are of interest to the user. (Whether a
particular output parameter is of interest to the user may, of course, depend on the value of some other parameter.)

In **IRENA**, a list of all output parameters' names after a particular call is returned by each function. Each output parameter becomes a global variable, whose value may be accessed at will.

A trivial but irritating deficiency of Fortran is the restriction of names to six characters, which often prevents the use of clear, meaningful names for **NAG** routine parameters. Jazz allows us to define synonyms for **NAG** names in such cases.

2.2 Practicalities of Library Use

The **NAG** Library is designed to run on a very wide range of computer types, including systems of limited memory. Additionally, its matrix manipulation routines are frequently used to process very large matrices. Thus, to avoid wasting memory, information is often densely packed: for instance, two separate triangular matrices may be packed into a single two-dimensional array or a "ragged array" into a one-dimensional array (with a separate array of row lengths). In the environments in which **IRENA** is likely to be mounted, economy of memory usage will not be a critical consideration, so we have chosen to adopt more natural representations, using the **IRENA** jazz system to translate between these and the Fortran objects.

2.3 Historical Considerations

The **NAG** Fortran Library project began in 1970 and, since a major revision in 1975, the library has evolved continuously. Once they are incorporated into the library routines are rarely removed, and so the present mark contains material ranging from fifteen years old to brand new. Originally written in Fortran IV, Fortran 66, or Fortran 77, the routines use whatever were the currently accepted conventions for naming and providing parameters. **IRENA** uses jazz to remove the many inconsistencies which result.

In older **NAG** routines, the choice of parameters sometimes reflects the needs of the Fortran language rather than the convenience of the user. Thus a parameter may be a simple function of a "natural" parameter of the problem (for instance, KPLUS1 in the **NAG** routine E02ADF) or the user may be required to supply an array, the first or last elements of which are zeroes. More natural jazzed parameters may be used in **IRENA**.

3 Matrix Representation in IRENA

At present, all matrix processing is handled by functions (one for each matrix representation) which take two parameters, the matrix name and its value. Each function updates the appropriate property lists for the particular matrix. In addition, there are functions to convert **IRENA** matrices (of any type) to **REDUCE** matrices and **REDUCE** matrices to **IRENA** rectangular matrices. It is anticipated that interconversion functions between various types of **IRENA** matrices will be added as the need arises.

We are also investigating the possibility of defining a domain (in the **REDUCE** sense [Bradford *et al.* 1986]) of "numeric matrices", so that the **IRENA** matrix types may be more fully integrated into **REDUCE**.[1]

All **IRENA** matrices are represented as lists of lists. In most cases, the inner lists represent all rows (or partial rows) in the natural order. For strict upper (lower) triangular matrices, the last (first) inner list is empty, although this empty list may optionally be omitted, where there is no possibility of confusion between strict upper and lower triangular matrices (i.e. for strict triangular matrices whose order is more than 2). In general we do not differentiate between upper and lower forms, where the form can be detected automatically. A full list of **IRENA** matrix types appears in tables 1–3. There is, additionally, an **IRENA** vector type, represented as a single list.

We chose not to have a separate "diagonal" type as this can easily be represented by a band matrix: {a,b,c,d, ... z} has little advantage over {{a,b,c,d, ... z}}.

4 The Jazz System

As previously stated, the form of input parameters is changed by the *jazz* system. In this section we describe the various cases which occur. Each routine has a jazz file associated with it, which contains instructions to **IRENA** on how to interpret non-**NAG** parameters it may meet, and how to get values for **NAG** parameters from their jazzed components. There are two classes of jazzing: input and output, which act on input and output parameters respectively. In the first case the jazzed form of parameters is not compulsory and there may be multiple jazzings for any parameter, so that a user who is familiar with the Fortran routine may still use the old parameter names and

---

[1]Certain properties of **REDUCE** domains make this non-trivial. Only one domain may be "current" and all objects are coerced to this. Handling domains whose elements are structures built from elements of another domain is difficult. Domain elements are constants: a variable cannot be a member of a domain.

Type	Representation
full	each inner list specifies a row
symmetric	each inner list specifies that part of a row for which $i \geq j$ or $i \leq j$
skew-symmetric	each inner list specifies that part of a row for which $i \geq j$ or $i \leq j$
Hermitian	each inner list specifies that part of a row for which $i \geq j$ or $i \leq j$
strict upper triangular	each inner list specifies that part of a row for which $i < j$ (final list empty)
upper triangular	each inner list specifies that part of a row for which $i \leq j$
upper Hessenberg	each inner list specifies that part of a row for which $i \leq j + 1$
strict lower triangular	each inner list specifies that part of a row for which $i > j$ (initial list empty)
lower triangular	each inner list specifies that part of a row for which $i \geq j$
lower Hessenberg	each inner list specifies that part of a row for which $i \geq j - 1$
general band (variable bandwidth)	each inner list specifies that part of a row lying within the envelope, the list being packed out with zeroes for symmetry about the diagonal
symmetric band (variable bandwidth)	each inner list specifies that part of a row, lying within the envelope, for which $i \geq j$

Table 1: Matrices with row lists: uppermost row first throughout (i represents the row, and j the column index).

Type	Representation
band (fixed bandwidth)	each inner list specifies a "diagonal"
symmetric band (fixed bandwidth)	only the superdiagonal and diagonal (or diagonal and subdiagonal) lists

Table 2: Matrices with diagonal lists: uppermost diagonal first throughout

definitions, while particular interfaces may be specially defined for specific sets of users. Output jazzing is compulsory, since it makes no sense to return the same item in several different ways.

There is one other area where the **IRENA** interface differs markedly from that of the **NAG** Library, and that is in how parameters which are either Functions or Subroutines are defined. We differentiate between this and jazz for purely functional reasons, conceptually they are identical.

None of these processes effect the Fortran code which is generated, as the job of transforming the parameters is done at the Lisp level.

4.1 Input Jazzing

4.1.1 Aliases

The simplest way in which jazzing is used is to provide different names for parameters. There are a number of cases where this is useful:

- Fortran restricts names to six characters, and these are often not very meaningful;

- It is preferable to have the same names for equivalent parameters across a whole chapter;

Type	Representation
sparse	3 inner lists, each in the same arbitrary order: the first containing the row indices of the non-zero elements, the second the column indices, and the third the values
symmetric sparse	as sparse, restricted to either upper or lower triangle.
An additional representation of sparse matrices is allowed:[2]	
long sparse	a list of triples {r,c,v} representing the row index, column index and value, respectively, of the non-zero elements (in arbitrary order)
symmetric long sparse	as long sparse, restricted to either upper or lower triangle

Table 3: Sparse matrices

• Different groups of users use different terminology.

There can be several aliases for the same object, or even aliases to aliases, and of course the user is still free to use the original parameter name, if desired.

4.1.2 New Scalars

Sometimes the **NAG** parameter is not the natural parameter, as for example in the case of KPLUS1 described in section 2.3. This form of jazzing transforms the **IRENA** parameter, in this case k, to its **NAG** equivalent.

4.1.3 Keywords

Some **NAG** parameters can only take a limitted number of values: for example .TRUE. or .FALSE. In this case we define a set of keywords, each of which is equivalent to one of these. For example, the routine E02BCF evaluates a cubic spline and its first three derivatives from its B-spline representation. It has a parameter, LEFT, which specifies whether left or right handed values are to be computed, depending on whether its value is 1 or not. **IRENA** has a pair of keywords *left* and *right*, which can be interpreted as LEFT=1 and LEFT=0 respectively. Thus a typical call to E02BCF would look like:

```
3:  e02bcf(vec k {0,0,0,0,1,3,3,3,4,4,6,6,6,6},
3:         vec c {10,12,13,15,22,26,24,18,14,12,0,0,0,0}, x=0, right);
```

4.1.4 Rectangles

NAG normally represents a rectangular region either as two scalars (in the one-dimensional case), or two arrays of lower and upper bounds. In **IRENA** we define a rectangle to be a single object in its own right. An example of a rectangle is *bounds* in figure 1. This is transformed into the two arrays BL and BU by jazz.

4.1.5 Very Local Constants

Sometimes **NAG** attaches special meanings to certain values. For example, in the example shown in figure 1, the arrays BL and BU contain the lower and upper constraints on the values of the x_i. If the value given is a very large negative or positive number respectively, then this is taken to mean that the value of that particular x_i is unconstrained in that particular direction. In the example x_3 is completely unconstrained, and in the rectangle *bounds* its bounds are denoted by asterisks. Each asterisk in fact means something different. For the upper bound it means *fphuge* — the largest floating point number (see section 6) — while for the lower bound it means *-fphuge*. The asterisk is a *very local constant*, and it enables us to provide a uniform interface within a routine. In general the asterisk character is interpreted as meaning that a parameter is "unset", i.e. it is not given a value.

4.1.6 Jazzing Matrices

There are three main reasons for jazzing arrays on input:

1. **NAG** arrays are sometimes confusing, with different columns being used for different purposes (e.g. W in D02YAF which has a variable number of columns used for inputting values of derivatives, returning results, and workspace). Jazz allows the user to specify their logical components and then assembles them correctly.

2. As explained in section 2, matrices with a special structure are represented by **NAG** routines in a multitude of ways to save space. However, we have provided representations for matrices which preserve these structures, and so need to transform the **IRENA** or **REDUCE** representation to the **NAG** one. Note that we do not insist that e.g. a triangular matrix be represented explicitly as an **IRENA** triangular matrix, jazz will try and coerce any **IRENA** or **REDUCE** matrix to the required type.

3. **NAG** routines often expect the user to provide a large array, only some of whose elements are set. An example is MU in E02DAF whose first and last four elements are zeros. It is nicer to allow the user to provide the smaller structure, which jazz then "pads-out" to the larger one.

Because of the multiplicity of types of jazzing needed for arrays in category 2, **IRENA** treats the jazzing of matrices differently from the way it treats the jazzing of scalars. Each form of jazzing has three functions associated with it, which will:

---

[2]since, in some circumstances, entering these would be less error prone.

- Check that all the necessary components of the Fortran parameter have been provided;

- Return the dimensions of the Fortran array (for defaults, see section 4);

- Generate the assignment statements for the Fortran array (using a suite of special functions).

This makes the jazz system much more easily extensible, as new routines which don't fit into an old pattern are added to the Library.

4.2 Output Jazzing

There are four categories of output jazzing, the first three of which apply only to arrays:

1. Disentangling Fortran arrays into their logical elements, like W in DO2YAF mentioned above.

2. Trimming large structures into smaller ones. For example many of the quadrature routines return information about the operation of the algorithm as the first element of a workspace array, rather than return the whole array IRENA returns a single scalar.

3. Unpacking arrays to restore some structure to them. For example two triangular matrices are sometimes returned as a single array, IRENA unpacks them and returns the two matrices separately.

4. Returning complex numbers. NAG often returns complex numbers as pairs of reals representing the real and imaginary parts, and complex arrays as pairs of arrays (or some other array structure). IRENA returns a true complex item in these cases.

4.3 Subroutines and Functions

Many NAG routines take parameters which are themselves Functions or Subroutines. Unfortunately standardisation of parameters has been hindered by the need to maintain the interfaces of older routines and so, while many do precisely the same thing, they differ in some trivial way: the order they take their parameters or return their results, for instance. The following is an attempt to loosely categorise them, in all we believe there to be over seventy different types in the (Mark 13) Library.

4.3.1 Functions

The majority of parameter subprograms return either a single result, or an array of results. Thus they can be replaced by either one function, or a series of functions. The parameter *funct1* in Figure 1 is an example of this type.

4.3.2 Derivatives

Some subroutines return derivatives or Jacobians of user-supplied functions, either in the same, or a separate subprogram as the function values themselves. These subroutines can be generated automatically using the algebraic manipulation features of REDUCE and the symbolic code optimisation package of [van Hulzen *et al.* 1989].

4.3.3 Output Routines

Occasionally NAG routines require the user to provide a routine to output intermediate information during the execution of the algorithm. IRENA provides a procedure which may or may not require some input from the user, such as an array of points at which to generate diagnostics. Moreover the resulting information is available as an actual structure within REDUCE, rather than simply printed out.

4.3.4 Matrix manipulation routines

These are routines which manipulate matrices in some way, and where we ask the user to provide a matrix rather than a function as a parameter. In FO2FJF the user is expected to provide a function DOT which given two vectors w and z will return the product $w^T B z$ where B is a fixed matrix. In IRENA we instead ask the user to provide the matrix B and we generate DOT using the symbolic matrix manipulation facilities of REDUCE.

5 NAG Input Parameters and the IRENA Defaults System

Frequently, input parameters of a Fortran routine can be given default values appropriate for some or all instances of the routine's use. A feature of **IRENA** is the "defaults" system, which allows appropriate default parameter values to be specified by the system developers or the user. Once a default value is established for a parameter, it need not be specified in the **IRENA** function call, thus considerably simplifying the user interface, compared to the native Fortran call. The defaults system itself will be discussed in more detail below. First, we shall consider the types of parameters for which defaults should be provided.

Input parameters of Fortran routines fall into three general categories: *data*, *control* parameters and *housekeeping* parameters. A number of borderline cases occur in the **NAG** Library but these will not immediately concern us.

The concept of a data parameter is largely self explanatory: these parameters specify the data which the user wishes to process. Specifying default values for such parameters would be completely inappropriate.

Algorithmic control parameters, as their name suggests, control the execution of the algorithm. Examples are limits on the number of iterations of a process and convergence criteria. Appropriate defaults can often be found, perhaps for particular cases, by careful scrutiny of the **NAG** Library Manual or other sources. However, the user may well wish to override such defaults. Other types of control parameters exist, controlling, for instance, the levels of diagnostics or printing of intermediate results. These are included in the same category since users may, at times, be expected to override the defaults.

In the category of housekeeping parameters we include all parameters whose values do not logically form part of the statement of the problem or constraints on its mode of solution. This includes such things as the dimensions of input and workspace arrays. Although it is unlikely that the user would wish to override the default value of such a parameter, there is no mechanism preventing this.

NAG workspace arrays are required to have a certain minimum size. Below this size, the algorithm will simply not function. Increasing the array size above this will normally have no observable effect; occasionally it will cause the routine to run faster. In a very few cases, the array size effectively provides a limit on the number of iterations of the algorithm: in these cases, we would consider the array size to be an algorithmic control parameter. Defaults for the lengths of workspace arrays are therefore normally classed as housekeeping but occasionally as algorithmic control.

IRENA is almost completely non-authoritarian in its approach to parameter specification. Whilst values must, of course, be provided for data parameters, the user is completely free to choose whether or not to specify any other parameter or simply use its default value. Additionally, personal default files may be established, taking precedence over the system defaults. There are two exceptions to this pattern: the parameter IFAIL and workspace arrays.

IFAIL occurs in almost all **NAG** routines and its value on input determines whether, when an exception condition occurs, the **NAG** routines terminates execution ("hard fail") or returns control to the calling program ("soft fail"). To enable **IRENA** to detect the exception and display an appropriate message, the soft fail option is used throughout.

On input, a workspace array contains no useful information; only its dimensions are relevant. Consequently, **IRENA** ignores any user specification of a particular workspace array (but not the dimensional information). However, certain **NAG** routines use arrays, described as workspace, to communicate information: such arrays are not treated as workspace by **IRENA**.

The system and user defaults for a routine are each specified in an individual file, using a simple language with the following features:

- arithmetic may be performed on parameter values;

- conditional values may be specified;

- antecedents of conditionals may involve relational operators and tests on the existence of parameter values;

- functions exist to provide the dimensions of arrays, the maximum and minimum of arrays or sets of values, the number of parameters in a user-specified function and the size of a set of related functions provided by the user;

- a special value "unset" may be used for parameters which will be ignored in a particular call;

- special symbols *userabserr*, *userrelerr*, *usermixerr* and *userinputerr* provide a second level default mechanism, in that they are set globally and used to specify parameter defaults. Their values may be reset at the **REDUCE** level by the user, thereby redefining default values throughout the system.

In addition to the above special symbols, **IRENA** provides a number of other symbols which represent mathematical and "machine" constants, which are discussed further in section 5. These may also be used in specifying defaults.

An annotated example of a fairly typical system defaults file is shown in Figure 2. The **NAG** routine E04GBF finds the unconstrained minimum of the sum of squares of M nonlinear functions of N variables.

```
% Defaults for E04GBF
      M : muliplicity(F)       % The number of functions F(1) ... F(M) defined
      N : dim(X)               % The length of the array "X"
      LSQLIN : 'E04HEV         % One of two available auxiliary NAG routines
      LSQMON : 'E04FDZ         % Dummy routine giving no intermediate printing
      IPRINT : if LSQMON = 'E04FDZ then -1 else 1
                               % Level of intermediate printing chosen
      MAXCAL : 50*N            % Maximum number of iterations in the minimisation
      ETA : 0.9                % Controls individual iterations' accuracy
      XTOL : !*USERMIXERR!*    % Acceptable accuracy of the solution.
      STEPMX : 100000.0        % Possible distance from starting point to solution
      LIW : 1                  % Length of an integer workspace array
      LW : if N = 1 then 9 + 3*M else 7*N + M*N + 2*M + N*N
                               % Length of a real workspace array
end; % of E04GBF defaults file
```

Figure 2: A Typical Defaults File, Annotated

This routine is unusual in having seven control parameters: LSQLIN, MAXCAL, ETA, XTOL, STEPMX, LSQMON and IPRINT. The parameters M and N would both be classified as "housekeeping". Only two NAG parameters are classified as "data": LSQFUN, which specifies the functions to be minimised, and X, which gives a starting point in the search for a minimum. (We consider it inadvisable to give a default value for X, as the starting point can determine which of several minima is found.) Thus, in calling E04GBF, the user need only specify the equivalent of two NAG parameters. In the Fortran calling sequence, a total of twenty-five parameters, including output parameters, is necessary.

In this example, the values of M and N are determined from characteristics of the problem. All of the algorithmic control parameters' defaults, except XTOL's, are based on suggestions in the NAG Fortran Library Manual. XTOL's default, *USERMIXERR*, is set to 0.00001 when IRENA is loaded but can be reset at any time by the user. *USERMIXERR* is provided as a means for the user to specify an error tolerance which is acceptable in a range of problems.

The fact that IRENA (unlike Fortran) is designed as an interactive system influences the choice of some defaults. The most obvious instance of this is perhaps print control parameters: generally, users of an interactive system do not wish to see large amounts of intermediate printing while a problem is being solved. Thus IPRINT is given a low default value in this example. This is true in general of print control parameters, if a result is unsatisfactory it is usually trivial, in an interactive environment, to resubmit the problem with a higher level of diagnostic printing specified. This could be more troublesome in a Fortran batch environment.

6 The Software / Hardware Interface

For many implementations of numerical algorithms there are a number of parameters which are dependent on the underlying hardware. These include the machine precision, the largest positive floating point number and so on. The NAG Library contains a number of functions to return such values: for example the routine X02AJF returns the machine precision and X02ALF returns the largest positive floating point number. There are also routines which return an estimate of the active set size in a paged environment or indicate how the system treats underflow. Such functions are essential if a user is to write portable code, and since one use of IRENA is to generate code on one machine (e.g. a desk-top workstation) to be run on another (e.g. a mainframe) it is essential that the code it produces uses them. The way such quantities are treated in IRENA is as follows: at the REDUCE level they are treated as constants so that, for example, the largest floating point number is called *fphuge* but, at the code generation stage, we generate assignments for the returned function values of any of these quantities used, along with the necessary type declarations and EXTERNAL statements.

As well as the above machine constants there are various mathematical constants whose values depend on the precision of the implementation. With the exception of e, which is replaced by EXP(1.0) (or its double precision equivalent), IRENA handles these in the same way. The most obvious example is *pi*.

IRENA depends on various attributes of the underlying system, in particular the ability to spawn child processes in order to perform compilations and to carry out the *oload* phase (see later). At present IRENA is only implemented under Unix, though a VMS version is planned. The need to spawn processes does, however, seem to rule out the possibility of an implementation on an operating system such as CMS.

REDUCE has been implemented in many different dialects of Lisp. The particular version **IRENA** uses is based on Portable Standard Lisp, or **PSL** [Galway *et al.* 1987]. This runs on a wide variety of machines including Suns, Apollos, VAXs and Crays. Although there are a few syntactic differences between the Lisps, the main area where we are tied to **PSL** is in the use of its *oload* utility (see below), an equivalent to which does not exist in every dialect.

When **IRENA** has written and compiled a subroutine to call a particular **NAG** routine, it must be loaded into the running Lisp system before it can be called. In **PSL** this can be done using a utility called *oload*. **PSL**'s binary program space (BPS) is organised so that data grows down from the top while text grows up from the bottom[3] and, as there is no garbage collection done on BPS, when the text and data portions collide it is irrevocably full. There are two components of *oload*, one a unix shell script, the other a set of Lisp functions. Calling the Lisp function *oload* spawns a child process to execute the script, which does the following:

- It generates a file containing the text portion of the file(s) being *oload*ed.

- It generates a file containing the data portion of the file(s) being *oload*ed.

- It creates a file containing the memory locations at which to load these files.

- It creates a file of Lisp statements telling the **PSL** compiler the names and entry points of the *oload*ed functions.

- If requested, it creates a new symbol table, so that the user may produce a new **PSL** with the *oload*ed code as an integral part.

Oload takes as argument a string containing the names of the executable load modules and various options either for *oload* or *ld*, the Unix linker. The *oload* options control how much the user is told about the progress of the *oload*, whether a symbol table is produced etc.. The ld options tell it which libraries to scan, where to find them and so forth. The script also receives the addresses of the end of the text segment and the beginning of the data segment.

The problem is caused by having to arrange matters so that the data segment of the new code *ends* at the *beginning* of the current data area of BPS. *Oload* does this through a tortuous sequence of steps:

1. using *ld*, it creates a relocatable code file containing all the load modules;

2. using the Unix pattern scanner *awk*, it determines the relative sizes of the two segments. At this point it checks to see if BPS is going to be exhausted and, if so, terminates;

3. using these figures it works out how much bigger the text segment would need to be to "shunt" the data forward so that it was contiguous with the current data area;

4. it creates a blank piece of text this size by creating a file of null characters and then assembling it;

5. it then does a second *ld*, this time including the blank text, to create the final executable file;

6. this file is then split in two, the "truncated" text (i.e. ignoring the blanks) and the data;

7. using the Unix utility *nm* the list of names and entry points is created;

8. if required, a further *ld* is performed to generate the symbol table.

The Lisp routine then reads in the files telling it where to put the pieces of code and loads them at the appropriate places.

There are three problems with this approach. The first one is that the whole process can be agonisingly slow. Up to three passes of the linker, the *awk* scripts and, worst of all, writing millions of zeros onto disc[4] can take a long time. The second problem is that the user needs to have enough free disc space for these big temporary files (there are two — one unassembled and one assembled) and, in a distributed networking environment such as that used by the authors, there can be problems with connections timing out. The third problem is to do with the way we are using *oload*. Each time we *oload* a routine we load all the **NAG** library routines it calls along with it and so BPS becomes rapidly exhausted. Enlarging BPS was found to exacerbate the first two problems to an almost unbearable degree.

In fact, *oload* does far more than **IRENA** needs. We never call a routine more than once, so we don't need to preserve it in BPS. Since we never "dump out" our system we don't need to produce a new symbol table, or even align the text and data segments correctly. Thus we have created our own version of *oload*, called *IRENAoload*, which is designed to be used with our "one-shot" problems. We need only one pass of the linker, and the text and data

---

[3] Technically the data doesn't go into BPS but into the word array space but, in **PSL**, these are both parts of the same structure, so the distinction can be ignored.

[4] In the authors' standard **IRENA** system, the gap in the middle of BPS starts at well over a megabyte.

portions are placed in memory exactly as they would be by the loader. The pointers to the top and bottom of BPS are unchanged so, the next time anything is loaded into BPS, the foreign function is overwritten. This method is much faster, doesn't require lots of temporary disc space and doesn't exhaust BPS.

Finally in this section, let us note that calling Fortran directly from **PSL** can cause some difficulties:

- Fortran has no global variables, so setting up "foreign global variables" is impossible.

- **PSL** is written in C and stores its arrays in row order, Fortran stores them in column order.

- ANSI Fortran cannot manipulate pointers explicitly.

The first is not really a problem since C has global variables and, in Unix, C and Fortran can be mixed, providing one remembers their different calling conventions and that the compiler prefixes a C name with an underscore, whereas it both prefixes and suffixes Fortran names. The second requires care if passing an array as a parameter. The third does cause difficulties with **IRENA**, and so we use a small C routine as "syntactic glue" between the **PSL** and Fortran routines. This is then *oloaded* along with the Fortran. The price we pay is one extra compilation.

7 Conclusions

We have provided an interactive interface to the **NAG** Library which uses a natural, mathematical style for parameters, rather than the space saving style of the Fortran routines. To do this we have had to investigate both the structure of parameters in the Library and how we can translate from one representation to another. In the process we have provided default values and expressions for many parameters and automated the process of generating code to call **NAG** Library routines.

IRENA caters for three different kinds of users. The first group are those who want an easy-to-use, interactive numerical analysis package. Here, we have shown that it is possible to develop a modern interface without throwing away the tried, tested and efficient code which has been the product of many years work by a wide range of individuals.

The second group consists of more experienced users of the **NAG** Library, who want to avoid the tedium of writing and testing large segments of code (for example to generate Jacobians) and who will take the code generated by **IRENA** and use it elsewhere. They may rely on the code being correct and, due to the symbolic code optimisation facilities available in **REDUCE**, of high quality.

The last group are those who genuinely wish to mix symbolic and numerical computation, using the facilities of both **REDUCE** and the **NAG** Library to solve their problems. Of particular interest to the authors is the possibility of using the algebraic power of **REDUCE** to help in the choice both of individual **NAG** routines and their control parameters ("intelligent", rather than "dumb" defaults).

Because of the way it has evolved, there are problems in working with a large software library such as **NAG** — in particular lack of consistency in the style and naming of the parameters. The work done in developing **IRENA** has also had some spin-offs here. Organising default information and categorising parameters as input, output etc. will, at Mark 14, lead to better documentation, both online and printed. The design of an "ideal" interface for each routine, through the jazz system, may also be useful in other areas, for example the design of a Fortran 8x Library.

References

[ANSI 1989]   ANSI. Fortran 8x. Technical Report X3J3/S8.112, American National Standards Institute, June 1989.

[Bradford *et al.* 1986]   R. J. Bradford, A. C. Hearn, J. A. Padget, and E. Schrüfer. Enlarging the REDUCE domain of computation. In *Proc. of SYMSAC '86*, pages 100–106, 1986.

[Dewar 1989]   Michael C. Dewar. IRENA —an integrated symbolic and numerical computation environment. In *Proceedings of ISSAC 1989*, pages 171–179. ACM, 1989.

[Galway *et al.* 1987]   W. Galway, M. L. Griss, B. Morrison, and B. Othmer. *The PSL 3.4 Users Manual*. University of Utah, 1987.

[Hearn 1987]   A. H. Hearn. *The REDUCE User's Guide*. The RAND Corporation, 1987.

[NAG LTD. 1988]   NAG LTD. *The NAG Fortran Library Manual — Mark 13*, 1988.

[van Hulzen *et al.* 1989] J. A. van Hulzen, B. J. A. Hulshof, B. L. Gates, and M. C. van Heerwaarden. A code optimization package for REDUCE. In *Proceedings of ISSAC 1989*, pages 163–170. ACM, 1989.

The design and specification of the ASSPEGIQUE database

M. BIDOIT, F. CAPY; C. CHOPPY

Laboratoire de Recherche en Informatique, U.A. 410 du C.N.R.S
Université Paris-Sud, Bâtiment 490, F 91405 ORSAY Cédex, FRANCE
Tel: 33 - (1) 69 41 66 29   Telefax: 33 - (1) 64 46 19 92
E-mail: mb or cc, uucp: sun8.lri.fr bitnet: frlri61

1   INTRODUCTION

Among the design issues for symbolic computation systems, a non trivial one is the design of the database where various pieces of information (specifications, proofs, test sets, program modules, etc.) are stored together with constraints and links between them. In this paper we address the design of a database for the algebraic specification environment ASSPEGIQUE, and provide an algebraic specification for this database management. In order to make use of algebraic specifications the essential ingredients are a specification language and a set of tools, or, better, an environment where tools to design, verify and use specifications are integrated : these two requirements lead to solve a problem of adequate database management for a specification library.

Complex problems yield complex specifications ; in order to cope with complex specifications, one needs to decompose them into smaller specification units, that we call specification *modules*. A specification language [B&G 77, Bro 84, EFH 83, EM 85, FGJM 85, G&H 86 ...] provides primitives to build a complex specification out of specification modules ; using specification building primitives thus enables to decompose specifications into modules, to reuse them, to hierarchically compose them in order to obtain more complex specifications. In the PLUSS specification language these building primitives are : enrichment, parameterisation, renaming and visibility control [Gau 85, Cap 88, BGM 89, Bid 89]. A specification is therefore composed of several specification modules related together through specification building primitives : these links have to be recorded - and updated as needed - in the specification library database.

An environment for algebraic specifications should include tools for editing specifications, and for performing symbolic computations (such as executing them when possible - for instance by means of term rewriting systems, logic programming, ... -, proving theorems about specifications, etc) : the use of these tools requires access to various pieces of information through the database. When designing the ASSPEGIQUE environment, library management problems were addressed ; in particular, the requirement that a flexible "middle-out" development strategy should be allowed (as opposed to either a top-down or a bottom-up approach) raises constraints to be taken care of in order to preserve the library consistency. One of the issues in the ASSPEGIQUE database design was to distinguish between "static" aspects, i.e. the attribute updating that is necessary to preserve the database consistency when a single action takes place, and the "dynamic" aspects, that take into account the management of concurrent accesses to the database. When a new module is introduced (or when some other operations take place) links between modules have to be updated : this is done through the "static" management of the library. The "static" database management is expressed w.r.t. states of the database, that is situations where no action is under process ; this database management viewpoint suffices when only one user performs one action at a time. The "dynamic" database management specification details how concurrent accesses may be allowed or blocked, and reflects not only the result of completed actions, but also actions that are under process (in particular, the management of the database when an action begins, ends with failure, and ends with success, is specified).

Since various cases of attribute dependencies are studied (transitive dependence of a given module attributes, and dependence w.r.t. other module attributes), the specification may be easily modified to take into account modifications in the environment architecture (when new tools are added, some new attributes may be necessary).

*now at : DIGITAL, Paris Research Laboratory, 85 Avenue Victor Hugo, 92563 Rueil Malmaison Cedex - Tel : 33 - (1) 47 08 97 33, E-mail: capy@decprl.dec.com

In the same way, this specification could be adapted to specify other symbolic computation systems database management.

The second Section of this paper is a short introduction to the PLUSS specification language constructs that are used here, the third Section details the processing of modularity in ASSPEGIQUE ; in Section 4 a specification of the static database management of the library is given.

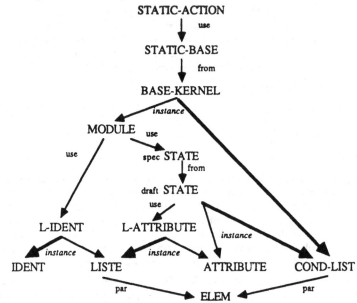

Figure 1 : Specification of the "static" data base management

2   A short introduction to the PLUSS specification language

The design of the PLUSS specification language is the result of numerous experiments in writing large specifications, some of them being done in cooperation with industry [B&H 85, BGM 89, BGHM 89]. The experience gained from these experiments led to put strong emphasis on modularization facilities. Moreover, these experiments have proved the need to state a careful distinction between "implementable" ("achieved") specification modules, and "not yet implementable" ("under development") specification modules.

In the following, we shall restrict ourselves to presenting those characteristics of PLUSS that will be used in the database specification (for more details see e.g. [Cap 88, BGM 89] ; the semantics of PLUSS is presented in [Bid 88, 89]). Using specification building primitives to build a complex specification out of specification modules, one gets a DAG (directed acyclic graph) of specification modules (Figure 1 shows the DAG of specification modules for the static management of the database). A straightforward way to add new domains, objects, properties, to a specification is through *enrichment*, denoted by the keyword "use", as e.g. the MODULE specification in Section 4 :

```
Spec : MODULE;
    use : STATE ;
``etc.''
```

Parameterization saves the writing of many instances of the same specification ; in the example below, ELEM is a *formal parameter* specification ("Par"), LIST (ELEM) is a *parameterised specification* ("Generic Spec"), and L-IDENT is an *instance* of LIST (ELEM) where ELEM is instanciated by IDENT through a "fitting" morphism "m" that maps "Elem" to "Ident" ; in addition, a *renaming* of the sort "List" into "L-ident" and of the operation "Empty" into "none" is performed in order to customize names for this particular instance.

```
Par : ELEM;
    Sort : Elem;        ``this is a comment''
```

```
End

Generic Spec : LIST (ELEM);
    Sort : List;
 Generated by :
    Empty :               -> List;
    _ :    Elem          -> List; ``a coercion : any Elem is a one element List''
    _ _ : Elem * List -> List; ``anonymous operation to add an Elem to a List''
 Operation :
    _ union _ : List * List -> List; ``the _'s indicate the argument locations''
 Predicates :
    _ is in _ : Elem * List;
    _ all in _ : List * List;
 Axioms :
    ``..., due to lack of space easy axioms are omitted''
End

Spec : L-IDENT
    use : LIST (ELEM => IDENT by m);
       where : m : Elem => Ident;
       renaming : List into L-ident, Empty into none;
End
```

As a means to improve readability of specifications, and to allow a maximum flexibility in the choice of identifiers, the specification signature may contain (as in LIST (ELEM) above) coercions, anonymous operations, overloaded operator symbols, etc. The price to pay is that the resulting language may be ambiguous, and may not be parsed using classical techniques : a tool called CIGALE was designed to generate the corresponding grammar and the appropriate parser [Voi 86].

As mentioned above, the main originality of PLUSS is to state a careful distinction between "implementable" specification modules ("Spec"), and "not yet implementable" ones. The specification modules under development are introduced by the keyword "Draft". They have a more flexible semantics than "Spec"s ; the signature and the axioms are not fully fixed and may be further refined by means of appropriate combination of enrichments and instanciations. A draft may enrich another draft ("with") or a specification ("use") - as in the draft STATE in Section 4 :

```
Draft : STATE
    use : L-ATTRIBUTE;
    with : COND-LIST (ELEM => spec ATTRIBUTE by m);
       where : m : Elem => Attribute;
``etc.''
```

A draft may also be parameterized ("Generic draft") as in the following COND-LIST example. In this conditional list, one may notice that the coercion (_ : Elem → C-List) is no longer a generator as in LIST (ELEM) since only "addable" elements can be used ; however, no axiom describes yet the "addable to" predicate :

```
Generic Draft : COND-LIST (ELEM)
    Sort : C-List;
 Generated by :
    Empty : -> C-List;
    _ _ : Elem * C-List -> C-List;
 Predicates :
    _ addable to _ : Elem * C-List;
    _ is in _ :      Elem * C-List;
    _ all in _ :    C-List * C-List;
 Precondition :                      ``only addable Elem are allowed''
    consistency : (E L) is defined iff E addable to L;
 Axioms :
    is1 : E is in Empty is-false;
    is2 : E is in (E' L) iff (E = E' | E is in L);
    al1 : Empty all in L is-true;
    al2 : (E L) all in L' iff (E is in L' & L all in L');
```

```
  Where : E, E': Elem; L : C-List;
End
```

When some operations are defined under some conditions, these conditions are expressed as logical expressions, and these expressions are listed in the "precondition" part using an "is defined when" construction (as in the above COND-LIST specification). Suitably instanciated, the preconditions are implicit premises for each of the axioms where the partially defined operation occurs.

When the properties of a draft (e.g. the properties of "addable to") are fully described, it is possible to convert the draft into an "achieved" specification using the keyword "from" (again, semantics attached to the various keywords is developed in [Bid 88, 89]) ; in Section 4 COND-LIST is instanciated and enriched in the draft BASE-KERNEL, then BASE-KERNEL is in turn converted into a specification STATIC-BASE were the properties of "addable to" are fixed :

```
Draft : BASE-KERNEL
     with : COND-LIST (ELEM => spec MODULE by m);
     where : m : Elem => Module;
     renaming : C-List into Base, Empty into empty base;
 Operations :
''etc.''

Spec : STATIC-BASE from BASE-KERNEL;
''etc''
 Axioms :
    ad1 : < M no-req-spec (present no-attribute) > addable to B iff M may be present in B;
''etc.''
```

3   ASSPEGIQUE: specification module handling issues

ASSPEGIQUE [BCV 84, B&C 85, Cap 87] is intended to be a flexible structure where new tools may easily be integrated ; its present components are browsing tools, a specification editor, symbolic evaluation tools, theorem proving tools (initially, a theorem prover that makes explicit use of induction ; more recently, interfaces with the REVE system [Les 83, F&G 84] and with the SLOG system [Fri 85, Slo 86] were realized), and a tool for assistance to Ada implementation.

Experiences with large specifications show that freedom of development strategy is desirable : when dealing with a complex problem it may be uneasy to use a top-down approach since it may not be clear yet how to analyse the problem as a whole, moreover it may lead to make assumptions about subsystems that will be checked only in the end and errors will be discovered too late ; using a bottom-up approach leads to start with too elementary specifications, that is with a degree of detail that yields a cumbersome design process, and with an increased probability of having to modify too early decisions ; it should then be possible to develop specifications starting "somewhere in the middle", at points where the degree of complexity is apprehensible without having to deal yet with too low level details. Moreover, this "middle-out" approach promotes the reuse of specifications.

ASSPEGIQUE was designed to support such a middle-out approach : when using ASSPEGIQUE, the user deals with specification modules. When a new module is introduced in the library (or when an existing one is modified), the library database is updated, in particular to express links between this module and others ; in addition, information concerning the modules related to this new (or modified) module has to be updated too. Therefore allowing a flexible way of introducing new modules in the library requires an appropriate database management to preserve the integrity of the database.

Two language levels can be distinguished in a PLUSS specification : the specification language level (with the specification building primitives, etc.), and the level of the language defined by the specification signature, i.e. the sorts and operations declared in the specification module and in the other modules of the relevant DAG - called *required* modules -. The syntactic analysis relative to the specification language level (denoted by *validation*) may be achieved with the specification module alone : its required modules need not be already validated or even present in the database. The situation is different for the analysis that uses the specification signature (denoted by *integration*) which cannot be achieved if some required modules are not yet provided (in particular, if some operation symbols and arity are not yet declared, it will not be possible to parse axioms that use them). Since this analysis checks the well-formedness of the specification terms across modules, we call it *integration* [1]. In order

---

[1]Other checks not detailed here are performed during this step.

to allow some degree of checking together with a flexible development approach, it is thus necessary to perform the two analyses separately.

The tools available in the ASSPEGIQUE specification environment can access to a specification module under some conditions which vary with the tool. Moreover, these conditions may concern not only the specification module itself, but also its required modules. For instance, in order to integrate a specification module, this module should be validated, and its required modules should be already integrated. In order to express these conditions, we first define various attributes for a specification module (e.g. *present, valid, integrated,* etc.). Then two kinds of relationships between attributes are expressed : (i) relationships between attributes of a given module (e.g. a module cannot be integrated if it is not present), and (ii) relationships between attributes of a given module and attributes of its required modules (e.g. a module cannot be integrated if its required modules are not integrated). Once integration of a module is achieved, the list of attributes for this module should be consequently updated. When a module is modified (and possibly operation names are changed, etc.) its integration is no longer valid, and integration of modules that use it are no longer valid too ; and again the database should be consequently updated.

In the following section, the database management specified is expressed w.r.t. states of the database, that is situations where no action is under process ; this database management viewpoint suffices when only one user performs one action at a time. This specification has been extended to take into account situations where several actions on the database may be active at the same time, but is not given here due to lack of space.

4 The static database management

As a consequence of supporting the PLUSS structuration primitives, a specification library itself is a DAG of specification modules ; within a library, a specification is a DAG that is (usually) a connected sub-component of the library. It is therefore necessary that the information attached to a specification module in the corresponding database provides the other modules of the DAG, e.g. through the list of its son modules.

In order to express the conditions under which ASSPEGIQUE tools may access specification modules, attributes are defined. Three basic attributes are : *present* means that a specification module is in the library, *valid* that the module was checked w.r.t. the specification language, and *integrated* that the required modules are integrated and the root module was checked w.r.t. the required modules, the grammar generated by the signatures, etc. As a matter of fact, since it produces an internal representation of the specification, integration is required by most tools (symbolic evaluation, theorem proving, etc.). Other attributes may be required : for instance, it is possible under some conditions to orient the axioms and then compile them into Lisp code, in order to speed up symbolic evaluation [Kap 87a, 87b] ; to use such an evaluation requires that the axioms are already compiled (*ax-compiled* attribute).

```
Spec : ATTRIBUTE;
    Sort : Attribute;
 Generated by :
    present :        -> Attribute;
    valid :          -> Attribute;
    integrated :     -> Attribute;
    ax-compiled : -> Attribute;
    ''etc...''
End
```

Fig. 2 : Module attribute hierarchy

There is of course some hierarchy between the attributes (as shown in Figure 2), this point will be further explained when dealing with the L-ATTRIBUTE and STATIC-BASE specifications.

In the database, the information concerning a given module contains the list of attributes of this module, also called the "state" of the module. Now, a module is defined as a triple : an identifier, the list of its son required modules, its state.

```
Spec : MODULE;
    use : STATE;    ''the draft STATE was converted into a Spec STATE''
    use : L-IDENT renaming : none into no-req-spec;
    Sort : Module;
 Generated by :
    < _ _ _ > : Ident * L-Ident * State -> Module;
       ''a module = a name, a list of son modules, a list of attributes''
 Precondition :
```

```
     req : < M-id Req-list S > is defined iff
             S # no-attribute        ''since a module has at least the present attribute''
             & {Req-list = no-req-spec | valid is in S};
                            ''the son module list is not known before validation''
   Where : M-id : Ident; Req-list : L-ident; S : State;
End
```

In the following the variable M-id is abbreviated in M, and Req-list in R.

Before going into details concerning the relationships between attributes, and concerning the STATE specification, let us present the architecture of the static database specification. Given the MODULE specification, the database, BASE-KERNEL, is specified as a conditional list of modules : the conditions under which a module may be added to the database ensure that the database consistency is preserved. These conditions are given in the specification STATIC BASE which also specifies how attributes in a module state may be modified ; it is used in the STATIC ACTION specification which describes the actions of inserting, validating, integrating, removing, etc., a module in terms of modifications of the database.

Let us now go back to the STATE specification. First, we define the specification L-ATTRIBUTE that expresses relationships between attributes by means of the "needed by" predicate and the "requested by" operation. The presence of an attribute in the state of a module may depend on the other attributes already in that module state (this is what is expressed in the L-ATTRIBUTE specification) and on attributes of the required modules (this second relationship is expressed at the STATIC BASE level - cf. the "intg" axiom, etc.).

```
Spec : L-ATTRIBUTE;
    use : LIST (ELEM => ATTRIBUTE by m);
      where : m : Elem => Attribute;
      renaming : List into L-attribute, Empty into no-attribute;
Operation :
    requested by _ : Attribute -> L-attribute;
Predicates :
    _ needed by _ : Attribute * Attribute ;
    _ needed by list _ : Attribute * L-attribute;
Axioms :
    re1 : requested by present = no-attribute;
    re2 : requested by valid = present;
    re3 : requested by integrated = valid;
    re4 : requested by ax-compiled = integrated;
    ''etc. in general, it may also be the case that an attribute A requests some
    attributes B and C ; this is why the arity of requested by is not Attribute -> Attribute''
    ne : A needed by A'
            iff A is in (requested by A') | A needed by list (requested by A');
    nl1 : A needed by list no-attribute is-false;
    nl2 : A needed by list A' iff A needed by A';
    nl3 : A needed by list (A' L) iff A needed by A' | A needed by list L;
  Where : A,A': Attribute; L : L-attribute;
End
```

When new tools are integrated in the specification environment, this may cause new attributes to be added in the ATTRIBUTE specification, as well as new axioms for the operation "requested by" (the STATIC BASE specification will also have to be completed).

The state of a module is defined as the (conditional) attribute list of a given module ; this list has to be coherent (i.e. it should respect relations between attributes) : the predicate "addable to" is used (cf. the axiom "add") to express the consistency.

```
Draft : STATE
    use : L-ATTRIBUTE;
    with : COND-LIST (ELEM => spec ATTRIBUTE by m);
      where : m : Elem => Attribute;
      renaming : C-List into State       ''a State is a conditional list of attributes'',
```

```
                Empty into no-attribute;
Operations :
   _ : State -> L-attribute;
   remove _ from _ : Attribute * State -> State;
Axioms :
   co1 : (no-attribute : State) = (no-attribute : L-attribute);
   ''the notation (term : type) may be used to solve parsing ambiguities''
   co2 : ((A S) : State) = ((A S) : L-attribute);
   add : A addable to S iff (requested by A) all in S & A is in S is-false;
   re1 : remove A from no-attribute = no-attribute;
   re2 : remove A from (A S) = S;
   re3 : A # A' & A' needed by A => remove A' from (A S) = remove A' from S;
   re4 : A # A' & A' needed by A is-false =>
                              remove A' from (A S) = A (remove A' from S);
  Where : A, A' : Attribute ; S : State;
End
```

The axiom "add" shows that a state is a somehow ordered list : an attribute A may be added to a state only if those attributes requested by A are already in the state. Therefore, removing properly an attribute from a state should yield another coherent state - in other words, when, through some modification done for instance by a user, an attribute is no longer part of a module state, the resulting module state should still be a coherent list of attributes. The COND-LIST specification is both instanciated in the above STATE draft, and in the following BASE-KERNEL draft, a Base being a conditional list of modules. BASE-KERNEL defines observers ("state of _ in _", "required modules of _ in _", etc.) ; the conditions under which a module may be added to a base will be given in the next STATIC-BASE specification.

```
Draft : BASE-KERNEL
    with : COND-LIST (ELEM => spec MODULE by m);
     where : m : Elem => Module;
     renaming : C-List into Base, Empty into empty base;
Operations :
   state of _ in _ : Ident * Base -> State;
   required modules of _ in _ : Ident * Base -> L-ident;
Predicates :
   _ is _ in _ : Ident * Attribute * Base;
   _ are _ in _ : L-ident * Attribute * Base;
Axioms :
   st1 : state of M in empty base = no-attribute;
   st2 : state of M in < M R S > B = S
   st3 : M # M' => state of M in < M' R S > B = state of M in B;
   isi : M is A in B iff A is in (state of M in B);
   ''etc.''
  Where : M, M' : Ident; R : L-ident; A : Attribute; S : State; B : Base;
End
```

The "ad1" and "ad2" axioms together with "pres", "intg", etc. (specifying "_ may be _ in _") express the conditions under which a module may be added to a base : as e.g. in "intg", these conditions may reflect conditions both on the attributes of the module (cf. the axiom "add" in STATE) and on the required modules ; in the same way that the axiom "add" showed that there is some order in which the attributes may be added to a state, an axiom such as "intg" shows that there is also some order in which an "integrated" module may be added to a base (namely, the base should already contain the "integrated" required modules). This has consequences on the way "remove-att _ from _ in _." together with the updating operations specify the repercussions of a module attribute modifications on the database.

```
Spec : STATIC-BASE from BASE-KERNEL;
 Operations :
   remove-att _ from _ in _ : Attribute * Ident * Base -> Base;
   update : Module * Base -> Base;
   update-aux1 : Ident * L-ident * State * Base -> State;
   update-aux2 : Ident * L-ident * Attribute * State * Base -> State;
 Predicate :
```

```
    _ may be _ in _ : Ident * Attribute * Base;
Precondition :
    p-r : remove-att A from M in B is-defined iff M is A in B;
Axioms :
    ad1 : < M no-req-spec (present no-attribute) > addable to B iff M may be present in B;
                ''recall from the MODULE specification that the required module list
                is not known (-> no-req-spec) before validation''
    ad2 : S # no-attribute => < M R (A S) > addable to B
                                iff < M R S > addable to B & M may be A in < M R S > B ;
    pres : M may be present in B iff M is present in B is-false;
    intg : M may be integrated in B iff integrated is addable to state of M in B &
                                        required modules of M are all integrated in B;
    ''etc.''
    rm1 : remove-att present from M in < M R S > B = B;
    rm2 : remove-att valid from M in < M R S > B =
                                    < M no-req-spec (remove valid from S) > B;
    rm3 : A # present & A # valid =>
                remove-att A from M in < M R S > B = < M R (remove A from S) > B;
                                        ''remove is specified in STATE''
    rm4 : M # M' => remove-att A from M in < M' R S > B =
                                update (< M' R S >, remove-att A from M in B);
    ''etc.''
    Where : M : Ident; R : L-ident; A : Attribute; S : State; B : Base;
End
```

Once the modifications of the database (either by adding a new module, or by modifying an attribute) are specified, an action is easily translated in terms of modifications in the database. Checking (axiom "chk") or integrating (axiom "itg") a module is expressed as (i) removing the module (in fact removing its "present" attribute), (ii) adding it with the proper state to the database ; other actions, like compiling axioms (axiom "axc") are expressed through "add-att" that is adding the corresponding attribute to the module state [2].

```
Spec : STATIC-ACTION;
    use : STATIC-BASE;
 Operations :
    insert _ in _ : Ident * Base -> Base;
    check _ requiring _ in _ : Ident * L-ident * Base -> Base;
    integrate _ in _ : Ident * Base -> Base;
    compile axs of _ in _ : Ident * Base -> Base;
    ''etc.''
    remove _ from _ : Ident * Base -> Base;
    add-att _ to _ in _ : Attribute * Ident * Base -> Base;
 Preconditions :
    ck : check M requiring R in B is defined iff M may be valid in B;
    it : integrate M in B is defined iff M may be integrated in B;
    ''etc.''
    rm : remove M from B is defined iff M is present in B;
 Axioms :
    ins : insert M in B = < M no-req-spec (present no-attribute) > B;
    chk : check M requiring R in B =
                < M R (valid present no-attribute) > remove-att present from M in B;
    itg : integrate M in B =
        < M R (integrated valid present no-attribute) > remove-att present from M in B;
    adat1 : add-att A to M in < M R S > B = < M R (A S) > B
    adat2 : M # M' =>
            add-att A to M in < M' R S > B = < M' R S > add-att A to M in B;
    axc : compile axs of M in B = add-att ax-compiled to M in B;
    ''etc.''
    rmv : remove M from B = remove present from M in B;
    Where : M, M': Ident; R : L-ident; A : Attribute; S : State; B : Base;
```

---

[2] Remember that what we are doing here is specifying, i.e. expressing required properties of operations. Thus, it is quite natural to specify that some change is equivalent to removing x and then adding a new x, even if, of course, the "change" operation will be implemented in a different (hopefully more efficient) way.

End

The above specification of actions in the database is done with a *static* perspective, i.e. it determines whether the states of the library specifications allows some given action execution, and how to traduce the result of that action in terms of possibly adding a new attribute, and repercuting the modification in the whole database. This approach is sufficient when dealing with an environment where only one user may request one action at a time on a given library. This specification has been extended to the *dynamic* situation where the environment would allow a given user to make several requests in parallel, and several users to work at the same time on the same library: the "dynamic" state of a module is a list of "dynamic" attributes (a dynamic attribute is a couple : Attribute * Access), and the dynamic base reflects not only the result of completed actions, but also actions that are under process (in particular, the management of the database when an action begins, ends with failure, and ends with success, is specified).

5 Conclusion

Among the design issues for symbolic computation systems, a non trivial one is the design of the database where informations (specifications, proofs, test sets, program modules, etc.) that are necessary to use the various tools available are stored. In this paper we address the design of a database for an algebraic specification environment, and provide an algebraic specification for this database management. One of the issues in this design is to distinguish between "static" aspects, i.e. the attribute updating that is necessary to preserve the database consistency when a single action takes place, and the "dynamic" aspects, that take into account the management of concurrent accesses to the database. The specification language modularity was crucial in order to correctly specify such notions as "coherent list of attributes", "coherent list of modules", etc.. Since various cases of attribute dependencies were studied (transitive dependence of a given module attributes, and dependence w.r.t. other module attributes), the specification may be easily modified to take into account modifications in the environment architecture (when new tools are added, some new attributes may be necessary). In the same way, this specification could be adapted to specify other symbolic computation systems database management.
Due to lack of space the extension of the specified database to the dynamic one is not given here, but this extension is a further argument to demonstrate the feasability and interest of our approach.

6 References

[ADJ 78] Goguen J., Thatcher J., Wagner E. : **An initial algebra approach to the specification, correctness and implementation of abstract data types** ; Current Trends in Programming Methodology, Vol. 4, Yeh Ed., Prentice Hall, 1978.

[Bid 88] Bidoit M. : **The stratified loose approach : a generalization of initial and loose semantics** ; Recent Trends in Data Type Specification, Selected Papers of the 5th Workshop on Specifications of Abstract Data Types, Gullane, Ecosse, Springer-Verlag L.N.C.S. 332, pp. 1–22, 1988.

[Bid 89] Bidoit M. : **Pluss, un langage pour le développement de spécifications algébriques modulaires** ; Thèse d'Etat, University of Paris-South, 1988.

[B&C 85a] Bidoit M., Choppy C. : **ASSPEGIQUE : an integrated environment for algebraic specifications** ; Formal Methods and Software Developments, Proc. International Joint Conference on Theory and Practice of Software Development (TAPSOFT), Berlin, Mars 1985, Vol. 2 : Colloquium on Software Engineering (CSE), L. N. C. S. 186, Springer Verlag, pp 246-260.

[BCV 84] Bidoit M., Choppy C., Voisin F. : **The ASSPEGIQUE specification environment, Motivations and design** ; Proc. of the 3rd Workshop on Theory and Applications of Abstract data types, Bremen, Nov 1984, Recent Trends in Data Type Specification (H.-J. Kreowski ed.), Informatik-Fachberichte 116, Springer Verlag, Berlin-Heidelberg, 1985, pp 54-72.

[BCC 87] Bidoit M., Capy F., Choppy C., Choquet N., Gresse C., Kaplan S., Schlienger F., Voisin F. : **ASSPRO : an interactive and integrated programming environment** ; Technology and Science of Informatics, Vol. 6, Num. 4, pp. 259–278, 1987. Techniques et Sciences Informatiques, vol 6, n° 1, Janvier 1987.

[BGHM 89] Bidoit M., Gaudel M.C., Hagelstein J., Mauboussin A. : **From an ERAE requirement specification to a PLUSS algebraic specification: A case study** ; Proc. of the METEOR Workshop "Methods based on Formal Specifications", Eindhoven, Netherlands, September 1989.

[BGM 89] Bidoit M., Gaudel M.C., Mauboussin A. : **How to make algebraic specifications more understandable ? An experiment with the PLUSS specification language** ; Science of Computer Programming, 12(1), 1989.

[B&H 85] Biebow B., Hagelstein J. : **Algebraic specification of synchronisation and errors : a telephonic example** ; in Mathematical Foundations of Software Development - Proc. TAPSOFT, Berlin, L.N.C.S. n° 186, Springer Verlag, 1985, pp 294-308.

[Bro 84] Broy M. : **Algebraic methods for program construction : the project CIP** ; in Program transformations and programming environments, Pepper P. (ed.), NATO ASI Series F : Computer and System Sciences, Vol. 8, Springer, 1984, pp 199-222.

[B&G 77] Burstall R.M., Goguen J.A. : **Putting theories together to make specifications** ; Proc. 5th Int. Conf. on Artificial Intelligence, Cambridge MA, 1977, pp 1045-58.

[Cap 87] Capy F. : **ASSPEGIQUE : un environnement d'exceptions ... Une sémantique opérationnelle des E,R-algèbres prenant en compte les exceptions. Un environnement intégré de spécification algébrique : ASSPEGIQUE** ; Thèse de 3ème cycle, Université d'Orsay, Dec. 1987.

[Cap 88] Capy F. : **ASSPEGIQUE - Le langage de spécification : PLUSS - Manuel de référence** ; L.R.I. Research Report n° 418, March 1988.

[Cho 86] Choppy C. : **Techniques et aspects du prototypage** ; Génie Logiciel n° 3, pp 4-12, Janvier 1986.

[EFH 83] Ehrig H., Fey W., Hansen H. : **ACT ONE : An algebraic specification language with two levels of semantics** ; Technical Report 83-03, Department of Computer Science, TU Berlin, 1983.

[EM 85] Ehrig H., Mahr B. : **Fundamentals of Algebraic Specifications 1** ; Springer Verlag, 1985.

[F&G 84] Forgaard R., Guttag J.V. : **REVE : a term rewriting system generator with failure-resistant Knuth-Bendix** ; Proc. of an NSF workshop on the rewrite rule laboratory, and : Report n° 84GEN008, Avril 1984, General Electric.

[FGJM 85] Futatsugi K., Goguen J.A., Jouannaud J.P., Meseguer J. : **Principles of OBJ2** ; Proc. 12th ACM Symp. on Principle of Programming Languages, New Orleans, Jan. 1985, pp 52-66.

[Fri 85] Fribourg L. : **Handling function definitions through innermost superposition and rewriting** ; Proc. 1st Conference on "Rewriting Techniques and Applications", Dijon, Mai 1985.

[Gau 85] Gaudel M.C. : **Towards structured algebraic specifications** ; Proc. ESPRIT Technical Week, Bruxelles 1985, Springer Verlag.

[G&H 86] Guttag J.V., Horning J.J. : **Report on the Larch Shared Language** ; Sci. of Comp. programming, 6, 2, 1986, pp 103-134.

[Kap 87a] Kaplan S. : **A compiler for conditional rewriting systems** ; Proc. 2nd Conf. on Rewriting techniques and applications, Bordeaux, L.N.C.S. n° 256, Springer Verlag, pp 25-41, May 1987.

[Kap 87b] Kaplan S. : **Simplifying conditional term rewriting systems : unification and confluence** ; Journal of Symbolic Computation, Vol. 4, n_o 3, pp 295-335.

[Les 83] Lescanne P. : **Computer experiments with the REVE term rewriting system generator** ; Proc. 10th Symp. on Principle of Programming Languages, A.C.M., Austin TX, USA, pp. 99-108.

[Sho 83] Shooman M. L. : **Software Engineering** ; International Student Edition, McGraw Hill Book Company, 1983, p 40.

[Slo 86] **Slog 1.1, User's Manual** ; C.G.E. Report, Route de Nozay, 91460 Marcoussis, France, August 1986.

[Voi 86] Voisin F. : **CIGALE : a tool for interactive grammar construction and expressions parsing** ; Science of Computer Programming, Vol. 7, n° 1, 1986, pp. 61-86.

A Functional and Logic Language with Polymorphic Types
(Extended Abstract)

Michael Hanus

Fachbereich Informatik, Universität Dortmund

D-4600 Dortmund 50, W. Germany

e-mail: michael@ls5.informatik.uni-dortmund.de

This paper presents a typed language with a precisely defined semantics that integrates functional and logic programming styles. To detect programming errors at compile time, the language has a polymorphic type system. The type system restricts the possible use of functions and predicates and ensures that a function or predicate is only called with appropriate arguments at run time. In contrast to many other type systems for logic programming, this type system has a model-theoretic semantics (types are subsets of domains of interpretations) and allows the use of typical logic programming techniques. For instance, it is possible to add specialized clauses and to apply higher-order programming techniques.

1 Introduction

During recent years, various attempts have been made to amalgamate functional and logic programming languages (see [DL86] for a collection of proposals). A lot of these integrations are based on Horn clause logic with equality which consists of predicates and Horn clauses for logic programming and functions and equations for functional programming. Because of the underlying single-sorted logic, a lot of these languages are untyped which is a disadvantage from a practical point of view. Modern functional programming languages, like ML [HMM86], Miranda [Tur85] and HOPE [BMS80], have polymorphic type systems to detect specific programming errors at compile time. Due to the polymorphism, the restrictions of the type system are acceptable for practical programming.

The lack of types for logic programming was recognized by several people, and therefore a lot of research for types in logic programming languages have been done. In contrast to functional languages, where types have a declarative meaning (e.g., [DM82], but a model-theoretic semantics for types in functional languages is also an area of ongoing research), many proposals for type systems for logic languages have a notion of a type that is not directly related to the declarative semantics. For instance, the polymorphic type systems in [MO84] and [DH88] require declarations for types and predicates but do not define the semantics of such declarations. Declarations are not required in the proposals [Mis84], [Klu87] and [Zob87] but are inferred by a type checking algorithm. These and other type systems have only a syntactic notion of a type, i.e., types are sets of terms rather than subsets of carrier sets of interpretations. Moreover, the inference of types from a completely untyped program yields only in a few cases the types expected by the programmer. For instance, assume *list* denotes the set of all terms of the form [] or [E|L] where L is a term from *list*. Then the inferred type for the predicate append defined by

```
append([],L,L) ←
append([E|R],L,[E|RL]) ← append(R,L,RL)
```

may be "$list \times \alpha \times \alpha \ \cup \ list \times \beta \times list$" [XW88], where α and β denote arbitrary types. The problem is the first clause which defines append to be true not only for lists but also for other terms. E.g., append([],3,3) is true but usually considered as an ill-typed goal, i.e., the expected type is "$list \times list \times list$". This example shows that inferring types from a completely untyped program is generally not acceptable since an untyped logic program does not contain the type information expected by the programmer (see also [Nai87]). A type system should *allow user declarations for types*. Such declarations frequently documents the expected meaning of predicates and improves the readability of large programs. Therefore the language presented in this paper is *explicitly typed*, i.e., each variable, function and predicate has an explicitly given type. A program where the types of some variables are not declared is viewed as a short-hand for an explicitly typed program. A type inference procedure can be used to insert the missing type declarations for variables.

Since pure functional and logic languages are declarative languages, an integration of these languages should be also declarative. Hence each declaration in the language should have a clearly defined model-theoretic semantics. If such a language is enriched by a type structure, the semantics of the type structure must be defined. But this have been done only in a few proposals. For instance, Padawitz [Pad88] has proposed a Horn clause logic with equality with a many-sorted type structure. Each type corresponds to a non-empty subset of the carrier set of the interpretation. Goguen and Meseguer [GM84] have shown that the common deduction rules for untyped equational logic become unsound if types denote empty sets. Hence the definition of the model-theoretic semantics of types is necessary to establish exact soundness and completeness results.

The simple many-sorted type structure was extended in several directions: Goguen, Meseguer [GM86] and Smolka [Smo86b] have proposed order-sorted type systems for Horn clause logic with equality where the ordering of types implies a subset relation on the corresponding sets. Aït-Kaci and Nasr [AN86] have proposed a logic language with a type system that includes subtypes and inheritance based on a similar semantics. From an operational point of view the approaches with subtypes need a unification procedure that considers types, i.e., types are present at run time. Smolka [Smo88b] has proposed an equational logic language with a polymorphic type system [Smo88a]. Since his language also includes an order-sorted type system, he has some restrictions on his type system and therefore the application of higher-order programming techniques, well-known from functional languages, is not possible (see below). A polymorphic type system for pure logic programming, based on a model-theoretic semantics, has been proposed in [Han89a]. Since it is rather general, it allows the application of higher-order programming techniques [Han89b]. Therefore it is the basis of the type system of the language presented in this paper.

Higher-order programming is a useful feature in functional languages. Therefore we are also interested in the application of higher-order programming techniques in our (first-order) framework. Warren [War82] has shown that higher-order programming techniques can be simulated in first-order logic if higher-order predicates are specified by clauses for an apply predicate. For instance, the following clauses define two binary predicates not and inc and the predicate map which applies a binary predicate to corresponding elements of two lists:

```
map(P,[],[]) ←
map(P,[E1|L1],[E2|L2]) ← apply2(P,E1,E2), map(P,L1,L2)
not(true,false) ←
not(false,true) ←
inc(N,s(N)) ←
apply2(not,B1,B2) ← not(B1,B2)
apply2(inc,I1,I2) ← inc(I1,I2)
```

The following goal shows an application of the map predicate:

```
?- map(not,[true,false,true],L).
L = [false,true,false]
```

Since such a specification is first-order, the result is not a higher-order logic, but predicate variables are universally quantified over all predicates defined in the program. One reason not to leave first-order logic in contrast to [MN86] is efficiency: The higher-order unification problem is undecidable in general [Gol81] and a complete unification procedure is a very complex task. But there is still another reason: Higher-order unification means searching new functions that satisfy a given set of equations. This feature is not available in functional languages and, in our opinion, not necessary for programming. From a practical point of view it is sufficient to apply only user-defined functions to appropriate arguments at run time.

Since Warren's proposal is concerned with Prolog and its untyped logic, it is not type secure and there is no clear distinction between first-order and higher-order objects (predicate variables). Therefore a type system is needed. But the proposed polymorphic type systems for logic programming [MO84] [DH88]

[Smo88a] are not applicable because of the clauses for the apply2 predicate: apply2 has the polymorphic type "$pred2(\alpha,\beta),\alpha,\beta$" (where $pred2(\ldots,\ldots)$ denotes the type of binary predicate abstractions), but the type of apply2 in the clause

    apply2(inc,I1,I2) ← inc(I1,I2)

is the specialized type "$pred2(nat,nat),nat,nat$". Hence this clause is ill-typed w.r.t. these type systems.[1] If we want to avoid any type-checking at run time, then it is not possible to construct a type system that can type the above program. For instance, consider the following goal (the constant 0 is of type nat):

    ?- map(P,[N1],[N2]), apply2(P,0,N3)

If the Prolog computation rule is used and no type-checking is made during the resolution process, then P, N1 and N2 are bound to not, true and false, respectively, and the goal

    ?- apply2(not,0,N3)

is derived after four resolution steps. The last goal is ill-typed, because the predicate not is defined on Booleans, but not on naturals. If we use type information at run time, then this resolution can be avoided, because variable P has type $pred2(nat,nat)$ and may not be bound to not which is of type $pred2(bool,bool)$. This example shows that the translation of higher-order programs into first-order programs (as proposed for IDEAL [BG86]) is generally not type secure if the target language does not perform any type-checking at run time. Since type security is the main purpose of our language proposal, our operational semantics includes type information whenever it is necessary.

The rest of this paper presents the syntactical part of our language and an outline of the declarative and operational semantics. Let us summarize the main features of our language:

- The language combines functional programming with equations and logic programming with Horn clauses in a type secure way. The type system has parametric polymorphism, i.e., types may contain type variables that are universally quantified over all types [DM82].

- The language has a declarative semantics that is based on Horn clause logic with equality. The types have a declarative meaning, i.e., types are subsets of carriers sets of interpretations.

- Only well-typed programs have a declarative meaning. Therefore all programs are explicitly typed. A program with some missing type annotations is viewed as a short-hand for an explicitly typed program and the missing type annotations have to be inserted by a type inference procedure.

- The operational semantics is based on resolution for predicates and narrowing for functions. Because of the general type system the unification must be replaced by the typed unification of [Han89a]. The typed unification procedure is more expensive than the untyped one but may help to reduce the search space in the resolution process.

- Each variable, function and predicate has a distinct (polymorphic) type. The function and predicate types must be declared by the programmer and all clauses have to meet the declared type requirements. Thus our language is explicitly typed. But the implementation of the language has a type inference system based on [DM82] that deduces the types of variables in the given untyped clauses.

- The type system is rather general and allows the application of higher-order programming techniques in a type secure way. Some restrictions of the polymorphic type systems in [MO84], [DH88] and [Smo88a] are dropped.

2 The polymorphic equational logic language

The typing rules of our language are quite simple. We start by defining the language of types which must be specified for a program. First the programmer has to declare the basic types like int or $bool$ and type constructors like $list$ which he wants to use in the program. Each type constructor has a fixed arity (e.g., $list$ has arity 1, denoted by $list/1$). Basic types can be seen as type constructors of arity 0. We assume

---

[1] In these type systems the left-hand side of a clause must have a type that is equivalent to the declared type of the predicate.

$$\frac{}{V \vdash x{:}\tau} \qquad (x{:}\tau \in V)$$

$$\frac{V \vdash t_1{:}\tau_1, \ldots, V \vdash t_n{:}\tau_n}{V \vdash f(t_1{:}\tau_1, \ldots, t_n{:}\tau_n){:}\tau} \qquad (f{:}\tau_1, \ldots, \tau_n \to \tau \text{ is a generic instance of a function declaration, } n \geq 0)$$

$$\frac{V \vdash t_1{:}\tau_1, \ldots, V \vdash t_n{:}\tau_n}{V \vdash p(t_1{:}\tau_1, \ldots, t_n{:}\tau_n)} \qquad (p{:}\tau_1, \ldots, \tau_n \text{ is a generic instance of a predicate declaration, } n \geq 0)$$

$$\frac{V \vdash L_0, \ldots, V \vdash L_n}{V \vdash L_0 \leftarrow L_1, \ldots, L_n} \qquad (\text{each } L_i \text{ has the form } p(\cdots), i = 0, \ldots, n)$$

Figure 1: Typing rules for the polymorphic equational logic language

a given infinite set of **type variables** and we denote members of this set by α and β. A (**polymorphic**) **type** is a term built from basic types, type constructors and type variables (see [HO80] for the notion of term). A **monomorphic type** is a type without type variables. For instance, $list(int)$ and $list(\alpha)$ are types which denote lists of integers and lists of elements of an arbitrary type, respectively.

Next the argument and result types of functions and predicates occurring in the program must be declared. A function declaration has the form

func $f{:}\tau_1, \ldots, \tau_n \to \tau$

(where $\tau_1, \ldots, \tau_n, \tau$ are arbitrary types) and means that the function f takes n arguments of types $\tau_1, \ldots, \tau_n$ and produces a value of type τ. f is called *constant* of type τ if $n = 0$. For simplicity we have no distinction between constructors for data types and functions defined on data types [HH82], but in practice this distinction can be made by the form of equations (constructors do not occur as the top symbol of the left-hand side of an equation). This distinction is unnecessary from a declarative point of view. A predicate declaration has the form

pred $p{:}\tau_1, \ldots, \tau_n$

(where $\tau_1, \ldots, \tau_n$ are arbitrary types) and means that the predicate p has n arguments of types $\tau_1, \ldots, \tau_n$. The **equality predicate** is always defined by

pred $\equiv{:}\alpha, \alpha$

In order to compute the most general type of a term automatically, we forbid overloading: For each function and predicate symbol there is only one type declaration.

The type variables in a declaration are universally quantified over all types, i.e., functions and predicates can be used with an arbitrary substitution of types for type variables in the declaration. Hence we call a function/predicate declaration a **generic instance** of another declaration if it can be obtained from the other declaration by replacing each occurrence of one or more type variables by other types (cf. [DM82]). For instance, $length{:}list(nat) \to nat$ is a generic instance of the function declaration

func $length{:}list(\alpha) \to nat$

We embed types in terms, i.e., each symbol in a term is annotated with an appropriate type expression. These annotations are useful for the unification of polymorphic terms (see below). The type annotations need not be provided by the user because most general type annotations can be computed. We assume a given infinite set Var of variable names distinguishable from type variables. A **typed variable** has the form $x{:}\tau$ where $x \in Var$ and τ is an arbitrary type. We call V an **allowed set of typed variables** if V contains only typed variables and $x{:}\tau, x{:}\tau' \in V$ implies $\tau = \tau'$. We call $L \leftarrow G$ a **polymorphic program clause** if there is an allowed set of typed variables V and $V \vdash L \leftarrow G$ is derivable by the inference rules in figure 1 (analogously for **terms**, **atoms** and **goals**). Note that we have no restrictions on the use of types and type variables in a clause in contrast to [MO84], [Smo88a] and similar type systems. For instance, facts with specialized types are allowed in our type system. A **polymorphic equational logic program** is a finite set of polymorphic program clauses. If the left-hand side of a clause has the form $t_1{:}\tau_1 \equiv t_2{:}\tau_2$

(we use the infix notation for '≡'), we call the clause **conditional equation**. Conditional equations define the semantics of functions, whereas other clauses define the semantics of predicates. Since there are no restrictions on the use of predicates and functions in clauses, our language is a genuine amalgamation of a functional and a logic language. The declarative semantics of the language is Horn clause logic with equality, where types are interpreted as subsets of carrier sets. Before we present more details, we give some examples for polymorphic equational logic programs in the next section.

3 Examples

For the examples in this section it is sufficient to have an intuitive idea of the semantics of polymorphic equational logic programs: The equality symbol denotes identity, clauses are implications and type variables are universally quantified over all types.

The first example defines some operations on lists of any type. The constant [] represents the empty list, and the function • concatenates an element with a list of the same type. We write [E|L] instead of •(E,L) (throughout this paper we use the Prolog notation for lists, cf. [CM87]). The function **append** that concatenates both argument lists is defined in a functional style by two equations (with empty conditions). The predicate **member** is defined in a logic programming style. We omit type annotations in program clauses because they can be simply produced by an ML-like type checker [DM82] since the types of all functions and predicates are explicitly given.

```
type list/1
func []:              →  list(α)
func • :   α, list(α) →  list(α)
func append: list(α), list(α) →  list(α)
pred member: α, list(α)
```

```
clauses:
append([],L) ≡ L ←
append([E|R],L) ≡ [E|append(R,L)] ←
member(E,[E|L]) ←
member(E,[F|L]) ← member(E,L)
```

Next we show the application of higher-order programming techniques in our framework. As stated above we do not want to leave first-order logic for the sake of efficiency. But we can apply Warren's technique [War82] in our typed framework because we have an unrestricted mechanism of polymorphic types. As shown in the first chapter and in [Han89b], this is *not* possible in other polymorphic type systems for logic programming, e.g., [MO84].

4 Declarative Semantics

We want to give an outline of the declarative semantics. More details can be found in [Han88]. Polymorphic equational logic programs will be interpreted by algebraic structures with a particular sort structure [Poi86]. If there are no type constructors in a program, i.e., all types are monomorphic, then the notions of interpretation and validity for polymorphic programs are equivalent to untyped [Llo87] or many-sorted [GM84] logic.

Variables in untyped logic vary over the carrier set of the interpretation. Consequently, type variables in polymorphic programs vary over all types of the interpretation and typed variables vary over appropriate carrier sets. Hence an interpretation of a polymorphic equational logic program consists of a single-sorted algebra that describes all types in the interpretation and a structure for the derived polymorphic signature. A structure is an interpretation of types as sets, function symbols as operations on these sets and predicate symbols as predicates on these sets where the equality predicate '$\equiv$' is always interpreted as identity on the carrier sets [Pad88]. In the following we will give more precise definitions of these notions. We assume familiarity with notions from algebraic specifications [EM85].

In order to give a precise definition of "universal quantification over all types", we view a specification of basic types and type constructors as a single-sorted signature H (where *type* is the only sort): Each basic type is a constant and each type constructor of arity n is an n-ary function in the signature H. If we denote by X the infinite set of all type variables, the term algebra over H and X, $T_H(X)$, contains all polymorphic type expressions. Hence we can use the notion of an H-algebra for the interpretation of types and the notion of H-homomorphisms from $T_H(X)$ into A to formalize "universal quantification over all types":

Let $\Sigma = (H, Func, Pred)$ be the type declarations of a polymorphic equational logic program, where H is the signature that specifies the basic types and type constructors and $Func$ and $Pred$ are the sets of function and predicate declarations, respectively. Σ is called a **polymorphic signature**. Let A be an H-algebra with carrier set Ty_A. The **polymorphic signature** $\Sigma(A) = (Ty_A, Func_A, Pred_A)$ **derived from Σ and A** is defined by

$$Func_A \quad := \quad \{f{:}\sigma(\tau_f) \mid f{:}\tau_f \in Func, \sigma\colon X \to Ty_A \text{ is an assignment for type variables}\}$$
$$Pred_A \quad := \quad \{p{:}\sigma(\tau_p) \mid p{:}\tau_p \in Pred, \sigma\colon X \to Ty_A \text{ is an assignment for type variables}\}$$

This is well-defined since each assignment for variables from X can be uniquely extended to an H-homomorphism from $T_H(X)$ into A and H-homomorphisms are extended to tuples over $T_H(X)$ by componentwise application. An **interpretation** of a polymorphic signature Σ is an H-algebra A together with a $\Sigma(A)$-**structure** (S, δ), which consists of a Ty_A-sorted set S (the **carrier** of the interpretation) and a denotation δ with:

1. If $f{:}\tau_1, \ldots, \tau_n \to \tau \in Func_A$, then $\delta_{f{:}\tau_1,\ldots,\tau_n\to\tau}\colon S_{\tau_1} \times \cdots \times S_{\tau_n} \to S_\tau$ is a function.

2. If $p{:}\tau_1, \ldots, \tau_n \in Pred_A$, then $\delta_{p{:}\tau_1,\ldots,\tau_n} \subseteq S_{\tau_1} \times \cdots \times S_{\tau_n}$ is a relation.

3. If '$\equiv$'$:\tau, \tau \in Pred_A$, then $\delta_{\equiv:\tau,\tau} = \{(a,a) \mid a \in S_\tau\}$

If A and A' are H-algebras, then every H-homomorphism $\sigma\colon A \to A'$ induces a **signature morphism** $\sigma\colon \Sigma(A) \to \Sigma(A')$ and a **forgetful functor** $U_\sigma\colon Cat_{\Sigma(A')} \to Cat_{\Sigma(A)}$ from the category of $\Sigma(A')$-structures into the category of $\Sigma(A)$-structures (for details, see [EM85]). Therefore we can define a Σ-**homomorphism** from a Σ-interpretation (A, S, δ) into another Σ-interpretation (A', S', δ') as a pair (σ, h), where $\sigma\colon A \to A'$ is an H-homomorphism and $h\colon (S, \delta) \to U_\sigma((S', \delta'))$ is a homomorphism between $\Sigma(A)$-structures. The class of all Σ-interpretations with the composition $(\sigma', h') \circ (\sigma, h) := (\sigma' \circ \sigma, U_\sigma(h') \circ h)$ of two Σ-homomorphisms is a category.

In the following we assume that X is the set of all type variables and V is a set of typed variables. The notion of a **term interpretation** can be defined as usual, where '$\equiv$' denotes the identity relation on terms and all other predicate symbols denote empty relations. By $T_\Sigma(X, V)$ we denote the free term interpretation over X and V where the carrier is the set of all well-typed terms that contain only symbols from Σ, X and V. A homomorphism in the polymorphic framework consists of a mapping between type algebras and a mapping between appropriate structures. Consequently, a variable assignment in the polymorphic framework maps type variables into types and typed variables into objects of appropriate types: If $I = (A, S, \delta)$ is a Σ-interpretation, then a **variable assignment** for (X, V) in I is a pair of mappings (μ, val) with $\mu\colon X \to Ty_A$ and $val\colon V \to S'$, where $(S', \delta') := U_\mu((S, \delta))$ and $val(x{:}\tau) \in S'_\tau \ (= S_{\mu(\tau)})$ for all $x{:}\tau \in V$. Similarly to the many-sorted case, any variable assignment can be uniquely extended to a Σ-homomorphism [Poi86]:

Theorem 1 (Free term structure) *Let I be a Σ-interpretation and v be an assignment for (X, V) in I. There exists a unique Σ-homomorphism from $T_\Sigma(X, V)$ into I that extends v.*

In the following we denote the Σ-homomorphism that extends an assignment v again by v. We are not interested in all interpretations of a polymorphic signature but only in those interpretations that satisfy all clauses of a given polymorphic equational logic program. In order to formalize that we define validity of atoms, goals and clauses relative to a given Σ-interpretation $I = (A, S, \delta)$ (we assume that the polymorphic atoms, goals and clauses contain only type variables from X and typed variables from V):

- Let $v = (\mu, val)$ be an assignment for (X, V) in I.

  $I, v \models L$ if $L = p(t_1{:}\tau_1, \ldots, t_n{:}\tau_n)$ is a polymorphic atom with $(val_{\tau_1}(t_1{:}\tau_1), \ldots, val_{\tau_n}(t_n{:}\tau_n)) \in \delta'_{p{:}\tau_1,\ldots,\tau_n}$ where $U_\mu((S, \delta)) = (S', \delta')$

  $I, v \models G$ if G is a polymorphic goal with $I, v \models L$ for all $L \in G$

  $I, v \models L \leftarrow G$ if $L \leftarrow G$ is a polymorphic clause where $I, v \models G$ implies $I, v \models L$

- $I, V \models \mathcal{F}$ if $\mathcal{F}$ is a polymorphic atom, goal or clause with $I, v \models \mathcal{F}$ for all variable assignments v for (X, V) in I

Let C be a set of polymorphic program clauses. A Σ-interpretation I is called **model** for (Σ, C) if $I, V_0 \models L \leftarrow G$ for all clauses $L \leftarrow G \in C$, where V_0 is the set of all typed variables occurring in $L \leftarrow G$. A polymorphic goal G is called **valid in** (Σ, C) relative to V if $I, V \models G$ for every model I of (Σ, C). We shall write: $(\Sigma, C, V) \models G$.

This notion of validity is the extension of validity in untyped or many-sorted equational Horn clause logic [Pad88] to the polymorphic case: In untyped or many-sorted logic an atom, goal or clause is said to be true iff it is true for all variable assignments. In the polymorphic case an atom, goal or clause is said to be true iff it is true for all assignments of type variables and typed variables. We have defined validity relative to a set of variables because carrier sets in our interpretations may be empty in contrast to untyped Horn logic. This is also the case in many-sorted logic [GM84]. Validity relative to variables is different from validity in the sense of untyped logic. An example for such a difference can be found in [Han89a], p. 231. Validity in our sense is equivalent to validity in the sense of untyped logic if the types of variables denote non-empty sets in all interpretations. But a requirement for non-empty carrier sets is not reasonable in our polymorphic framework.

"Typed substitutions" are a combination of substitutions on types and substitutions on well-typed terms: If V, V' are sets of typed variables, then a **typed substitution** σ is a Σ-homomorphism $\sigma = (\sigma_X, \sigma_V)$ from $T_\Sigma(X, V)$ into $T_\Sigma(X, V')$. Since σ_X and σ_V are only applied to type expressions and typed terms, respectively, we omit the indices X and V and write σ for both σ_X and σ_V. We extend typed substitutions on Σ-atoms by: $\sigma(p(t_1, \ldots, t_n)) = p(\sigma(t_1), \ldots, \sigma(t_n))$.

A polymorphic term t' with typed variables V' is called an **instance** of a term t with typed variables V if there is a typed substitution σ from $T_\Sigma(X, V)$ into $T_\Sigma(X, V')$ with $t' = \sigma(t)$. The definition of instances can be extended on atoms, goals and clauses. We omit the simple definitions here.

It can be shown that there exists an initial model for each polymorphic equational logic program. A particular initial model is the quotient of the term interpretation $T_\Sigma(\emptyset, \emptyset)$ and the least congruence generated by the axioms of equality [Han88]. Note that this is a set-theoretic model for logic programs with polymorphic types. This is not a contradiction to the result of Reynolds [Rey84], because Reynolds has a different semantic basis. Reynolds' foundation is the polymorphic typed lambda calculus which allows computations with higher-order functions. Our basis is not the lambda calculus but we use algebraic interpretations. All functions in our specifications are first-order and therefore we can construct a set-theoretic model in contrast to Reynolds. But Reynolds' result shows that the extension of typed logic programs to higher-order functions or predicates is a difficult task. Nevertheless we have seen in section 3 that it is possible to simulate some features of higher-order programming in our framework.

5 Operational semantics

There exists an efficient proof procedure that computes a correct answer if the initial goal is valid w.r.t. the given program. The proof procedure is similar to other equational logic languages, e.g., EQLOG [GM86]: It is the combination of resolution for predicates [Llo87] and conditional narrowing [Hus85] for the computation of functions but with a particular unification procedure for polymorphic terms: In [Han89a] it is shown that the unification of polymorphic terms can be reduced to common first-order unification [Rob65] if the annotated types are treated as first-order terms. Type terms are distinguished from other terms by their position (type terms occur only after a colon ':'). For instance, a unifier of the polymorphic terms $\square{:}list(\alpha)$

and v:*list(int)* is the substitution that replaces α by *int* and **v** by $\Box$. This could also be computed by a first-order unification algorithm if the symbol ':' is treated as a term constructor of arity 2.

Similarly to [HO80], we denote *positions* or *occurrences* in polymorphic terms or goals by sequences of naturals. If π is an occurrence in a polymorphic goal G, then $G[\pi]$ denotes the subterm of G at position π and $G[\pi \leftarrow t]$ denotes the result of replacing the subterm $G[\pi]$ by t. We specify the *basic operational semantics* of our language by describing a computation step from one goal to the next goal. Let $L_1, \ldots, L_n$ be a polymorphic goal.

1. (**Narrowing rule**) If there exist a non-variable occurrence π in L_1, a conditional equation $v \equiv w \leftarrow R_1, \ldots, R_m$ and a most general unifier σ for $L_1[\pi]$ and v, then

$$\sigma(R_1), \ldots, \sigma(R_m), \sigma(L_1)[\pi \leftarrow \sigma(w)], \sigma(L_2), \ldots, \sigma(L_n)$$

   is the next goal, otherwise:

2. (**Unification rule**) If $L_1 = v \equiv w$ and there exists a most general unifier σ for v and w, then

$$\sigma(L_2), \ldots, \sigma(L_n)$$

   is the next goal, otherwise:

3. (**Restricted resolution rule**) If there exist a program clause $L \leftarrow R_1, \ldots, R_m$ which is not a conditional equation and a most general unifier σ for L_1 and L, then

$$\sigma(R_1), \ldots, \sigma(R_m), \sigma(L_2), \ldots, \sigma(L_n)$$

   is the next goal, otherwise: fail.

The soundness and completeness of the operational semantics is proved in [Han88], where the completeness is only stated under the following assumptions: The polymorphic equational program is Church-Rosser (i.e., for each proof with applications of equations in both directions there exists a proof with applications of equations from left to right), the computed answer is irreducible (i.e., the solutions are in normal form) and there are no extra-variables in clauses (i.e., the left-hand-side of a conditional equation contains all variables occurring in the conditional equation). The first two restrictions are standard in equational logic programming [Pad88], but the last restriction is not acceptable from a logic programmer's point of view. Since we are interested in the influence of types into equational logic programming, we have not developed better results for this problem but we may adopt results from other work done in this area. For instance, Bertling and Ganzinger [BG89] have investigated the problem of extra-variables in conditions of conditional equations. They have no restrictions on the variables in conditional equations and give sufficient criteria for the completeness of the narrowing procedure. In some cases it is possible to transform a given program into another one which satisfies the completeness criterion. A particular variant of the Knuth-Bendix completion procedure which considers the particularly chosen rewrite relation is used to transform the programs.

The actual implementation of the language is done in a more efficient way than described above. For instance, the set of all function symbols are partitioned into a set of constructors and a set of defined operators [HH82], where constructors are function symbols that do not appear as the top symbol of the left-hand side in any conditional equation. The operational semantics considers the constructors so that equations between constructors are flattened and an innermost position is chosen in a narrowing step (this strategy is only complete under additional restrictions, see [Fri85]).

Since we have an unrestricted type system, the unification procedure has to consider the types of the polymorphic terms. Hence the polymorphic unification is more complex and less efficient than the unification in untyped logic languages. But it can be shown [Han88] that it is possible to omit type annotations at run time if the program satisfies particular syntactic conditions (compare [Han89a] and [Han89b] for the case of polymorphic logic programs without equality). For instance, if the left-hand sides of all clauses have a most general type w.r.t. the type declarations, then all types can be omitted at run time. Better optimization techniques are a topic for future research. On the other hand, type information may be useful to reduce the search space in the computation process [HV87]. Therefore the overall goal is not to omit all type annotations at run time but only those annotations that are unnecessary for correct computation. We have seen in the introduction that some logic programming techniques cannot be applied in a type secure way if all type annotations are omitted at run time.

Resolution combined with conditional narrowing is only a complete proof method for validity if all possible derivations are simultaneously computed. This is very expensive and therefore it is recommendable to use a backtracking strategy as in Prolog with the consequence that completeness is lost in general. The interpreter of our language is implemented in Prolog and uses the Prolog backtracking strategy for different derivations. Polymorphic terms are mapped into Prolog terms and therefore the built-in unification can be used to unify polymorphic terms. A lot of equational logic programs have been successfully executed by the interpreter.

6 Conclusions

We have presented an equational logic language with a polymorphic type system. The language integrates two interesting programming styles in a type secure way: functional and logic programming. In contrast to other proposals for polymorphically typed logic programming languages, it is possible to apply higher-order programming techniques in our framework. The language has a well-defined semantics and programs can be efficiently executed if the same drawbacks as in Prolog (incompleteness because of infinite derivations) are accepted. The language is explicitly typed, i.e., each syntactic unit is annotated with a type expression, but the implementation contains a type inference procedure so that the programmer can omit all type annotations in clauses. Further work remains to be done in the area of run-time optimizations with the aim to reduce the cases where type information is required for correct unification.

References

[AN86] H. Aït-Kaci and R. Nasr. LOGIN: A Logic Programming Language with Built-In Inheritance. *Journal of Logic Programming (3)*, pp. 185–215, 1986.

[BG86] P.G. Bosco and E. Giovannetti. IDEAL: An Ideal Deductive Applicative Language. In *Proc. IEEE Internat. Symposium on Logic Programming*, pp. 89–94, Salt Lake City, 1986.

[BG89] H. Bertling and H. Ganzinger. Completion-Time Optimization of Rewrite-Time Goal Solving. In *Proc. of the Conference on Rewriting Techniques and Applications*, pp. 45–58. Springer LNCS 355, 1989.

[BMS80] R.M. Burstall, D.B. MacQueen, and D.T. Sannella. HOPE: An Experimental Applicative Language. In *Conference Record of the 1980 LISP Conference*, pp. 136–143. ACM, 1980.

[CM87] W.F. Clocksin and C.S. Mellish. *Programming in Prolog*. Springer, third rev. and ext. edition, 1987.

[DH88] R. Dietrich and F. Hagl. A polymorphic type system with subtypes for Prolog. In *Proc. ESOP 88*, Nancy, pp. 79–93. Springer LNCS 300, 1988.

[DL86] D. DeGroot and G. Lindstrom, editors. *Logic Programming, Functions, Relations, and Equations*. Prentice Hall, 1986.

[DM82] L. Damas and R. Milner. Principal type-schemes for functional programs. In *Proc. 9th Annual Symposium on Principles of Programming Languages*, pp. 207–212, 1982.

[EM85] H. Ehrig and B. Mahr. *Fundamentals of Algebraic Specification 1: Equations and Initial Semantics*, volume 6 of *EATCS Monographs on Theoretical Computer Science*. Springer, 1985.

[Fri85] L. Fribourg. SLOG: A Logic Programming Language Interpreter Based on Clausal Superposition and Rewriting. In *Proc. IEEE Internat. Symposium on Logic Programming*, pp. 172–184, Boston, 1985.

[GM84] J.A. Goguen and J. Meseguer. Completeness of Many-Sorted Equational Logic. Report No. CSLI-84-15, Stanford University, 1984.

[GM86] J.A. Goguen and J. Meseguer. Eqlog: Equality, Types, and Generic Modules for Logic Programming. In D. DeGroot and G. Lindstrom, editors, *Logic Programming, Functions, Relations, and Equations*, pp. 295–363. Prentice Hall, 1986.

[Gol81] W. Goldfarb. The Undecidability of the Second-Order Unification Problem. *Theoretical Computer Science 13*, pp. 225–230, 1981.

[Han88] M. Hanus. *Horn Clause Specifications with Polymorphic Types*. Dissertation, FB Informatik, Univ. Dortmund, 1988.

[Han89a] M. Hanus. Horn Clause Programs with Polymorphic Types: Semantics and Resolution. In *Proc. of the TAPSOFT '89*, pp. 225–240. Springer LNCS 352, 1989. Extended version to appear in *Theoretical Computer Science*.

[Han89b] M. Hanus. Polymorphic Higher-Order Programming in Prolog. In *Proc. Sixth International Conference on Logic Programming (Lisboa)*, pp. 382–397. MIT Press, 1989.

[HH82] G. Huet and J.-M. Hullot. Proofs by Induction of Equational Theories with Constructors. *Journal of Computer and System Sciences 25*, pp. 239–266, 1982.

[HMM86] R. Harper, D.B. MacQueen, and R. Milner. Standard ML. LFCS Report Series ECS-LFCS-86-2, University of Edinburgh, 1986.

[HO80] G. Huet and D.C. Oppen. Equations and Rewrite Rules: A Survey. In R.V. Book, editor, *Formal Language Theory: Perspectives and Open Problems*. Academic Press, 1980.

[Hus85] H. Hussmann. Unification in Conditional-Equational Theories. In *Proc. EUROCAL '85*, pp. 543–553. Springer LNCS 204, 1985.

[HV87] M. Huber and I. Varsek. Extended Prolog with Order-Sorted Resolution. In *Proc. 4th IEEE Internat. Symposium on Logic Programming*, pp. 34–43, San Francisco, 1987.

[Klu87] F. Kluźniak. Type Synthesis for Ground Prolog. In *Proc. Fourth International Conference on Logic Programming (Melbourne)*, pp. 788–816. MIT Press, 1987.

[Llo87] J.W. Lloyd. *Foundations of Logic Programming*. Springer, second, extended edition, 1987.

[Mis84] P. Mishra. Towards a theory of types in Prolog. In *Proc. IEEE Internat. Symposium on Logic Programming*, pp. 289–298, Atlantic City, 1984.

[MN86] D.A. Miller and G. Nadathur. Higher-Order Logic Programming. In *Proc. Third International Conference on Logic Programming (London)*, pp. 448–462. Springer LNCS 225, 1986.

[MO84] A. Mycroft and R.A. O'Keefe. A Polymorphic Type System for Prolog. *Artificial Intelligence*, Vol. 23, pp. 295–307, 1984.

[Nai87] L. Naish. Specification = Program + Types. In *Proc. Foundations of Software Technology and Theoretical Computer Science*, pp. 326–339. Springer LNCS 287, 1987.

[Pad88] P. Padawitz. *Computing in Horn Clause Theories*, volume 16 of *EATCS Monographs on Theoretical Computer Science*. Springer, 1988.

[Poi86] A. Poigné. On Specifications, Theories, and Models with Higher Types. *Information and Control*, Vol. 68, No. 1-3, 1986.

[Rey84] J.C. Reynolds. Polymorphism is not set-theoretic. In *Proc. of the Int. Symp. on the Semantics of Data Types, Sophia-Antipolis*, pp. 145–156. Springer LNCS 173, 1984.

[Rob65] J.A. Robinson. A Machine-Oriented Logic Based on the Resolution Principle. *Journal of the ACM*, Vol. 12, No. 1, pp. 23–41, 1965.

[Smo86a] G. Smolka. Fresh: A Higher-Order Language Based on Unification and Multiple Results. In D. DeGroot and G. Lindstrom, editors, *Logic Programming, Functions, Relations, and Equations*, pp. 469–524. Prentice Hall, 1986.

[Smo86b] G. Smolka. Order-Sorted Horn Logic: Semantics and Deduction. SEKI Report SR-86-17, FB Informatik, Univ. Kaiserslautern, 1986.

[Smo88a] G. Smolka. Logic Programming with Polymorphically Order-Sorted Types. In *Proc. First International Workshop on Algebraic and Logic Programming (Gaussig, G.D.R.)*, pp. 53–70. Springer LNCS 343, 1988.

[Smo88b] G. Smolka. TEL (Version 0.9) Report and User Manual. SEKI Report SR-87-11, FB Informatik, Univ. Kaiserslautern, 1988.

[Tur85] D. Turner. Miranda: A non-strict functional language with polymorphic types. In *Conference on Functional Programming Languages and Computer Architecture, Nancy, France*, pp. 1–16. Springer LNCS 201, 1985.

[War82] D.H.D. Warren. Higher-order extensions to PROLOG: are they needed? In *Machine Intelligence 10*, pp. 441–454, 1982.

[XW88] J. Xu and D.S. Warren. A Type Inference System For Prolog. In *Proc. 5th Conference on Logic Programming & 5th Symposium on Logic Programming (Seattle)*, pp. 604–619, 1988.

[Zob87] J. Zobel. Derivation of Polymorphic Types for Prolog Programs. In *Proc. Fourth International Conference on Logic Programming (Melbourne)*, pp. 817–838. MIT Press, 1987.

Graphical Object Oriented Executable Specification for an Automation Oriented Paradigm of Software Development

Vincenzo Russi   Roberto Zompi

Olivetti Systems & Networks
Standard Platform Division
Case Technology Group
Via Jervis 77
10015 Ivrea - Torino (Italy)
Tel 39-125-528491
Fax 39-125-527689

Abstract — This paper presents PROTOB, an object-oriented CASE system based on high level Petri nets called PROT nets. It consists of several tools supporting object oriented specification, symbolic computation, code generation within the framework of an automation oriented software life cycle paradigm. As its major application area it addresses distributed systems, such as real-time embedded systems, communication protocols and manufacturing control systems.

Keywords — Automation oriented software process, Visual Programming, Executable specification, symbolic computation, Object-oriented design, Petri nets, PROT nets, Rapid prototyping, Real-time distributed systems.

1 Introduction

Effective software design for discrete event dynamic systems (DEDs), such as real-time embedded systems, communication protocols, manufacturing control systems and, in general, distributed systems, is a difficult undertaking because many critical aspects have not yet been tackled satisfactorily. In particular we focus the attention on two issues:

1. the need for specification models providing both symbolic computation and performance evaluation features;

2. the demand of an automated code generation for transforming a specification into standard third generation language.

The current approach to the specification of DEDs systems is to add a conceptual level to the traditional dataflow paradigm in order to capture control and timing information. Infact a key issue of a DED system is the dependency of its behavior, that is its response to external stimuli, upon its state. The state is a mode of operation determining which activities are appropriate and which are not: the mechanism by which a subsystem changes state is referred to as an event. An event can be a message received from another subsystem or the notification that a certain time interval has elapsed. A state-based behavior cannot be expressed using the traditional dataflow technique which accounts for data driven computations. For these reasons several extensions of Structured Analysis were proposed: the basic idea of such extensions is to add to the usual dataflow specification a control specification based on **state transition diagram** (STD). A STD describes the evolution of a subsystem's behavior through states depending on events: in each transition the proper dataflow transformations are enabled while the others are disabled.

Either with STD extension, current specification techniques, such as Hatley-Pirbhai's [7] and Ward-Mellor's [8], offer little more than documentation support, being bound to the waterfall approach of software life cycle. Recent research in software engineering, such as **Executable Specification** [2], **Object Oriented Programming** [3], **Visual Programming** [4], **Rapid Prototyping** and **Automation Oriented Paradigm of software process** [5], provide the necessary background to stimulate the development of more powerful integrated approaches which allow the designer to work with dynamical models offering both qualitative and quantitative results, to generate prototypes from such models in order to test the software architecture on a distributed hardware, and finally to produce the deliverable system by refining the prototype and adding suitable interfaces to the devices of the target application.

Alternative paradigms cannot be picked alone to support a real powerful automation oriented paradigm. Operational paradigm [9] suffers for the lack of model efficiency because operational specification does not have performance requirements, furthermore a transformation of specification into final implementation is left to the designer.

Prototyping paradigm [31] provides for an efficient working model of the system, but its major drawback is the cost of the prototype, furthermore the prototype if often thrown away because its purpose is just capture some performance evaluation or provide at early stages something to show to the committent. A cost-effective paradigm has to be based on "do it once" rather then "do it twice".

Trasformational paradigm [30] requires just formal specification to generate an implementation code, but specification language is not executable and model verification and validation cannot be perfomed at high level of abstraction.

Merging togheter Prototyping, Operational and Trasformational paradigms, results in the **Automation oriented paradigm** [5]. Symbolic computation plays an important role for the execution of a system. PROTOB, illustrated into the next section, can perform a symbolic computation of a model at different levels of abstraction.

2   PROTOB: an overview

This paper presents **PROTOB** which is a technique and a **CASE** — Computer Aided Software Engineering — tool for modelling, prototyping and implementing distributed systems according to a development cycle consisting schematically of four major phases:

1. **Modelling** - An executable model of the system is built according to the object-oriented paradigm. Since objects are elements of the PROTOB language, the graphical representation of the architecture (made of icons and edges) directly affects the model. Each object class has a graphical representation in terms of high level Petri nets, called **PROT nets** [14], which define the body of the class. Objects classes can be built on top of other objects in a hierarchical architecture. They communicate with each other by sending and receiving messages through their interface. The overall model is obtained by generating and interconnecting instances of PROTOB objects graphically.

2. **Symbolic computation and simulation** - The model can be executed in terms of discrete event simulation providing a graphical animation which allows the interactive validation of system behavior to be carried out. The simulation is obtained through symbolic computation of a PROT net. Depending on the level of details introduced into the model, PROTOB can convert a symbolic computation in a real computation.

3. **Emulation** - While the model of the system is actually constructed and tested in a design environment where the high level logic is of concern, in this phase the model is refined by taking into account implementation details. The aim of this phase is to build an emulator of the final system: it has all the functionalities of the final system, runs on the target

architecture but has no connection with real devices which are still represented by PROTOB objects. Such an emulator is produced automatically from the PROTOB representation by specifying the allocation of the instances of PROTOB objects to processors and tasks of the target distributed system. Since the target system is well defined, the communication and synchronization mechanisms are generated automatically. Moreover timing constraints are managed by the underlying operating system.

4. **Application Generation** - Exercising the emulator can results in the adjustment of the allocation as well as of implementation details. In this phase the link with target devices is performed. This implies the replacement of PROTOB objects emulating the devices with appropriate interfaces which can be generated automatically since the interaction with the devices is well known. The interface generation results from the definition of data and commands to be transferred, and also from the definition of the events to be perceived.

The strength of PROTOB is its modelling language which has a graphical representation and procedural semantics. The graphical representation based on the concepts of state, state transition and message passing allows the end user to easily understand the modelled behavior, and, due to the procedural semantics, the graphical representation can be associated with code in a standard programming language, thus allowing the automatic translation into a running program to be performed by exploiting compiling technology. Modelling, simulation, emulation and application generation are carried out in the same environment and in the same language through the cyclic refinement of the model.

PROTOB is based on high level Petri nets, called **PROT nets** [14]. As results from the literature, there is a growing interest in high level Petri nets not only for analysis and performance evaluation purposes but also for modelling and prototyping issues in the framework of software engineering [1]. The main advantages provided by high level Petri nets in software development are:

- the ability of graphically modelling a system at a conceptual level by means of the intuitive notions of state and state transition based on time and mutual interaction;

- the possibility of obtaining analytical results on some properties of the model;

- the capability of providing a symbolic computation model in order to produce behaviour of the intended system.

For such reasons, combining recent software engineering techniques with high level Petri nets can yield a powerful formalism which is able to integrate the phases of specification, symbolic computation and prototyping of discrete event dynamic systems, such as real-time systems and process control systems. In these applications, models based on high level Petri nets, at any level of detail, can provide more formal representations than those obtained using extended data flow concepts [7], [8]. Moreover, owing to their graphical interface they appear to be more user-friendly than textual executable specification languages such as PAISLey [9].

From this point of view software tools can be built to exploit the above-mentioned features of high level Petri nets: such tools can play an important role in the field of CASE moreover for next generation of Intel 80486-based workstations.

Like a Petri net a PROT net models a system's behaviour in terms of **State** and **State Transition**. Possible states are represented by circles called **Places**. The elementary event or action that causes a state transition is a **Transition** and it is represented by a rectangle. A state transition is **Caused** by certain states and has the **Effect** of activating other states. This is represented graphically with directed arcs going from places to the transition they cause and from the transition to the places which model its effects. A PROT net statically describes in a visual way the relationships of cause and effect among states and actions or state transitions. Names of places should be nouns that describe a state while names of transitions should be verbs describing an action. Marking the active states by putting a **Token** in the corresponding places — a number inside the place counts the contained tokens — makes a PROT net a dynamical model. This is quite similar to having a cursor pointing to the next instruction of a flow-chart. A transition will then activate its effect-places by moving the tokens from the cause-places to the effect-places when all the cause-places are active. It corresponds to moving the cursor onto the next instruction in an emulation of the execution of the flow-chart. In this sense PROT nets are executable models.

A criticism which is often raised against Petri nets is the unmanageable size of the models of complex systems; however this drawback has been reduced by using high level Petri nets, such as coloured Petri nets [12] and predicate/transition nets [13], which provide more compact descriptions. PROT nets allow tokens to be structured data on which actions, defined by pieces of sequential code and associated to transitions, may act.

Moreover a further improvement can be obtained if models based on those nets are structured within an object-oriented framework, where each object is represented by an autonomous net exchanging messages – i.e. tokens - with the other objects of the system. In particular, it is the object-oriented structure of PROT nets what distinguish them from other realizations of high level Petri nets, such as numerical Petri nets [15], and stimulates the design of reusable software components characterized by a graphical structure. To describe objects' interface, a new element — the **Gate** — was added to the PROT net to represent the output of a token to another object. A token reaching a gate is sent to a place of another net inside an object. They support process-oriented [18], transaction-oriented [19] and rule-oriented [20] programming paradigms. Depending on the paradigm, states can represent particular situations in the process life cycle or particular occurrences in a database or knowledge base.

PROT nets are a visual programming language. In fact pieces of code written in the target language can be associated with the transitions of the net. Transitions may therefore carry out well-defined actions while the overall control structure is visually established by the PROT net. The final program results from a translation phase which assembles these actions into the appropriate framework – i.e. tasks, transactions or rules.

3 Graphical Object-Oriented Design with PROTOB

Among its major properties, PROTOB was designed to support the Object Oriented Design methodology in its latest extended form also. HOOD (Hierarchical Object Oriented Design) methodology divides the system in a hierarchy of objects to improve its comprehensibility and to simplify modification and reuse of system elements.

The **Object** is the building block of a PROTOB model. It is a class of which several individuals may be instantiated all having the same structure but separate existence. Objects can be instantiated and put together to form objects at a higher level thus creating a hierarchy of objects. The model is itself an object at the highest level in the hierarchy.

Inside the object there is its **Body,** which is hidden from the ouside, and which implements the features offered through the **interface.** Body is a conceptually lower, but more detailed level where an object is described. The body of an object may be defined by a pure PROT net in an **Simple Object** or by other objects interacting with an optional PROT net in a **Compound Object.** The simple object is therefore at the lowest level in the hierarchy while compound objects permit the hierarchical decomposition of systems into subsystems that are again modeled by objects.

3.1 Connecting objects

Objects use other objects by requesting their services. This is defined graphically by connecting objects with lines. Connection is finally performed between the objects' PROT nets. PROT nets are connectable by setting **Links** — directed arcs — from gates to input places. For their common nature of being connectable by links,input places and gates are generically called **Ports.** The token that reaches a gate will leave its PROT net to go to another PROT net queueing up in the input place connected through a link to that gate. Considering the token as a message, the link acts as a transmission line. PROT nets thus communicate by message passing.

4 The PROTOB Language

A PROTOB object class is described visually by a **Graph** and textually by a **Script**. The graph is the primitive definition of an object's behavior given in terms of PROT nets. It is composed of the following elements:

Places - They are represented by a circle which is labelled by the name of the place, followed by the name of the type of tokens to be contained and optionally by the number of tokens present at the beginning of the execution (the initial marking of the net). Each place can contain more than one token, but they all have to be of the same type. Tokens are queued in arrival-time order and may leave FIFO according with an optional condition they must satisfy. Special places are the input places which allow objects to receive tokens from the outside: they are represented by a smaller circle inscribed in the circle that characterizes all places. During the animation of the PROT net, the current number of tokens queued is displayed at the center of the place.

Gates - They are the borderline of a PROT net and are represented by a circle with a triangle inscribed upsidedown. A token that reaches a gate is sent to the linked place. Gates do not queue tokens; everytime a token reaches a gate it is immediately send to input place connected where it is queued.

Transitions - A transition is graphically represented by a rectangle which is labelled by the name of the transition optionally followed by a number indicating its priority. When a transition fires, it moves a token from each input place to the corresponding output place: each input place is in fact implicitly mapped onto the output place of the same type. Consequently, a transition cannot have more than one input place or more than one output place of the same type, except for the **Nul** type because tokens of the nul type are undistinguishable. If an input place does not have a corresponding output port of the same type, its token is removed and destroyed. A token is created for every output port that has no corresponding input place of the same type. Each transition can be given an additional condition that must be satisfied for the transition to fire and a sequential activity to be carried out when the transition fires. When two or more transitions can fire at the same time — i.e. are in conflict — the one with the highest priority is chosen.

The release of the tokens in the output places of the transition may be delayed by a variable amount of time to model the finite delay time during which the activity associated to the transition is in progress. During the animation of the PROT net, the number of times the transition fired since the beginning of the execution and the number of token tuples yet to be released are displayed at the center of the icon.

Arcs - Arcs are edges connecting places to transitions and transitions to places. They graphically define the input places and the output ports of a transition.

In addition to the PROT net a PROTOB **Compound Object** can contain **Subobjects**, **Links** and **Superlinks**:

Subobjects - Are instances of object classes. The use of subobjects makes the definition of an object hierarchical by allowing instances of other objects to appear as components of more complex objects. Subobjects are graphically represented by an icon consisting of a square framed by another square: each icon is labelled with the name of the subobject, followed by the class name. To each subobject are associated its *state* (i.e. an integer value) and its *colour*. During the animation of the model, the state of each subobject is displayed by its colour and an integer at the center of the icon which represents the subobject.

Links and Superlinks - Links and superlinks are represented by directed edges. A link connects the gate of an object to a place of another object. Superlinks are interconnections between subobjects: they represent sets of links thus simplifying the connection of two subobjects. Since superlinks stand for many links with arbitrary orientation, the orientation of a superlink has no practical effect.

When a PROTOB graph is so complex that it does not fit on the screen, it can be logically partitioned into several **Views**. Cutting points are places which are duplicated in every view. Two views are adjacent when there is at least one place in common. On the contrary, subobjects, links, transitions and arcs cannot be duplicated, because the context of a transition — i.e. its input and output places — and the interface to a subobject — i.e. its sending and receiving ports — must be defined completely in only one view.

The **Script** of an object is an optional textual file which completes the graph defining in detail the entities that into the graph are only known by name, at a more conceptual level. It contains the definition of the token types defined into the class, of the local variables and a detailed description of the transitions' predicates and actions. Sections defining data and sequential operations are written in a standard programming language — Pascal, C, and Ada for now. External routines written in other languages may be called if needed, thus providing the way to call primitive functionalities of the target enviroment. The most rilevant parts compising a script are the following:

1. Description of **Token Types**. Tokens are *structured moving data*, similar to *Pascal records*. If a *scalar* field is preceded by a tilde, it is possible to examine its value during the execution of the model. Communication types are defined in separate files common to all the objects in the model. In the script only the names of the used communication types are mentioned after the keyword COMMUNICATION. The Nul type is a standard predefined type which has a null data structure: tokens of that type are only simple flags.

2. Declaration of the object **Parameters,**. Parameter can give to each instance a characteriztion in terms of attributes value. For example an object class 'car' may have 'colour' as parameter.

3. Description of the **Local Variables**, which are visible only to the PROT net they belong to. They can be of any type. It is clear that the values of the local variables of each instance will change separately from those of other instances. It is also possible to initialize the local variables by writing in the script a sequence of instructions – the *initial action* – which will be executed at the beginning of the program. Its remarkable that a strong information hiding is enforced not only among different object classes but inside an object definition too. In fact transitions can test and modify only token that are routed through them and local variables changing are not event for transition to be fired.

4. Definition of **Transitions** in terms of the following attributes:

    (a) Optional **Predicate** in *embedded Pascal or C or Ada*. It is a condition that must be satisfied for the transition to be enabled. The implicit condition set by the PROT net is that a transition may fire if all of its input places have at least one token in them — Petri condition. The predicate is an additional explicit condition, specified in the script by a boolean expression, which can be used to select the tokens from the input places according to a particular policy instead of FIFO. The predicate has also visibility on local variables and on parameters, but these do not influence the synchronization mechanism of transitions, which is only determined by the flow of tokens: in fact a change in a local variabile is not allowed to bring about the firing of a transition as a side effect. Therefore a transition can become enabled only when a new token arrives at one of its input places, and only then its predicate will be evaluated.

    (b) Optional **Action** in *embedded Pascal or C or Ada*. An action is a sequence of operations that a transition must carry out when it fires. External procedure calls are permitted,

Figure 1: View of a compound object

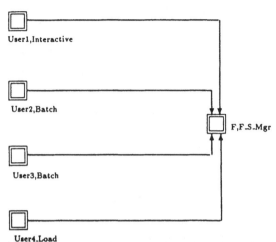

but the external code must be declared as such in the script. The action has visibility on local variables and parameters, on the output tokens of the transition and also on the input tokens that will be destroyed. In order to refer to a particular token involved in the firing of a transition, the name of the output place where it will be moved (or of the input one if the token will be destroyed) is to be used. Transitions can be timed so when they remove tokens from the input places, they do not add them to the output places until the associated delay has expired. This allows to add timing information to the model for a quantitative analysis by execution. Delay is expressed in term of time units where a time unit can have whatever value.

Figures 1 and 2 show an example of the definition af a compound object and of a simple object respectively.

5 The PROTOB Environment: Modelling and Generating Software

The kernel of PROTOB is composed of four separate but strongly interconnected tools.

Editor/Animator - It allows PROTOB objects to be edited and animated during the execution of the model. It is able to check the consistency of PROT nets during editing and also to call a graph-dependant textual editor which allows the user to write the text files associated with the graphical description. In particular, during the simulation of the model, the editor interacts with the simulator by sending commands to one mailbox and waiting for replies from a second mailbox. The editor displays on the screen the state of the net as received from the simulator. Simulation commands may be given to the editor that will send them to the simulator.

Translator - It translates the PROTOB model into an executable program written in the target language.

Each object class can be translated separately. Translator performs sintactical, semantical and lexical checking by comparing the graph and the script. If no error occurs a module is produced in target language. When each object of the model has been traslated, a linker can glue together each module and produces a unique module to

Figure 2: View of simple object

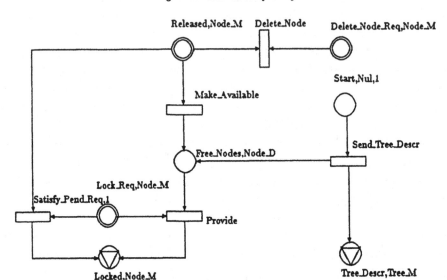

start compilation. The translator does not require a separate compilation for each object; the entire model can be translated directly. The translation can be accomplished for two porposes: logical time simulation or real time emulation. The emulation can be distributed over a computer network; in this case PROTOB generate the communication code to manage the communication between each task. One or more objects can run on each task.

The distributed program is also installed automatically by the translator according to the system configuration requirements.

Simulator/Emulator - It executes the PROTOB closed object through a symbolic computation based on the PROT net semantic. Simulation of the model is performed with logical timing: a cronograph monitors the elapsed time in term of *time unit* which can have whatever value. This is a very important feature to collapse very long simulation in a short time. Emulation of the model is perfomed in real timing mode and provide a fruitful way to collect performance evaluation directly from the model. Simulation and emulation are both presented through an animation of the model. Each icon of the model show its state: transition shows how many time it fired, place shows many token it contains, object shows its current state. Distributed simulation can be obtained allocating a simulator in every host.

Report generator - It assists the user in preparing the documentation of the model and produces a quality report combining both graphical and textual descriptions. For every object of the model a form is produced. It contains a reference to each entity of the model.

Even if the above-mentioned modules can be used independently, the editor is the natural access point to the environment since a WIMP (Windows Icon Menu Puntator) interface is provided for an easy use of all the tools.

6 Future enhancements of PROTOB

Olivetti Case Technology Group has experimented PROTOB in a real case study: the design
of a distributed file system manager with strong performance constraints. Results of this experiments are partially reported in [26]. Other applications range from Computer Integrated
Manufacturing to Communication protocols. Current activities with PROTOB relates to its
implementation in several operating systems, while research is open to add other important
capabilities. One of the most important enhancement is a *model validator* which exploits
the proof semantic of PROT nets to generate a first order predicate logic description for
theoreme proving. For practical applications, a Prolog program would be generated starting
from PROT net description, thus allowing an automated reasoning for model validation. This
would allow a static verification of specification through a mechanism of query; for example
it would be possible to ask: "given a scenario S can the model generate an output O?".
Another important topic relates to the report generation. Current reserch shows how Hyper-
texts can add a very powerful organization and an easy access to multiple kind of information
such as graphs, scripts, animations, statistics, etc. It is not difficult to envisage a PROT net
as the structure of an hypertext where each icon relates to an information item and edges are
hypertext links. For istance a place P of type T would has a *card* associated with complete
description of data structure and of its current value, a transition A would have a card with
a complete description of its predicate and action together with its current status, statistics,
delay, priority, etc. An object icon has a card with its script part and an implicit link to its
graph card, thus providing a hierarchical navigation throughout the model definition. Other
links are associated to each object to indicate its history, its past simulations, its description
in natural language and so on. Thus when a model is defined on the top of existing objects,
the hypertext part is completely inherited inside the model. To generate a complete document of a model, the hypertext is scanned and a standard text is produced.

7 Conclusion

We envisage that the PROTOB methodology and its support environment described in this
paper can be used in software development of distributed discrete event dynamic systems at
three different levels:

(a) **Specification** - the functionality of the system can be formally defined and also analysed quantitatively by building a PROT net based model, which is actually a simulation
model. Operational specification, object-oriented design and discrete-event simulation
are the main features of this approach.

(b) **Prototyping** - in this phase the model becomes more detailed and the timing of transitions is real being managed by the host operating system. Moreover the target architecture is taken into account by decomposing the model into distributed processes. At
this point we obtain a prototype of the system running on a distributed architecture –
for example a local area network of computers – where the environment of the system,
i.e. the plant, is still emulated by some PROTOB objects. The major result of this approach is the automatic generation of actual processes and synchronization mechanisms
which is an error-prone activity if it is done without any automatic support.

(c) **Application Generation** - at this level the PROTOB objects emulating the physical
environment are replaced by a suitable interface which has the task of transforming
signals coming from the plant into tokens to be introduced into the PROTOB model
and, likewise, of converting tokens coming from the PROTOB model into appropriate
commands Issued to the plant. Such interface depends on the devices – i.e. robots,
machining centers, programmable logical controllers – and can be standardised according
to the kind of application.

Maintainance is another issue directly addressed by PROTOB. Since code is generated directly from the specification, maintainance can be performed at specification level, thus preserving the system consistency at any level of detail. The same applies to documentation.

References

[1] W. Reisig. Petri nets for software engineering. In *Petri Nets: Applications and relations to Other Models of Concurrency*, pages 63–96, Springer-Verlag, Berlin, 1986.

[2] P. Zave. The operational versus the conventional approach to software development. *Comm. of the ACM*, 27:104–118, February 1984.

[3] G. Booch. Object oriented development. *IEEE Trans. on Soft. Eng.*, SE-12:211–221, February 1986.

[4] IEEE Computer special issue on visual programming. August 1985.

[5] R. Balzer, T.E. Cheatham, and C. Green. Software technology in the 1990's: using a new paradigm. *Computer*, 16:39–45, November 1983.

[6] T. De Marco. *Structured analysis and system specification.* Prentice Hall, 1979.

[7] D. Hatley and I. Pirbhai. *Strategies for real-time system specification.* Dorset House Publishing, 1987.

[8] P. T. Ward and S. J. Mellor. *Structured development of real-time systems.* Yourdon Press, 1985.

[9] P. Zave. An operational approach to requirement specification for embedded systems. *IEEE Trans. on Soft. Eng.*, SE-8:250–269, May 1982.

[10] V. Berzins and M. Gray. Analysis and design in MSG.84: formalizing functional specifications. *IEEE Trans. on Soft. Eng.*, SE-11:657–670, August 1985.

[11] IEEE Software special issue on CASE. March 1988.

[12] K. Jensen. Coloured Petri nets and the invariant-method. *Theoretical Comput. Sci.*, 14:317–336, 1981.

[13] H.J. Genrich and K. Lautenbach. System modelling with high level Petri nets. *Theoretical Comput. Sci.*, 13:109–136, 1981.

[14] G. Bruno and G. Marchetto. Process-translatable Petri nets for the rapid prototyping of process control systems. *IEEE Trans. on Soft. Eng.*, SE-12:346–357, February 1986.

[15] G.R. Wheeler, M.C. Wilbur-Ham, J. Billington, and J.A. Gilmour. Protocol analysis using numerical Petri nets. In *Advances in Petri nets 1985*, pages 435–452, Springer-Verlag, Berlin, 1986.

[16] J.M. Colom, M. Silva, and J.L. Villarroel. On software implementation of Petri nets and coloured Petri nets using high-level concurrent languages. In *Proc. Application and Theory of Petri Nets*, pages 207–241, Oxford, June 1986.

[17] R.A. Nelson, L.M. Haibt, and P.B. Sheridan. Casting Petri nets into programs. *IEEE Trans. on Soft. Eng.*, SE-9:590–602, September 1983.

[18] G. Bruno and A. Balsamo. Petri net-based object-oriented modeling of distributed systems. In *ACM Conf. on Object-oriented Programming*, pages 284–293, Portland Oregon, October 1986.

[19] G. Bruno and A. Elia. Extending the entity-relationship approach for dinamic modeling purposes. In *5th International Conference On Entity-Relationship Approach*, pages 327–339, Dijon, France, November 1986.

[20] G. Bruno and A. Elia. Operational specification of process control systems: execution of PROT nets using OPS5. In *10th World IFIP Congress*, pages 35–40, Dublin, September 1986.

[21] L. Brownston, R. Furrell, and E. Kant. *Programming expert systems in OPS5.* Addison Wesley, 1985.

[22] R. Valette, M. Courvoisier, and D. Mayeux. Control of flexible production systems and Petri nets. In *Informatik-Fachberichte 66: Application and Theory of Petri nets*, pages 264–277, Springer-Verlag, Berlin, 1983.

[23] J. Martinez, P. Muro, and M. Silva. Modeling, validation and software implementation of production systems using high level Petri nets. In *IEEE Int. Conf. on Robotics and Automation*, pages 1180–1185, Raleigh NC, March 1987.

[24] Y. Sagiv Concurrent operation on B-Tree with overtaking. In *Journ. of computer and system science* N.33, pages 275-296 1986.

[25] P.L. Lehman, S.B.Yao Efficient locking for concurrent operation on B-trees. In *ACM Trans. on database systems.* vol.6, No. 4. Dec. 1981, pages 650-670.

[26] M.Baldassari G.Bruno V.Russi R.Zompi PROTOB A Hierarchical Object Oriented CASE tool for Distributed Systems In *Lectures note in computer science: ESEC '89 Proceedings* vol. 387 pag. 424-445

[27] S. Shlaer, S. Mellor Object Oriented Systems Analysis Yourdon Press computing series 1988, Prentice Hall

[28] J. Bigelow Hypertext and CASE In *IEEE Software* march 1988, pages 23-27.

[29] P.Coad, E.Yourdon Object Oriented Analysis Yourdon Press computing series 1990, Prentice Hall

[30] R. Balzer Trasformational Implementation: An example. In *IEEE transaction on software engineering* Jan 1981, pages 3-14.

[31] T.Taylor, T.A.Standish Initial thoughts on rapid prototyping techniques. In *ACM SIGSOFT, software engineering notes* Dec 1982, pages 160-166.

Building graphic user interfaces for Computer Algebra Systems

Norbert Kajler

INRIA, Centre de Sophia-Antipolis
2004 route des Lucioles, 06565 Valbonne Cedex, France

1 Introduction

A quality user interface is nowadays a crucial element for a Computer Algebra System (in the sequel : CAS). First, it makes the use of main functionalities much easier for students and casual users. Second, it gives access to the whole range of possibilities of the system and makes programming easier for expert users. In all cases, it highly improves the visual comfort and offers many advantages during formulae editing. The aim of this paper is the concise study of the need for a CAS user interface. Furthermore, it represents an important and prior step to any effective realization.

2 Description of the existing user interfaces

According to their user interface, CAS can be classified in two large groups. The first one works on traditional video display terminals, inputs are typed on the keyboard and displayed in one-dimensional form, outputs are displayed in a pseudo two-dimensional form using alphanumerical characters combinations. MACSYMA , MAPLE , REDUCE , and SCRATCHPAD II systems support this kind of interface. The second one needs a high definition graphical terminal with a pointing device (mouse), the display of both inputs and outputs are in two dimensions, formulae are drawn with accuracy, and the mouse can be used to select subexpressions from previous inputs or ouputs and insert them in the current edited formula. Few systems already include such an interface; however we can think of : GI/S [22], MATHEMATICA [21] and MATHSCRIBE [18,20]. Of the above, GI/S and MATHSCRIBE are the one which have the most sophisticated user interface. More precisely, they are both user interfaces built upon traditional CAS, namely MACSYMA and REDUCE. In order to have a reference for the sequel, we will begin by studying the main characteristics of MATHSCRIBE.

MATHSCRIBE is a graphical man-machine interface for the REDUCE system. It enables the user to open many kinds of windows by pressing buttons on a control panel driving the whole interface. In each window, mathematical formulae appears in a specialized editor which includes the following possibilities and features : real time two dimensional edition, cut and paste, scrollbars, undoing, substitutions, local and global abbreviations, structured edition by menu. MATHSCRIBE also enables one to visualize the REDUCE flags in a separate window, to generate some EQN or TEX code from a formula, and to plot two or three dimensions graphs. MATHSCRIBE requires an extensive use of the mouse to select syntactical structures through menus. Nevertheless, it is possible to type alternative keyboard forms during edition. The error messages from the interface are presented in a terminal emulator which can also be used as a traditional textual interface with REDUCE. The setting of interface parameters is limited to static modification of some elements of the visual aspect of the interface (colors, fonts, and dimensions of the windows). Moving or enlarging a window requires the use the window manager. Buttons for iconification and lowering are provided for each window.

3 Problematic of the man-machine interface

GI/S and MATHSCRIBE are the first examples of a sophisticated graphical user interface for a CAS. They eases the MACSYMA or REDUCE systems access and bring a great deal of visual comfort.

However, many heterogeneous requests about user interface are brought up by different kinds of CAS users. An improved user interface would increase the use of CAS to various areas like education, engineering, and mathematical research. Consequently, the next step is to develop specific interface for each specific domain. At the same time, new software engineering techniques have been developed, including complex tools like graphical syntax-directed editors, and toolboxes for man-machine interface design. That is why a new methodology including the use of up-to-date software tools, and the generation of some important parts of the interface is now an interesting alternative to directly coding the interface in C for a particular CAS (as it is the case with MATHSCRIBE).

3.1 Existing tools

Building a man-machine interface for a CAS raises two major difficulties. The first one lies in editing formula in two dimensions. The second one deals with consistently combining a bunch of basic components such as editors, menus, graph plotters and so on. Related to these problems, more and more tools, including programming environment generation, are available and their development becomes one of the major challenges for the beginning of the next century. Some of these tools will be presented, including examples of available software and research projects under development.

Nowadays there are sophisticated editors of formulae such as Grif or The Publisher, as well as generators of graphical language based syntax-directed editors which can adapt to the handling of mathematical expressions. Gigas [4] is a prototype of it. It was built above the Cornell Synthesizer Generator [17]. It enables the generation of structured graphical editors by compiling an attributed grammar written in the Synthesizer Generator formalism. The drawing is the result of an incremental calculus on the semantical attributes included in the grammar. The whole works in an X Window System environment. Similarly, a system such as Centaur [11], designed to the generate programming environments, should in the future include such a tool. Among the commercialized systems we can also think of Graspin [1].

Most of the existing interfaces are directly built above toolboxes. A toolbox (also called toolkit) is a collection of high level functions based above the lowest level routines of a windowing system. There now exists a very large number of toolboxes. Some of them are proprietary (for instance the toolbox of the MacIntosh , that of the NeXT Machine, or those of the Lisp machines by Symbolics). Some others are linked to X Window System (Athena Toolkit [19], OSF/Motif [15], InterView [13], CLUE[1] [12], etc). The last ones are independent of any windowing system and may be adapted to several computer environments (Workstations, MacIntosh, IBM PC, etc). An example is Aïda [8], built on the LeLisp language. These toolkits are also differentiated by their programming language (C, C++, Objective C, Smalltalk or Lisp), their general conception (use of object-oriented programming for instance), and their content (some of them offer many variations to the basis graphical objects, some others include specialized display machines such as tree or vector editors).

Beyond the toolboxes, another kind of tool appears [14]. It is frequently named UIDS (User Interface Design System). The prototype is SOS Interface [7] (written in Lisp on MacIntosh.). For a short time a tool of this kind has been commercialized by the Ilog firm (which markets LeLisp and Aïda) : Masaï [9]. It is a graphical user interface editor which generates Aïda code. Masaï itself includes a user-friendly graphical user interface which enables one to realize interfaces rapidly and interactively. Moreover, the code generated may be hand-altered by editing the corresponding Aïda program or edited again under Masaï. Of course, that greatly improves the ability to modify or adapt such a generated interface. Examples of UIDS also exist for the Lisp Machine. In the X

---

[1]CLUE (Common Lisp User Interface Environment) is an object-oriented programming system suitable for developing user interfaces in Common LISP under X Window System. It is built above CLOS (Common Lisp Object System) and CLX (Common Lisp programmer's interface to X).

Window System domain many tools are under development (such as Egerie [2]). There is also an equivalent tool already available for the NeXT machine : Interface Builder.

A more general approach is proposed by the man-machine dialogue specialists through the concept of UIMS (User Interface Management System) [3,16]. This time the point is to divide the user interface under the form of three modules made up in layers which strongly separates the application from its interface. The communication between one layer and another is done in an asynchronous way by function calls. The three modules have specific roles. The first one is the "application interface". Its role is to ensure the communications between the application and the other parts of the interface. In a system such as Serpent [10], it consists of a shared data base of the variables of the application usable by the user interface. The second one is the "Dialogue Control". It is responsible for all interactions which need no semantical control (such as the syntactical checking of the data given by the user) and imposes the behavior of the interface (the "feel"). The third module is the "Presentation Manager", it carries out the display operations and manages the visual aspect of the interface (the "look"). Corresponding to the UIMS concept we find development environments integrating specification languages which allow one to generate interfaces on this model. Such complete and operational tools are rare; however many studies are being held. As an example we shall mention the Alberta UIMS [6], Serpent [10] and UIMX.

3.2 Methodology

The techniques of man-machine interface have greatly progressed from the conception of MATH-SCRIBE. That is why a new approach seems desirable to create user interfaces meeting the constraints of portability and upgrading capability.

Indeed, instead of designing the user interface under the form of a graphical extension of a given CAS, we can begin with the users' needs to realize a precise specification of the desired interface. This is advantageous as it yields an interface largely independent of a particular system. The second step should consist of building an interface meeting these specifications for a target CAS. It is carried out by bringing into play the best suited software tools available. These tools must be chosen according to the needs expressed in the specifications. Moreover they evolve very quickly; hence separating the interface from the CAS allows one to derive benefits from the progresses realized by these tools.

The advantages brought by the use of generating tools are well known : much higher productivity during the interface developing, reliability of the code, and the possibility to quickly and easily modify the code by altering the high level language used by the generating tool instead of the code itself. In return we must mention the risks of inefficiency and memory space wastage when the chosen tools are not optimized. However the positive evolution of workstations (both in terms of powers and memory space availability) and the coming of industrial versions of these software tools enable us to foresee the success of this approach. Furthermore, we must note that most of these tools are themselves under development. But the needs related to CAS interfaces are complex enough to interest the designers of these tools and to realize their perfection.

Thus the development of a man-machine interface for a CAS sets a new problem. It consists first in clearly defining the needs. This is the aim of the remaining part of this paper. Then the point will be to study in details the different tools, participate in their perfection and fix the choices related to the effective realization of the interface.

4 Specification of the needs for the user interface

4.1 Elementary manipulation of formulae

Multiple window editing of 2D formulae display is provided both through the keyboard and mouse-based events. Editing is interactive and real time on the screen, while interaction with the CAS results from plain request by the user.

- **Formulae display**

  The point is to take advantage of the high resolution graphic screen to display formulae in the most pleasant form for the user, without performance penalty or additional constraints. A quality display implies the use of different size character sets and accurate positioning of graphical components. To be efficient the display must be made in an incremental way (i.e. only modified parts of a formula must be refreshed on the screen). This is not a trivial problem as small changes made in a complex formula can bring about major revisions of the whole formula drawing.

- **Cursor scanning**

  The cursor is a graphical symbol pointing out, on the screen, the place of the formula which is likely to receive the next insertion (there is one cursor in each editing window). Unlike traditional editors, it does not perform scanning left to right and top to bottom , but follows the syntactical structure of the formula.

- **Editing with the mouse**

  The mouse is intended to act globally : it makes block manipulation easier. The following editing facilities must be done easily and accurately with the mouse : positioning the cursor at the mouse location, selecting a block, and other usual block manipulations like cut and paste.

- **Marked block**

  This is a concept local to the interface. For the user, the goal is to select, using the mouse, a sub-formula in a mathematical editing window. Once marked, the block can be easily seen (for instance, it may appear in a rectangular colored area) and is used as an implicit parameter for a large number of operations (erase, copy, print, etc).

- **Editing with the keyboard**

  The keyboard is the most suitable device for the manipulation of elementary lexical units. It is used for moving the cursor throughout the formula, and deleting or inserting textual elements. The highest number of sophisticated interface functionalities must also be usable from the keyboard. More, the bindings of the editing commands with the corresponding key sequences may be altered and displayed in a window.

- **"Undoing"**

  During the edition of a mathematical formula, it is handy to be able to go back step by step, in order to retrieve the formula as it was at each stage of the edition (as the undo command of a text editor does). This mechanism will have to work separately in each editing window, and is independent of the history, which deals with the requests and the results of the CAS.

- **Transmission of the formula to the CAS**

  It happens on an explicit command and concerns the expression edited in the active window. As edition is syntax directed, the expression won't be transmitted to the CAS unless it is syntactically correct. The feedback expression sent in answer by the CAS could be displayed either following the request (as it is for all traditional CAS), either in another window dedicated to the answers of the system (and laterally pained with the first one) or in the same location, replacing the request.

4.2 Manipulation of complex formulae

A CAS usually handles very large formulae (thousands of characters). In most cases, displaying them just as they are is useless. So, an essential capability of the interface will be to master the size of these complex formulae in order to make them readable and suitable.

- **Displaying of long formulae**

  The problem is to display expressions longer than the width of the editing window. According to the user preferences, the expressions will be either cut in accordance with caesura rules used by mathematicians (like MACSYMA does), either partially displayed, with the window linked to a horizontal scrollbar (solution adopted in MATHSCRIBE), or printed on a single line, without scrollbars, and using the reduction mechanism.

- **Reductions and expansions**
  The point is to substitute to a block in a formula a graphical object which denotes the initial object. The icon created will include a generated piece of text, according to the nature of the replaced subexpression (Sum[100], Cos(...) or Matrix[20,20] for example). The expansion may then be achieved directly by spotting with the mouse, or indirectly with the magnifying glass.

- **Local abbreviations**
  The matter is to substitute, locally in a formula, all occurrences of an expression by an abbreviation. The expression corresponds to the marked block. The abbreviation can be typed on the keyboard in a dialogue window or be set to a default value (LOCAL$_i$ if i is the i-th local abbreviation requested for the current formula).

- **Simple local abbreviations**
  They work on the same model as local abbreviations except that only the marked area is substituted by the abbreviation. The default value is : LOCAL$_i^p$, the p (for partial) symbol records that the substitution was not applied to all occurrences.

- **Global abbreviations**
  The principle is the same as for local abbreviations excepted that the couple abbreviation/content is defined globally, and is then available in each editing window. The default value is ABBREV$_i$. The index numbering being also common to the whole application.
  Two commands realize global abbreviations : the first one consists in abbreviating the marked block (this defines a new couple abbreviation/content). The second one consists in realizing all possible substitutions of subexpressions according to the abbreviations already defined.
  All the couples corresponding to defined global abbreviations may be displayed in a window by pressing a button on the main control panel.

- **Simple global abbreviations**
  They work the same way as global abbreviations, except that the subject of the substitution is the marked block only. The default value is : ABBREV$_i^p$.

- **The magnifying glass**
  The magnifying glass is a graphical feature made for displaying in a separate window the content of a reduction or abbreviation. It is selected by pressing a button on the main control panel and changes the design of the cursor onto a kind of magnifying glass. The user can drag it above an icon corresponding to a reduction or an abbreviation, and click on the mouse button to get a new window with the content of the abbreviation inside it. Such magnifying windows can be either killed at the release of the mouse button, or "pined up" on the screen.

4.3 Global manipulations

- **The scratch paper**
  A window named "scratch paper" is available by clicking a button on the main control panel. Its use is to collect parts of formulae cut by the user in mathematical editors. These parts of formulae may be syntactically incorrect and could be freely manipulated on the scratch paper.

- **Previously marked block manager**
  Most of the advanced interface functionalities use as argument the expression contained in the marked block. For this reason, it would be useful to keep the last marked blocks in memory.

Help could be provided by a graphical component managing the current and previously marked blocks. For example, this could be done by a window including on the right the current marked block and on the left a sub-window linked to a vertical scrollbar displaying in five buttons the five previous marked blocks in an iconic form. Clicking on one of the five buttons would change the current marked blocks. Using the scrollbar would allow the retrieval of the oldest marked blocks. Such a mechanism presents two major advantages : it makes edition easier for the user who can access five permanently updated blocks, and it increases the feeling of security during complex manipulations (a block erased accidentally remains available for a while).

- **Using the history**
  The history mechanism is similar in systems such as MACSYMA or MAPLE and in MATHSCRIBE. It enables the user to retrieve and use in the currently edited formula the previous or the n-th expression given to the CAS. To generalize the use of this facility it seems desirable to bring the following improvements : pattern-matching based research, insertion of comments usable as research keys. More, the history must be connected to a kind of vertical scrollbar.

- **Scrollbars**
  Each mathematical window includes two kinds of scrollbar. The first one is horizontal and is suited for a latteral scan of the formula. The second one is vertical and is linked to the history. It is desirable to let the user chose between connecting the vertical scrollbar to the requests, to the answers or both (like in MATHSCRIBE). In effect when the results are long a scrollbar exclusively connected to the requests is best suitable for a research in the history. In return, retrieving a precise result is easier if the scrollbar is connected to the results only.

- **Comments usage**
  In addition to the comments used in the history mechanism, it may be useful to attach another kind of comments to any object of the CAS. This is particularly true inside an unorganized structure such as the scratch paper. These comments will be a concept local to the interface and will never be transmitted to the CAS. For each elementary lexical unit (as a number or an operator), it will be possible for the user to create, modify and erase comments freely and at any time. The comments will be displayed in a particular font. Furthermore, they could be iconified by clicking on them with the mouse.

4.4   Utilization of a command language

All CAS include a command language which enables one to master all the possibilities of the system. The user interface will have to provide specialized tools to ease the use of this command language.

- **syntactical edition**
  In the mathematical windows the edition of expressions will be directed by the syntax of the command language. This includes the edition of mathematical formulae.
  For the interface this implies a precise knowledge of the syntax of the manipulated form and an abstraction level superior to a simple characters editor. The objective is to apply powerful treatments to the edited text, such as dynamical verification of the syntactical validity. For the user that means that the editor will try for each recognized lexical unit to match the text with a valid syntactical pattern. Thus, the editor will be able to reject unacceptable syntactical units in a given context. It will also be able to insert empty blocks that the user will have to fill. Moreover, the editor will take advantage of its syntactical knowledge to anticipate the user stroke. For instance, after the the character $\wedge$ is typed, the cursor will go up and the editor will expect an exponent entry.
  Hence the use of a syntax-directed editor presents numerous advantages : the guaranty of the syntactical validity of the expressions given to the CAS, the automatic indentation of the expressions, the anticipation of the user stroke and the correct positionning of the cursor.

- **syntactical scheme generation**

  Clicking in an edition window will cause menus to pop-up offering sub-formula schemes. These schemes correspond to the different constructions available in the command language. Selecting a scheme with the mouse will make it appear at the cursor location. Here are for instance the syntactical scheme corresponding to an undefined integral : $\int \boxed{expr}\ \mathbf{d}\ \boxed{var}$

  These menus will make the edition of complicated mathematical formulae easier and faster. At the same time they will offer a quick view on all possible constructions of the CAS command language and will constitute a tempting alternative to the lecture of the documentation.

  These syntactical schemes will also be automatically generated and displayed during keyboard edition, with the editor identifying the beginning of a known lexical unit.

- **Interactive help for the programmer**

  When programming a system like MACSYMA or SCRATCHPAD II the advanced user has to face a great number of concepts : very long list of available modules, complicated graph of types, existence of thousands of functions, etc. That's why the user interface has to provide adapted tools for quick scanning in the on-line documentation. Many ways are possible : use of pattern matching for the look-up of an identifier name, function name completion, fast access to the technical documentation, etc.

  More, the interface can provide assistance for the use of the debugging facilities of the command language. At the very least it will include a graphic version of *debug* or *trace* commands.

4.5 Usage of the color

Color is helpful for immediate perception of the main components of the interface. It is essential to establish for the whole application, a constant relation between a color and an identical concept of the interface. It is also important to limit the number of colors simultaneously present on the screen. This will allow a faster reading based on the contrast of the colors. When many applications are simultaneously present on the screen, using a uniform subset of colors also makes the quick identification of the windows composing the CAS interface easier. More, the user interface will have to be usable on monochrom screens. That is why the colors will never carry supplementary original information but will be strictly used to emphasize existing concepts.

4.6 Communication with the CAS

All the information about the system must be complete, widely available and easily understandable. In the same way, commanding the system must be simple and handy for an unexperienced user. Menus or control panels, offering all the possibility linked to a particular concept, will be available each time these possibilities can be known in advance.

- **Main control panel**

  A window named "Main control panel", always present on the screen, drives the system. It is used to display essential informations about the System and gathers the buttons corresponding to the main functionalities of the interface. Each button, in addition to the name of the triggered action, includes a complementary graphical indication on the nature of the corresponding effect (instant action, scrolling of a menu, opening of a dialogue box, etc). In the case of a menu or a dialogue box, the current and the default value will be displayed nearby the button on the control panel and will be reminded in the menu or the dialogue box.

- **Global variables of the CAS**

  A window must enable one to visualize and modify all the global variables of the system. This window will come in the form of a chart, each line presenting the following information : name of the variable, current value (editable), value by default and indication on all the possible values (for example : boolean, numerical interval, string of characters, etc).

- **Access to the documentation**

  The documentation of the CAS must be available for consultation at any time and the way to do it must be easy and obvious. To do this the main control panel will include a "HELP" button. Its effect will be to pop up a menu offering the two following possibilities : to select and display the different sections of the on-line CAS reference manual or to get a specific help by pointing out with the mouse a function or a global variable. The different elements of the interface should also be self-documented. That is why it should be possible to use the "HELP" button to get an information on a precise concept of the interface.

- **Algorithms driving**

  The command language of the CAS must offer the one who programs an algorithm the opportunity to communicate with the user during the execution of the code.

  Some complex algorithms such as Knuth-Bendix or Gröbner' basis, derive some benefits from an information exchange between the system and the user. Thus the program can inform the user of the achieved steps and show intermediate calculation results. This can interest the user who can manually modify some important parameters during the execution. In some other simpler cases the program may only tell the user about the launching of a particular subroutine or warn that the coming calculation may take a long time.

  The interaction between the program and the user can be designed according to two different ways : either as a dialogue exclusively mastered by the calculator (the program keeps the user informed and asks him to take some decisions), or as a driving of the algorithm by the user (the program keeps the user informed by regularly displaying some variable contents or plotting a graph, and the user can at any time impose his options by pressing buttons).

  Concerning the interface, this technique will require a dedicated window linked to the algorithm code execution. Besides, the options chosen by the user during calculation will be memorized in the history. A particular symbol will go with the requests which have generated such choices. This symbol will also be used as a switch to visualize the options corresponding to a request of the history. Concerning the algorithm, the one who codes it, will have to integrate relatively simple instructions into the program allowing the interface to generate the dialogue window. These instructions will indicate the kind of dialogue desired, the information to be displayed and the buttons to create with the corresponding actions.

- **Plotting graphs**

  A button on the main control panel must ease the use of the plotting facilities integrated in the CAS. The effect of clicking this button will be to pop up a dialogue window linked to the plot window where the graph will be displayed. The dialogue window will help the user to point out an equation and the different parameters needed by the plot program.

4.7 External communication

In most cases, the user wants to transfer a formula to another application or a printer. On some occasions, the subject of the transfer can be different : algorithms, session abstracts, hardcopies of a window or of the screen, etc. In all cases, the interface must offer a fast and easy way to realize this kind of manipulations.

Thus, we could have three buttons on the main control panel. The first two buttons would pop two menus onto the screen. Selecting in the first one would assign an output format (TEX, PostScript, C, Fortran, Lisp, etc.), selecting in the second one would define an output channel (file, printer, X Window System cut buffer, etc.). Then, the transmission of the content of the marked block would be done by clicking on the third button. Once selected, the output format and channel would be permanently displayed nearby the transmission buttons.

Beyond these possibilities, we can imagine a mechanism which would enable the user to write and to integrate into the interface a function generating code in a particular output format from an internal reference format, syntactically simple and semantically lightened (a Lisp format for example).

This would allow the user to establish a communication between the CAS and an application with a particular input format (a spreadsheet or a data base for instance).

4.8 Help in the writing of scientific texts

This is a particular case of communication between the CAS and an external application (text editor). The aim is to answer to three wishes expressed by many CAS users. The first one is the plain integration to a document of a formula obtained with the help of the CAS. The second one is the insertion of a figure (such as a curve drawn by the CAS in a window or just a screen copy). The third one is the generation of a CAS session abstract. This could work in the following way : when given a relevant sequence of couples request/answer, freely selected in the historics of mathematical windows, the system would automatically generate the abstract (in TEX or PostScript format).

4.9 Relation with the window manager

Under X, the following actions : *move* (the moving of a window), *resize* (enlargement or contraction) and *iconify*, (substitution of a window by a graphical icon), are usually uniformly carried out through the window manager. However, the programmer has to write, if necessary, the non-standard methods to achieve each of these actions on the different kinds of windows which make up the interface. This will be the case for the windows including formulae editors. In all cases, it is important that the CAS interface has a familiar look and feel, and is driven by the user's preferred window manager.

4.10 Parametring the interface

Beyond the possibilities offered by the window manager, a large subset of visual characteristics of the interface might have to be modified by the user. This includes : fonts, colors and default window sizes. Moreover, one should be able to carry out some choices dynamically : the use of one or two windows for the dialogue with the CAS, the criteria of caesura of the too long formulae, etc.

5 Conclusion

The absence of convenient graphical man-machine interface has certainly been a serious obstacle to the broadcasting of CAS in the scientific community. Today, the available powerful workstations and software tools for the interface developers allow the creation of more and more sophisticated graphical interfaces for an acceptable cost in term of developing effort. The main problem with realizing such a user interface for a CAS is to satisfy the desire for quality : respecting the typography and the habits of work, while presenting a set of performant and user-friendly tools.

The aim of this document was to give a preliminary impression of what a CAS user interface could look like in the near future. It does not constitute the specification of the best imaginable interface for a CAS, but just a picture of the needs expressed by the users. In the framework of the Safir project at Inria, it will be used as a model for the specification of the user interface of SISYPHE [5].

This paper also presented a development methodology based on the use of high level software tools. From this point of view, the next step of our work will discover new problems. After evaluating them, the point will be to choose among all the existing software tools adapted to our problem, those which are able to be integrated in a large system, and are efficient enough to produce a useful interface corresponding to the initial specifications.

References

[1] M. Bologna, M. Chesi, S. Mannucci, I. Montanelli, P. Torrigiani, and N. Zuffi. The Kernel System of Graspin. In *CASE 87*, Cambridge, MA, 1987.

[2] V. Bouthors and V. Joloboff. *Editeur d'interface EGERIE*. Rapport interne du centre de recherche BULL, Septembre 1989.

[3] J. Coutaz. A Layout Abstraction for User System Design. ACM SIGCHI, January 1985.

[4] P. Franchi-Zanettacci, B. Chabrier, and V. lextrait. GIGAS : a Graphical Interface Generator for Attribute Specifications. In *Actes du colloque "Le Génie logiciel et ses Application"*, Toulouse, Décembre 1988.

[5] A. Galligo, J. Grimm, and L. Pottier. The design of SISYPHE : a system for doing symbolic and algebraic computations. In *Proceedings of DISCO'90*.

[6] M. Green. The University of Alberta User Interface Management System. In ACM, editor, *Computer Graphics*, pages 205–213, SIGGRAPH'85, San Fransisco, July 1985.

[7] J. M. Hullot. SOS Interface: Un générateur d'interfaces Homme-Machine. In *Actes des journées AFCET sur les Langages Orientés Objets*, Bulletin BIGRE+GLOBULE, Janvier 1986.

[8] Sté ILOG. *AIDA Environnement de développement d'applications*. Paris, 1988.

[9] Sté ILOG. *MASAI L'outil de développement interactif d'interfaces graphiques*. Paris, 1989.

[10] Software Engineering Institute. *SERPENT Overview*. Carnegie Mellon University, April 1989.

[11] G. Kahn and al. CENTAUR: The System. In E. Brinksma, G. Scollo, C. Vissers, editor, *Proc. of 9th IFIP WG6.1*, Intern. Symp. on Protocol Specification, Testing and Verification, 1989.

[12] Kerry Kimbrough and Oren LaMott. *Common Lisp User Interface Environment*. Texas instrument Incorporated, February 1988.

[13] Mark. A. Linton, Paul. R. Calder, and John. M. Vlissides. *InterViews: A C++ graphical interface toolkit*. Technical Report CSL-TR-88-358, Stanford University.

[14] B. A. Myers. *Tools for creating user interfaces: An introduction and survey*. Technical Report CMU-CS-88-107, Carnegie Mellon University, January 1988.

[15] OSF/Motif. *OSF/Motif Programmer's Guide, Programmer's Reference Manual & Style Guide*. Eleven Cambridge Center, Cambridge, MA 02142, Open Software Foundation edition, 1989.

[16] G. E. Pfaff. User Interface Management Systems. In *Proceedings of the workshop on user interface*, Springer, Seeheim, FRG, November 1983.

[17] Thomas Reps and Tim Teitelbaum. *The Syntesizer Generator Reference Manual*. Cornell University, NY 14853, August 1985.

[18] Carolyn J. Smith and Soiffer Neil M. MathScribe: A User Interface for Computer Algebra Systems. In ACM, editor, *Conference Proceedings of Symsac 86*, pages 7–12, July 1986.

[19] Ralph R. Swick and Terry Weissman. *X Toolkit Athena Widgets*. MIT edition, 1988.

[20] TEKTRONIX. *MathScribe User's Manual VERSION 1.0*. edition, 1988.

[21] S. Wolfram. *Mathematica, A System for Doing Mathematics by Computer*. Addison-Wesley, 1988.

[22] Douglas A. Young and Paul S. Wang. GI/S: A Graphical User Interface For Symbolic Computation Systems. *J. Symbolic Computation*, (4):365–380, 1987.

A System Independent Graphing Package for Mathematical Functions

Paul S. Wang [1]
Department of Mathematical Sciences
Kent State University
Kent, Ohio 44242-0001

Abstract

SIG is a compact graphics system for the display of curves and surfaces defined by mathematical ormulas in a symbolic system. It is available from Kent State University. SIG consists of two parts: graph and mgraph that run as concurrent processes. Xgraph is a stand-alone graphics facility written C to work with the X Window System. Mgraph is the part that is symbolic system dependent. SIG chieves display device independence through X and portability through mgraph. Capabilities of SIG, s design and implementation, as well as plans for further development are presented.

. Introduction

The availability of modern workstations with high-resolution graphics displays has revolutionized the ser interface for many computer systems. One important development in this direction is the emergence X, a protocol for system independent windowing and graphics from the Massachusetts Institute of echnology (MIT). X is now the acknowledged industry standard. Major vendors who support the irrent X11 standard include IBM, DEC, HP/Apollo, and SUN. A graphics system using the X11 rotocol will work on any workstation or graphics terminal that supports the standard. This factor has significant influence on the design and implementation of SIG, a system independent graphics package r symbolic systems.

At Kent we have been interested in the integration of symbolic, numeric and graphics computing cilities [9], [10] for some time. A convenient environment for scientific computations must include owerful and easy to use facilities for graphics display of mathematical functions. The SIG package presents the first steps of our research in ways to provide such graphics capabilities and to integrate em with an advanced user environment for scientific computing. Earlier graphing facilities for symbolic stems exist [11], [13]. These are mostly tied to particular symbolic systems and to specific display ardware. SIG provides two and three dimensional monotone and color plots either directly from a mbolic system or from a file of coordinate points. Either functional or parametric forms are allowed specify the curve or surface to be displayed. SIG is system independent because it is implemented sing two separate modules: a mathematical module that works within a target symbolic system and graphics system, called xgraph, that works with X11. Xgraph is written in C and uses straight X11 brary [2] function calls. A mathematical module, mgraph, has been written to work with the franz SP based Vaxima [6] system. It is very easy to convert mgraph to work under other symbolic systems. or example, simply rewriting mgraph in Common Lisp will allow it to work with Reduce [3] or DOE ACSYMA; writing mgraph in C allows it to run under Maple [1].

After a brief introduction to the X Window System, we describe how SIG is used from Vaxima; the esign and implementation of mgraph and xgraph; and the way they are interfaced. Ongoing work and ans to evolve SIG will also be discussed.

. Overview of X11

1 System Architecture

---

[1] Work reported herein has been supported in part by the National Science Foundation under Grants CCR-8714836 and EET-8714628

The X Window System [12] provides software facilities to support a window-mouse oriented use interface environment. X11, the latest version of X, is supported by a consortium of hardware an software vendors who have made a commitment to use this standard across their product lines. Th X11 software is in the public domain and is distributed freely by MIT and also redistributed by other The basic X11 consists of two major components: the X *server* and the *Xlib*. On top of the basic X1 there are also easy to use *toolkits* [5], [7]. The X server uses device dependent drivers that handl I/O with one or a set of graphics *displays* (keyboard, mouse and CRT display) being controlled by th server. An X server performs actual I/O on behalf of *client* processes which make requests of desire I/O operations to the server. The X server defines a standard protocol for I/O requests. Any progra that operates a graphics terminal through the X server is a client. And the X sever can simultaneous take care of multiple clients and displays. The X client is always device independent and will work wit any graphics equipment that comes with an X server. The distributed X11 package already contai servers for most popular graphics workstations and displays. The client program may run on the san graphics workstation as the server or on another computer, in which case it can communicate with th server through a network.

The Xlib is a library of C functions that can be used by a client program to interact with the X serve Xlib provides, for example, a function to initiate connection with a particular X server, a function t establish a window of a certain size and type, and a function to draw a line or a polygon in a graphi window. Once a client program is compiled and linked with the Xlib, it will work without change wit any X server transparently across the network. X also supports multiple networking protocols includi TCP/IP [8], DECnet and Chaos. Figure 1 illustrates the current way xgraph and mgraph fit in the architecture.

2.2 Advantages

Based on the above described architecture we can point to the following advantages for building SIG top of X11.

- Hardware independence – SIG can establish graphics windows on any X supported display. There no need to rewrite or recompile xgraph for a different display device. This makes SIG very portabl

- Network transparent – X is a network-based system defined by an inter-process communicatio protocol based on an asynchronous character stream. Therefore the client SIG can run on on machine and display the results on another machine, on a local area network, or even the Intern Furthermore, these two computers need not have the same operating system or architecture. Th SIG can run on a compute server where the symbolic computing is done and send the graphics any graphics display.

- Integration with other tools – In a scientific computing environment interactive graphical displ of curvers and surfaces plays only a part. The user must be provided with control and interacti with complimentary symbolic, numeric, text process and other computing tools. The same X serv can handle multiple clients. It provides convenient ways to provide concurrent user control a program defined interactions between these tools. At Kent we are pursuing a *system independe user interface* project which can cooperate with a graphics system such as SIG.

- Xlib support – The xgraph part can be programmed using the library support provided by Xl Thus the program is free from low level considerations of graphics and interactions with the us Details such as a mouse click event etc. are all handled by X.

- Nonproprietary – Last but certainly not the least is the fact that the X window system is in t public domain. The full source is available either free or for a nominal fee. Further developmer and redistributions are also encouraged.

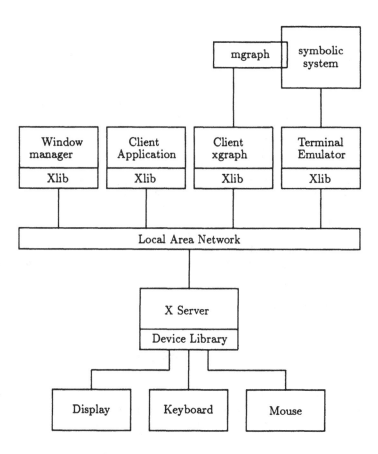

Figure 1: X Window System Architecture

SIG is useful even for a symbolic system with built-in graphics facilities that are tied to specific hardware and are likely not to work after a port of the symbolic system. For example, we have Vaxima running on VAX-11/780, SUN3, HP9000, and Encore Multimax and the same SIG is used for graphics.

SIG Functionalities

The SIG package contains functions to generate plots and graphs of mathematical functions, and to display them in a graphics window established under X11. The mgraph part of SIG is dependent on the symbolic system and the xgraph part uses X11. Xgraph can also be used independently to display curves and surfaces stored in files. In this section we describe the capabilities and usage of SIG. To discuss specifics we will assume that the symbolic system used is Vaxima.

1 The graph Command

Once the mgraph part is loaded into Vaxima, the Vaxima top-level command **graph** is defined. It used to generate both two dimensional curves and three dimensional surfaces. A simple example is plotting the Sine curve.

```
graph(sin(x),x,[-%pi,%pi,30]);
```

This produces in an X11 graphics window a plot of sin(x) from $-\pi$ to π using 30 points. Here is a sample surface

```
graph(sin(x*y),[x,y],[-%pi,%pi,30],[0,2*%pi,20]);
```

taking 30 points in the x direction and 20 in the y direction, resulting in 600 points on the surface
Curves and surfaces can also be given in parametric forms. For instance

```
graph([sin(r),cos(r)],r,[0,2*%pi,30]);
```

plots a circle using 30 points (values of r). And the command

```
graph([(1-r^2)*cos(s),(1-r^2)*sin(s),r],[r,s],
      [-1.4,1.4,25],[0,2*%pi,25]);
```

draws a blimp-shaped surface with 625 points. The **graph** command first creates a file of points then
request the independent xgraph process to display the graphics.

3.2 Graphing Options

The **graph** command uses a default name for the file of points. The user can also specify what file
name to use. This and other options are specified as the last argument of the **graph** command which
given as a list of one or more items each in the form

option-name = option-value
For example,

```
graph(sin(x*y),[x,y],[-%pi,%pi,30],[0,2*%pi,20],
      [filename = surface1, hidden = true, color = blue]);
```

will use "surface1" as the file name and request **xgraph** to display the graphics with hidden line remove
and with lines drawn in the color blue. There are many options for displaying graphics. Options for 2-
graph, with defaults for color display indicated in parenthesis, include

color	(cyan)
background	(white)
axiscolor	(black)
capcolor	(black)
overlay	(false)
grid	(false)

The color of the graphics window is set using **background**. Colors are specified by name such as black
white, red, yellow, green, cyan, blue, or magenta. Two axes with labels are displayed for a 2D plot
The **axiscolor** and **capcolor** options control the color of the axes and the labels respectively. If **grid**
is true then a coordinate grid is drawn instead of the axes. If **overlay** is true then the graph is ren
dered on top of the existing graph in the graphics window. For surfaces the options are shown in Figure

The default values for all the options can be modified using the command

graphdefault(*options*);

To restored mgraph supplied default option values a user can use

graphdefault(true);
graphdefault(false);

for a color or black-and-white display respectively.

Option	Default	Meaning
color	cyan	color of the polygon lines
hidden	false	requests hidden line removal
background	white	the background color of the window
fillcolor	white	color to fill inside of polygons
xangle	30	rotation about x axis
yangle	40	rotation about y axis
zangle	50	rotation about z axis

Figure 2: 3D Graphing Options

It is also possible to generate a file of points without displaying any graphics. This is done by setting the Vaxima flag gfileonly to true. To display a file of points already there, the command

graphfile (*dim*,[filename = *name*]);

used where *dim*, 2 or 3, indicates the dimension of the plot. Other options can be included with the filename specification as well.

nce the **graph** command is used, **xgraph** remains ready to process new requests from Vaxima. When aphics is no longer needed, the command

graphclose();

used to close the connection between Vaxima and **xgraph** which will then delete the graphics window nd terminate.

. Implementation of Xgraph

As mentioned before, xgraph is a stand-alone graphics system written in C to display curves and urfaces in an X11 graphics window. It is decoupled from the symbolic system that generates the formulas nd the points of the graph. The **xgraph** command takes arguments that specify the dimension, filename, reground, background colors and other options. It then displays the graphics in an X11 window. If **graph** is invoked with no arguments then it takes graphing requests from *standard input* which is the eyboard if **xgraph** is invoked at the UNIX shell level or mgraph if it is invoked by the **graph** command Vaxima. The set of points defining the curve or surface is contained in a file that has been established efore **xgraph** is called. For example,

    -2d -fg black -bg white -file circle;

quests **xgraph** to display a 2D curve whose points are given in the file circle using black lines on white ackground. The trailing semicolon (;) is a command terminator. After processing a command, **xgraph** turns to process another command until an *end-of-file* condition (EOF) is met. EOF is a line with a ngle control-D typed on the keyboard or the closing of the lisp port used by mgraph to send commands xgraph. **Xgraph** terminates after EOF.

Xgraph contains five modules written in C.

• *xmain.c* – This is the user interface module. It defines routines to process the command line, to parse a command string in case it is supplied through the standard input. The defaults and settings for options are handled here. The top-level is a loop that executes *get next request, parse request, set option values, call 2D or 3D display routines* repeatedly until the end of file condition is encountered.

- x11plot2d.c – The plotting of 2D curves is handled in this module. The file of points is assumed to contain an integer n, the number of points on the curve followed by n pairs of floating point numbers representing (x,y) values of the points on the curve. After the points are read in from the given file, the point values are first *normalized* to fit into the graphics window. The logical graphics window is a square of x and y values between 0 and 1 inclusive. The normalization involves shifting and scaling in both the x and y directions so that the curve fits in the 0.1 to 0.9 part of the window without distorting the form of the curve. This leaves a boarder of width 0.1 around the graphing area for the display of axis and labels. Once the points are normalized, they can be translated into pixel addresses in the graphics window and lines can be drawn to link successive points to form the desired curve.

  There is a separate function that handles the axis, grids, tick marks, and labels. Lines with tick marks and labels appear on the appropriate sides of the square boarder depending on whether the curve lies entirely or partially in a quadrant. If the origin (0,0) is in the window, the x and y axes are drawn. These are made to coincide with the tick marks on the boarder. If the grid option is chosen, then no tick marks are used, instead a coordinate grid covering the entire window is displayed over the curve.

- x11graph3d.c – A common graphics technique for displaying an arbitrary 3D object is to approximate its surface with a set of plane, polygon surfaces. This *polygon-mesh* representation can be displayed quickly to give a good indication of the form of the object. In xgraph a surface is represented by drawing a mesh composed of quadrilaterals by connecting neighboring points on the surface, the finer the mesh the better the graphics. Xgraph uses standard graphics techniques to render a three-dimensional object on a two-dimensional viewing plane. Figure 3 shows a typical mesh represented surface inside an X11 graphics window .

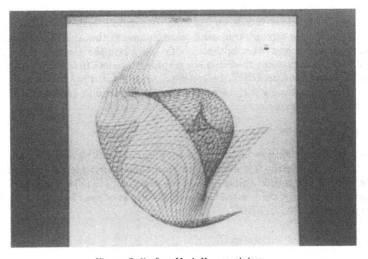

Figure 3: Surface Mesh Representation

The file to be displayed consists of two integers m and n followed by $m*n$ triples (x, y, z) each representing a point on the surface. The points are taken to be x(r,s), y(r,s), z(r,s) from m values of r and

n values of s. After the points are read in, a *transformation matrix* is constructed based on the high-low ranges of the points in the x, y and z directions and the distance of the view point. The matrix can also take into account any user specified rotations of the object to be displayed. The rotations are specified as three independent rotation angles with respect to the x, y, and z axis respectively. The x, y directions are in the plane of the graphics window and the z axis is perpendicular to it. The view point is from the negative z direction into the x-y plane (see Figure 4). After the matrix transformation, the data points are normalized to lie within the plot area in the graphics window. Finally, the neighboring points are put into the four vertices of polygons to be drawn with X11 calls.

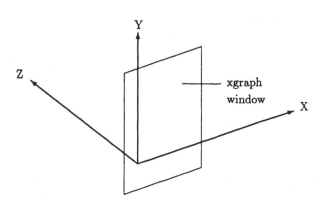

Figure 4: Coordinate System and the Graphics Window

A fast, but not necessarily water tight, hidden line removal algorithm is used. To remove hidden lines, the polygons are sorted by their z values so that the ones with high z value are plotted first. Each polygon is plotted with its internal region filled with the background color. This wipes out any lines further away that have been drawn already (Figure 5).

- x11graphics.c – This file is the xgraph-X11 interface. It contains all the X11 dependent functions. These include setting up a graphics window, setting color options, pixel position computations, drawing of line, polygon, axes, and labels. It also controls overlay and closing of the graphics window.

- x11graphics.h – This is a header file that defines point and color structures, constants and declares external quantities used in X11.

- xgraph.demo – A set of commands that show how to use **xgraph** as a stand-alone system is included here. It is used to test **xgraph** when modifications are made. It also serves to document the usage of xgraph.

With the above described implementation, the 2D and 3D graphing functions are separate and independent. Furthermore, the dependence on X11 is collected in a single file. Let us now turn our attention the mgraph part of SIG.

Implementation of mgraph

Mgraph is the part of SIG that is dependent on the symbolic manipulation system. Here we discuss w mgraph is implemented to run under Vaxima. This implementation is written in Franz lisp and can

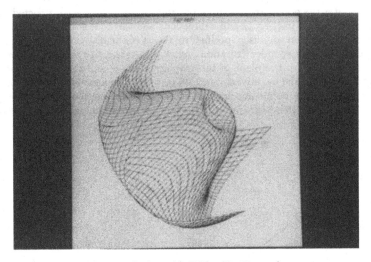

Figure 5: Surface with Hidden-Line Removal

be easily ported to other systems.

Mgraph defines a **graph** command at the Vaxima top level. Curves and surfaces defined in function
or parametric forms can be plotted with a variety of graphics options. The **graph** command parse
its arguments and determines whether the request is 2D or 3D. It transforms the given functions in
parametric forms and calls either a 2D or 3D routine to generate the points on the curve or surface
The points are written out to a file under a name specified on the command line or a default name. The
xgraph process is started if it has not been started already. The mgraph process also has a port that
connected to the standard input of **xgraph**. A command is composed from the filename, the dimensi
and the graphics options and sent to **xgraph** via this port. The **graph** command then returns with the
value "Done".

There is also a flag, **gfileonly**, which when set to true will cause mgraph to generate a file of poin
but no graphics display.

Option Handling

Mgraph supports a variety of graphing options for the display of curves and surfaces. A set of defau
options are set initially depending on whether the display used is monotone or color which is indicat
by the setting of the flag **color**. The default values can be modified with the command

graphdefaults(*options*);

with the desired list of *options*. If the argument is **true** or **false** then the system defined default optio
for color or monotone display are restored. The graphics options used are set to the default values aft
each invocation of the **graph** command. This set of options is then modified by the per comma
options given inside the **graph** command to arrive at the effective options for the current graph reque

Function Evaluations

In a single (2D case) or double (3D case) loop, the independent parameters are varied within t
plotting ranges given and the (x, y) or (x, y, z) values are computed and written out to a file. T

loating point evaluation of the points uses Vaxima evaluation and can handle any function that can be valuated in this system. The speed of the evaluation computation is reasonable for 2D plots and for oarse 3D surfaces. For fine 3D surfaces, it takes some amount of time.

One way to speed up the point evaluations is to use lisp level floating point evaluations rather than he evaluation mechanism of Vaxima. This can be done by first converting the functions defined in Vaxima representation into the corresponding lisp representation which can be done quite easily. For xample the Vaxima function

```
((mtimes simp) $r ((%sin simp) $s))
```

s converted to

```
(times rr* (sin ss*))
```

The lisp expressions can then be evaluated repeatedly with much increased speed. Of course, there re functions that can not be converted into lisp and evaluated, these will be detected and evaluated in Vaxima. To give an idea of the speed up achieved with this technique we show the results of a timing est performed in Vaxima running on our Encore Multimax, a multiprocessor with 12 CPU's each rated t 0.75 MIPS. The command

```
graph([(1-r^2)*cos(s),(1-r^2)*sin(s),r],[r,s],
      [-1.4,1.4,30],[0,2*%pi,30],[filename=ship]);
```

s executed to compute 900 points with the lisp and Vaxima evaluations resulting in the following timings.

```
Lisp evaluation:    totaltime= 22950 msec  (gctime=   9666  msec.)

Vaxima evaluation: totaltime= 121716 msec  (gctime=  24483  msec.)
```

he timings do not include writing out the points into a file or displaying them. The lisp level evaluation s not exactly fast but is tolerable, the Vaxima level evaluation is very slow.

nterface to Xgraph

Mgraph invokes **xgraph** with the Franz lisp statement

```
(setq gport (*process $xgraph nil t))
```

The variable $xgraph is the UNIX file name of the **xgraph** command. The ***process** call returns an utput port, **gport**, which can be used to send command strings to **xgraph**. **Xgraph** exits only after port is closed. Thus, once **xgraph** is invoked, it can take multiple commands from mgraph to display esired curves and surfaces.

Discussion and On-going Work

SIG is a compact graphics system for the display of curves and surfaces defined by mathematical rmulas in a symbolic system. It uses X11 to achieve device independence and a two-part architecture) achieve portability among symbolic systems. Since the xgraph part runs as an independent process can be executed concurrently with the mgraph part which runs inside a symbolic system. On a ultiprocessor system such as the Sequent Balance [14] or Encore Multimax, the symbolic system and e xgraph processes can run in parallel. This can result in significantly improved performance.

Following SIG, interactive features and other improvements to xgraph have been under study at ent [4]. Work is on going to build a substantially more sophisticated graphics system with the basic chitecture of SIG. Major new features include:

Definition of a graphics interface protocol between mgraph and xgraph.

- Add to xgraph a networking front end so that it can be used via socket [8] connections as well.

- Provide xgraph with the ability of interactive manipulation of the displayed graphics using the mouse and menus.

- Establish a library of common mathematical curves and surfaces as graphical objects which is extendible by the user.

- Include in mgraph more geometry expertise and the ability to analyze the formulas being plotted to make decisions such as the plotting range of the independent variables, ununiform spacing of the sample points, and identification of *critical points* like extremum points, and axes crossings.

- Experiment with System V shared memory as a way to pass the data points from mgraph to xgraph. This will enhance performance especially on shared-memory multiprocessors.

In the meantime, the SIG system is available for distribution and it is quite satisfactory for displaying most mathematical curves and surfaces.

References

[1] Bruce W. Char, Keith O. Geddes, Gaston H. Gonnet, M. B. Monagan and Steven M. Watt, "*Maple Reference Manual, 5th Edition*, WATCOM Publications Limited, Waterloo, Ontario, Canada, 1988.

[2] Jim Gettys, Ron Newman, and Robert W. Scheifler "*Xlib - C Language X Interface*" Protocol Version 11, Release 2, September 1987.

[3] Anthony C. Hearn, ed. *Reduce User's Manual*, Version 3.0, The Rand Corporation, Santa Monica, California. April 1983.

[4] Chia-Kai Hsu, "An Object-oriented Interactive Graphics Package Based on the X Window System" Master thesis, Department of Mathematical Sciences, Kent State University, Kent Ohio, Dec. 1989.

[5] Joel McCormack, Paul Asente, and Ralph R. Swick "*X Toolkit Intrinsics - C Language X Interface*" X Window System, X Version 11, Release 2, 1988.

[6] Richard Pavelle and Paul S. Wang, "MACSYMA from F to G", Journal of Symbolic Computation, vol. 1, 1985, pp. 69-100, Academic Press.

[7] Ralph R. Swick and Terry Weissman "*X Toolkit Widgets - C Language X Interface*" X Window System, X Version 11, Release 2, 1988.

[8] Paul S. Wang, *Introduction to Berkeley Unix*, Wadsworth Publishing Company, Belmont, California, USA, 1988.

[9] Paul S. Wang, "Integrating Symbolic, numeric, and graphics computing techniques", *Mathematical Aspects of Scientific Software*, The IMA Volumes in Mathematics and Its Applications, vol. 14, Springer-Verlag, 1988, pp. 197-208.

[10] Douglas A. Young and Paul S. Wang, GI/S: A Graphical User Interface For Symbolic Computation Systems, Journal of Symbolic Computation, Academic Press, Jan. 1988, pp. 365-380.

[11] Douglas A. Young and Paul S. Wang, "An Improved Plotting Package for Vaxima" Proceedings EUROCAL'85, Lecture Notes in Computer Science, Vol. 204, Springer-Verlag, April 1985, pp. 431-432.

[12] Douglas A. Young *X Window Systems: Programming and Applications with Xt*, Prentice Hall, Englewood Cliffs, New Jersey, USA 1989.

[13] *Macsyma Reference Manual*, version nine, the MATHLAB Group, Laboratory for Computer Science, M.I.T., Cambridge, Mass. USA 1977.

[14] *Guide to Parallel Programming on Sequent Computer Systems*, Sequent Computer Systems Inc.

A Model of Interaction for Graphical Systems

G.P. Faconti, R.D. Bettarini, F. Paterno'
C.N.R. – Istituto CNUCE
Via S.Maria 36, 56100 Pisa, Italy

Abstract

In this paper we present a model suitable for the description of interactive graphics programs within the framework defined by the Reference Model for Computer Graphics Systems, actually under development within the International Organization for Standardization. An overview of the state of the art techniques currently used to describe user interfaces is given togheter with the Seeheim model. The attention is focused on the Presentation Component, where problems resulting from different approaches are outlined and discussed. The architecture defined by the Computer Graphics Reference Model, at its actual state of development, is then presented. Following, the components of an interaction are identified and described as a set of processes within a logical device or interactor. Interactors are the basic components from which interactive graphics programs can be modeled; that is an interactive graphics program is seen as a set of independent processes that make use of interactors. Relationships between interactors are described by means of acyclic graphs that realize the control structure of the dialogue. In that way it is possible to allow for modularity and parallelism: in particular the user may interact with several parts of the program (or with several programs) simultaneously.

Introduction

In the last decade a large amount of work in human–computer communication has been devoted to the development of models and tools to support the design and the implementation of user interfaces. These models and tools are often referred to as User Interface Management Systems (UIMS) although the literature doesn't have a consistent view of this term.

The traditional view of a UIMS is a piece of software which controls all communication between the user and the application program; the underlying idea being that of a strong separation of the semantic component and the user interface component.

In our view, the concept of UIMS applies to all the software that provides for the management of user interfaces and not only to the specification of the control of the dialogue. Starting from this assumption, our goal is to define the basic components from which interactive graphical programs can be modeled. Such components are described as a set of interaction units, namely *interactors*, each consisting of an *input* part, that has the task of managing measure values, and an *output* part, that contains corresponding pictures and provides for semantic feedback.

An interactive graphics program is seen as a set of independent processes that make use of interactors. Relationships between interactors are described by means of acyclic graphs that realize the control structure of the dialogue. In that way it is possible to allow for modularity and parallelism: in particular the user may interact with several parts of the program (or with several programs) simultaneously.

The model we are addressing has been first put forward in 1979 [1], and further reworked by several authors [2, 3, 4, 5, 6]. We differs from the previous approaches in that interactors are uniformly applied at different levels of abstraction and their internal components are differently specified in order to meet the requirements of the Reference Model for Computer Graphics Systems [7].

The Seeheim Model of UIMS Structure

The description and specification of user interfaces have been based for many years on the linguistic model first proposed by Foley and Wallace [8] and subsequently reinforced by Foley and Van Dam [9], and adopted by the Seeheim model of UIMS [10].

The Seeheim model defines a layered architecture of UIMS composed by a Presentation, a Dialogue, and an Application layers that correspond to the lexical, syntactic, and semantic analysis phases derived from the theory of formal languages and from the compiler practice (figure 1).

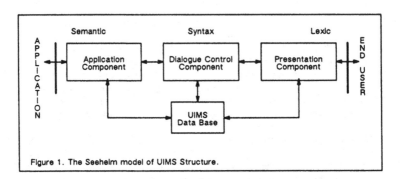

Figure 1. The Seeheim model of UIMS Structure.

The model by itself doesn't specify how to separate an interface into the layers making often difficult to understand where the boundaries between these layers lie. In fact, the model defines a framework within which UIMS may be described rather than providing for a functional description, either formally specified or not, of a system.

As a result, many of the actual UIMS address only the specification of the Dialogue component. They are based mainly on sequential control models that may be specified by using context-free grammars, state transition diagrams, or equivalent specification techniques, and that are good enough to describe several styles of dialogues such as command-oriented, form filling, menu-based, and question/answer interactions [11].

However such models fail in describing dialogue styles based on the direct manipulation of graphical images, as recently demonstrated by several authors [12, 13, 14, 15]; the most important reason being that direct manipulation interfaces require an extensive use of the semantic information for controlling feedback as it cannot be broken down into a lexical, syntactic, and semantic components; rather, the process of feedback is best defined as a continuum based on the amount of application semantic knowledge that is required [16].

Current trends in UIMS show that one of the most important requirements of user interfaces is the support for multi-thread input, that is the capability to asynchronously process input from different logical or physical devices to realize human-computer dialogues through different interaction paths. This control model of dialogues is implied by the use of direct manipulation techniques.

The event control model, as introduced by Green [17], allows to describe parallel asynchronous dialogues, and it is demonstrated to have a greater descriptive power than the other mentioned techniques. However, it has been developed to only apply to the specification of the control of the dialogue, leaving the presentation component relying on a generic graphics library.

The Presentation Component of UIMS

As already said, the Seeheim model makes the assumption that the presentation component of a UIMS is built from a graphical system without any further discussion on the matter. However, a complete specification of the presentation component must take into account the functionalities that are to be provided by a graphical system to meet the dialogue requirements.

There exist two viable solutions for this purpose: the first one is to address a traditional graphics system such as the GKS or the PHIGS standards [18, 19], and the other one is to use the functionalities provided by a window system.

At the actual state of the art, both solutions show many drawbacks.

The logical input device model of graphics system is an abstraction of the physical input devices that effectively hides the specific hardware peculiarities with major advantages considering as a primary goal the portability of application programs across systems. The mapping of logical to physical devices is hidden within the system so that an application programmer can neither inquire what physical input device the logical input device relates to, nor choose a particular mapping scheme.

A logical input device belongs to a set of predefined classes distinguished by the type of data they return to the application program. There is no way to specify input data types differing from the predefined set. Moreover, input data types do not match with data types used to describe output pictures leaving to the application program the task of providing a consistent mapping between the two sets. Also, this may cause inconsistencies in the specification of prompt, echo, and acknowledgement functions.

Although this model has been succesfully applied to graphics standards, it has been recognized that it is not sufficient to describe an interaction process [20]. For the purposes of graphical user interfaces development, there is a need for the programmer to be able to have full control over the mapping mechanism between logical and physical input devices as well as over the control of feedback.

Window systems provide better support from the input side of an interaction as they are able to handle physical events. Logical input devices shield such events and return logical events instead. The problems with this approach is that physical events and logical devices are differently specified, and that the support for picture handling is missing. In fact, current window systems provide a quite naive support for the generation of graphical images. This means that the mechanisms to let graphics systems provide the functions to generate pictures in a window must be reinforced [21, 22].

In order to overcome these drawbacks, and to provide a uniform mechanism to describe an interaction, we extend the use of the event model to the specification of the presentation component. The resulting model defines a set of processes directly connected to physical devices from where logical devices can be built by the programmer instead of by the system.

The model leads someway far from the Seeheim model in that the layering technique can be applied within each logical device while the control of the dialogue of the overall system is implicitly specified by the relationship occuring between the logical devices.

The Reference Model for Computer Graphics Systems

The Computer Graphics Reference Model [7], actually under development within the International Standardization Organization (ISO) and to which we are contributing, defines an architecture for computer graphics. Its purpose is to define the internal behaviour of graphical systems and establish the relationship between the concepts which make up the reference model.

Computer graphics is described as an environmental approach. An environment consists of a picture, a set of collections, an input memory and possibly associated state information, defined at a specific coordinate space. There are five environment as shown in figure 2. They are:

- Application Environment
- Virtual Environment
- Projection Environment
- Logical Environment
- Physical Environment

The five environments are always present in the description of a graphics system but some of them may be transparent or null. The main characteristics of each environment are given below:

Application Environment: in this environment, output information is composed into abstract graphics fragments with editing, composition and transformation applied. Input memory stores values of data types as they are required by the application.

Virtual Environment: in this environment the graphical output is defined in terms of a set of virtual output primitives. The geometry of this primitives is completely defined so that virtual pictures are geometrically

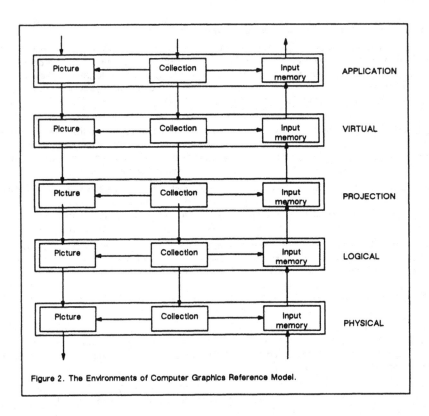

Figure 2. The Environments of Computer Graphics Reference Model.

complete. Input memory is defined in the coordinate system used in the virtual environment and similar input primitives can only be differentiated by their associated properties.

Projection Environment: in this environment, a specific view of the graphical output is taken which produces the picture to be presented. In 3 dimensions, a variety of projections onto a plane may be used.

Logical Environment: associated with graphical output primitives are a set of aspects associated with rendering. Input data are converted to device independent form with input values properties added to differentiate the origin of the input if required.

Physical Environment: the environment consistes of a picture in device coordinates with a specific device. Input memory contains input values as received from the physical input device.

Collections

A collection is a named structured assembly of entities which can be transformed into a (part of a) picture within the same environment and to the corresponding collection within the next lower level by the *traversal* and *post* operations. A partially evaluated collection can be computed with data from the input memory to provide for values of specific input data types. This provides with the capability of extending the input device classes so that they are be able to return values of data types that can be dynamically defined depending on a specific instance of graphics system, and also of controlling the feedback provided by a specific instance of an input device.

Pictures

A picture is defined as a spacially structured set of output primitives at a given environment level. Output primitives are the atomic units from which graphical output is composed and are defined as:

<output_primitive> ::= <output_primitive_class> <geometric_shape> <properties>.

Pictures are transformed from one environment level to the next lower environment level by the *post* operation.

Input Memory

Input memory is composed by input primitives at a given environment level. They are the atomic units from wich graphical input is composed ad are defined as:

<input_primitive> ::= <input_primitive_class> <geometric_shape> <properties>.

Specific functions exist for triggering an input memory at one environment to generate some part of input memory at the next higher environment level.

Components and Frameworks

The Reference Model sees a graphics system as constructed from a collection of components set in a framework. Components define the different entities of a graphics framework and would include data types and operations. A framework describes a glue of the components which can be grouped togheter to establish an instance of graphics system.

The Interaction Components

We describe the behaviour of graphical interactive programs in terms of manipulating I/O units. Logical and physical devices, or interactors, are made of an input module, an output module and a control module; that is they are specified by the triple

$$Interactor = <CNTL, IN, OUT>.$$

The input component is an abstract internal representation of a possibly complex user input, while the output component is the representation of a picture that is in relation with the user input. Either the *IN*–component or the *OUT*–component may be empty, in which cases pure input and pure output devices can be realized.

The *IN*–component is defined as a trigger–measure–collection triple:

$$IN = <T, M, Ci>,$$

and the *OUT*–component is defined as a feedback–collection pair:

$$OUT = <F, Co>.$$

When both *IN*–component and *OUT*–component are present (e.g. are not empty) within an interactor they share the same collection; that is:

$$C = Co \cup Ci.$$

Interactors are distinguished by *classes* that univoquely specifiy the data type generated by the interactors belonging to a specific class. The class of an interactor is defined as a function of the entities contained in the Ci component as:

$$InteractorClass = \{ \ f(c) \ | \ c \in Ci \ \}.$$

Interactors may be grouped into a set defined as:

$$InteractorSet = \{ \ Interactor_1, \ Interactor_2, \ ..... \ \}.$$

Binding an InteractorSet to an InteractorClass defines a *subclass* for that class which completely describes its input data type. This can be specified as:

$$InteractorSubclass = \{ \ g(c,i) \ | \ c \in Ci \ \land \ i \in \prod InteractorClass_j \ \}$$

where *InteractorClassj* is the class of the jth component interactor of the InteractorSet.

The Interactor Processes

An interactor is modeled as a set of comunicating processes [24] each one realizing one of the components previously identified. In the most general case, five components may be found as represented in figure 4.

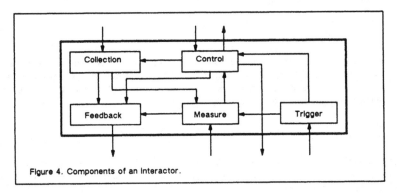

Figure 4. Components of an Interactor.

When the interactor is activated, it activates the associated control, collection, measure, trigger and feedback processes which then function independently.

The **control** process is responsible for the overall operation of an interactor and its associated component processes. It notifies other interactors of the triggers and measures is interested in, and receives similar requests from other interactors. When the trigger firing report is received, it reads from the measure process the value of the appropriate input primitive, which was current at the time of the trigger firing, and broadcasts it to all the interactors that have an active link to this control process.

The **collection** process is composed by a structured set of entities as defined in the Computer Graphics Reference Model, and by a process performing the traversal operation. The collection process refers both to input and output components of an interactor, however the result of traversing a collection provides for different semantics. As for the input side, the subsequent filtering of the traversal operation uniquely defines the data type generated by a specific interactor, that is it defines its class. As the for the output side, the traversal of a collection produces a picture that represents the appearance and behaviour of the interactor as perceived by the user. A given graphics system completely defines the entities which can be made part of a collection, and consequently the set of the classes of the available interactors for that system.

The **trigger** is defined as a set of conditions which, when satisfied, identifies a significant moment in time. Traditionally triggers define what a user has to do to engage an interaction and are generally intended as the manipulation of real input devices. We give here a more general definition as they may be generated from within any interactor although it can trigger only if it was itself just triggered. Then a trigger can be specified as a function of time that returns a value of *true* or *false*; that is given the domain S

$$S = \left\{ \text{true} , \text{false} \right\}$$

then a trigger function can be defined as

(1) $\qquad T = f(t) : [0, t_\infty] \rightarrow S$

A trigger is said to have *fired* when $f(t) = \text{true}$, that is the conditions are meet. This can be formalized by saying that given the left and right neighbourhoods of $t_0 \in [0, t_\infty]$ such that:

$$U^- = \left\{ t_0 \in [0, t_\infty] \mid t \in] t_0 - \epsilon , t_0 [\right\} \forall \epsilon > 0 ,$$

$$U^+ = \left\{ t_0 \in [0, t_\infty] \mid t \in] t_0 , t_0 + \epsilon [\right\} \forall \epsilon > 0 ,$$

then the following conditions apply:

(2) $\qquad f(t_0) = \text{true}$ if $\exists U^-, U^+ \mid f(t_1) \neq f(t_2) , \forall t_1 \in U^-, \forall t_2 \in U^+$

that describes a generic trigger (i.e. a key event), and

(3) $\qquad f(t_0)^- = \text{true}$ if $\exists U^-, U^+ \mid f(t) = \text{true} , \forall t \in U^-$, and

$\qquad\qquad\qquad\qquad\qquad f(t) = \text{false} , \forall t \in U^+$

(4) $\qquad f(t_0)^+ = \text{true}$ if $\exists U^-, U^+ \mid f(t) = \text{false} , \forall t \in U^-$, and

$\qquad\qquad\qquad\qquad\qquad f(t) = \text{true} , \forall t \in U^+$

that describe specific triggers (i.e. respectively a key press and a key release).

While a trigger process is activated, it continously monitors one or more set of conditions as specified by $f(t)$. The trigger firing is reported to both the control and the measure processes. The trigger is mandatory for each interactor for which the *IN*-component in not empty.

The **measure** process, when activated, continously updates the data value for the data type defined by the interactor class. It receives named data streams from the collection process, applies the filter provided by the control process, and builds a new data value eventually derived from input values. This value is continuously made available to the feedback process, and to the control process upon trigger firing.

The result of a measure process is an input primitive specified as

(5) $\qquad m = M (F(c), x_1, x_2, \ldots, x_n)$

where x_i are the input values, c is the result of the traversal operation over a collection, and F is the filtering. The following conditions apply:

$$m \in D_m , \phi \in D_m$$

where D_m is the domain of definition of the data type for this interactor. D_m may be regarded as the cartesian product of the domains d_i so that:

$$D_m = \prod_{i=1}^{n} d_i , \quad \phi \in d_i , \forall i$$

and $\qquad\qquad f_j (F(c),x) : I_j \rightarrow d_i , j_{max} \leq i_{max}$

where l_j are the domains of definition for the input data x, and f_j is the set of functions that can be applied to every x. As the filtering of c is a unique data type for a given interactor class the expression (5) for a given interactor can be specified as:

$$(6) \qquad m = M \ (\ k, f_1 \ (x_1 \ ), f_2 \ (x_2 \ ),....., f_n \ (x_n \ ))$$

The **feedback** process within a specific interactor is responsible for generating an output picture that gives the appearance of that interactor. Whenever a measure process is activated, its value is made available to the corresponding feedback process. This value is used to apply a filtering function to the result of the traversal operation on a collection. The resulting picture is added to the current picture for display purposes.

Unlike measure process, the feedback process may generate pictures composed by the full set of output primitives defined by the underlying graphics system regardless of its interaction class. This allows for the creation of dynamically defined visual representations of any complexity for any class of interactors.

Conclusions

The interactors model is being developed for the purposes of describing graphical interactive programs in the framework defined by the Computer Graphics Reference Model. Although it is at a very early stage of development it is very promising for its applicability to a wide range of applications and environments. Especially, it has been proved to be useful in the specification of user interfaces relying on multi-tread input and on multiple feedback.

Further researches are expected to be carried on in order to use languages for concurrent programming to specify the relationship between interactors and exploit the full capabilities of parallelism of operations implied by the model.

References

[1] R.A. Guedj at al., **Proceedings of Seillac II, IFIP Workshop on methodology of Interaction**, Seillac, France, May 1979, North-Holland, 1980.

[2] H.G. Borufka, P.J.W. Ten Hagen, H.W. Kuhlmann, **Dialogue Cells, a method for defining interaction**, *IEEE Computer Graphics & Applications*, 2(5), 1982.

[3] D.S.H. Rosenthal, J.C. Michener, G. Pfaff, R. Kessner, M. Sabin, **The detailed semantic of graphical input devices**, 1982

[4] D.S.H. Rosenthal, **Managing Graphical Resources**, *Computer Graphics*, 1983.

[5] G. Pfaff, **Proceedings of IFIP Workshop on User Interface Management Systems**, Seeheim, F.R.G., Springer-Verlag, 1985.

[6] D. Duce, **Configurable Input Devices**, *Proceedings of Eurographics Workshop on GKS Review*, ed. W.T. Hewitt, Manchester, U.K., 1987.

[7] ISO/JTC 1/SC 24/WG 1/N 84, Information processing systems, Computer Graphics, **Computer Graphics Reference Model**, 1989.

[8] J.D. Foley, V.L. Wallace, **The Art of Natural Graphic Man-Machine Conversation**, *Proceedings of IEEE 62*, 1974.

[9] JU.D. Foley, A. Van Dam, **Fundamental of Interactive Computer Graphics**, Addison-Wesley, 1982.

[10] M. Green, **Report on Dialogue Specification Tools**, *User Interface Management Systems*, G. Pfaff ed., Springer-Verlag, 1985.

[11] B. Betts et al., **Goals and Objectives for User Interface Software**, *Computer Graphics*, **2**(21), 1987.

[12] D. Olsen et al., **A Context for User Interface Management**, *IEEE Computer Graphics & Application*, 12, 1984.

[13] K.A. Lantz, **Multi-process Structuring of User Interface Software**, *Computer Graphics*, **2**(21), 1987.

[14] R.D. Hill, M. Herrmann, **The Structure of Tube – A Tool for Implementing Advanced User Interfaces**, *Proceedings of EUROGRAPHICS'89*, Hamburg, F.R.G., 1989.

[15] W. Hubner, M. de Lancastre, **Towards an Object-Oriented Interaction Model for Graphics User Interfaces**, *Computer Graphics Forum*, **3**(8), 1989.

[16] J.R. Dance et al., **The Run-time Structure of UIMS-Supported Applications**, *Computer Graphics*, **2**(21), 1987.

[17] M. Green, **A Survey of Three Dialogue Models**, *ACM Transaction on Graphics*, **3**(5), 1986.

[18] ISO/IS 7942, Inpormation processing systems, Computer Graphics, **Graphica! Keinel System – Functional Description**, 1985.

[19] ISO/IS 9592:1989, Information processing systems, Computer Graphics, **Programmers Hierarchical Interactive Graphics System – Functional Description**, 1989.

[20] R. van Liere, P.J.W. Ten Hagen, **Logical Input Devices and Interaction**, *Computer Graphics Forum*, **4**(7), 1988.

[21] G. Lux-Mulder et al., **An approach for the integration of general purpose graphics systems and window management**, *The Visual Computer*, 4, 1988.

[22] G.P. Faconti, F. Paterno', **Providing an Initial Geometry for a Graphics Workstation in a Windowing Environment**, *Joint Workshop on the Inpact of Windowing on Graphics Standards and on Windowing Environments*, Amsterdam, Holland, 1989.

[23] ISO/IEC JTC 1/SC 24/WG 1, **Report of the Study Period on Windowing Environment**, P.J.W. Ten Hagen ed., 1989.

[24] G.P.Faconti, F.Paterno', **An Approach to the Formal Specification of the Components of an Interaction**, to be published on the *Proceedings of EUROGRAPHICS'90*, Montreaux, Switzerland, 1990.

Praxis: A Rule-Based Expert System for MACSYMA

Mike Clarkson,
ISTS, York University,
North York, Ontario, CANADA, M3J 1P3

Extended Abstract

1   Introduction

General purpose computer algebra (CA) systems such as FORMAC, Reduce, MACSYMA, SMP and Maple provide a wide range of techniques to help scientists solve problems in mathematics. Despite the fact that these systems have been in widespread use in academia for more than a decade, and despite their wide applicability, we have found that they have proven to be very difficult systems to use. These systems are very large, and the biggest hurdle has been the difficulty of learning how to use them. Simply learning the proper command syntax and arguments can be a major hurdle, especially when there may be many different ways to solve any given problem. In addition, for inexperienced users there is often the temptation to try and solve a problem with brute force, without applying any of the finesse that mathematics requires. Beyond the problems associated with using any individual CA program, there is also a degree of difficulty that arises from the lack of semantic uniqueness that is inherent in mathematics.

Perhaps one of the poorest systems from a user's point of view has been MACSYMA, the symbolic and algebraic manipulation system developed at MIT during the 1970's. MACSYMA is a very large CA system, with over 1000 global variables and functions defined and documented. MACSYMA was developed by a large number of people over a ten year period, and grew without the benefit of a coherent naming scheme for the functions and variables. At the same time, MACSYMA is probably the most powerful of the generally available CA systems, and with the requisite skill, can be an excellent system to solve problems in the physical sciences. In fact, the skills needed to operate an CA system like MACSYMA are in themselves a considerable body of knowledge. One has to have good understanding of mathematics to know how to approach any non-trivial problem, as well as extensive training on how to implement the chosen approach. Further consideration must also be given to selecting implementation strategies based on efficiency. Given the structured nature of this knowledge and expertise, it immediately suggests the idea of combining CA systems with rule-based expert systems in order to provide an intelligent guide to aid in mathematical problem solving.

At first glance, the ideal solution might be to design and write a hybrid expert system that was part rule-based expert system and part CA system. Some work towards this end is already underway, notably at Karlsrüe [Calmet, 1988]. That system will incorporate an object-oriented relational database of facts based on mathematical objects, and will use a graphical functional language for the specification and implementation of the knowledge base. We distinguish a "hybrid" expert system from a "combined" expert system in that the former has integrated the rule-based knowledge into the same system as the procedural knowledge, whereas the later may keep the two kinds of knowledge separate, and evolve a method by which the two parts of the combined system can talk to each other. We feel that a "shallow" coupling of the two expert systems is preferable to designing a monolithic hybrid system [Kowalik, 1986]. This would use the expert system for the parts that it can do best: to provide a consistent user-interface that allows the user to succinctly specify his goal; to correlate high-level knowledge about the CA system syntax is needed to solve the problem, and to perform rule-based error checking and optimization of the MACSYMA input. The rule-based system is essentially separate from the CA system, and the two sub-systems can run as processes, not necessarily even on the same CPU. By using separate packages we can use existing rule-based and CA systems, so that they do not have to be written from scratch. The two sub-systems can be maintained separately, and we also gain a measure of portability, as the rule-based system is capable of running small workstations and micro-computers such as an IBM PC/AT.

2   Implementation

The system we have developed is a synthesis of three separate sub-systems; a *Computer Algebra System* using the symbolic algebra system MACSYMA, a *Rule-Based Expert System* using the Personal Consultant Expert System from Texas Instruments, and an *On-line Help System* using the Gnu Emacs TEXInfo system. The rule-based system prompts the user for a definition of what he or she wants to do, which becomes the goal of the consultation. This goal is refined by a series of questions posed in the form of multiple choice menus. The information in the menus is structured similarly to an algebra and calculus textbook, and its organization is intended to be intuitively apparent to a physical scientist. The system requires very little knowledge of the syntax or functions of the underlying CA system, making it suitable for the novice user. At the same time, it is an organized catalogue of most of the functions and variables available in MACSYMA, and is therefore useful to the more advanced user. The system has been integrated with a context sensitive on-line help system at every point in the consultation. The help system is relational in the sense that it allows the user to move up or down the tree of sections of the on-line versions of the *Macsyma Reference Manual* for detailed information about MACSYMA's functions and variables, and the *Praxis User's Guide* which provides a more tutorial style of presentation. Both manuals are organized similarly to the organization of the knowledge base, so that it is easy to follow the path of the consultation in the manual.

The expression and any associated parameters are prompted for, and the structure of the expression is analysed by the knowledge base to determine the best computer algebra approach to solving the problem. The system constructs the MACSYMA command, and presents any related MACSYMA flags or variables that may effect the MACSYMA command. The user's inputs then are checked for data type and acceptable value. At the end of the consultation when the final MACSYMA command has been constructed, the user is presented with the option of entering a terminal emulator session to connect to MACSYMA. The user can have the MACSYMA command transmitted to the MACSYMA session, after which he or she can continue to work in the terminal emulator session until he needs to consult the expert system again.

Currently the expert system and the MACSYMA session are simply linked together using Unix pseudo-terminal devices. This limits the amount of expression parsing that can be done by the expert system for use by the rule–based knowledge, and therefore forces the expert system to ask the user for information about the structure of the expression that is being operated on. Work is underway to have the portion of MACSYMA that formats the output into the two–dimensional displayed form integrated with the expert system. This would allow the expert system to receive output from MACSYMA as its raw list structure, which can be more effectively analysed by the expert system. Moreover, just as we can pass information to the rule-based system via the first list in MACSYMA's list structure, it is also possible to return information to MACSYMA, by adding flags to this list. In order to take advantage of these added flags, it would be necessary to make modification to MACSYMA's source code at a fairly fundamental level. Whether the improved functionality of the system would be worth the problems associated with maintaining the changes remains to be seen, but at the very least, this work should provide valuable insights into how this might be done for highly integrated hybrid systems of the future.

3   Conclusion

We have implemented a rule-based expert system for MACSYMA. Although the system has been written with MACSYMA in mind, we must stress that it is not intimately tied to this particular computer algebra package. We feel that it would not be a difficult task to port this system to other computer algebra systems such as Maple, SMP or Mathematica.

Bibliography

Jacques Calmet. Intelligent Computer Algebra System: Myth, Fancy or Reality? In R. Janssen, editor, *Trends in Computer Algebra*, volume 296 of *Lecture Notes in Computer Science*, Berlin-Heidelberg-New York, 1988. Springer-Verlag.

J. S. Kowalik, editor. *Coupling Symbolic and Numerical Computing in Expert Systems*, New York, 1986. Elsevier Science.

WILL DELiA GROW INTO AN EXPERT SYSTEM ?

A.V.Bocharov

Program Systems Institute , USSR Academy of Science
Pereslavl , P.O.Box 11 , 152140 USSR ,Tlx : 412531 BOAT

DELiA in its present state

DELiA (meaning originally "Differential Equations with S.Lie Approach") is a concise and efficient software system for exact algebraic investigation of differential equations on personal computers [BOBR , DEL] . DELiA project has been developed by the author and Dr.Mich.L.Bronshtein [1] .

Originally DELiA had rather strong facilities for computing generalized symmetries and conservation laws of partial differential equations and limited facilities for solution-hunting. All the computations within DELiA were made in purely algebraic mode . Only well-defined closed math algorithms were implemented .

Presently DELiA contains the following items : *Symmetry* analyzer, *Conservation laws* handler and a *Simplifier* for differential systems. The symmetry and invariance analysis is implemented in most general setting (found e.g. in [OLV] , [VIN]) . The simplifier includes a general passivization algorithm together with a set of integration rules well tested on linear and quasilinear systems of p.d.e.

DELiA has been implemented on a totally original algorithmic and computer-algebraic basis : Standard Pascal has been used for the implementation , the present MS DOS releases (1.2x , 1.3x) make restricted usage of Turbo Pascal 5.5 facilities. DELiA's symmetry analyzer (less than 35 % of the system) essentially covers what has been done in the REDUCE SPDE package (see [SCH]) but it compares favorably with the SPDE in that it makes optimum usage of the scarce MS DOS resources thus gaining in speed and memory efficiency.

DELiA's further evolution

In course of the present evolution DELiA will acquire special facilities for ordinary differential equations , some knowledge on integro-differential equations , general symbolic-numeric interface facilities , means for analyzing initial-value and boundary-value

---

[1] With partial support from the Program Systems Institute

problems. Still more important is the project to incorporate into DELiA knowledge , know-how and heuristics relevant to hunting for solutions. With this DELiA will tend to become an intelligent expert system on differential equations.

It is well-known since the time of [LIE] that if a finite-type differential system admits a sufficiently ample abelian or solvable symmetry algebra , then its general solutions may be obtained in quadratures in terms of characteristic functions of that algebra (see also quite recent [STE]).

A version of an algorithm for building such quadratures will be added in DELiA together with an algorithmic test for finiteness of type . This will enhance the power of DELiA's simplifier/integrator.

Ordinary differential equations are always of finite type - so the algorithm mentioned in the previous section always applies to sufficiently symmetrical o.d.e's.

Otherwise powerful invariance methods may be used to test for linearizability of an o.d.e , or , what is more general , to test whether the o.d.e under investigation is equivalent to one of the "model" ones , well-described in textbooks and reference books.

If all the rigorous methods fail for an o.d.e , then it comes to heuristics that is to hunting for lucky substitutions . A knowledge base on such matters is to be added to DELiA .

Why using AI methods for differential equations

All the above-mentioned novelties are still in the scope of traditional rigorous mathematics .

The crucial thing however is the strategy of applying rigorous math methods to a system of differential equations , because even if solutions of a differential system in a closed form are guaranteed by a theorem they are seldom provided by this theorem in a constructive way . The cases when nothing is guaranteed exactly are still more numerous.

The expert knowledge how to deal with such cases is an important part of "differential science" .

A no-joke job is ahead of selecting a reasonable and flexible set of expert parameters providing an adequate description of a differential system . (Conservation laws , differential invariants , classical point symmetries without doubt are the first candidates for the role of such parameters).

Then it comes to the task of accumulation and implementation of expert rules making it possible to infer a class of probable investigation strategies for a specific differential system judging from the values of its expert parameters.

Thus exact algebraic methods to compute invariance properties of differential systems implemented in DELiA now may be considered as a basis and a prolegomena to its future intelligent editions.

References

[BOBR] A.V.Bocharov,M.L.Bronstein// *Acta Appl.Math.*,16(1989),P.143-166.
[DEL] DELiA 1.2x User's Guide/ *OIPS*, 1990.
[OLV] P.J.Olver   Lie Group Applications to Differential Equations / N.Y.: Springer , 1986 .
[VIN] A.M.Vinogradov //*Acta Appl.Math.*,2 (1984), P.21 - 78 .
[SCH] F.Schwarz // *Computing* 34 (1985),91-106 and 36 (1986),279-280 .
[LIE] S.Lie   Vorlesungen uber Differentialgleichungen mit bekannten infinitesimalen Transformationen / Leiptzig : Teubner , 1891.
[STE] H.Stephani , Differential Equations : Their Solutions Using Symmetries / Cambridge Univ. Press , 1989

The GANITH algebraic geometry toolkit*

Chanderjit Bajaj   *Andrew Royappa*

Department of Computer Science
Purdue University
West Lafayette, IN 47907

Abstract

We are building a general-purpose tool for computing and visualizing solutions to systems of algebraic equations. Diverse algorithms exist for this problem and related sub-problems, and we shall incorporate several of them. We are also developing a new set of solution techniques using multi-polynomial resultants and birational maps between arbitrary algebraic sets and hypersurfaces. Our designed tool shall be portable and allow rapid prototyping of new and existing algorithms, in an intelligent blend of algebraic and numeric methods, and real solutions. Complex solutions can also be computed, but visualizing them is difficult. The software shall also take advantage of any parallel hardware that is present. In all, we anticipate improving the state of the art of algebraic equation solving by devising novel techniques, blending existing methods to form new ones, and comparing the relative efficacy of the various methods.

A prototype system implementing some of these goals is built and evolving. It is written in Common Lisp and C, and runs under version 11 of the X window system. The system is portable to any machine that runs vanilla Common Lisp, supports the X window system, and has at least a rudimentary Lisp/C interface. At the present time it can solve systems of up to two equations in any number of variables. Example applications of this are curve and surface display, curve-curve intersections, surface-surface intersections, etc. A graphical user interface allows the display and manipulation of 0D (points), 1D (curves) or 2D (surface) solutions.

1   Functionality & Implementation

1.1   Platforms

We have built a prototype toolkit that implements many of the features sketched above. Although the prototype w implemented on a Sun-4 workstation running the Unix operating system, with Sun Common Lisp, it is written entirely standard Common Lisp. The only Sun-specific parts pertain to the Lisp/C interface. The GANITH toolkit is meant be portable to any machine that supports Common Lisp, the X11 window system via the Xlib library and Athena Widg toolkit, and has a Lisp/C interface that allows strings to passed between Lisp and C. The entire tool runs within one Li process, however due to the X Window system the user interface window may appear on any X window server. The advanta of this is that the tool may run computations on non-graphics machines. Thus one may compute on a powerful non-graphi supercomputer and interact with the tool on a lightweight workstation with poor computation but good graphical facilitie

1.2   User Interface

The graphical user interface is contained in an X window, and can be manipulated (e.g. moved, resized) by the windc system as usual. It contains within itself three subwindows.

Input: This an editor buffer where commands are entered. The default editing commands are Emacs-like (Emacs is UNIX screen editor) although the user may substitute alternate editing commands.

Graphics: This window is used to display solutions to systems of equations. For curve-curve intersections the two curv are plotted in different colors and their intersection points are circled. For surface-surface intersections, the space curve intersection is displayed in the mouse-sensitive graphics window. The space curve may be viewed from different viewpoin by moving the mouse. See pictures.

Output: This is a text window used to annotate the solutions displayed in the graphics window. For instance, in t curve-curve intersection case the output window will display the (x, y) coordinates of the intersection points in the plane (t points that are circled in the graphics window). This window also contains a scrollbar so the history of the session can I perused. One can also cut text from the output window to paste into the input window, if necessary.

---

*Supported in part by NSF grant DMS 88-16286, ARO contract DAAG29-85-C-0018 under Cornell MSI and ONR contract N00014-88-K-0402

.3 Algorithms

very system of algebraic equations has three main parameters: the number of equations (n), the maximum total degree of ny equation (d), and the number of variables (r). For certain values of n and d, good methods already exist. A chart of ke "problem space" can be seen in the table below. The new algorithms we are developing for $n \geq 2$ and $d > 1$, are based n multi-polynomial resultants and birational maps, and shall handle all dimensionality of solutions. Details are in the full aper [1]. One of the public domain and available Gröbner basis packages shall be used for comparison purposes.

$n \geq 3$		Macaulay's Resultant Gröbner Basis
$n = 2$	Linear System Solving (Established Methods)	Parameterizations Birational Maps Sylvester's Resultant
$n = 1$		Polynomial Root Solving (Established Methods)
	$d = 1$	$d > 1$

.4 Layers Of Computation

he computation part has a layered design. Higher layers are built on top of the lower layers.

Level 4: High-level algorithms: Intersect curves and surfaces; Display curves and surfaces; Piecewise, low degree approxi- ation of curves and surfaces; Irreducible decomposition of curves and surfaces.

Level 3: Mid-level algorithms: Conversions from implicit to parametric ; Resolution of singularities by "blowing up" ; ranch computations at singular points .

Level 2: Low-level algorithms: Sylvester's resultant, subresultant p.r.s (by modular and non-modular methods); Macaulay's ultant.

Level 1: Multivariate polynomial manipulation: Add, subtract, multiply, divide, pseudo-divide, differentiate, evaluate ; terpolate/chinese remainder by both iterative and other (divide-and-conquer) methods; Conversion from sparse to recursive rms, and from power to Bernstein to B-spline representations.

References

1] Bajaj, C., and Royappa, A., (1989), "GANITH: A Package for Algebraic Geometry", Comp. Science Tech. Rept. 914, and CAPO report CER-89-21, Purdue University.

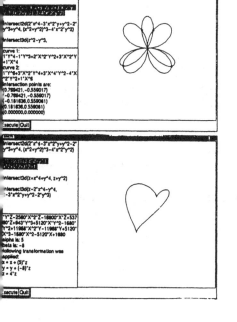

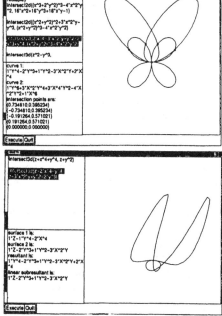

MAS MODULA-2 ALGEBRA SYSTEM

HEINZ KREDEL

UNIVERSITY OF PASSAU, FRG

1. Overview. MAS is an experimental computer algebra system and not a symbol manipulation system. The goal of the MAS system is to provide:

1. an interactive computer algebra system
2. comprehensive algorithm libraries, including the ALDES / SAC-2 system [Collins 82],
3. a familiar program development system for algebraic algorithm design and study with an efficient compiler,
4. algorithm documentation open to the users.

Key attributes of the MAS system are:

1. portability (it is portable to a computer during a student exercise 'Praktikum'), machine dependencies isolated in a small kernel,
2. extendability (it is possible to add and interface to external algorithm libraries), open system architecture,
3. transparent storage management (garbage collection is provided without user cooperation), stable error handling (no system break down on misspelled expressions and runtime exceptions), transparent input / output facilities with streams (so that no changes are required to existing libraries).

The goals and attributes have been achieved by the following main design concepts:

MAS replaces the ALDES language [Loos 76] and the FORTRAN implementation system of SAC-2 by the Modula-2 language (N. Wirth). Modula-2 is well suited for the development of large program libraries, the language is powerful enough to implement all parts of a computer algebra system and the Modula-2 compilers have easy to use program development environments.

To provide an interactive calculation system a LISP interpreter is implemented in Modula-2 with full access to the library modules. For better usability a Modula-2 like (interaction) language was defined with a type system and function overloading capabilities.

Further design issues are:

Contrary to other computer algebra systems (e.g. Scratchpad II [Jenks 85]) the MAS system has very limited knowledge of built-in data structures. The only data objects are atoms, symbols and lists over atoms and symbols. Data types provided by the compiled algorithms (arbitrary precision integers, rational numbers, polynomials etc.) are handled by the respective library procedures.

The type declaration concept equips the MAS system with the knowledge that some variables and objects have types. Generic functions applied to these typed variables or objects causes the interpreter to look for an executable function, which can work with the specific object types. This approach is different to typed lambda calculus (e.g. in SML [Appel 88]) were the types of functions are deduced from the function text. In MAS function types and overloading of functions must be explicitly defined, since most functions are compiled Modula-2 programs.

2. Achievements and Current State. The steps towards the MAS system have been:

1. definition of a syntax transformation scheme between ALDES and Modula-2; development of a translator and translation of most of the ALDES / SAC-2 libraries to Modula-2;

2. development of a storage management system in Modula-2 with automatic garbage collection in an uncooperative environment; implementation of a input / output system in Modula-2 with streams;

3. implementation of a LISP interpreter in Modula-2 with access to the compiled procedures (using Modula-2 procedure types and variables)

4. definition of an interaction language with type system and function overloading;

5. implementation of a parser for the interaction language and corresponding modifications to the LISP interpreter.

Steps 1 and 2 were subject to the restriction that the interface had to be compatible with the existing ALDES / SAC-2 libraries. Steps 1 - 3 have been reported in [Kredel 88].

Currently all steps have been completed. Versions of the MAS system are running on Atari ST, IBM PC and Commodore Amiga. A version for IBM VM/CMS is in work.

The ALDES / SAC-2 libraries have been implemented including the Polynomial Factorization System and the Real Root Isolation System. From the DIP system the Buchberger Algorithm System and the Ideal Decomposition and Ideal Real Root System have been implemented. Gröbner Bases are also available for non-commutative polynomial rings of solvable type. The combination of the MAS programs with numerical Modula-2 libraries has been tested.

3. Next Steps and Future Plans. The current development concentrates on filling some gaps in the ALDES / SAC-2 system, namely: a linear algebra package, some logic programming facilities and more arbitrary precision numeric facilities. Further the system documentation is completed.

Naturally the MAS system is used to evaluate the design and to see how serious are its limits in practical use:

1. static Modula-2 compiler and LISP interpreter, incremental compilation,

2. 'string expressions' instead of symbolic expressions and restrictive typing requirements, no mathematical knowledge in the parser, only in the libraries,

3. reusing the ALDES / SAC-2 data representations.

Cooperation is welcome especially in the areas:

- algebraic algorithm libraries: commutative and non-commutative polynomial rings,
- interaction language: symbolic expressions, possibly functional and / or logic programming extensions, etc.

Under consideration is also a switch from Modula-2 to Oberon [Wirth 89] to be able to join the type system of the compiler with the type system in the interaction part.

Availability: MAS is available on the electronic networks (usenet, eunet) from the groups for the respective machines (comp.binaries.atari.st, etc.) or from the author.

REFERENCES

[Appel 88] A. W. Appel, R. Milner, R. W. Harper, D. B. MacQueen, *Standard ML Reference Manual (preliminary draft)*, University of Edinburgh, LFCS Report, 1988.

[Collins 82] G.E. Collins, R. Loos, *ALDES/SAC-2 now available*, SIGSAM Bulletin 1982, and several reports distributed with the ALDES/SAC-2 system.

[Jenks 85] R. D. Jenks *et al.*, *Scratchpad II Programming Language Manual*, Computer Algebra Group, IBM, Yorktown Heights, NY, 1985.

[Kredel 88] H. Kredel, *From SAC-2 to Modula-2*, Proc. ISSAC'88 Rome, LNCS 358, pp 447-455, Springer, 1989.

[Loos 76] R. G. K. Loos. *The Algorithm Description Language ALDES (Report)*, SIGSAM Bulletin 14/1, pp 15-39, 1976.

[Wirth 89] N. Wirth, J. Gutknecht, *The Oberon System*, pp 857-893, Software-Practice and Experience Vol. 19(9) (September 1989).

PROTOTYPES FOR THE AUTOMATIC TRANSLATION OF COMPUTER ALGEBRA LANGUAGES

Denis Constales
Research Assistant of the Belgian National Fund for Scientific Research
Seminar for Algebra and Functional Analysis
State University of Ghent
Galglaan 2, B9000 Belgium

Today, computer algebra software is available in nearly all research and higher education institutions concerned with mathematics, computer science, physics or engineering; they range from relatively small and inexpensive general-purpose programs to highly specialized software packages.

Considering the various general-purpose packages, we see that they share some features, among which :

- the most common type for their objects is 'a rational function of kernels' (in the Reduce terminology), i.e. they are aimed at the manipulation of polynomials and rational functions, possibly involving transcendental functions. Such packages will allow the substitution of variables, the factorization of polynomials and the differentiation and integration of expressions, but may, for instance, lack the built-in ability to distinguish variables over a modular field from general ones, to factor over field extensions etc., so they are at their best when dealing with real analysis, real or complex matrices and the like.

- some of these packages are written in LISP, some are not but remain close to LISP; most of them offer a programming language whose syntax is ALGOL-like.

This makes it possible for an experienced user to translate his programs and data from one of these languages to another—a very tiring job, because the language designers seem to have done all they could to create misunderstandings. Here are some examples :

- both Reduce and Macsyma have a valued if construct, allowing the expression of the C language ?: operator, but Maple's if cannot simply be used as in

```
a := b + if c > 0 then 1 else 0 fi
```

you should write instead :

```
a := b + map(proc () if c>0 then 1 else 0 fi end, 0)
```

where the 0 has no special meaning and might be any 'scalar', but not a list or a set

- matrix elements are accessed and modified in slightly different ways

- polynomial manipulation functions may act differently in special cases (e.g. when the polynomial does not involve the specified variable)

- Reduce simplifies automatically while Macsyma offers dozens of different simplification functions

Our aim is to offer software that might prove useful in the translation process, even though it is very unlikely that there ever will be a fully automatic translation capability for computer algebra software. Indeed, this would require the formalization of the complete knowledge of the target languages along with the human expertise which guides the developer in his choice of an optimal coding, given the strengths and weaknesses of a particular language. But at least we may hope to be able to translate the 'objects' (such as expressions, Taylor series, matrices etc.) faithfully from one language to another, and to automate the most tiresome and... automatic part of the translation process.

The programs were written at the State University of Ghent (Belgium) as part of the CAGe project on the integration of computer algebra systems, supported by the Belgian National Fund for Scientific Research N.F.W.O. They are filters translating each of the languages Reduce, Maple and Macsyma to and from an intermediary language, called CAIL, which was designed to be trivial to parse, since it essentially serves to export n-ary trees.

The translators consist of

- a 'backbone' built from a yacc parser and a lex scanner, adapted to the particular source language

- shared modules for the manipulation of the different structures used internally :

  - lookup tables
  - hash tables
  - n-ary trees
  - parser utilities for the manipulation of the n-ary tree used to represent the structure of the successive top-level expressions. They include :
    * building associative and non-associative binary operations
    * building ternary and higher-arity nodes of the tree corresponding to other CAIL constructs (such as the valued if, for statements etc.)
    * the non-recursive navigation of a subtree, calling certain functions at every node
  - a pattern-matching module, whose importance may be illustrated by the example involving the if statement in Maple : a valued if in a Macsyma program is translated to a map(proc () ... end, 0) in Maple. If the produced Maple code is fed to the Maple translator, this construct must be recognized as a valued if and expressed by the corresponding CAIL construct, rather than by a CAIL 'map' of a lambda expression.

The latter modules are shared with the translators from CAIL to Macsyma, Reduce and Maple, which also consist of :

- a CAIL lexical analyzer and parser written in C language

- a code generator tailored to the particular target language

- a line-breaking output module.

To derive a final product from these prototypes will require the integration of some extra knowledge on the idiosyncrasies of the supported languages, and some speed optimization. For the latter, profiling indicates that the slowest component is the lexical scanner, accounting for about half the computer time. To illustrate the speed (or slowness), the Macsyma translator handles about 5K of input data per CPU second on a 20MHz 68020 workstation.

The Implementation of A PC-Based List Processor for Symbolic Computation

K.H.Lee,
K.S.Leung and
S.M.Cheang

Department of Computer Science
The Chinese University of Hong Kong

Abstract. The Arithmetical and Symbolical List Processor (ASLP) is a purpose-built processor for list handling and processing. Multiple buses and multiple memory principles are applied for pipelining and parallel data movements. This micro-programmable ASLP is a stand-alone processor which connects to an IBM/AT personal computer. The IBM/AT personal computer works as the host for software development. The prototype of the ASLP is constructed using standard chips. A special micro-assembler is written for the ASLP micro-assembly program translation. Most standard list functions are programmed and evaluated. In parallel with the evaluation, the core part of the original hardware design of the ASLP is being redesigned using ASICs. This paper will present the design and the evaluation results of the ASLP.

1. INTRODUCTION

List is one of the most important data structures in computer programming, especially in AI and expert system applications which demand an efficient list data structure. Although using list as the main data structure for programming is flexible, the execution time overhead is high in a Von Neumann computer. Thus a purpose-built processor is designed and implemented for an IBM/AT personal computer to support list manipulation functions.

The **Arithmetical and Symbolical List Processor (ASLP)** [1,2] is a micro-programmable hardware processor for list data structure handling and manipulation. The structure of a list handled in the ASLP is the same as that in LISP language. [2,3,4] The ASLP speeds up list processing by pipelining, parallel data movements and processing. The functional block diagram of the ASLP is shown in figure 2.1. To facilitate fast list processing, special function registers and two separate memory modules are used in the processor. Dedicated functional units, such as the internal stack for non-linear list handling, are also included in the architecture of the ASLP. The detailed discussion on the architecture of the ASLP will be discussed in section 2. The techniques that are used for hardware design and implementation of the ASLP will be given in section 3.

Since the ASLP is a micro-programmable architecture, the function of the processor can be redefined and experimented with by loading different micro-codes into the micro-controller of the ASLP. For efficient micro-code programming, a micro-assembler is built on the host computer to translate micro-assembly programs into micro-codes. Moreover, many list function calls are needed for application program developments. These software tools will be discussed in section 4. A list function library written in C has been completed and an evaluation on the performance of these functions are presented in section 5.

As we can see in figure 2.1, the structure of the ASLP is highly modular. Two partition methods, the functional and bit-slice partitions, can be used to construct the hardware. Due to construction difficulties, the functional partition method is more suitable for the prototype ASLP. In parallel with the evaluation experiment, an eight-bit slice VLSI chip, **LP1**, is being designed to replace some parts of the hardware of the ASLP. Using LP1 will reduce the size of the ASLP by as much as 30%. More about the bit-slice chip will be explained in section 6.

References

[1]   Lee K.H., Leung K.S., And Cheang S.M., *A Microprogrammable List Processor for Personal Computer*, IEEE Micro. (To be published)

[2]   Leung K.S., Lee K.H. And Cheang S.M., *List Processing for Artificial Intelligence Applications*, Microprocessing and Microprogramming - EUROMICRO. (To be published)

[3]   Steele G.L., Jr.(1984), *Common Lisp*, Digital Press.

[4]   Winston P.H., Horn B.K.P.(1984), *Lisp*, Addison-Wesley.

[5]   Wilensky R.(1986), *Common LISPcraft*, W.W.Norton and Company, New York and London.

[6]   AMD(1985), *Bipolar Microprocessor Logic and Interface*, Advanced Micro Devices.

IMPLEMENTATION OF THE SYMBOL ANALYTIC TRANSFORMATIONS LANGUAGE FLAC

S. V. Chmutov, E. A. Gaydar, I. M. Ignatovich,
V. F. Kozadoy, A. P. Nemytykh, V. A. Pinchuk

Program Systems Institute AS USSR
152140 Pereslavl-Zalessky, USSR.

The language FLAC (Functional Language for Algebraic Computations) was developed by V. L. Kistlerov in 1986. We are describing the version of FLAC implemented by the authors.

Data. Data in FLAC are sequences (possibly empty) of trees. Thus, they differ substantially from LISP data. For example, the sequence of trees

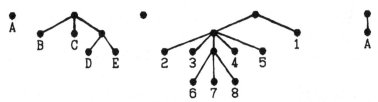

is represented as   A (B C (D E)) () ((2 3 (6 7 8) 4 5) 1) (A).   In this representation parentheses correspond to unlabelled nodes. A single tree is referred to as *term*, while a single tree with unlabelled root is called an *applicative term*. The *name* of an applicative term is its maximal left subtree. The syntax representation of a sequence of trees is non-unique: the name of applicative term may be extracted from inside the brackets. In the above example we have four applicative terms. The name of the first is B; the name of the second is empty; the third name is (2 3 (6 7 8) 4 5) and the fourth is A.   Our sequence may be represented also as   A B(C (D E)) () (2 3 (6 7 8) 4 5)(1) A().

Programs. *A FLAC program* is a term rewriting system with the following two features:
1. The pattern matching procedure should comply with the order of sentences in the program.
2. There exist variables of two kinds:
   - &x, &y, ... - which may take values consisting of only one term.
   - #x, #y, ... - whose values are *sequences* of terms (including the empty sequence).

In more detail. A FLAC - program consists of descriptions of *functions*. Descriptions of functions consist of *sentences*. Each sentence has the form ⟨ left-hand part ⟩ = ⟨ right-hand part ⟩; .
Here   ⟨left-hand part⟩ ::= ⟨function name⟩(⟨sequence of terms⟩)
         ⟨right-hand part⟩ ::= ⟨sequence of terms⟩
The program's work begins with the call of a function. The FLAC - machine makes an attempt to match the initial call with the left-hand part of the first sentence of this function. During the pattern matching process variables take certain values. If the matching is successful, then the initial call of the function is replaced by the right-hand part of the sentence with the appropriate values. Then the applicative terms involved in the right-hand part are called. If the matching is impossible, then an attempt is made to match the call with the left-hand part of the next sentence. If no match was found throughout the program, then the result of the called function is the call itself, i.e. the applicative term :
         ⟨function name⟩(⟨sequence of terms⟩).
This phenomenon is referred to as *suspension*.

Remarks. 1. There is a restriction on the use of variables: the left-hand part of a sentence cannot contain two variables of the # kind at the same level in the expressions with parentheses.

2. FLAC has modularity mechanism.

Examples. I. Reverse of a sequence.
Program: rev() = ;
           rev(&x #y) = rev(#y) &x;
Initial call: rev(a b c);
Trace: rev(a b c) ⟶ rev(b c) a;   /* #y equals b c ,
                                       but not (b c) ! */
       rev(b c) a ⟶ rev(c) b a;   /* #y is equal to c */
       rev(c) b a ⟶ rev() c b a; /* #y is empty   */
       rev() c b a ⟶ c b a;
Result: c b a

II. Chose the maximal subsequence beginning with A and ending with B.
Program: ch(A #y B) = A #y B;
           ch(A #y &x) = ch(A #y);
           ch(&x #y)   = ch(#y);
Initial call: ch(1 2 A B B (B));
Result: A B B
Initial call: ch(1 2 B B (B));
Result: ch()   /* suspension */

III. Evaluation of a sequence of term.
Program: eval(&f(#y) #z) = &f(#y) eval(#z);
                           /* eval is a higher-order function */
           eval(&x   #z) = &x eval(#z);
           eval() = ;

IV. Replace all occurences of A in a sequence by B.
Program: Rep()   = ;
           Rep(A #x)   = B Rep(#x);
           Rep((#y) #x) = (Rep(#y)) Rep(#x);
           Rep(&y #x)   = &y Rep(#x);
Initial call: Rep((1 A) B);
Result: (1 B) B
Initial call: Rep('(Rep A))   /* (Rep A) is data */
Trace: Rep((Rep A)) ⟶ (Rep(Rep A)) Rep();
 (Rep(Rep A)) Rep() ⟶ (Rep Rep(A)) Rep();
 (Rep Rep(A)) Rep() ⟶ (Rep B) Rep(); /* (Rep B) ≈ Rep(B) */
       Rep(B) Rep() ⟶ B Rep();   /* !!! */
       B Rep() ⟶ B;
Result: B.   But we wanted to obtain (Rep B). The reason of our failure is that the data (Rep B) was evaluated at /* !!! */. It should be noted that FLAC does have tools for suspension control, which allow to write correct programs.

Implementation. The system is implemented as a compiler from FLAC to a special assembly language and as an interpreter of this language. Inner representation of the tree (A B) looks like

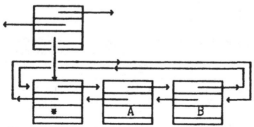

Here * means the number of references to the lower "storey".

Design and development of ENprover,
an automated theorem proving system based on EN-strategy

Fabio Baj, Massimo Bruschi, Antonella Zanzi
Dipartimento di Scienze dell'Informazione, Università degli Studi di Milano
Via Moretto da Brescia 9, 20133 Milano
email: mbruschi@imiucca.bitnet

Hsiang has presented a refutational proof method based on term rewriting for the first order predicate calculus with equality [Hs87]. His approach relies on translating sets of first-order formulas into a set of boolean rewrite rules and then applying various superposition rules to obtain critical pairs. ENprover is a theorem prover which incorporates Hsiang's method.

The connection between resolution theorem proving and the critical-pair / completion procedures for term rewriting is quite recent [Hs81][Hs82][DH]. Few running systems have been presented in the literature [HJ][ADM][SW]. See also [AHM][Ch][KZ][BS] for experimetations made with systems developed for the equational theory.

The development of ENprover gave rise to three prototypes, two written in Prolog [Le][Ba] and one in C language [Fe]. The program is composed by a set of interacting modules specialized in: formula to clauses transformation, clause to rule transformation, rules' normalisation by the canonical term rewriting system for the boolean ring, rule-base management, match and unification, simplification by rewriting, superposition.

Some of the techniques employed in the implementation of ENprover are similar to those of TeRSe [Hs85]: classifying the rules, sorting the terms and rules, giving higher priority to the simplification procedure than the superposition one. Improved algorithms have been developed for the clause to rule tranformation, for the semplification process and to test of rules' uniqueness into the base [Ba].

A theorem bank, collecting theorems from various sources like [Pe][KM][BLMOSW], has been developed, to verify and stress the prover. A controlled execution of the program with automated collection of statistical data follows all the main modifications.

OTTER [McC], the powerful and well known theorem prover based on resolution, has been choosed as a reference point and to make a comparison with another theorem proving approach. In the following graphics a comparison between the efficiency of OTTER and ENprover is shown. The first shows the useful rule generation rates evaluated on sets of theorems with proof time belonging to a given interval. In the second graphic this rate is evaluated on sets of theorems that halt for out-of-mem problems. The main difference is memory wasting. OTTER actually relies on a better and engineerized data structure than the ENprover one.

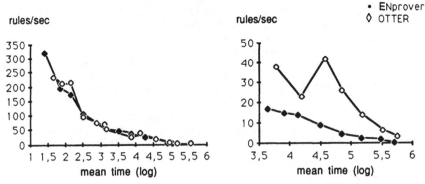

From a user point of view the main difference between OTTER and ENprover is in the interface. OTTER has a lot of parameters to control many aspects of the proof process, but few to choose the search strategy. Actually OTTER has a (SOS) hard-coded search strategy. On the other hand ENprover has an external definition of the search strategy. In the Prolog version the search strategy is defined by an algorithm which manages sets of rule indexes whereas in the C version it is based on rules' weight evaluation functions. This approach allows to study the effectiveness of different search strategies. The relationships between completeness and efficiency is not well investigated. One possibility is to work with a lot of (incomplete) search strategies.

A transputer system, to get a parallel execution of proof processes by independent search strategy, has been developed [BFG]. This system runs on a Meico Transputer Surface with 16 processors. A Sun 4-110 behaves as host. OTTER and the C version of ENprover has been set into this environment.

The next graphic, realised with data collected with the Prolog version of ENprover, can give an idea of the impact of using parallelism. Working on a sample of 200 theorems and with a set of 10 strategies (set-of-support, linear input, ancestry filtered, ordered fifo, and some restricted variants) the curve of the best succeding strategies k-uple is plotted. Every point identifies the number of theorems proved in a given time by the "k-best-strategy".

The impact of the parallelism is less evident as k grows. This is mainly due to the naive choose of the set of strategies that are probably not "independent" each other. The interesting aspect is that no strategy alone is able to prove the number of theorems proved by a set of strategies.

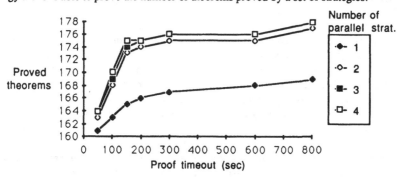

Acknowledgements
ENprover has been developed at the Department of Computer Science, Study University of Milan. Prof. Giovanni Degli Antoni followed, encouraged and supported the development of ENprover since its very beginning. We also thank M.P.Bonacina and G.Ferrari for their innumerable suggestions.

This work was partially supported by IBM Italy SpA in the context of a Joint Study with the Comp. Sci. Dep. of the Univ. of Milan, by CEE in the context of the KWICK-ESPRIT Project and by TECOGRAF in the same context, by the Italian National Research Council and by the Ministry of Public Instruction 40% grant.

References
[AHM] S.Anantharaman, J.Hsiang, J.Mzali, "SbReve2: A Term Rewriting Laboratory with (AC-Unfailing Completion", in RTA89, LNCS 355, 1989
[ADM] J.Avenhaus, J.Denzinger, J.Muller, "THEOPOGLES - An efficient Theorem Prover based on Rewrite-Techniques", in RTA89, LNCS 355, 1989
[Ba] F.Baj, "Development of an ATP for FOPC+=" (in Italian), Thesis, Comp. Sc. Dep. Milan, 1989
[BFG] F.Baj, G.Ferrari, D.Galli, "Theorem proving in supercomputing", Supercomputing Tools for Science and Engineering - Workshop Proc., 1989
[BS] M.P.Bonacina, G.Sanna, "KBlab: An Equational Theorem Prover for the Macintosh", in RTA89, LNCS 355, 1989
[BLMOSW] R.Boyer, E.Lusk, W.McCune, R.Overbeek, M.Stickel, L.Wos, "Set theory in first order logic: clauses for Goedel axioms", JAR 1, 1986
[Ch] J.Christian, "Fast Knuth-Bendix Completion: Summary", in RTA89, LNCS355, 1989
[DH] N.Dershowitz, J.Hsiang, "Rewrite methods for clausal and non-clausal theorem proving", Proc. ICALP 83, LNCS 154, 1983
[Fe] G.Ferrari, "ENprover in C Language on Transputers" (in Italian), Thesis, Comp. Sc. Dep. of Milan, 1989
[Hs81] J.Hsiang, "Refutational Theorem Proving Using Term Rewriting Systems", AI J. 1985, Manuscript, Univ of Illinois at Urbana, Dep. Comp. Scie., 1981
[Hs82] J.Hsiang, "Topics in Automated Theorem Proving and Program Generation", AI J., 1985, PhD Thesis, Univ of Illinois at Urbana, Dep. Comp. Scie., 1982
[Hs85] J.Hsiang, "Refutational theorem proving using term rewriting systems", Art. Int. 25, 1985
[Hs87] J.Hsiang, "Rewrite Method for Theorem Proving in First Order Theory with Equality", J. Symb. Comp., 1987
[HJ] J.Hsiang, N.A.Josephson, "TeRSe: A Rewriting Theorem Prover", in Proc. Rewrite Rule Laboratory Workshop, Schenectady, NY, 1983
[KM] D.Kalish, R.Montague, "Logic, thechniques of formal reasoning", H.Brace & World Inc, 1964
[KZ] D.Kapur, H.Zhang, "An Overview of Rewrite Rule Laboratory (RRL)", in RTA89, LNCS 355, 1989
[Le] G.Leidi, "An ATP for FOPC+=" (in Italian), Thesis, Comp. Sc. Dep. Milan, 1988
[McC] W.W.McCune, OTTER 1.0 Users' Guide, Argonne National Lab. Report, ANL-88-44, 1989
[Pe] F.J.Pelletier, "Seventy-five problems for testing automatic theorem provers", JAR 2, 1986
[SW] B.Smith, R.Wilkerson, "Non-Obviousness - Again", AAR Newsletter 11, 1989

TOWARDS A LOGIC LANGUAGE:
AN OBJECT-ORIENTED IMPLEMENTATION
OF THE CONNECTION METHOD

Giorgio Forcellese †, *Marco Temperini* ‡

† Dipartimento di Informatica e Sistemistica, Università degli Studi di Roma "La Sapienza", Via Buonarroti 12, 00185 Roma, Italy.

‡ Istituto di Analisi dei Sistemi ed Informatica del C.N.R. Viale Manzoni 30, 00185 Roma, Italy; student of Dottorato in Informatica at Università degli Studi "La Sapienza", Roma.

The aim of this work is to present an automated deduction tool designed and implemented by following an object-oriented (OO) paradigm. Our work is developed in the frame of the definition of a programming language for mathematical objects manipulation. For this general project, some requirements have been considered as mainly important: they are the OO methodology to be supported, and the inclusion into the language of mechanisms for the axiomatic specification of data structures and for dealing with the properties of such mathematical structures.

In this work we refer to the last subject, describing the chosen inference method to be implemented, the language and the methodology exploited in the preliminary implementation, and some examples of actual use, from both the points of view of the pure automated reasoning and of the integration of a logic tool into the more general environment for mathematical structures handling. The implementation language is Loglan [Log]. It includes very powerful features of the OO paradigm, such as the *class* unit, the multi-level *prefixing* (that is supported together with *nesting* features: this is remarkable for the construction of effective modules), *virtual* definition of attributes, the generalization to the *coroutine* unit of the class construction.

Some distinctive features have been selected for the choice of an automated deduction mechanism to be implemented. They are: clearness and trasparency, human-orientedness possibility to have a description of the proof (or of the causes of the failure) in a natural text, efficiency in terms of space and time, extendibility to higher order logic. In order to reach these aims, the Connection Method (CM) has been chosen, as the most suitable deduction mechanism for an OO implementation. A full description of CM is in [Bib]; an introduction to the method, through its close relationships with the Tableaux Proof, with some technical notes about the implementation, is given in [FoTe], showing the equivalence between these mechanisms from a constructive point of view, and the technical advantages of the former, with regard to space-efficiency and its adaptability to an OO implementation. As regarded to the distinctive features a deduction method we wanted to have, we can give the following observations: CM has been implemented for the FOL, but it is adaptable to higher order logics; in this direction the possibility to apply this method to Algorithmic Logic [MiSa] seems to be evaluated. Having to work with the same untouched matrix, the problem to generate a proof for a formula is always clear at any step (there exists a simple and exhaustive algorithm to find a spanning set of connection in a given matrix). The facts that we don't have to negate the formula (CM is not originally based on refutation) and that the method can be applied also to formulae not in disjunctive normal form, make the method surely human oriented. CM was derived from Gentzen Natural Calculus and there is an automatic way to obtain a Gentzen proof from a CM one, and consequently to obtain a description of the proof in natural language. CM is efficient in term of space because the initial form remains untouched during the proof (even when many istances of the matrix are needed in the predicative case, according to the Herbrand theorem, we can make it virtually). The only structures we have to build and store in memory are the connections. Moreover, the decision to use this deduction mechanism lays also on features making it suitable for an implementation in an OO programming language. CM is based

Research partially supported by MURST: "Calcolo Algebrico, Sistemi di Manipolazione Algebrica"; CNR: "Matematica Computazionale", Progetto Finalizzato "Sistemi Informatici e Calcolo Parallelo"; Olivetti System and Networks.

on the manipulation of a unique data structure: the matrix, representing the formula we want to prove to be valid, which, once generated as an object, remains untouched, reducing the space occupation; its features of trasparency and clearness allow an incremental way of realization, with an easy development towards the parallelism, the introduction of equality and induction and easy changes in order to refine the efficiency feature of the method implementation.

Therefore the CM allows full use of the rules of OO design methodology: the clearness and trasparency of the CM, enhanced by the use of an OO language, allows to built a reusable and modifiable module, always available in the system (through inheritance or clientness) for example in the construction of a PROLOG-like language.

The actual module can be used directly as a Theorem Proving Tool for FOL, by validating an input formula and producing a set of unificated connections (if success occurs). In this sense the actual implementation has been tested on a significant set of formulae of the propositional and predicative logic [Pel]. Moreover the programming techniques standing at the basis of this implementation allow more interesting developments, by means of few modifications.

An interesting application concerns the possible completion of a set of hypotheses: starting from a given formula represented from a matrix which is not complementary, the adding of some atoms can be attempted, to determine a spanning set of connections; it worths to note that a new atom comes out from the consideration about a literal having no possibilities to be connected, but occurring in some path that doesn't contain other detected connections. This type of application is meaningful towards applications concerning the use of "Abduction" in automated reasoning [EsKo]. As another enhancement, the insertion of this module into the programming system has been considered: the module can become a system service tool designed to work on instances of variables of type "formula".

The actual implementation supports proofs in full FOL, without any limitations on multiplicity nor on arity of functions, but to reach the above aims, a more general version is actually under development, in order to improve the performance of the existing module, allowing the general nested matrices use; this characteristic doesn't provide more expressive power, but results in a human orientation feature; moreover there is a gain in terms of space and time usage.

The possibilities offered by the programming system and methodologies allow to enterprise the next extensions by an incremental logic. Two main directions for such extensions are listed below. The first step concerns the possibility, if it is needed, to perform parallel computations (for example creating a new process when multiplicity is incremented): in fact, the coroutine-choice for the implementation of the deductive module is motivated by such an observation. The second direction concerns the improving of the Unification mechanism, with a more efficient algorithm [PaWe].

References

[Bib] W. BIBEL: *Automated theorem proving.* Friedr. Vieweg & Sohn, Braunschweig, (1982).

[Log] W.M. BARTOL et al: *Report on the Programming Language LOGLAN 82*, Polish Scient. Publ. Warsaw (1984).

[EsKo] K. ESHGHI, R.A. KOWALSKI: *Abduction Compared with Negation By Failure*, Proc. 6th ICLP, G.Levi & M.Martelli Eds. MIT Press, (1989).

[FoTe] G. FORCELLESE, M.TEMPERINI: *A System for Automated Deduction Based on the Connection Method*, R.268 IASI-CNR, Roma.

[MiSa] G. MIRKOWSKA, A. SALWICKI: *Algorithmic Logic*, Polish Scient. Publ. Warsaw (1987).

[PaWe] M.S. PATERSON, M.N. WEGMAN: *Linear unification.* JCSS 16, (1978).

[Pel] F.J. PELLETIER: *Seventy-Five Problems for Testing Automatic Theorem Provers*, JAR 16 (1986).

SUGGESTIONS FOR A FRIENDLIER USER INTERFACE

Ron Avitzur
Physics Dept., Stanford University
Stanford, California

The importance of the user interface in math systems has long been recognized [1]. As an undergraduate, I have well-defined needs for a math system. It must not only perform calculations, but also produce documents quickly and easily. Currently, students do mathematically-oriented problem sets almost exclusively with pencil and paper, despite the increasing availability of powerful symbolic computation systems. Existing systems, by concentrating on difficult or large problems, neglect the student interested only in completing easy manipulations and presenting the results more quickly. Users need to learn a new syntax for entering mathematics as well as a command language for manipulating expressions. This intimidates those with no computer experience and is time consuming even for experienced computer users. Questions encountered in undergraduate problem sets are computationally trivial. They may be tedious, but not enough to warrant the time needed to enter the formulas, interpret the output, and create a document using existing systems. This is entirely a user interface problem.

I encourage developers to create better user interfaces by focusing on two criteria: speed of learning and speed of use. New users should be able to learn the system quickly, while experienced users should be able to use it efficiently. WYSIWYG (What You See Is What You Get) word processors provide a model for a friendly user interface. They have become the standard tool on college campuses for writing assignments. Users with no computer experience can learn to use them quickly and easily without documentation. Developers of user interfaces should make this level of friendliness a goal.

To address this, the interface to a math system must satisfy several requirements. It should be part of a document preparation system which supports editing text and graphics as well as equations. Expressions should be entered and manipulated with a structure editor. The system should use menus and palettes and provide on-line help.

FrameMaker 2.0 [2] implements these suggestions. It is a document preparation system suitable for publishing technical documents. Math objects are simply another tool alongside text and graphical objects which allows the user to concentrate on creating a document for presentation. One can enter and manipulate math expression in a WYSIWYG manner within documents. The math system built into Frame-Maker is very easy for a novice to use.

The user enters math expressions with a structure editor designed to make editing equations as similar as possible to editing text. As expressions are entered, they are displayed in standard textbook notation. Gestures invoked with the keyboard or the mouse operate on the current selection, which is always a meaningful mathematical object. Complex expressions are built by wrapping templates such as an integral or a summation around the selection. By displaying the expression in standard notation at all times, the structure editor provides immediate feedback during input. This reassures new users and decreases the learning time. Also, by allowing selection of subexpressions, the structure editor enables experienced users to edit expressions more quickly.

Manipulating expressions in a structure editor allows for more specific commands. For example, most systems have a command such as Mathematica's *TrigReduce* to simplify a line containing trigonometric expressions. However, it is much more difficult to select a particular sine in a large expression and rewrite it in terms of cosine without affecting the form of the rest of the expression. Manipulating expressions can be made more friendly and less intimidating by offering low-level manipulation commands as well as powerful black box commands which hide algebraic complexity. I call these low-level commands "generalized movement" commands. The user may select a subexpression and issue the gesture *Move Right*. The system then attempts a correctness-preserving transformation on the expression, which visually moves the subexpression to the right. For example, the system may commute two terms in a product or a sum, or it may move the term across an equal sign, reciprocating or negating the term, as appropriate. Similarly, moving a subexpression from the denominator to the numerator raises the subexpression to the -1 power. Figure 1 demonstrates the *Move Left* gesture repeatedly applied to a selection.

Each command is simple. Combined, they allow the user to quickly massage a complicated expression by issuing only graphically oriented commands. This method is powerful both for new users who need not remember commands and for experienced users who want to express an expression in a nonstandard form. Simple algebra is reduced to the visual metaphor of dragging boxes across the screen.

$$y = \blacksquare x + b \qquad y = \blacksquare\left(x + \frac{b}{a}\right) \qquad y\,\blacksquare = \left(x + \frac{b}{a}\right)$$

Figure 1

Still, I can usually write expressions on paper faster than I can type them into any system because the keyboard and mouse must serve the double function of both positioning the selection range and entering the symbols. With pencil and paper I can place the symbols as I write them. Happily, the technology for a handwriting interface exists. Commercial systems now exist on personal computers which can recognize handwriting. A math interface incorporating handwriting would combine the flexibility and convenience of pencil and paper with the power and speed of symbolic computation systems.

References

[1] Smith, C.J. and Soiffer, N.M., "MathScribe: A User Interface for Computer Algebra Systems," Technical Report No. CRL-86-35, 1986.
[2] FrameMaker 2.0, Frame Technology Corporation, 1989.

Index of Authors

Vol. 379: A. Kreczmar, G. Mirkowska (Eds.), Mathematical Foundations of Computer Science 1989. Proceedings, 1989. VIII, 605 pages. 1989.

Vol. 380: J. Csirik, J. Demetrovics, F. Gécseg (Eds.), Fundamentals of Computation Theory. Proceedings, 1989. XI, 493 pages. 1989.

Vol. 381: J. Dassow, J. Kelemen (Eds.), Machines, Languages, and Complexity. Proceedings, 1988. VI, 244 pages. 1989.

Vol. 382: F. Dehne, J.-R. Sack, N. Santoro (Eds.), Algorithms and Data Structures. WADS '89. Proceedings, 1989. IX, 592 pages. 1989.

Vol. 383: K. Furukawa, H. Tanaka, T. Fujisaki (Eds.), Logic Programming '88. Proceedings, 1988. VII, 251 pages. 1989 (Subseries LNAI).

Vol. 384: G. A. van Zee, J. G. G. van de Vorst (Eds.), Parallel Computing 1988. Proceedings, 1988. V, 135 pages. 1989.

Vol. 385: E. Börger, H. Kleine Büning, M.M. Richter (Eds.), CSL '88. Proceedings, 1988. VI, 399 pages. 1989.

Vol. 386: J.E. Pin (Ed.), Formal Properties of Finite Automata and Applications. Proceedings, 1988. VIII, 260 pages. 1989.

Vol. 387: C. Ghezzi, J. A. McDermid (Eds.), ESEC '89. 2nd European Software Engineering Conference. Proceedings, 1989. VI, 496 pages. 1989.

Vol. 388: G. Cohen, J. Wolfmann (Eds.), Coding Theory and Applications. Proceedings, 1988. IX, 329 pages. 1989.

Vol. 389: D.H. Pitt, D.E. Rydeheard, P. Dybjer, A.M. Pitts, A. Poigné (Eds.), Category Theory and Computer Science. Proceedings, 1989. VI, 365 pages. 1989.

Vol. 390: J.P. Martins, E.M. Morgado (Eds.), EPIA 89. Proceedings, 1989. XII. 400 pages. 1989 (Subseries LNAI).

Vol. 391: J.-D. Boissonnat, J.-P. Laumond (Eds.), Geometry and Robotics. Proceedings, 1988. VI, 413 pages. 1989.

Vol. 392: J.-C. Bermond, M. Raynal (Eds.), Distributed Algorithms. Proceedings, 1989. VI, 315 pages. 1989.

Vol. 393: H. Ehrig, H. Herrlich, H.-J. Kreowski, G. Preuß (Eds.), Categorical Methods in Computer Science. VI, 350 pages. 1989.

Vol. 394: M. Wirsing, J.A. Bergstra (Eds.), Algebraic Methods: Theory, Tools and Applications. VI, 558 pages. 1989.

Vol. 395: M. Schmidt-Schauß, Computational Aspects of an Order-Sorted Logic with Term Declarations. VIII, 171 pages. 1989. (Subseries LNAI).

Vol. 396: T. A. Berson, T. Beth (Eds.), Local Area Network Security. Proceedings, 1989. IX, 152 pages. 1989.

Vol. 397: K. P. Jantke (Ed.), Analogical and Inductive Inference. Proceedings, 1989. IX, 338 pages. 1989. (Subseries LNAI).

Vol. 398: B. Banieqbal, H. Barringer, A. Pnueli (Eds.), Temporal Logic in Specification. Proceedings, 1987. VI, 448 pages. 1989.

Vol. 399: V. Cantoni, R. Creutzburg, S. Levialdi, G. Wolf (Eds.), Recent Issues in Pattern Analysis and Recognition. VII, 400 pages. 1989.

Vol. 400: R. Klein, Concrete and Abstract Voronoi Diagrams. IV, 167 pages. 1989.

Vol. 401: H. Djidjev (Ed.), Optimal Algorithms. Proceedings, 1989. VI, 308 pages. 1989.

Vol. 402: T. P. Bagchi, V. K. Chaudhri, Interactive Relational Database Design. XI, 186 pages. 1989.

Vol. 403: S. Goldwasser (Ed.), Advances in Cryptology – CRYPTO '88. Proceedings, 1988. XI, 591 pages. 1990.

Vol. 404: J. Beer, Concepts, Design, and Performance Analysis of a Parallel Prolog Machine. VI, 128 pages. 1989.

Vol. 405: C. E. Veni Madhavan (Ed.), Foundations of Software Technology and Theoretical Computer Science. Proceedings, 1989. VIII, 339 pages. 1989.

Vol. 407: J. Sifakis (Ed.), Automatic Verification Methods for Finite State Systems. Proceedings, 1989. VII, 382 pages. 1990.

Vol. 408: M. Leeser, G. Brown (Eds.) Hardware Specification, Verification and Synthesis: Mathematical Aspects. Proceedings, 1989. VI, 402 pages. 1990.

Vol. 409: A. Buchmann, O. Günther, T. R. Smith, Y.-F. Wang (Eds.), Design and Implementation of Large Spatial Databases. Proceedings, 1989. IX, 364 pages. 1990.

Vol. 410: F. Pichler, R. Moreno-Diaz (Eds.), Computer Aided Systems Theory – EUROCAST '89. Proceedings, 1989. VII, 427 pages. 1990.

Vol. 411: M. Nagl (Ed.), Graph-Theoretic Concepts in Computer Science. Proceedings, 1989. VII, 374 pages. 1990.

Vol. 412: L. B. Almeida, C. J. Wellekens (Eds.), Neural Networks. Proceedings, 1990. IX, 276 pages. 1990.

Vol. 413: R. Lenz, Group Theoretical Methods in Image Processing. VIII, 139 pages. 1990.

Vol. 414: A.Kreczmar, A. Salwicki, M. Warpechowski, LOGLAN '88 – Report on the Programming Language. X, 133 pages. 1990.

Vol. 415: C. Choffrut, T. Lengauer (Eds.), STACS 90. Proceedings, 1990. VI, 312 pages. 1990.

Vol. 416: F. Bancilhon, C. Thanos, D. Tsichritzis (Eds.), Advances in Database Technology – EDBT '90. Proceedings, 1990. IX, 452 pages. 1990.

Vol. 417: P. Martin-Löf, G. Mints (Eds.), COLOG-88. International Conference on Computer Logic. Proceedings, 1988. VI, 338 pages. 1990.

Vol. 419: K. Weichselberger, S. Pöhlmann, A Methodology for Uncertainty in Knowledge-Based Systems, 1989. VIII, 136 pages. 1990. (Subseries LNAI).

Vol. 420: Z. Michalewicz (Ed.), Statistical and Scientific Database Management, V SSDBM. Proceedings, 1990. V, 256 pages. 1990.

Vol. 421: T. Onodera, S. Kawai, A Formal Model of Visualization in Computer Graphics Systems. X, 100 pages. 1990.

Vol. 423: L. E. Deimel (Ed.), Software Engineering Education. Proceedings, 1990. VI, 164 pages. 1990.

Vol. 424: G. Rozenberg (Ed.), Advances in Petri Nets 1989. VI, 524 pages. 1990.

Vol. 426: N. Houbak, SIL – a Simulation Language. VII, 192 pages. 1990.

Vol. 427: O. Faugeras (Ed.), Computer Vision – ECCV 90. Proceedings, 1990. XII, 619 pages. 1990.

Vol. 428: D. Bjørner, C. A. R. Hoare, H. Langmaack (Eds.), VDM '90, VDM and Z – Formal Methods in Software Development. Proceedings, 1990. XVIII, 580 pages. 1990.

Vol. 429: A. Miola (Ed.), Design and Implementation of Symbolic Computation Systems. Proceedings, 1990. XII, 284 pages. 1990.